The Spectre of Hegel

The Spectre of Hegel

Early Writings

◆

LOUIS ALTHUSSER

Edited with an Introduction by
François Matheron

Translated by
G. M. Goshgarian

VERSO
London · New York

First published by Verso 1997
This edition © Verso 1997
Translation © G. M. Goshgarian
First published in *Écrits philosophiques et politiques. Tome I.*
© Stock/IMEC 1994
All rights reserved

Verso

UK: 6 Meard Street, London W1V 3HR
USA: 180 Varick Street, New York NY 10014–4606

Verso is the imprint of New Left Books

ISBN 1–85984–964–4
ISBN 1–85984–099–X

British Library Cataloguing in Publication Data
A catalogue record for this book is available from the British Library

Library of Congress Cataloging-in-Publication Data
Althusser, Louis.
  The spectre of Hegel : early writings / Louis Althusser : edited
with an introduction by François Matheron : translated by G.M.
Goshgarian.
    p.   cm.
  Includes index.
  ISBN 1–85984–964–4 (hbk.) — ISBN 1–85984–099–X (pbk.)
  1. Hegel, Georg Wilhelm Friedrich, 1770–1831.   I. Matheron.
  François.   II. Title.
  B2948.A48   1997
  193—dc21   96–50054
                                                            CIP

Typeset by CentraCet Limited, Cambridge
Printed by Biddles Ltd, Kings Lynn and Guildford

Contents

Translator's Note   vii

Introduction   1

Preface   14

1 The International of Decent Feelings   21

2 On Content in the Thought of G. W. F. Hegel   36

   Introduction   36
   I Origins of the Concept   41
   II Cognition of the Concept   61
   III Miscognition of the Concept   99
   Notes   156

3 Man, That Night   170

4 The Return to Hegel   173

5 A Matter of Fact   185

6 Letter to Jean Lacroix   197

7 On Conjugal Obscenity   231

   Appendix: On Marxism   241

   Index   259

Translator's Note

The present English text is a translation of approximately the first half (pp. 7–339) of Louis Althusser, *Écrits philosophiques et politiques. Tome I* (Stock/IMEC, 1994), containing comprehensive selections from Althusser's published and unpublished texts of 1945–51, together with an essay entitled 'On Marxism', published in two parts in the *Revue de l'enseignement philosophique* in 1953. 'On Marxism' has been included because it marks the transition from the 'early' to the 'mature' Althusser, outlining a research programme that was to bear fruit in the path-breaking texts of the 1960s.

The editor's original French introduction, translated here, was intended to introduce the whole of Vol. I of the *Écrits philosophiques et politiques*, which, as the introduction indicates, also includes a selection of unpublished texts from the 1970s and 1980s. The French preface, likewise translated in the present volume, is specifically devoted to the early writings.

In preparing these texts for publication, the editors have been guided by a twofold concern for readability and fidelity to the original texts. The usual emendations of minor slips or faulty punctuation have been made; occasional interpolations indispensable to a clear understanding of the text have been enclosed in brackets and placed in the body of the text. All passages the author has underlined for emphasis are set in italics; his capitalization has generally been respected. Many of Althusser's longer paragraphs – especially in the 'Letter to Jean Lacroix' – have, however, been divided.

Author's notes, marked with an asterisk, have been placed at the foot of the page, except in the case of the master's thesis, *On Content in the Thought of G. W. F. Hegel*, where they are extensive; here, to avoid overburdening the page, they have been numbered consecutively throughout the text and put at the end. The editor's notes have been placed at the end of each text, except, again, in the case of the master's thesis, where they have been enclosed in brackets and included within the author's notes. Variant passages have been given in the notes when they seemed significant. To avoid placing notes within notes, the occasional editorial comment on a note has been placed in brackets and included in the note itself. Translator's notes are indicated with superior letters and placed at the foot of the page throughout, except in the master's thesis, where they are marked with an asterisk.

Althusser's bibliographical references have been systematically retained; errors have been silently emended whenever possible. When English translations of French or German works cited by Althusser could be found, the English-language references are given in brackets after the original reference. In the notes to the master's thesis on Hegel, the translator has also, as indicated at the beginning of the notes, provided references to standard German editions of works by Hegel or Marx which Althusser cites in French translation.

The translator thanks the following people for practical help, criticisms, and suggestions: Olivier Corpet, Alexandra Gruebler, Jane Hindle, Malcolm Imrie, Joseph McCarney, François Matheron, Markar Melkonian and Sandrine Samson. Special thanks to Gregory Elliott and Catherine Lesimple.

INTRODUCTION
François Matheron

'In full possession of my faculties, I declare you my depositary before all eternity, that you may bear witness to my act in centuries to come, when my posthumous works and correspondence with Franca are published.'[1]

'We do not publish our own drafts, that is, our own mistakes, but we do sometimes publish other people's ... Marx *did not publish* the famous – alas – '1844 Manuscripts' on philosophy and political economy ... he did not even publish *The German Ideology* ... though it is a crucially important text for us (nor did he publish the *Theses on Feuerbach*, our alpha and omega).'[2]

All Althusser lies in the gap between these two strictly contemporaneous texts; even, indeed, in the gap at the heart of the second. The thesis about the 'break' that was to make him famous was based on a meticulous study of Marx's early works: his personal copy of the 1844 *Manuscripts* constitutes an impressive archival document in itself. Yet he sometimes regretted that these works had been published, occasionally even going so far as to deplore the fact that they had been written. As to the eventual fate of his own unpublished writings, if it is impossible to speak of any *intention* of Althusser's in this connection, he was incontestably no stranger to the idea of posthumous publication.

Althusser certainly had sharply mixed feelings about his own work. He never disavowed his early writings. Thus he authorized the belated republication in Spanish of 'A Matter of Fact',[3] a text his French readers would not get to see. He built up a myth, for those close to him, around his long letter to Jean Lacroix, but never showed them the letter itself. On the other hand, he did let a few friends read his diatribe 'On Conjugal Obscenity' in the 1970s, adding a complementary text 'on the woman question' to it in 1978. He kept his master's thesis on Hegel secreted away, but felt the need to declare in 1963 that Merleau-Ponty had wanted to publish it.[4] Moreover, not long after the publication of *For Marx* and

Reading Capital, he invented what might be called texts with semi-public status, which he had typed and mimeographed by a secretary at the École normale supérieure for wide distribution to those around him. These texts had so powerful an impact that the criticisms Jacques Rancière later levelled at him[5] were largely based on one of them, written in 1965: 'Theory, Theoretical Practice, and Theoretical Formation: Ideology and Ideological Struggle', a text still unavailable in France, though it was published in Latin America.[6] Althusser was likewise not averse to publishing anonymous texts, a practice he had already experimented with in the early 1950s, and resorted to again, rather successfully, in 1966, when he published an unsigned article entitled 'On the Cultural Revolution' in *Cahiers marxistes-léninistes* (nos 13–14). Finally, his projects to publish certain texts came so close to realization that it is no exaggeration to say that his publicly acknowledged work was several times on the point of moving in a direction utterly different from the one history tells us it ultimately did – for better or for worse.

Known for his brief, incisive texts, Althusser nevertheless wrote two manuals on Marxism-Leninism[7] and another two on philosophy for non-philosophers,[8] and it was only at the last moment that he withdrew a book announced in a note to his 'Preface to *Capital* Volume One':[9] 'cf. *A Revolutionary Science: Introduction to Book I of* Capital, Éditions Maspero, Paris, 1969'. What is more, he several times refused to send the page proofs of a text to the printer after he had corrected them. Thus French readers never had an opportunity to read 'The Historical Task of Marxist Philosophy', though this work saw partial publication in Hungarian[10] after being commissioned, and then declined, by the Soviet journal *Voprossi Filosofi* in 1967; a paste-up found in Althusser's archives indicates that it had been slated for publication in his collection *Théorie*. Similarly, the fifth 'Philosophy Course for Scientists', which was to have been published in the *Revue de l'enseignement philosophique* in 1968 or 1969, well before the other four, ultimately went unpublished, and was not included in *Philosophy and the Spontaneous Philosophy of Scientists* in 1974.[11] If Althusser does not seem to have regretted the fact that these texts did not appear in print, the same cannot be said of his 'Machiavelli and Us' (written between 1972 and 1976), as is shown by a letter of 28 May 1986 to his Mexican publisher Arnaldo Ofrila Reynal, director of the publishing house Siglo XXI.[12] It is certainly strange to note the imbalance between the nine, often short, books Althusser published in French in his lifetime, and the thousands of pages discovered in his archives – including the typescripts of some ten books, many of them containing instructions for the printer. It is even stranger that his voluminous correspondence, all the more complete in that he generally kept copies of his own letters, contains virtually no mention of his reasons for abandoning any of his publication plans. His illness, the exacerbated attention he paid to the political conjuncture, and the often contradictory advice he received from friends he asked to read his texts all have something to do with this reluctance to publish; but we are doubtless also entitled to see in it the mark of the aleatory.[a]

The present volume offers a selection of texts drawn from Althusser's prolific output. It was put together on principles that are by definition subjective. We have privileged texts which, in subject-matter, style, or content, diverge from the already well-known books and essays; hence we have given relatively small space to writings that tend merely to ring changes on familiar themes. Moreover, out of a concern for readability, we have opted to leave out the manuals on Marxism and philosophy.[13] Often written in a style that pays heavy tribute to the notion Althusser then had of the demands of the theoretical conjuncture, these manuals have ironically not stood the test of time as well as earlier works. Finally, although the two volumes of the *Écrits philosophiques et politiques* are made up almost exclusively of hitherto unpublished material, a wish to offer the reader coherent groupings of texts has led us to reprint a few already published essays, which are either completely unknown or else have gone largely unnoticed.

The first [French] volume has been organized chronologically; the organizing principle of the second is essentially thematic. We could hardly have broken up the group of texts on art, or those on the history of philosophy which Althusser wrote for courses he gave in different periods; accordingly, these texts appear in the second volume. On the other hand, the early writings, whatever their themes, must be read together: though it would have been possible to group the 1947 master's thesis on Hegel with the writings on the history of philosophy, the other texts of the period shed a great deal more light on it.

The internal organization of this first volume rests on a very simple principle. A political-philosophical subject named 'Althusser' emerged in the course of the 1960s, becoming, with the publication of *For Marx* and *Reading Capital* in 1965, one of the major poles of reference of intellectual life in France and elsewhere. A product, like many others in Gaullist France, of converging factors that seemingly had as little to do with one another as the advent of structuralism, the rediscovery of epistemology, the highly problematic repercussions of de-Stalinization on the French Communist Party, the Sino-Soviet split, the emergence of the student movement, and, let us not forget, the Catholic past and very special psychological make-up of an individual ensconced in an École normale supérieure that was forced to invent new strategies to compete

[a] *L'aléatoire*, a notion that was to take on crucial importance in Althusser's writings of the 1980s; see pp. 10–11 below.

successfully with other institutions, this subject would, as such, disappear during the events of May 1968. The philosopher's celebrity remained intact, and there was no sudden drop in his theoretical production. But the world had changed; certain ruptures had been consummated. Althusser served notice of his new situation by publishing, for the first time, an article in *L'Humanité*, the main organ of the French Communist Party.[14] If there had indubitably been an Althusserian school before this date, it had now practically ceased to exist.

The object of the present [French] volume is to introduce readers to, or, at least, afford them an opportunity to become better acquainted with, Althusser's output in the years preceding and following the 1960s;[a] the general contours of his development in the 1960s are already familiar. Althusser's early works, written between 1946 and 1951 by a subject still in the process of emerging, undeniably correspond to a precise moment in his evolution, one marked by a double transition: from Hegel to Marx and from Catholicism to Communism. These texts make up the first part of the present volume [entitled, in the original French edition, 'Louis Althusser before Althusser']. As to the 1970s, they were extremely problematic years. Althusser was still a figure to be reckoned with; his writings were cited more frequently than ever, at least in the first half of the decade, and he was publishing texts seemingly very sure of their foundations, among them the 1972 *Reply to John Lewis*, in which he defined philosophy as 'class struggle in the field of theory'.[15] But, below the surface, profound changes were underway. Althusser's unpublished work was in fact highly variegated: a new subject was trying to make himself heard at the cost of provoking a generalized crisis of which only a few publications provide even a glimpse.[16] Because the specificity of this new Althusser has, for the most part, gone largely unnoticed, the second part of the present [French] volume, entitled 'Texts of Crisis', has been given over to him. When Althusser killed his wife on 16 November 1980, he ceased to be a political-philosophical subject for good and all. Beyond the continuities with his earlier work, his often strange texts on aleatory materialism constitute the final moment of his theoretical activity, a moment inseparable from a renewed preoccupation with the question of his own first name:[17] 'Louis Althusser after Althusser'.[b]

French philosophy in the post-war period was profoundly marked by Hegel, little read since the nineteenth century. To be sure, important essays had occasionally been devoted to him earlier in the twentieth century:[18] Jean Wahl published *Le Malheur de la conscience dans la*

---

[a] A number of texts from the 1970s and 1980s have been published for the first time in *Écrits philosophiques*, Vol. I, pp. 341–582 and Vol. II, *passim*.
[b] This is the subtitle of the second half of the *Écrits philosophiques et politiques*, Vol. 1.

philosophie de Hegel in 1929,[19] together with a translation of selected passages from the *Phenomenology of Spirit*; Henri Lefebvre and Norbert Guterman, after publishing their *Selections* from the work of Karl Marx in 1934, edited an anthology of selections from Hegel in 1939;[20] from 1933 to 1939, Alexandre Kojève gave a series of courses on the *Phenomenology of Spirit* at the École pratique des Hautes études, which were attended by a public with a brilliant future ahead of it.[a] Yet none of this was enough to induce people actually to read Hegel. It was not until 1939 that Aubier undertook publication of the first full-length translation, by Jean Hyppolite, of the *Phenomenology of Spirit*, the second volume of which came off the presses in 1941; the *Philosophy of Right* and the *Aesthetics* appeared during the war under circumstances that were, to say the least, disagreeable.[21] The *Lectures on the Philosophy of History* were published in 1945, followed, in 1947 and 1949, by the first French translation of the *Science of Logic*, by Samuel Jankélévitch; *The Spirit of Christianity and its Fate*, translated by Jacques Martin, to whom Althusser was to dedicate *For Marx*, was released by Vrin in 1948. Thus, in the space of a few years, Hegel's major work was made available to the French public. Studies now began to mushroom. Two monuments emerged: Jean Hyppolite's *Genesis and Structure of Hegel's Phenomenology of Spirit* (1946),[22] and Alexandre Kojève's *Introduction to the Reading of Hegel* (1947).[23] Among the other works to appear in this period were Father Henri Niel's *De la médiation dans la philosophie de Hegel*.[24] Untold articles on Hegel were published by Kojève, Hyppolite, numerous theologians, such as Rev. Father Fessard, and many others. In a context in which Karl Marx was also assuming central importance, the dialectic of master and slave, the struggle unto death, the for-itself and the in-itself, consciousness and self-consciousness, and the other and alienation were on everyone's lips. Hegel was becoming familiar, if only by way of Sartre's *Being and Nothingness*.

There is thus nothing astonishing about the fact that Althusser should have been working on Hegel in 1947. His master's thesis[25] is all the more solid because he was twenty-nine when he wrote it, an unusual age to be engaging in an academic exercise of this type: matured by the war and his experiences in a POW camp, the 'young Althusser' was no longer a young man. The volumes found in his library at his death show that, subsequent disclaimers notwithstanding, he had read Hegel with great care. He made extensive annotations in his copy of the *Phenomenology*, the *Lectures on the Philosophy of History*, and the *Philosophy of Right*, and he was plainly familiar with the old translation of the *Encyclopædia* by Véra;[b] he read *Faith and Knowledge* in German, along with *The Difference*

---

[a] Notably Raymond Aron, Georges Bataille, Roger Caillois, Pierre Klossowski, Jacques Lacan, Maurice Merleau-Ponty, Raymond Queneau, Jean-Paul Sartre.
[b] Auguste Véra, whose French translation of the *Encyclopædia* began to appear in 1859.

Between Fichte's and Schelling's System of Philosophy and the early theological writings – especially *The Spirit of Christianity and its Fate*, which he
very probably discussed with Jacques Martin, then at work on a translation of it. If he knew *The Science of Logic* only imperfectly, he had
nevertheless read the preface and the last chapter in German. Like most
of those who have written about Hegel, he was captivated by his subject:
not only did he write about Hegel, he was, incontestably, an Hegelian.

Althusser's study of Hegel in this period was inseparable from his
study of Marx, whom he devoured in Jacques Molitor's translation.[26] He
did not altogether neglect *Capital* or the *Histoire des doctrines économiques*
[Theories of Surplus-Value], a few volumes of which he annotated,
although his interest in the *Contribution to a Critique of Political Economy*
did not, in this period, go much beyond the 1859 Preface and the 1857
Introduction. However, he covered his copies of Marx's *Œuvres philosophiques* with annotations, especially *Philosophy and Political Economy* (as the
'1844 Manuscripts' were then called), *The German Ideology* and the *Critique
of Hegel's Philosophy of Right*. His master's thesis, informed by a histor-
icism that is rather surprising for those who know his later works,
describes the relations between Marx and Hegel in the following anything but unambiguous terms:

> Yet Hegel clearly saw another point as well, one Marx neglects. How was one
> to think the essence of philosophy, that is, the alienation of thought, without
> becoming the prisoner of the essence of one's own thinking? ... As philo-
> sopher, Marx was thus a prisoner of his times and hence of Hegel, who had
> foreseen this captivity. In a sense, Marx succumbed to the necessity of the
> error he wished to retrace in Hegel, in that Hegel had exposed this necessity
> in the philosopher, while overcoming it in himself so as to engender the Sage.
> Marx's error lay in not being a sage.[27]

We are inevitably reminded of this passage by the early Althusser when
we read a work like 'Marx in his Limits'.[28]

In Althusser's case, the confrontation between Hegel and Marx was
played out in the ideological context of a transition from Catholicism to
Communism. Althusser's Catholicism went back a long way; it did not
always have a leftist bent.[29] If his political positions changed radically
after the war, he nevertheless continued to call himself a Catholic. Thus
he took part in a journey to Rome and gave an account of it in *Témoignage
chrétien* under the pseudonym Robert Leclos;[30] he published a review of
Georges Izard's *L'homme est révolutionnaire* in the review *Dieu vivant;*[31]
and his article 'The International of Decent Feelings,' which opens the
present volume, was initially intended for publication in another Catholic
review, *Les Cahiers de notre jeunesse*.

Althusser took an interest in the activities of two Catholic groups: the
'Union of Progressive Christians' [*l'Union des chrétiens progressistes*] and

'Youth of the Church' [*Jeunesse de l'Église*]. Founded on the initiative of André Mandouze, the Union of Progressive Christians was politically very close to the Communist Party, which many of its members, including Maurice Caveing, Jean Chesneaux and François Ricci, would soon join. Although numerous documents connected with the group were preserved in his archives, Althusser did not really help shape its thinking: progressive Christians were doubtless too political in his view, and failed to establish a satisfactory link between their secular commitment and their faith. 'Youth of the Church'[32] was very different. In January 1936, the Dominican father Maurice Montuclard founded, in Lyons, a group he then called 'The Community'; out of it would evolve a centre for religious studies, 'Youth of the Church', which from 1942 to 1949 published, among other things, ten *Cahiers*, including *L'Incroyance des croyants* [The Unbelief of Believers], *Le Temps du Pauvre* [The Time of the Poor Man], and *L'Évangile captif* [The Captive Gospel]. One of the paradoxes of Althusser's evolution is that the moment he chose to join the Communist Party coincided with the period of his closest collaboration with this religious community, which settled in Petit-Clamart[33] after the Liberation. The following passage by Maurice Montuclard, to whose anti-humanism Althusser was doubtless not indifferent, provides some idea of what might have brought Althusser to take this step:

> It is of crucial importance to the Gospel and the Church that Christians cast off
> . . . the bonds of humanism and a civilization that was once Christian, and is
> now 'bourgeois'; that they bring to today's historical developments their
> active, lucid presence, and, with it, the influence and reality of grace. This
> entails . . . 1) A Christian vision of secular History which is distinct from the
> historical action of the Church visible, though never opposed to it, and is a
> progressive force to the extent that God chooses to make this vision too an
> instrument of Salvation in Jesus Christ. 2) A subordination of politics to
> religion, and, more broadly, of the temporal to the spiritual, different . . . from
> the kind of subordination authorized by Christianity's post-medieval regime.[34]

Or, again, the following passage:

> If we want the Christian message to be heard, we have to preach the Gospel –
> *the Gospel, not Christian humanism.* If we want people to believe in the Church,
> we have to present it, and consequently experience it, in such a way that it
> will show it is capable of relying on its own supernatural means, not
> superfluous human help, to bring a reborn humanity to life, liberty, fraternity,
> and the worship of the true God . . . A world is disappearing; as it falls, it is
> taking with it, along with our privileges and certitudes, all the sources of
> support the Church once fell back on to facilitate and promote its mission by
> human means. This world is disappearing in favour of a better humanity in a
> new civilization. How can we not wish that its fall will create new oppor-
> tunities, as yet unknown but already certain, for the progress of evangeliza-
> tion? How can we not choose to free the Gospel of its trammels so as to pave

the way, in this nascent world, for a Church wholly attuned to the freedom of the Gospel, and wholly based, in its teaching, methods, and institutions, on the sovereign power of grace? No, we no longer have a choice: we have chosen the Gospel.[35]

If Althusser, for his part, chose the Communist Party, Catholicism would never entirely cease to hold a place in his thinking: an article published in 1969 in the review *Lumière et Vie* bears witness to this,[36] as does the transcription, made in 1985 and discovered in his archives, of a discussion he had with Father Stanislas Breton on the subject of liberation theology.[37]

It would have been surprising if Althusser had not been a Stalinist. No-one who joined the Communist Party in November 1948, as he did, and remained faithful to it as few others have, could have avoided it. His Stalinism, which was at all events predictable, is amply attested by his writings: the great post-war trials did not trouble him in the least, and he apparently entertained no doubts as to Rajk's guilt.[38] But, by itself, the adjective 'Stalinist' does not tell us much. There are different ways of being a Stalinist, and the history of the phenomenon cannot really be understood if one fails to recognize its diversity: the 'Letter to Jean Lacroix' probably has no equal. If Althusser indicates his agreement with Zhdanov's lecture on philosophy,[39] nowhere in his work does one find the least trace of a defence of socialist realism; yet the theory of socialist realism had itself been propounded by Zhdanov. Althusser took a close interest in the Lysenko affair, reading and annotating several propaganda pamphlets, and yet it is not easy to guess what he thought of it. Unlike, for example, Jean-Toussaint Desanti, then a member of the editorial board of *La Nouvelle Critique*, he does not seem to have succumbed to the folly of the theory of the 'two sciences', 'bourgeois' and 'proletarian'; it is hard to imagine him writing a panegyric to 'Stalin, scientist of a new type'.[40] If, despite all, he did approve Lysenko's doctrines, he clearly did so, even at this early date, in the name of *science*, in the singular; his position was thus diametrically opposed to the one Aragon took on the same question. To be sure, these texts of Althusser's have something disturbing about them. Yet one whole facet of his later work can be fully understood only after a reading of these early writings: thus the preface to *For Marx* acquires a dimension that has largely escaped notice. Moreover, in this light, the relationship to Hegel appears in all its complexity.

The 1970s were dramatic years for Althusser. Cut off from the movements of the far Left after 1968, he had also ceased to utilize the École normale supérieure as the centre of a complex politico-philosophical strategy: the era of the seminar on *Capital* or of the 'Philosophy Course for Scientists' was definitively over. He now chose to wage a struggle essentially internal to the Communist Party, at the very moment when it was going into a phase of decline that, at the time, could be only dimly foreseen: its position within the academy was still very strong, and the Union of the Left had bright days ahead of it. Publications continued to appear at the usual slow pace, as if nothing had changed: *Reply to John Lewis*[41] was published in England in 1972 and in France a year later, *Elements of Self-Criticism*[42] and *Philosophy and the Spontaneous Philosophy of Scientists* in 1974,[43] *Positions* in 1976.[44] Yet the success of these works, especially that of *Reply to John Lewis*, which was considerable, could not hide the depths of Althusser's disarray – witness the self-parody he wrote in the same period.[45] Something had definitely snapped. The crisis of the middle of the decade did nothing to improve the situation: France's intellectuals suddenly rediscovered the horrors of Stalinism, and, in time, a reference to Marx became a mark of ignominy.

Althusser's reaction was by no means all of a kind. His most noticeable impulse, at least initially, was to rise to the defence of basic principles. Thus he undertook a vigorous campaign in defence of the concept of the dictatorship of the proletariat, the most conspicuous result being the pamphlet 'On the Twenty-Second Congress of the French Communist Party'.[46] He took part in several public debates on this theme, in France and in Spain, and wrote a long work, which would remain unfinished, called 'The Black Cows: An Imaginary Interview'. At about the same time, he drew up an unsparing account of the crisis in the Communist Party in a series of articles published in *Le Monde* and reprinted in the book *What Must Change in the Communist Party*.[47] He also embarked on a full-scale review of the crisis of Marxist theory; this time, the primary objective was not to defend principles, but to show that a renewal of Marxist thought could take place only on the basis of an analysis of its inherent limits. Thus, attentively rereading Gramsci, he tried to define Marx's 'absolute limits', in particular with regard to the question of the state. This procedure had its own dark side: the crisis was perhaps even deeper, it was perhaps time to do something completely different – that was at least one of the senses of the 'return to philosophy' which began at the same moment, to say nothing of the writing of the first autobiography, *The Facts*, in 1976. Thus, in the two philosophy manuals mentioned above, we find what for Althusser were unusual references: he evokes Epicurus, Heidegger, and also Derrida, whom he had been reading for a long time, but had never publicly discussed. It is in this period that the metaphor of the train makes its appearance in his theoretical writings; it was to become one of the main preoccupations of his last years. If Althusser's thought had always had many facets, the divergence amongst them was here extreme.

*

In the last years of his life, Althusser no longer had, in a certain sense, to answer to anyone for anything. Despite the fidelity of his friends, this state of extreme solitude had a shaping influence on his theoretical writing, which now displayed a pronounced tendency to take on a prophetic tone. There is often only a thin line between the philosophical work and texts whose often immense import is primarily clinical. We have decided not to publish such writings here; in our judgement, they belong somewhere else. Indeed, the only book to be published in Althusser's lifetime after the murder of Hélène – it appeared in Mexico in 1988[48] – was the end result of so complex a process of production that a lengthy narrative would be required to give a full account of it.

The relation these late writings bear to Althusser's work as a whole is not simple. In one sense, the break is obvious: to borrow one of Althusser's favourite expressions, the concept of 'aleatory materialism' was not explicitly present [trouvable] in his earlier work. 'Aleatory materialism' combines two terms in a way totally foreign to the tradition of dialectical materialism; and yet the phrase forcibly brings 'theoretical practice' to mind. Moreover – indeed, above all – the theme of the encounter had long been at the centre of Althusser's thinking about history and the concept of mode of production.[49] The ideas about the conjuncture that he worked out in the 1960s had obviously emerged against the backdrop of a projected theory of the conjuncture that was never to crystallize. After the initial surprise has worn off, we are finally not puzzled to find, in working notes dating from 1966, comments that would be repeated almost word for word in his last writings: '1. Theory of the encounter or *conjunction* (= *genesis*...) (cf. Epicurus, clinamen, Cournot), chance etc., precipitation, coagulation. 2. Theory of the *conjuncture* (= structure) ... philosophy as a general theory of the *conjuncture* (= *conjunction*).' And it is not without a certain emotion that we discover, suddenly surging up in the midst of notes on Pierre Macherey's book *Towards a Theory of Literary Production*, phrases which, at first sight, are very far removed from the subject: 'Theory of the clinamen. First theory of the *encounter*!' If, finally, the image of the train elaborated in the 'Portrait of the Materialist Philosopher', the text that rounds off this [French] volume,[50] occurs in most of Althusser's late writings, it does not materialize out of nowhere in the 1980s. It can, for example, also be found in a letter to René Diatkine probably written in 1972: 'There is no point of departure and no destination. One can only ever climb aboard moving trains: they come from nowhere and are not going any place. Materialist thesis: it is only on this condition that we can progress.'

Althusser has left us no word of conclusion: his work stops in mid-course, essentially unfinishable. But if we had to identify something like the motor of his theoretical production, we would hazard calling it the void. From the conjuring away of the necessary void in the master's thesis on Hegel, through the 'void of a distance taken' in *Lenin and Philosophy*, to, finally, the void as the 'one and only object' of philosophy, fascination with a word doubtless underlies the construction of a philosophical object.

We wish to thank all those who have helped make publication of this volume possible: first and foremost, François Boddaert, Louis Althusser's heir, Olivier Corpet, and Yann Moulier Boutang, whose day-to-day support has been invaluable. Our thanks also go to Étienne Balibar, Madame Behr, chief librarian of the Library of the Catholic University of Lyons, Madame Bely, Dean of the Philosophy Faculty at the Catholic University of Lyons, Gilles Candar, André Chabin, Marcel Cornu, Dominique Lecourt, Jacqueline Pluet-Despatin, Robert F. Roeming, Jacqueline Sichler. And a special thanks to Sandrine Samson.

Notes

1. Louis Althusser, Letter to Franca Madonia of 18 November 1963. On Madonia, see *L'avenir dure longtemps*, suivi de *Les Faits*, 2nd edn, Le Livre de poche, Paris, 1994, p. 162 [*The Future Lasts a Long Time*, trans. Richard Veasey, Chatto and Windus, London, 1993, pp. 141–2].
2. Louis Althusser, 'Réponse à une critique', appendix, 30 November 1963, in *Écrits philosophiques et politiques*, Vol. 2, Stock/IMEC, Paris, 1995, pp. 385, 387.
3. 'Une question de faits', *Jeunesse de l'Église*, *Cahier X* ('L'Évangile captif'), translated as 'Situación histórica de la Iglesia en perspectiva marxista', in Louis Althusser, *Nuevos escritos: La crisis del movimiento comunista internacional frente a la teoría marxista*, Laia B, Barcelona, 1978, pp. 137–63; pp. 185–96 in the present volume.
4. See Yann Moulier Boutang, *Louis Althusser: Une biographie*, Vol. 1: *La formation du mythe*, *1918–1956*, Grasset, Paris, 1992.
5. Jacques Rancière, *La Leçon d'Althusser*, Gallimard, Paris, 1974.
6. In *La filosofia como arma de la revolución*, Cuadernos de Pasado y Presente, Cordoba, 1970. [This text, whose French title is 'Théorie, pratique théorique et formation théorique: Idéologie et lutte idéologique', has also appeared in English, trans. James H. Kavanagh, in *Philosophy and the Spontaneous Philosophy of the Scientists and Other Essays*, trans. Ben Brewster *et al.*, Verso, London, 1989, pp. 1–42.]
7. Extracts from the first were published in 1966 in *Cahiers marxistes-léninistes*, no. 11, April 1966 pp. 90–122, under the title 'Matérialisme historique et matérialisme dialectique' [Historical Materialism and Dialectical Materialism]; extracts from the second, whose original title, 'Qu'est-ce que la philosophie marxiste-léniniste?' [What is Marxist-Leninist Philosophy?], was later changed to 'De la superstructure' [On the Superstructure], were brought together in the famous essay 'Idéologie et appareils idéologiques d'État', *La Pensée*, no. 151, June 1970, repr. in *Positions*, Éditions Sociales, Paris, 1976, pp. 79–137 ['Ideology and Ideological State Apparatuses', trans. Ben Brewster, in *Lenin and Philosophy and Other Essays*, New Left Books, London, 1971, pp. 127–86, repr. in *Essays on Ideology*, Verso, London, 1984, pp. 1–60]. The full text of 'De la superstructure' was published in 1995 under the title 'La Reproduction des rapports de production', in Louis Althusser, *Sur la reproduction*, ed. Jacques Bidet, Presses Universitaires de France, Paris.
8. 'Être marxiste en philosophie' [To Be a Marxist in Philosophy] (1976); 'Initiation à la philosophie (pour les non-philosophes)' [Introduction to Philosophy (for non-

philosophers)] (1978). A brief extract from the first work has appeared under the title 'Une conversation philosophique' in *Digraphe*, no. 66, December 1993, pp. 55–62.

9. Trans. Ben Brewster, in *Lenin and Philosophy*, pp. 71–106. This note is not included in the English translation of the Preface; it may be found on p. 18 of the original French version, entitled 'Avertissement aux lecteurs du Livre I du "Capital"', in Karl Marx, *Le Capital*, Livre I, Garnier-Flammarion, Paris, 1969.

10. As 'A Marxista Filozófia Történelmi Feladata', in Louis Althusser, *Marx-az elmélet forradalma*, Kossuth Könyvkiadó, Budapest, 1968, pp. 272–306. The French title is 'La Tâche historique de la philosophie marxiste'.

11. *Philosophie et philosophie spontanée des savants* (1967), Maspero, Paris, 1974 ['Philosophy and the Spontaneous Philosophy of Scientists (1967)', in *Philosophy and the Spontaneous Philosophy of Scientists*, trans. Warren Montag, pp. 69–165]. The fifth course is now available under the title 'Du côté de la philosophie', in *Écrits philosophiques et politiques*, Vol. 2, pp. 257–96.

12. Cf. *L'avenir dure longtemps*, p. 21. The essay may be found in *Écrits philosophiques*, Vol. 2, pp. 44–161.

13. Furthermore, anyone may consult these and all other materials in Althusser's archives at the IMEC (Institut Mémoires de l'édition contemporaine, Paris).

14. 'Comment lire *Le Capital*?', *L'Humanité*, 21 March 1969; repr. in *Positions*, pp. 49–60 ['How to Read Marx's "Capital"', *Marxism Today*, October 1969, pp. 302–5].

15. Originally published in English in *Marxism Today*, October 1972, pp. 310–18, and November 1972, pp. 343–9, then in a revised and expanded French version, *Réponse à John Lewis*, Maspero, Paris, 1973, pp. 7–68 [translation of the latter version by Grahame Lock, in *Essays in Self-Criticism*, New Left Books, London, 1976, pp. 33–77; repr. in *Essays on Ideology*, pp. 61–114. The formula in question appears on p. 67 of *On Ideology*].

16. For example, 'Ce qui ne peut plus durer dans le parti communiste', *Le Monde*, 25–28 April 1978; revised version published under the same title, Maspero, Paris, 1978 ['What Must Change in the Party', trans. Patrick Camiller, *New Left Review*, no. 109, May/June 1978, pp. 19–45]; or Althusser's contribution to the Venice Conference organized in 1977 by *Il Manifesto*: Il Manifesto, *Pouvoir et opposition dans les sociétés postrévolutionnaires*, Paris, Seuil, 1978, pp. 242–53 ['The Crisis of Marxism', trans. Grahame Lock, *Marxism Today*, July 1978, pp. 215–20, 227; repr. in Il Manifesto, *Power and Opposition in Post-Revolutionary Societies*, Ink Links, London, 1979, pp. 225–37].

17. *The Future Lasts a Long Time*, written in 1985, bears witness to the dramatic nature of this question of the first name.

18. Thus the July–September 1931 issue of *Revue de métaphysique et de morale* is devoted to Hegel.

19. *Le Malheur de la conscience dans la philosophie de Hegel*, Rieder, Paris, 1929.

20. Paris, Gallimard, 1939.

21. *Principes de la philosophie du droit* [Elements of the Philosophy of Right], Gallimard, Paris, 1940, appeared without mention of the translator's name – André Kaan! *L'Esthétique*, Aubier, Paris, 1944, likewise appeared without mention of the name of the real translator, Samuel Jankélévitch; worse, the first volume carried the notice 'original translation by J. G.'!

22. [Partial translation by Samuel Cherniak and John Heckman, Northwestern University Press, Evanston, Ill., 1974. The French title is *Genèse et structure de la Phénoménologie de l'Esprit de Hegel*.]

23. [Ed. Allan Bloom, trans. James H. Nichols, Jr., Cornell University Press, Ithaca, New York, 1969; a partial translation of *Introduction à la lecture de Hegel*.]

24. Aubier, Paris, 1945.

25. *Mémoire de DES*, the equivalent of the current French *maîtrise* [or Anglo-American M.A.].

26. [Alfred Costes, Paris, 1924–38.]

27. See p. 132 in the present volume.

28. 'Marx dans ses limites', *Écrits philosophiques*, Vol. 1, p. 357.

29. See Moulier Boutang, *Althusser*, Vol. 1, pp. 99–171.

30. [While in Rome, Althusser participated in a collective audience with Pope Pius XII. His article on what he saw in Rome is entitled 'En attendant le blé américain, Rome

sommeille' [While it waits for the American wheat, Rome dozes], *Témoignage chrétien*, 10 May 1946 et 17 May 1946.]

31. *Dieu vivant*, no. 6, Seuil, 1946, pp. 149–52.

32. See *L'Instituant, les Savoirs et les Orthodoxies (en souvenir de Maurice Montuclard)*, ed. Nicole Ramognino, Publications of the University of Provence, 1991 (especially Émile Poulat, 'La formation religieuse et sociale d'un sociologue'), and Moulier Boutang, *Althusser*, Vol. 1, pp. 276–341. On the dissolution of 'Youth of the Church', which was directly linked to the repression of the worker-priests carried out by the Vatican, see also Pierre Pierrard, *L'Église et les ouvriers en France, 1940–1990*, Hachette, Paris, 1991, and François Le Prieur, *Quand Rome condamne*, repr. Plon, Paris, 1989.

33. [Part of the city of Clamart, a suburb just south of Paris.]

34. Lettre, *Jeunesse de l'Église*, no. 2, January 1949.

35. This passage closes the tenth *Cahier* of *Jeunesse de l'Église*, entitled 'L'Évangile captif', which contains Althusser's article 'A Matter of Fact', pp. 185–96 in the present volume.

36. ['Crise de l'homme et de la société'], *Lumière et Vie* ('L'Église aujourd'hui'), no. 93, May/June 1969, pp. 26–9.

37. See Stanislas Breton, 'Althusser aujourd'hui', *Archives de la philosophie*, July/September 1993, pp. 417–30.

38. See the 'Letter to Jean Lacroix', pp. 197–230 in the present volume.

39. See p. 222 of the present volume.

40. See Jean-Toussaint Desanti, 'Stalin, savant d'un type nouveau' [Stalin, Scientist of a New Type], *La Nouvelle Critique*, no. 11, December 1949. A comparative study of Althusser's and Desanti's Stalinist writings would certainly be fascinating.

41. See n. 18.

42. [*Éléments d'autocritique*, Hachette, Paris; 'Elements of Self-Criticism', trans. Grahame Lock, *Essays in Self-Criticism*, New Left Books, London, 1976 pp. 101–61.]

43. See n. 11.

44. [Éditions Sociales, Paris. The essays collected in *Positions* had all been published previously. English translations of these essays are scattered in a number of publications: (1) 'Freud and Lacan', trans. Ben Brewster, *New Left Review*, no. 55, May/June 1969, pp. 49–65, repr. in *Lenin and Philosophy*, pp. 177–202, and in *Essays on Ideology*, 141–71; (2) 'Philosophy as a Revolutionary Weapon', trans. Ben Brewster, *New Left Review*, no. 64, November/December. 1970, pp. 3–11, repr. in *Lenin and Philosophy*, pp. 13–25; (3) 'How to Read Marx's "Capital"' (see n. 14); (4) 'Ideology and Ideological State Apparatuses' (see n. 7); (4) 'Marxism and Class Struggle', trans. Patrick Lyons, *Radical*, no. 1, Oxford, November 1985, pp. 12–13; (5) 'Is it Simple to be a Marxist in Philosophy?', trans. Grahame Lock, in *Essays in Self-Criticism*, pp. 163–207, repr. in *Philosophy and the Spontaneous Philosophy of the Scientists*, pp. 203–40.]

45. 'Une question posée par Louis Althusser', in *Écrits philosophiques*, Vol. 1, pp. 345–56.

46. The first version of this work was published in English in Étienne Balibar, *On the Dictatorship of the Proletariat*, trans. Grahame Lock, New Left Books, London, 1977, pp. 193–211; a revised French version, entitled *22ᵉ Congrès*, was published by Maspero the same year. Ben Brewster's English translation of the revised version may be found in *New Left Review*, no. 104, July/August 1977, pp. 3–22.

47. See n. 16.

48. *Filosofía y marxismo: Entrevistas con Fernanda Navarro*, Siglo XXI, Mexico, 1988; French trans. by Fernanda Navarro, Bernard Vasseur, Dolorès Gallago, and Olivier Corpet, 'Philosophie et marxisme: Entretiens avec Fernanda Navarro (1984–1987)', in Althusser, *Sur la philosophie*, Gallimard, L'Infini, Paris, 1994, pp. 17–79.

49. See, for example, 'Contradiction and Overdetermination: Notes for an Investigation', trans. Ben Brewster, in *For Marx*, Allen Lane, London, 1969, pp. 87–128; or Étienne Balibar's contribution to *Reading Capital* (trans. Ben Brewster, New Left Books, London, 1970, pp. 199–308), which Althusser continued to refer to in 1982.

50. 'Portrait du philosophe matérialiste', *Écrits philosophiques*, Vol. 1, pp. 581–2.

PREFACE
François Matheron

This volume contains the essential output of 'the young Althusser'. Philosophically, these texts are dominated by their author's relationship to Hegel. Ideologically, they are marked by an anything but linear transition from Catholicism to Communism.

Dated 20 December 1946, 'The International of Decent Feelings' is the first text in which Althusser's talent for polemic comes fully to the fore. Written by a young philosopher who called himself a Christian and, though already attracted by the Communist Party, had not as yet had to grapple with Stalinist rhetoric, this essay was intended for publication in the *Cahiers de notre jeunesse*, a review edited by Althusser's friend François Ricci, who was later to join the Party. Althusser notes in a letter to his parents of 20 December 1946: 'I'm about to write a rather virulent essay for the *Cahiers de notre jeunesse* (a little Catholic review, which was founded during the Occupation by students[a] from Lyons and has come a good way since) on "The International of Decent Feelings".' If this text finally went unpublished, it was not at all because Althusser had the kind of second thoughts that often assailed him in later years, but rather for the simple reason that the editor to whom he sent it, alarmed by its virulence, rejected it.[1]

Althusser was not to forget this rejection, which, curiously, he chalked up to the account of the review *Esprit* in a letter of 4 July 1958 to his friend Claire:[2] 'Malraux. A lot to tell you about him. I even wrote an essay once about one of his lecture-prophecies in 1947, but the essay never came out, because I refused to change a single line – it had been intended for the review *Esprit*.'

To read 'the young Althusser's' three texts on Hegel one after the other is to experience a number of surprises. There is, of course, the surprise of

---

[a] *Cagneux*: graduates of a lycée on a two-year course that prepares them for the entrance examination for the École normale supérieure.

discovering an Hegelian Althusser; but there is also the surprise of seeing just how quickly he arrived at an extremely negative judgement of Hegel – or, at any event, of the 'return to Hegel' then underway in French philosophy.

'On Content in the Thought of G. W. F. Hegel' is Althusser's *Diplôme d'études supérieures*, the equivalent of today's master's thesis. Written, in all likelihood, between August and October 1947, the thesis was defended before Gaston Bachelard. In an undated letter, probably written in October or November 1947, Althusser describes the defence for Hélène, who had typed his thesis:

> Yesterday I took the orals for my master's degree with Bachelard, who said, what do you mean by the circularity of the concept, isn't it rather circulation of concepts? I shot back a few words that drove him back into his beard, but he didn't flinch: he said he would reread my 'very interesting' text, but that doesn't commit him to much of anything. Besides, I can't count on him, because he's not familiar with the questions that interest me. Naturally he told me not to worry about anything. I hope he'll give me 'with distinction', for the greater glory of the administration, the honour of my parents, and the merits of the typist.

These hopes were well-founded, because Althusser received a mark of 18 out of 20[a] for the thesis.[3]

Althusser's friend Jacques Martin[4] wrote his master's thesis at about the same time as Althusser. Entitled 'Remarks on the Notion of the Individual in Hegel's Philosophy', it too was typed by Hélène and defended before Bachelard. The two texts were discovered lying side by side in Althusser's library. Althusser had not had his name printed on the binding of his thesis: all that appears there is 'G. W. F. Hegel: On Content in the Thought'. Martin took his own life late in August 1963. Still in shock over the suicide of the friend he would later call his 'only contemporary', Althusser discussed Martin's work at length in a letter of 7 October 1963 to his friend Franca:

> Franca, in my office this morning I looked – I had a sort of vague memory that I'd kept it, in spite of him, and almost without his knowledge – for the only text he ever produced for an anonymous reader, his master's thesis on Hegel, which he wrote in 1946–47, the same academic year I was working on mine. I found it. It's here, on my table. He brought it to me a year and a half ago I think it was, asking me to read it and tell him 'if it might still be of some interest' – he'd doubtless come across it again himself, and I had the feeling he still valued it, at least as far as certain theoretical points he'd worked out in it went. He was right: it was an extraordinarily mature text. At an age when most of us, and I more than anyone, were still turning out 'literature' about philosophy, his text was that of a master; it was above all temptation, especially

---

[a] The equivalent of A+. 16 out of 20 usually suffices for highest honours.

the temptation to be facile. Because of the way things were in that strange youth and this strange school, I had no more read his thesis than he had mine. We kept these things close to our chests, kept a tight grip on them so as not to have to acknowledge them. Merleau-Ponty, whom you may have heard of, a famous philosopher here who knew us because he had taught a number of courses at the École [normale supérieure], wanted to publish our theses, J[acques] M[artin]'s, mine, and that of another friend who has since taken a teaching job outside Paris. We put up fierce resistance, saying that these texts had merely provided an opportunity to rid ourselves of our youthful errors. 'One doesn't publish one's youthful errors.' Merleau was very annoyed, we fought him off as best we could, though to tell you the truth we weren't so much fighting him as his line of thinking: we didn't want to give him any sort of support or approval. Merleau has since died, as you know. The theses haven't been published. But I know that our excuse, which was valid in my case, wasn't in J[acques] M[artin]'s. His thesis may have contained errors, or, at any rate, propositions he wouldn't have subscribed to in later years. But they were not youthful errors by any means. They were the errors of a mature man, a man thinking had made mature.

We can detect, just beneath the surface of this passage, Althusser's thinking of the time about Marx's early works, which he had been reading and rereading even as he was going so far as to question the wisdom of the decision to publish them. There is nothing to prevent us from concluding that Althusser was here airing a certain regret over the fate of his own work.

Written while he was working on his thesis, 'Man, That Night' was published in the second half of 1947 in the *Cahiers du Sud*, a journal edited by Jean Ballard, whom Althusser had met through Hélène. The essay, a review of Alexandre Kojève's *Introduction to the Reading of Hegel*, appeared in the section of the journal entitled 'Chronicles'. The *Cahiers* did not retain the title 'Man, That Night', which is to be found in the typescript. In an undated letter, probably written in September 1947, Althusser tells Hélène about his reading of Kojève's book: 'I've read Kojève (in Ballard), there are some silly remarks in it but some very interesting things which are simply Hegel *understood* (from which I see that I had *surmised* a great deal in a dim way but had understood very little), things that are in any case very useful for my thesis (and the *agreg*[a]).'

'The Return to Hegel, the Latest Word in Academic Revisionism' was published in November 1950 in *La Nouvelle Critique*, no. 20. It was signed by 'the Commission for criticism of the circle of Communist philosophers'; here again, the title differs from that of the typescript ('Hegel, Marx, and Hyppolite, the Latest Word in Academic Revisionism'). The

---

[a] Academic jargon for *agrégation*, the highest competitive examination for teachers in France.

Cold War was well underway; the time for subtly shaded criticism had passed, and Althusser's style had become more peremptory. The philosopher's archives show that he worked a long time on this article: they contain several different typed versions, along with a great many notes Althusser took on his reading and catalogued under the evocative heading 'contemporary Hegelia–nanities'.[a]

Anonymous though it was, Althusser's entry into the fray did not go unnoticed. Émile Bottigelli, who would later translate Marx's 1844 *Manuscripts*, published a reply with the straightforward title 'Disagree About the "Return to Hegel"' in *La Nouvelle Critique*, no. 21. Declaring that he was in agreement with Althusser's thesis, Bottigelli nevertheless rejected his conception of the relationship between Hegel and the German bourgeoisie. A friend of Althusser's, the Germanist Pierre Grappin, rallied to his support in a letter of 22 November 1950 which included a long quotation from Franz Mehring tending to corroborate Althusser's argument. 'Your opponent wants to make a show of his knowledge,' Grappin concluded, 'but his knowledge is short of the mark.' In *La Nouvelle Critique*, no. 22, Henri Lefebvre published a 'Letter on Hegel', in which he said, notably:

> The article in *la N[ouvelle] C[ritique]* leaves the impression that a 'return to Hegel' inevitably has a reactionary or fascistic character. Should it not have been made clearer that this 'return' has that character only if it ignores the work of Marx, Engels, Lenin, and Stalin? Should the writer not have recalled that Lenin 'returned' to Hegel in the autumn of 1914, at a particularly difficult moment; that he reread Hegel's *Logic* before writing *Against the Current*, and took the notes known as the *Philosophical Notebooks*? Should the writer not have cited this book, rather than limiting himself to the extremely well-known (and, be it noted in passing, essential) Preface to *Capital*? The article creates the impression that the 'Hegel question' (Zhdanov) has been settled by simply relegating Hegel to a now closed past. I cannot accept this position, at least not without hearing new arguments; it seems to me incompatible with the texts of all the Marxist classics, from Marx to Stalin. This could not have been the meaning of Zhdanov's sentence, which must not be taken in isolation.

Besides these documents, Althusser's archives contain two letters from René Schérer, then a member of the French Communist Party. The first begins with a 'Dear Comrades', follows it up with a classically threatening set phrase – 'I am in complete agreement with your analysis of the current vogue of Hegelian philosophy in the Academy' – and then goes on to defend Hegel for seven pages. The second, dated 19 December 1950, is friendlier: the first had been transmitted to Althusser, who had obviously answered Schérer, thereby revealing that he was the author under attack. All the indications are that Althusser, taking cover behind

---

[a] *Hégéliâneries. Ânerie* means 'inanity'; *Hegelianer* means 'Hegelian(s)' in German.

a prudent anonymity, had carved out a coign of vantage for himself. And it is not hard to imagine the 'ulterior motives' involved in his relationship – which was, moreover, extremely courteous – with Jean Hyppolite, who would be named director of the École normale supérieure in 1954.

'A Matter of Fact' was published in February 1949, in the tenth *Cahier* of 'Youth of the Church', entitled 'The Captive Gospel'. Divided into two main sections, 'The Real Conditions of Evangelization' and 'Possibilities for Evangelization', this collection of essays is a series of responses, of widely varying length, to a single question: 'Has the Good News been announced to the men of our day?' The question is discussed in a 'Foreword' in which we find, notably, this:

> On the one hand, we cannot purely and simply call an end to our activities because of the economic, political, and social obstacles we are encountering today in our efforts to evangelize. The 'impossibility' of spreading the Gospel in fact means only that the Christian message and the Church must take a new historical form, one which will be especially disconcerting for the 'faithful'. Yet we must not be too quick to credit the spiritual possibilities for evangelization of today's world by the Christian world: 'it would be enough if we were all saints.' It would not be enough, because the way to evangelization is blocked by an internal barrier, or, rather, a barrier internal to those who evangelize: not personal unworthiness, but perhaps practical ignorance of the Gospel as the Good News announced to every man. What, indeed, do we call Gospel? Might it be that our habits, our set ideas, our modes of life have failed to make the Gospel *our* Gospel?

'A Matter of Fact' reveals the complexity of Althusser's intellectual itinerary with particular clarity: he wrote this text shortly after joining the Communist Party in November 1948, precisely the moment he chose to take a close interest in the activities of 'Youth of the Church', an organization of which his sister Georgette was, for a time, a staff member. Thus it is not surprising that his should have been the opening essay in the tenth *Cahier* published by this extraordinarily complex group. Althusser must not have been dissatisfied with the result, since he authorized a Spanish publisher to bring out a translation of the essay in 1978.[5]

Begun on 25 December 1949 in Paris, laid aside for a time, and finally finished on 21 January 1950 in the Limousin region, the 'Letter to Jean Lacroix' is much more than a personal letter to a former teacher. Indeed, Althusser built up a kind of myth around this lengthy, seventy-page epistle, upon which he conferred the status of a semi-public act simply by talking a great deal about it to his friends and associates.[6] A sharp critique of Lacroix's book *Marxisme, Existentialisme, Personnalisme*, and one not entirely lacking in bad faith, this text is in many respects disconcerting for anyone familiar with Althusser's books. Defending the

Rajk trial in language which was certainly not yet that of a 'left critique of Stalinism', he nevertheless declares that he has, in a certain sense, continued to uphold the ideals of his Catholic past, and defends the idea of a Marxist humanism in terms diametrically opposed to those he would later employ. At the same time, he rejects the problematic of alienation which he had defended in the thesis on Hegel.

Despite its vehemence, this letter was by no means intended to provoke a break in Althusser's relations with Lacroix, of whose reaction we know nothing, since Althusser's archives contain no trace of a response. If, in later years, Althusser rarely read the books the personalist philosopher still sent him, he nevertheless continued to treat his political positions with the utmost respect, and kept up a regular correspondence with him. It was thanks to Lacroix that Althusser published his book on Montesquieu with Presses Universitaires de France. Furthermore, Lacroix was the first person in France to accept for publication – in the June 1964 *Cahiers de l'Institut de science économique appliquée* – Althusser's most controversial essay: 'Marxism and Humanism'.

Written in a style like no other, 'On Conjugal Obscenity' dates from January 1951, if we are to believe what Althusser said about it in 1978, in the opening lines of a text devoted to the women's movement:

> To this text, written in January 1951 – at a moment when, still close to the student organizations of the *Action catholique* in which I had been active, but already a member of the French CP (1948), I was pursuing, taking an apparently unrelated theme as my pretext, a reflection about my own past and also about the 'politics' of the French Church, then in the 'forefront' of a revival movement that had not yet become the *aggiornamento* of Vatican I and II – I would like to append the following remarks, which, this time, have a direct bearing on the women's movement and, secondarily, 'feminism'.

In this piece, in which he says nearly the opposite of what one might expect, Althusser, literally haunted by his subject, deploys a talent often put to work in his letters: that of plunging the reader into a situation which seems, at first sight, completely unfamiliar.

Notes

1. See Yann Moulier Boutang, *Louis Althusser: Une Biographie*, Vol. 1: *La formation du mythe, 1918–1956*, Grasset, Paris, 1992, pp. 283–90.
2. On Claire, see *L'avenir dure longtemps*, suivi de *Les Faits*, 2nd edn, Le Livre de poche, Paris, 1994, pp. 161–2. [*The Future Lasts a Long Time*, trans. Richard Veasey, Chatto and Windus, London, 1993, pp. 141–2].
3. See Moulier Boutang, *Althusser*, p. 275. Althusser tells this story after his own fashion in *Les Faits*, p. 361 [*The Future Lasts a Long Time*, p. 327].
4. On Martin, to whom *For Marx* is dedicated, see Moulier Boutang, *Althusser*, Vol. 1, especially pp. 449–60.

5. 'Une question de faits', *Jeunesse de l'Église, Cahier X* ('L'Évangile captif'). The essay appears in Spanish under the title 'Situación histórica de la Iglesia en perspectiva marxista', in Louis Althusser, *Nuevos escritos: La crisis del movimiento comunista internacional frente a la teoría marxista*, Laia B, Barcelona, 1978, pp. 137–63.
6. See Moulier Boutang, *Althusser*, Vol. 1, pp. 314–24.

The International of Decent Feelings
(1946)

All of us have taken André Malraux's words to heart: 'At the end of the last century, Nietzsche proclaimed the death of God. Now it is for us to ask ourselves whether, today, man is not dead.'[1] I am quoting from memory; those were perhaps not his exact words. I will not forget the emptiness we felt within us then. The crowd watching from the steps of the Sorbonne as this tragic actor[2] struggled in solitude suddenly saw that it was itself this solitude, and that in this desert of the conscience[a] a small, gesticulating man was wrestling with the death of man. 'We must reconstruct an image of man that man can recognize as his own.' Malraux's pathos lay, not in the death whose imminence he proclaimed, but in this desperate consciousness of imminent death haunting someone still alive. Even those who did not share his fears could not help but feel a profound apprehensiveness: one does not watch a man *treat his destiny as an enemy* with impunity.

But in this world that provides us shelter, it is becoming a little clearer every day that men are, in ever increasing numbers, breaking the ties which silently bound them to their fate, and cursing it. Two years after the most atrocious of wars, on this earth covered with peace and ruins, in the mists of the winter that is drawing nigh, silent assemblies are taking place. The murmurs stifled by the clamour of arms, the protests that went unheard amidst the din of war – we can hear them now that calm has been restored. Remarkably, it is from the old lands of Europe that the plaints of peacetime arise. To the east, the immense Russian people has gone back to work, and is reconciling itself to history through work. 'Anguish is a bourgeois state of mind. We are rebuilding' (Ehrenburg).[3] To the west, America, intact, counts its dead and its victories, tests its future strength in the air and on the seas, takes up its place in

---

[a] *Conscience*, which means both 'consciousness' and 'conscience', an ambiguity Althusser exploits in this essay.

the world as it settles into its future: the American century lies before it, stretching outward to the horizon, like a long summer holiday: 'our destiny is to be free Americans.' To be sure, the optimism of effort and freedom continues to mean something to the French and British, most of whom seek in it the justification[4] for the hard life they are leading.[5] Yet it is in the midst of the 'Western' ruins that men are beginning to see that the war waged with arms has not brought the war for souls to an end, that the peace is as murderous as the war, and still more terrible; for now, in peacetime, murder no longer has the clamour of arms for an excuse.

In France we have Malraux, whose tragic discourse has already been mentioned; we have the Camus* of the articles in *Combat*,[6] in which fate seizes men as they murder and releases them only in death; we have Gabriel Marcel, bitterly opposed to the modernity of the world and its 'techniques of debasement';[7] we have the movement called the 'Human Front',[8] which thinks it can avert the fatality of war by conducting an international moral campaign; we have examples of commercially minded agitation, like the issue of *Franchise* about *Le Temps des assassins*.[9] In England, Koestler[10] denounces the way totalitarian regimes enslave men, feeding his contemporaries' resentment of their history with novels. The extraordinary success of his work proves[11] that the curses of these modern prophets are finding a broad public response. And certain echoes from Germany give us reason to believe that the defeated ask nothing better than to join the voice of their all too untroubled conscience to that of the victors' bad conscience – that they too are ready to curse the recent peace and conclude a holy alliance of protest against it. We must ask ourselves what this alliance really signifies. For we are confronted with a phenomenon that is international in scope, and with a diffuse ideology which, though it has not yet been precisely defined, is capable of assuming a certain organizational form: it is said that Camus envisages creating protest groups bent on denouncing crimes against humanity before the conscience of the world, while the 'Human Front' is contemplating the use of cinema or radio[12] to induce humanity to abandon war. One senses, in these attempts, a mentality in search of itself, an intention[13] eager to embody itself in concrete form, an ideology seeking to define itself, entrench itself, and also furnish itself with means of action. If this mentality is international, and in the process of taking institutional form, then a new 'International' is in the making.

---

* It is not the least paradox of our times that the most eloquent protests come to us, in peacetime, from those who were the bravest and staunchest in war: Malraux and Koestler fought in the Republican ranks in Spain, Malraux took part in this war, Camus played an admirable role in the Resistance, like many others who rank amongst the best of these modern crusaders. That they have laid down their arms is troubling.

There is perhaps something to be gained from trying to discover what it conceals.

This 'International' of humane protest against destiny rests on a growing awareness that humanity is threatened, and has become, in the face of the threat, a kind of *'proletariat' of terror*. Whereas the labouring proletariat is defined by sociological, economic, and historical conditions, this latter-day 'proletariat' would seem to be defined by a psychological state: intimidation and fear. And, just as there is proletarian equality in the poverty and alienation of the workers, so too this *implicit proletariat* is said to experience equality, but in death[14] and suffering. According to our authors, the latest inventions, whether in the domain of atoms or torture, *are now and will henceforth be the human condition in which all men are equal*. This is a *de facto* equality, which governs all our acts, in which we live and move unawares, just as a man lives and moves unawares in gravity. And, just as the unity of the proletariat existed before Marx, but only became consciousness [*sic*][15] with Marx, so this unity in terror of the humanity-proletariat exists for us in consciousness thanks only to the revelations of our modern prophets. In their appeals, we hear the same historical pathos (they, at any rate, think we do) that transpires in Marx' and Engels' famous slogans, the pathos common to all appeals to conscience (this conscience which, as Malraux shows, is our sole glory and sole good in the 'night' in which we are plunged); we sense the tragic overtones of the words in which men are summoned to be *born* to the truth, to come to know their condition and master it. Man, know thyself: your condition is death (Malraux), is to be a victim or an executioner (Camus), is to draw steadily closer to the world of prisons and torture (Koestler), or to nuclear war, your total destruction, or to the end of what makes you man and is more than your life: the gaze of your brothers, your freedom, the very struggle for freedom. Humanity, says Camus, is racing towards the abyss like a train hurtling ahead at full speed, while the passengers pursue their petty quarrels. We are madmen grappling on the brink of the abyss, unaware that *death has already reconciled us to one another*. What sensible man, seeing humanity about to perish, can still put faith in class struggle and revolution? What good is it for an activist in a modern workers' party to know that he is threatened by the bourgeoisie, if he does not realize that he is threatened by death as a man before being threatened by servitude as a worker, if he does not realize that this threat overshadows all others, and that the proletariat of the class struggle is an historical diversion? We have only one recourse left, they bluntly tell us, in the face of catastrophe: an holy alliance against destiny. *Let men learn, if there is still time, that the proletariat of class struggle can only divide them, and that they are already united unawares in the proletariat of fear or the bomb, of terror and death, in the proletariat of the human condition.*

The old proletariat having been 'reduced' by the new, we need to examine the essential nature of the latter. What is the *'proletariat' of the human condition?* Camus says in *Combat*[16] that the condition of modern man is *fear*, and, in a certain sense, this is incontestable. It is of the order of everyday experience; and, whatever the reason, that humanity currently lives in fear may be regarded as an *historical fact*. But it is also noteworthy that the causes of this authentic phenomenon are hard to identify: if this fear strikes observers because it so plainly exists, it also disconcerts them by virtue of a kind of inherent irrationality. There is a paradox to fear: if human reason has no control over it, it offers little resistance to the reason that examines it and can be defined without[a] difficulty.[17]

Let us note that fear is, first of all, a *psychological context* of a very general sort. It is neither inscribed in law codes nor entrenched in institutions; it does not even haunt, as fear, the domains over which it holds sway – the prisons, the death camps. Fear haunts the rich man and the poor, the free man and the prisoner, it holds the soul of every man in its grip, whatever his legal or social status, from the moment he looks his destiny in the face and sees that *his destiny awaits him.* There are powerful reflections in Bossuet on the proletariat of death, whom the Middle Ages brought together in the stone of the cathedrals and whom history reconciled in the brotherhood of dust. What unites men is not today, where the rich are not attired like the poor, but tomorrow, where they will lie down together in the same death, or be subjected to the same torture. What unites them is the fact that they await a common fate which will make them all equals. *The proletariat of the human condition is a proletariat of the morrow.* We could quibble with words here, and say that, at this level of abstraction, if human unity is defined by the imminence of a common destiny, it is hard to see why the destiny of daily routine should not also be taken into account: since it 'rains on the good and the evil alike',[18] there is also a proletariat of the rain and another of good weather, and, since the sun shines upon all, a proletariat of daytime and another of night, a proletariat of Sunday, and Monday, and Tuesday – but we will not play the Preacher's[b] game any longer.[19,20] If fear were in reality nothing but a psychological context, an expectation with no object, it would be an abstraction with no escape. But fear is more than a context; it is also a psychological reaction in the face of a certain real threat. Here the object of fear draws closer to it – and the paradox of fear

[a] Althusser writes 'with difficulty', doubtless a slip of the pen.
[b] The preacher of *Ecclesiastes*.

bursts into view: however intense the obsession, the object of fear always lies outside it, and ahead of it. It is this which distinguishes the labouring proletariat from the proletariat of fear. The worker is not a proletarian by virtue of what-will-happen-to-him-tomorrow, but by virtue of what happens to him every minute of the day. As Camus said so well, not long ago, 'There is no tomorrow'; the *labouring proletariat is an everyday reality, like our daily bread*. The proletariat is that which has no future, not even the future of fear: poverty, in the proletariat, is not the fear of poverty, it is an actual presence that never disappears, it is on the walls, on the table, in the sheets, in the air the worker breathes and the water he drinks, in the money that he makes and that is made from his poverty, in the very gestures that conjure fear; proletarians are in poverty the way one is in the night, the way certain sick people are in their suffering, which is so closely bound up with them that it becomes part of their nature. The man who is afraid lives with his back to a wall,[21] says Camus, but we do not want to live like dogs. The wall is a horizon, the only horizon, but at least there is a horizon.[22] *The fearful man lives with his back to the wall; the proletarian is walled in*. Thus he does not see his destiny before him, he does not take the coming war or the bombs that churn the seas at the other end of the world for signs of Fatality, he does not fear the peace he has conquered; his condition is his labour, his needs, his daily struggle. *He knows that tomorrow will be a today, and that the proletariat of the morrow is, today, a smoke-screen for the proletariat of every day.*

Let us add that fear and its object are not things of the same kind, which suggests that a dialectic of fear is inconceivable. The fearful man is at one with his fear, but the object of his fear is not present to him the way his fear is: I am not afraid of another as other, I am afraid of the destiny that awaits me in the other. I am not afraid of the war as war, but of being the wounded man, the invalid, the man in pain the war will make me. The war does not really enter into my fear, in which I find only my body mutilated by war. The true object of my fear *is myself imagined as suffering pain at some point in the future; that is, not another, but I myself, and not a real, but an imaginary I. The content of fear is something imaginary, non-existent*: that is why, unlike the proletarian, who finds in the proletariat the means of emancipating himself from the proletariat, *the man who is afraid cannot convert the object of his fear into the abolition of his fear*.[23] Prisoners can escape, because theirs is an objective condition, because the bars are real; real bars can be smashed: freedom now! The man who is afraid is a prisoner without a prison and without bars; he is his own prisoner, and threats stand guard in his soul. This is an adventure from which there is no escape, because there is no fleeing a prison without bars: *fear is captivity without possibility of flight*.

Servitude, however, does have a content: the master and labour. Whereas the object of fear is merely imaginary, the workers' condition involves appropriating, amidst the domination of the capitalist world, a real object that grounds the real dialectic of proletarian emancipation and provides the means of achieving it. In other words, *servitude can transform itself into freedom* by reflecting on its own content and transcending its content through action. There can be no emancipation from fear through the consciousness of fear.[24] *Servitude, in contrast, is a form of captivity from which one can escape, because it is a real prison, with real walls and real bars.* That is why anguish is not the proletariat's lot: *there is no emancipating oneself from the human condition, but it is possible to emancipate oneself from the workers'*. No matter the price and the patience with which this freedom will be purchased; at least one knows that it is possible, that man can reconcile himself with his destiny and live in the expectation, not of the end of the world, but of freedom; not in despair and absurdity, but in hope. Every day, the proletarian experiences the concrete reality of the content of his condition; every day, he repeats his efforts to get the better of it, and this daily experience furnishes him the double proof that he is not wrestling with shadows, but confronts a real object in his struggle, and that this object, inasmuch as it exists and resists, can be overcome. It is for this reason that the workers' condition is dialectical, for *it can transform its content, converting concrete servitude into concrete freedom*. Let us, finally, note that a community forged in fear and the community forged through the emancipation of the proletariat do not have the same import. Apprehension is a collective expectation, an *advent*, in which human beings are united in spirit but not in truth, and are all the more disoriented in that *they already dwell in the same void*. But it is not possible to live outside the truth forever. Because the man who is afraid has not grasped the truth of his fear, he makes his fear come true.

Alain[a] liked to point out that wars are myths thus translated into reality, that wars are born of the fear of wars, as sins are born of the fear of sin. This communion in catastrophe is a herd phenomenon, whereby everyone ends up fearing an object endowed with existence only by everyone else's fear, and no-one can account for the non-existent object all are afraid of. The result is the misunderstanding known as panic. History offers no lack of examples, from the Great Fear of the year 1000 to that of the summer of 1789, from the stock market crashes of the nineteenth century through the atomic panics touched off by radio programmes to, finally, the diffuse panic we live in, precipitated by ill-advised acts that are the fruits of disarray, like a certain issue of *Témoignage chrétien*[25] on the-outbreak-of-war-in-two-weeks'-time. This apocalyptic fraternity is a pure creation of language. Looking back, we can make out anticipations of it in certain formulations of *Man's Hope*,

[a] Pseudonym of the philosopher Émile-Auguste Chartier (1868–1951).

perhaps the most sombre[26] book of our times: is it still possible to speak of a 'fraternity beyond death'? Fear is not a fatherland, nor is courage (we have learned this from the fascists, who now attempt to exonerate themselves by talking about their courage); more, *the human condition is not a human fatherland*. It is, perhaps, the fatherland of men as they appear to God; because we are Christians, we call this condition original sin. For the man who is not a Christian, and for the Christian who does not usurp God's place, the human fatherland is not the proletariat of the human condition, it is the proletariat *tout court*, leading the whole of humanity towards its emancipation. This proletariat has a real content. Speaking of the French socialists, Marx wrote in 1844: 'For them, the brotherhood of man is no empty phrase but a reality.'[27] For us, brotherhood is no longer to be found in fear or words; it can only be found in the truth.

We may say here that the 'proletariat of the human condition' (in its present form, based on fear) not only does not call the reality of the labouring proletariat into question, but also turns out, upon analysis, to be an abstraction, i.e., something which has no reality beyond that of discourse and intentions. *The proletariat of fear is a myth, but a myth that exists, and it is particularly important that it be exposed as such by Christians.* For, as Christians, we believe that there is a human condition; in other words, we believe in the equality of all men before God, and his Judgement, *but we do not want the Judgement of God to be spirited away before our very eyes; nor do we want to see non-Christians and, occasionally, Christians as well, commit the sacrilege of taking the atomic bomb for the will of God, equality before death for equality before God* (this needs to be said, since Bossuet and certain other preachers have not gotten beyond this position), *and the tortures of the concentration camps for the Last Judgement.* Yet no-one is more vulnerable to blackmail based on this confusion of terms than Christians. When people talk to them about the equality of men in their unhappy condition, they take this psychological truth for a religious one, and when the panic-stricken declare that the end of time and the destruction of the planet are at hand, they hear echoes of St. John and the Apocalypse: one need only play on the religious ambiguity to take them in as one does a child. What has been written and uttered in the genre 'theology of the atom bomb', in Christian circles, beggars the imagination; we have not even been spared the speeches of Churchill or Truman, representatives of 'Christian civilization'! Whenever he suspects that the political is turning religious, Gabriel Marcel immediately goes into a prophetic trance:

> ... this war, if it takes place, will in fact be a bilateral crime. But the paradoxical notion of a bilateral crime calls for closer examination. It appears to be indistinguishable from that of sin itself. This would suggest that we shift

our attention to the religious plane.... Are we not approaching the moment in history when sin will exactly coincide with its own punishment, appearing as the very expression of the wrath of God?[28]

Gabriel Marcel is a dupe who seeks the reasons for his delusion, and is astute enough to find the real ones. Mauriac, for his part, is a man of disconcerting and disarming naiveté. Childishness, in his case, is a chronic state of mind; he confesses his faith according to St. Koestler with the fervour of a convert, discovers the Passion in the Moscow trials, and divides people up into the good and the bad the way one cleaves an apple.[29] We will not be swayed by the talent[30] of these novelists turned prophets, or by the fact that Christians and non-Christians alike have come together around a common theme. Although Camus and Mauriac have begun chanting in unison,[31] we know very well that the same words do not mean the same thing to both of them; if they are sincere (as I believe they are), they are fooling themselves, and us to boot. *This false end of the world is teeming with false prophets who announce false Christs and treat an event as the Advent.* But Christ has taught us that we must beware of false prophets, and also that they will reappear as the Last Days draw nigh. The paradox is plain: the end that is close for every Christian is not the end of the false prophets of history.

This 'International' of protest does not, then, hold any religious meaning for us; but the fact remains that it is an historical event, one noteworthy in that it cannot explain its own existence, resting as it does on a myth. Thus we are faced with a real phenomenon lacking all internal necessity: an *ideology*, that is, a trend of opinion which remains historically incomprehensible if we do not refer to the context in which it appears. We have shown that this ideology does not call real historical distinctions into question, since its content is imaginary. We need, then, to confront this ideology with the history it appears in, and to elucidate, in a real history, the reasons for this imaginary construct.*

---

* Let us forthrightly admit that this enterprise is a hazardous one, and that we do not claim to be able to carry it off successfully in a few pages. Lack of information and of detachment are valid excuses that would have deterred us from publishing these remarks, if we had not thought it necessary to call attention to a trend of opinion that is now sufficiently broad to inspire reflection, if not concern. On the other hand, it is all too clear that any 'reduction' of human protest to psychological or political causes, even if they are obscure, will necessarily offend the sensibilities of all self-respecting people; it would be absurd to suppose that the risk that their protest might be perverted had escaped them. Today it is always being proven to all of us that we have misunderstood our own intentions, their meaning, and their consequences; the world is full of fortune-tellers more or less in league with history. There is something healthy in the reaction of protesters, we need protesters, but one might also be permitted to wish that they would pay some attention to what becomes of their generous words; or, if they are too profoundly purist for that, that they let outsiders who wish them well signal the dangers it is hard to perceive from the inside.

By way of explanation, let us first note the disequilibrium caused by the war. The transition from war to peace is not risk-free. War feeds on war; peace is initially a void, and dizziness in the face of this void. Those for whom war is a fatherland enter peace as they would a desert: German youth do not know what to do with their hands, they no longer have any future because peace – *terra incognita* – has been established. How many, even among the victors, fail to recognize in this peace what they sought to achieve during the war, either because they approved of the war for reasons of courage and morality they seek in vain in peacetime; or because they disavow, in the peace, the consequences of a war they accepted?

Those who were willing to accept the concentration camps (I mean the fascists), and those who were willing to accept the 300,000 deaths in Hamburg (I mean the Allies); those who lived off the deaths of millions of enslaved human beings, and those who reluctantly consented to become 'murderers' to prevent the massacre from continuing; those who assumed responsibility for their own deaths, and the deaths of those dear to them, and the deaths of their enemies, so that life might become possible again; those who, on the one side as on the other, but in opposite senses (because the cause was enslavement in one case, and liberation in the other), bear the responsibility for millions of deaths – all these people sometimes mingle their voices, now that peace has returned, in curious lamentations. We are all murderers! cries Camus. I think that 'Europe' can find reconciliation on the basis of this obvious truth; the first to hearken to it will assuredly be those who, with Camus' help and contrary to his intentions, are going to clear their consciences at bargain rates. Our crimes make us all equals, they will say, equals because we have killed – behold, we have been absolved by crime, made indistinguishable by crime, reconciled by crime! It is impossible to hear such a monstrosity without a sense of shame. And, when one knows the echo it is finding in Germany, and knows too that the German Churches have, in a perversion of religion, appropriated this secular absolution, one truly wonders whether words and deeds still mean something – whether, in the eyes of men, *the act of killing to enslave and killing to set free is the same act, whether man is ultimately defined not by his reasons for living and dying, which are what make him a man, but by the life and death that make him a dog.* No death transcends the reasons for dying it; our reasons judge our dead, distinguishing between the corpses united in the corruption of death. *But this unity in death is corruption, and corruption everything that entrenches it in the human spirit.* We must surely free ourselves of this shame: we are not dogs, and those who wrested freedom from fascism for all of us are not dogs – this freedom we accept without asking its price, forgetting that, if some died to abolish it, others died to defend it! Who stands to gain from this confusion? Obviously, those who died fighting for slavery and those who honour their memory in the country of their birth, and also those who, in certain nations, want to buy, with forgiveness, mercenaries for the next war . . .

The same desire to conceal real reasons and present realities behind a confusing myth also has something to do with the aforementioned reaction to the end of the war. We are aware that a war does not begin when it is declared; *but we have yet to realize that it does not end with the armistice.* Peace is supposed to be essentially different from war; in war, they say, death may be inflicted by man, but it must occur naturally in peace (Camus speaks of abolishing capital punishment!*). The laws governing these two situations are supposed to differ so sharply that one can stop fighting a war the way a child stops playing a game, by changing the rules or shouting 'truce!' Today one meets people with the best of intentions who explain that the war is over, that we must now put aside its rules, arms, and methods – that this peace is not a peace because war is not only being prepared, but is also being conducted in it, because it has not done away with the concentration camps, because it fosters social antagonisms, because men have, after all, earned the right to live in serenity, and yet the struggle goes on. There is only one means, they say, of combating this scandal of a war that continues in peacetime: protest, the cry of conscience – and we have come back round to our International of Decent Feelings, the creation of all those who have given up the idea of achieving peace in and through action, who want to obtain *immediately,* by raising an outcry, what they have not quite had the patience to conquer: the sincere (generous religious natures who have strayed into politics by mistake), the indignant, the impatient, those suffering from persecution complexes (*not* the persecuted). Of course, all these good intentions are inoperative in the short term, and mystified. 'Not everyone that saith, Lord, Lord . . .'[32] *When we merely invoke the Lord, we serve, not the Lord we invoke, but another whom we do not.* And when we see Koestler holding up, in his sermon to the 'European Left', the example and ideal of English Labour in power, or Malraux turning out luminous myths on the theme of the Western bloc (the world's freedom has to be saved from America and the USSR), or Mauriac extending Léon Blum[33] the vote of confidence of all right-thinking people,[34] we are entitled to ask *if these desperate people are not nurturing a secret hope, and are not serving a cause or master they do not invoke*: the cause of a 'Western' socialism without class struggle, that is, the cause of a Europe united in a verbal, moralizing socialism which conjures away social antagonisms, thus maintaining in actual fact, despite concessions of form, the essential positions of capitalism. As to the master who is not invoked, it might well be the kind of capitalism that, as we are seeing in England,[35] puts

---

* Provisionally, to be sure, and as a therapeutic measure.

socialism in the government as the best means of ensuring that there will be none in the economy, and would like to extend this system of protection against Communism to the rest of Europe. Here we are afforded a glimpse, perhaps, of the objective significance of the phenomenon under consideration and of the meaning of this hysteria over war, this atomic neurosis from across the Atlantic, nourished by American news reports and Bikini;[36] they mean *to tear the men of this old world from the very reality of their existence, from their daily political and social struggles, and leave them in the clutches of the myths of fear.*

The present reflection has no relevance to Christians as Christians, but it does aspire to reach Christians as men. The vast operation (little matter whether conscious or unconscious) we are here exposing tends to give men the sense *that they cannot reconcile themselves with their destiny, that they will not succeed in mastering their technology* and will be destroyed by their own inventions, *that, far from emancipating them, their labour enslaves and kills them.* This is the theme of the sorcerer's apprentice – and of the childishness that is invading the world, shadowed by a political pessimism (man has not reached adulthood, one cannot depend on man to save man) which all decent souls interpret in the religious mode. Unfortunately, it is still men who preach this kind of morality to men, or who inspire it, or who allow others to propagate it. Unfortunately, these good apostles are precisely those who, before the world ends, have the greatest interest in shaking mankind's confidence in itself and its destiny, and, in particular, in discouraging those in our camp who have already undertaken to reconcile humanity with its history – those[37] who hold that technology liberates rather than enslaves humanity, that humanity's labour emancipates rather than destroys it. It would be monstrous if man, who is discovering atomic energy, were not also to discover a way of using it for man's benefit. But this perversion of the atom is nothing new: the bomb is simply a product of human labour, *and the world in which humanity trembles before what it has itself wrought is an extravagant image of the proletarian condition, in which the worker is enslaved by his own labour*; it is, quite simply, the same world. One sees, then, which 'proletariat' encompasses the other, and one also understands where the human will may find a solution: the road to man's reconciliation with his destiny is essentially that of the appropriation of the products of his labour, of what he creates in general, and of history as his creation. This reconciliation presupposes a transition from capitalism to socialism by way of the emancipation of the labouring proletariat, which can, through this act, rid not only itself, but also all humanity of contradiction, delivering it, moreover, from the apocalyptic panic besetting it. Destiny, said Hegel, is the consciousness of oneself as an enemy.[38] We look for the advent of the human condition and the end of destiny. But we know the price of this effort, and the lucidity it calls for. The solution will be attained only in struggle, but we are not so naive as to believe that war does not haunt peace; on the contrary, we . . .[39]

In this combat, we will also be battling the myths that are meant to conceal the truth from us: we are hungry for truth, we love it as we love the bread it tastes of. In this combat, we do not reject good will, *but we need good will and comrades who are willing to hear and to see. It is not the deaf and the blind who will lead men to befriend their destiny.*

Notes

1. Allusion to a lecture on 'L'homme et la culture' that André Malraux delivered on 4 November 1946 at the Sorbonne in the framework of 'Unesco Month'. According to the account of the lecture given in *Combat* on 5 November 1946, the sentence Althusser evokes ran as follows: 'Since Nietzsche, God has been dead, but we need to know whether or not, in this old Europe, Man is also dead. Europe today is not more desolate nor bloodier than the figure of Man.'
2. First draft: 'this little actor'.
3. *Franchise*, no. 3, November/December 1946 (see n. 9). The exact wording of the sentence is: 'Anguish is a bourgeois luxury. As for us, we are rebuilding.'
4. First draft: 'find in it the meaning'.
5. A passage has been struck in the manuscript: 'But it is from old Europe that complaints of exhaustion and revolts of conscience arise.'
6. Albert Camus, 'Ni victimes ni bourreaux', a series of eight articles published in *Combat* between 19 November and 30 November 1946 (also in Camus, *Essais*, Pléiade, Gallimard, Paris, 1965, pp. 331–52) ['Neither Victims nor Executioners', in Camus, *Between Hell and Reason: Essays from the Resistance Newspaper* Combat, *1944–1947*, trans. Alexandre de Gramont, University Press of New England, Hanover (NH), 1991, pp. 115–45].
7. See, for example, the article 'La propagande comme technique d'avilissement' [Propaganda as a Technique of Debasement], *Les Nouvelles Paroles françaises*, 9 March 1946 (also in *Les Hommes contre l'humain*, Éditions du Vieux-Colombier, Paris, 1951, repr. 1991, Les Éditions Universitaires, with a preface by Paul Ricœur); or, in the same collection, 'Technique et péché' [Technology and Sin].
8. A movement that described itself as 'born under the German occupation, out of the experiences of a handful of leaders of Resistance groups belonging to the National Service of the Maquis Schools', the Human Front published, beginning in 1945, some ten 'letters to the citizens of the world', as well as several instalments of the 'working papers of the Human Front of Citizens of the World', an offshoot of the 'International Centre for World Research and Expression'. One collection of 'working papers' was placed under Einstein's patronage. The following appeal is ascribed to him: 'I urgently request that you send a check to me, the president of the committee of despair of atomic research.'
9. *Franchise*, no. 3, November/December 1946. The whole issue is presented as if it were a play entitled 'The Day of the Murderers, Tragedy in Five Acts' by Pierre Garrigues, Louis Pauwels, and Jean Sylveire; the 'characters in the play' are the contributors to the issue, among them Albert Einstein ('23 May 1946 . . . To the Press'), Albert Camus ('We Murderers'), Emmanuel Mounier ('General Mobilization'), Aldous Huxley ('Hunger'), Ilya Ehrenburg ('I Cannot Tell You Anything'), Gabriel Marcel ('Our Sole Refuge: Grace'), and Jean-Paul Sartre ('The War of Fear'). The 'Curtain-Raiser' that stands in lieu of an editorial statement includes, notably, the following: 'The vast multitude pays, in blood and hunger, the lesson that the only reality is its absolute anguish and absolute poverty, in a world in which increasingly "satisfactory" political principles

proliferate, ravaging the earth ... We stand on the very brink of the abyss. A handful of men are frenetically active, pretending, without realizing it, to be acting responsibly.'

10. *Darkness at Noon*, Modern Library, New York, 1941. A copy of *The Yogi and the Commissar* was discovered in Althusser's library at his death. In 1946, *Thieves in the Night* was being published in instalments in *Combat*.

11. First draft: 'is the sign'.

12. First draft: 'is thinking of utilizing modern propaganda tools like cinema...'. In the first 'Letter to the Citizens of the World', which is undated, but was most probably published in 1946, we do, indeed, find the following: 'In four months' time, it would be possible to produce a fifty-minute film that could be dubbed and distributed throughout the world. It could be put to good use by thousands of lecturers active in the movement.... In six months' time, it would be possible to produce a daily and weekly for the citizens of the world.... It is possible ... to obtain time slots for radio programmes in a number of countries, and use them to address all mankind in the world's major languages.'

13. First draft: 'a form of psychological behaviour'.

14. First draft: 'before death and suffering'.

15. First draft: 'but did not exist for the proletariat in consciousness'.

16. The first article in the series 'Neither Victims nor Executioners' was entitled 'The Century of Fear'.

17. A handwritten page, attached to the typed text with a paper clip, was found among Althusser's papers; it was probably to be inserted at the beginning of the next paragraph. 'These reasons are powerful ones. It is not only their outwardly logical form that pleads in their favour, but also the weight of a certain experience, which they reveal in a sudden flash of illumination. Koestler, Camus, and Malraux show us our fate, the greatest risk humanity has ever run. Until today, only our civilizations were mortal; we learned this rather late in the day, but were then quick to draw the lesson: that we should hasten the death of the old societies and invent new ones. Today we can no longer play these games. Death now threatens not only our ways of life, but our life *tout court*. There can no longer be any question of inventing new customs; what is at stake for us today is maintaining the life which, however old it may be, is the only one we have, and will not have a second [*sic*]. Here our prophets step in not only to draw our attention to the disease, but also to show us that the cure resides in the disease itself. Awareness of our perilous condition is enough, they say, to preserve us from the peril and reconcile us with our future. The state of apprehension we live in contains the principle of both its own destruction and our emancipation from it. The destiny that dominates us through fear could be brought to be as obedient as a child. We need only, by undergoing a cure of conscience and alarm, convert the content of our fear into tranquillity of soul, overcome our present neurosis, and extract from the future war, which we already inhabit, promises of peace. We do not, however, believe that this claim is warranted, or that words can cure humanity. The disease tormenting it has deeper causes than a troubled conscience, and we do not think that the treatment which will vanquish it can operate at the same level as the disease described. In other words, we do not believe that consciousness of the affliction can lead to its disappearance if that consciousness strictly limits itself to the affliction as described, without penetrating to the profound regions it stems from. We need to establish this point before proceeding. Let us, then, try to see, at the level of fear as such, if the affliction can transform itself; if it contains within itself reason enough to exorcize itself; if, like the labouring proletariat, humanity too can emancipate itself from its terrified condition by means of that condition – let us try to see, in a word, what the real nature of this fear is.'

18. An allusion to Malebranche; for example, the *Entretiens métaphysiques*, IX, §12 [*Dialogues on Metaphysics and on Religion*, trans. Morris Ginsberg, Macmillan, New York, 1923, p. 240], or the *Traité de la nature et de la grâce*, I, §14. Althusser was fascinated by these texts all his life, and was to evoke them again in his last writings. See *Écrits philosophiques et politiques*, Vol. 1, Stock/IMEC, Paris, 1994, p. 539.

19. A passage has been struck: 'The morrow of the human condition is not daily routine, but, rather, that which calls man into question by putting the best he possesses in

jeopardy, his life included. But this extreme situation does not alter the fact that what we are considering here is an abstraction; it is, perhaps, important to understand this if, as Christians, we do not wish to be misled into taking *equality before atomic death for the equality of men before God, and the proletariat of fear in 1946 for the proletariat of the Last Judgement.'*

20. A handwritten page has been intercalated here; it was doubtless intended to replace the typed version. Althusser probably meant to insert this passage immediately after the word 'Preacher,' though this is not explicitly stated. 'The object of our fear is not the distant limit constituted by death, towards which each of our days carries us, though only one attains it; nor is it simply our environment – the air we breathe, the space we move in – which accompanies our acts as the horizon insensibly accompanies a man walking. Such equality in an abstract condition would no more prevent us from living than equal access to the air prevents us from breathing – unless we waited to live in order to live, and died simply of the fear of dying. Our fear is something other than a simple psychological context: it is a psychological reaction to a genuine threat. Here we see fear's object draw closer to it. I am not apprehensive of death in general, but of death by the bomb, and, of these two terms, which I think of as necessarily linked, I know that one is real, even if I do not know its geographical location: I mean the bomb. The reality of the bomb constitutes the reality of my fear. Yet, if I examine matters more closely, I can also see that the bomb is, by itself, harmless. It is harmless at the moment I write, inasmuch as the effect of dropping it would doubtless be to prevent me from writing. What is dangerous is, then, its significance, its destination, its utilization. But, by saying this, I add a new dimension to the bomb itself, one by which it begins to be relevant to my existence. The bomb does not threaten me unless it is aimed at me, unless it can reach me, so that my fear becomes an anticipation of the threat. The object of my fear is no longer the bomb or the war, but the possibility of the bomb or the war; that is, a chain of events that does not yet exist when I envisage it as a possibility. Finally, to follow up my remark, I note that this possibility does not affect me as long as I do not feel it in my very body. The true object of my fear is no longer a real object (the bomb), nor an anticipated event (the explosion of the bomb), but myself as imagined victim of this possible event. My fear is not of the bomb as bomb, but of the destiny that awaits me in the form of the bomb. My fear is not of the war as war, but of being the wounded man, the invalid, the man in pain it will make of me. The real war is not actually part of my fear, in which I find only my body mutilated by war. In reality, I am the object of my fear, I myself imagined as suffering pain at some future time; not the real I that I am at this moment, but an imaginary I. Thus I have to grant that the object of my fear does not have the same reality as my fear. I apprehend the latter as a daily obsession; analysis shows me that the former is merely an imaginary object.'

21. 'Living with one's back to the wall is a life for dogs. Well, the men of my generation, those who today enter faculties and universities, are living more and more like dogs.' Albert Camus, 'Le siècle de la peur', in *Essais*, p. 331 ['The Century of Fear', in *Between Hell and Reason*, p. 117].

22. A passage has been struck: 'The true proletariat does not fear its condition, because this condition does not lie *before* it; it dwells in its condition as if this condition were its nature.'

23. The last part of the manuscript passage cited in n. 20 was to have appeared here.

24. A passage has been struck: 'In contrast, the slave who knows he is a slave thereby knows that he is the master of the master, and so knows that he is the master of his servitude, not only in his soul, but in life, because the master is at his mercy from the moment he ceases to work: his own servitude is therefore at his mercy. But fear is not at the mercy of the man who is afraid: we no more cry out against the night than we can pierce the sky with arrows. There is no fleeing fear, and that is why the condition of the man battling his destiny is tragic; we are executioners or victims, but are no longer men.'

25. *Témoignage chrétien*, 3 February 1946. The allusion is to the second of a series of two articles; the series is entitled 'Where is France Going?' and signed 'Témoignage chrétien'. In this article, subtitled 'War Is At our Doorstep', one finds, for example, the

following: 'In fact, war is at our doorstep; if events of a semi-miraculous sort do not occur in the next few months, France will again experience the horrors of war and occupation.'

26. First draft: 'despairing'.

27. Karl Marx, *Œuvres philosophiques*, Vol. VI, Alfred Costes, Paris, 1937, p. 64 [*Economic and Philosophical Manuscripts*, in *Early Writings*, trans. and ed. T. B. Bottomore, McGraw-Hill, New York, 1963, p. 176].

28. Gabriel Marcel, 'Un seul recours: la grâce', *Franchise*, no. 3, November/December 1946. See n. 9.

29. See, for example, 'La vocation trahie', an editorial in *Le Figaro* of 3 December 1946, in which Mauriac cites Koestler at length: 'There are but two conceptions of human morality, and they are poles apart. One is Christian and humanitarian: it says that the individual is sacred and that the rules of arithmetic must not be applied to human units. . . . The other starts out from the basic principle that a collective end always justifies the means, and not only permits, but indeed requires, that the individual be subordinated and sacrificed to the community, which may use him either as an experimental guinea pig or as a sacrificial lamb.'

30. First draft: 'by these great names, nor by the talent . . .'.

31. In October 1944, Camus and Mauriac had engaged in a sharp polemic over the purges that began in France after the Liberation.

32. *Matthew*, 7:21: 'Not every one that saith unto me, Lord, Lord, shall enter into the kingdom of heaven; but he that doeth the will of my Father which is in heaven.' (Found in his library after his death, Althusser's copy of the Segond edition of the Bible contained, curiously, a photograph of André Gide.)

33. Léon Blum was elected head of government on 17 December 1946. In his editorial in *Le Figaro* of 19 December 1946 ('The Inconsistency of the Communists'), Mauriac wrote: 'It is not because he appears to be a moderate that a socialist like Léon Blum is received without mistrust by the [National] Assembly and the country, but because he gives the word Republic or the word Democracy the meaning we too give them. The motives for his governmental acts will be easily discernible. He can be misled, we know, but he will not mislead us.'

34. A passage has been struck: 'or Camus catering to the German conscience with justifications for future use'.

35. Labour won the Parliamentary elections of 5 July 1945.

36. A reference to the first US atomic test on Bikini Atoll, which took place on 1 July 1946, in the presence of journalists from around the world expressly invited for the occasion.

37. A passage has been struck: '(the Marxists and their Christian or non-Christian allies)'.

38. G. W. F. Hegel, *L'Esprit du christianisme et son destin*; cf. the translation by Jacques Martin, Vrin, Paris, 1948, p. 53 [*The Spirit of Christianity and its Fate*, in *Hegel's Early Theological Writings*, trans. T. M. Knox, Philadelphia, University of Pennsylvania Press, 1971, p. 231].

39. Part of the last page of the typescript (which was discovered among Althusser's papers) has been torn away.

On Content in the Thought
of G. W. F. Hegel
(1947)

The Content is always young.

G. W. F. Hegel

Introduction*

1. The problem of the content in Hegel's philosophy is, first of all, an historical problem. If truth is nothing apart from its becoming, then the becoming of truth appears as the truth of truth, and the development of truth as the manifestation of what truth is in itself. In a certain sense, history provides Hegelianism with the moment it lacks: the test of the for-itself. Hegel was enveloped in his own thought as a child is wrapped up in his growth, ignorant of the law that makes him grow or the contradictions slumbering within him. We need to revive the dialectic of the ages of man, and to seek, in the maturity of history, the truth of Hegel, a philosopher who died young: it is we who are living his manhood.

For, by way of history, Hegel's thought escapes the prison of a dawning age and the confines of a civil servant's mentality, offering itself to our gaze in the freedom of its realization and its objective development. In a sense that is not un-Marxist, our world has become philosophy, or, more precisely, Hegel come to maturity now stands before us – is, indeed, our world: the world has become Hegelian to the extent that Hegel was a truth capable of becoming a world. We need only read: fortunately, the letters are there before our eyes, writ large in the text of history – letters become men.

* As Althusser's text already contains a great many notes, no explanatory notes have been added by the editors. Indispensable supplementary information has been given, in brackets, at the end of the author's notes; references to English translations of works in German or French have, when available, been supplied by the translator. So as not to overburden the page, the author's notes have been placed at the end of the text. Translator's notes, indicated by an asterisk, have been placed at the foot of the page.

But the lesson of history is unequivocal: Hegel come to maturity is the decomposition and decay of Hegel. Ten years after the Master's death, his work was already coming undone, splitting apart, developing in opposite directions, turning into a battlefield. Indeed, it was itself a battle: *Ich bin der Kampf* [I am the battle]. Those famous words, uttered long before, in Jena, found a strange sort of posthumous confirmation in the struggles of the Young Hegelians. With the peace of the final system, in the absolution of Spirit, opposites seemed to be reconciled. But the simple stroke of death was enough to set them free, as the fall of the Prussian despot unleashed the deep-seated forces of the opposition. Is this not a sign that the bond which held them at rest was external to them?

Engels distinguishes two basic elements in Hegel's thought: in his words, the dialectical method, adopted by the young revolutionaries, and the system, the set of political, religious, and aesthetic truths the young conservatives laid claim to. One and the same loyalty to the Master united his warring disciples, who professed to derive from Hegel himself 'the real consequences Hegel did not dare work out'.[1] In the course of the nineteenth century, the decomposition process grew more intense: the adverse parties abandoned, one by one, most of the truths of the Hegelian corpus, retaining only a certain spirit or general tendency. Although it can be argued that philosophy has not gone beyond Hegelianism, and that the struggles of our recent history are merely the conflict of Left against Right in Hegel himself, the fact remains that no-one is now fighting over the body of the system, over the logic or the aesthetics, the philosophy of nature or the philosophy of religion. Advanced Hegelianism has disintegrated in two ways: by abandoning a major part of its contents, for which contemporary thought has no use, and by revealing that the spirit which has survived this body is divided and antagonistic.

In the history of Hegel's philosophy, this double externality – of life to death and of life to life – raises the question of the nature of the body that is thus going to wrack and ruin before our very eyes. Marx did not rule out the possibility that history could decay; we are discovering in the dead Hegel the decay of truth. Improbably, Hegel announced in advance what the decomposition of his own thought signified: 'truth in philosophy means that the concept corresponds to reality. ... A dead body therefore still has an existence, but no longer a true one, for it is a conceptless existence; that is why the dead body decomposes.'[2] Life slips with ease from one body to another, it is survival:* Hegel survives in Marxism, in the existentialisms and fascisms, but the corpus of Hegelian truths is merely a corpse in history which displays its decay as does 'an

* *Survie*, which also means 'life after death'.

existence without a concept', a content without form, a content abandoned by an alien form.

2. This historical experience brings us back to Hegel. The development
of Hegelianism points to what its beginnings concealed. Hegel's decomposition is his truth, but it would be futile to seek the truth of this
decomposition outside Hegel himself. The problem of the content of
Hegel's thought is posed in Hegel; the dormant contradictions slumber
in this undeveloped in-itself. It is there that the externality of soul to
body or of form to content must manifest itself. Otherwise, the revelation
of history would be nothing more than the revelation of an error – not
the development of Hegel's truth, but the exhibition of a mythical,
misunderstood, falsified Hegel. Hegel's thought must furnish us the
truth by itself, appear in its profundity or its formalism, resolve, at last,
the debate that divides his commentators, by teaching us whether the
dialectic represents a form which is imposed from without, or one which
emerges from its content, whether it is formal or real, whether its
schematism is purely mechanistic or the very soul of things.

We might content ourselves with a classificatory method here, like
that Nicolai Hartmann recommends we adopt to sift real from formal
dialectics in Hegel, the authentic from the schematic. But that would be
to treat Hegel's thought as a fully formed historical object held up to our
critical judgement, i.e., subject to a criterion of discrimination from
without that would permit us to distinguish, on the basis of certain
presuppositions, the good sides of a given philosophy from the bad.
Thus it would be enough to retrace, in thought, the decomposition of the
system, sort the true from the false, and mime, from outside, the
historical breakdown of the system. But that would be to transform
Hegelian truth into something external, to convert the system into an
object analytical judgement could reduce to its constituent elements –
without noticing that such analysis destroys its object, arrogating unto
itself the truth of the object thus decomposed, and, in essence, discovering in the object only the truth of its decomposition, i.e., the externality
of this apprehension itself. To treat Hegel as an object is, then, to
presuppose the externality in question. The only way to throw off the
shackles of this judging consciousness is to penetrate to the heart of the
truth by plunging into its content, by coming into existence and growing
with it. We must treat Hegel as, literally, a subject.

3. Just as the historical evolution of the content directed our attention
back to the content itself, so the fully formed content of Hegel's thought
directs our attention back to its development. Now, however, we have
gone beyond historical externality and the externality of the judging
consciousness: what we have in view is the externality of the content
itself, and – as it is still development that is in question – what we must
take as the object of our analysis is the development of the content in

itself, in its concept, or, to put it another way, the development of the concept of the content. Indeed, in the system of Hegel's thought it is impossible to treat an element as a given, since Hegel's basic way of proceeding is to abolish givens. A given points back to that which establishes it as a given; what is a given content for the judging consciousness points back, within the system, to the process that produces it as its result, i.e., to its own internal development. The fully developed content that Hegel's work represents for us is, for Hegel, the moment of an immediate internality made explicit; in other words, the manifestation of the concept of that content. If, in Hegel, results are nothing apart from the process of their becoming, we need to examine the becoming of this concept in order to obtain the truth of the content as our result, and to distinguish between the truth and the error of this truth. Perhaps it will then be possible to say in what sense Hegelianism genuinely thinks its content, or is merely a formalism without depth; and to account for the paradox that this most rigorous of systems legitimized the least rigorous of institutions, and then underwent a natural decomposition process, as if its very rigour had been borrowed.

It is the emergence, growth, and decay of the concept that we shall attempt to describe in the course of this study.

I

ORIGINS OF THE CONCEPT

Nach dem Gehalte der Wahrheit
war mithin eine Sehnsucht vorhanden . . .

(*Geschichte der Philosophie*)

Hegel's philosophy presents itself not only as a corpus of truths, a finished whole we can consider in its place in the history of thought, but also as a totalizing whole; not only as an attempt to grasp reality, but also as the act by which truth is fulfilled or accomplished, *sich vollzieht*, achieves plenitude. The expression must be taken literally to mean that the *plenitudo temporum* is accomplished with Hegel, that his work is not merely the revelation of this event, but the event itself: in it, event is absorbed by Advent. Hence its ambiguity: it is both that by virtue of which the whole is accomplished, *vollzogen*, full, that which constitutes the whole as such – but, at the same time, it is that through which the lack it serves to fill is exposed. It is that which the whole lacked, and that which unveils this lack. It fills a void it discloses in the very act of filling it, revealing it to be, precisely, the void it is summoned to abolish. Thus it is impossible to separate the movement by which Hegel takes cognizance of the import of his thought from the development of his thought. At every instant, more or less clearly, the void which has been revealed calls for a content; but the void is also, in some sort, the revelation that this content already exists, as the unlimited is already present in awareness of the limit.[3] It is this appropriation of its own genesis as a fulfilment, in the very consciousness of the void, which the meditations of the young Hegel already put before us. There is, perhaps, no better introduction to his thought than its beginnings, which, in a sense, are already a fulfilment for us, but which, considered as an event, are for Hegel's phenomenological consciousness initially only the experience and horror of the void.

A. Hegel's Life

One might here be tempted to reduce the import of Hegel's work to its author, by showing that this fulfilment represented, first and foremost, personal fulfilment for Hegel.

His life, one of extreme self-effacement and unremitting effort, is remarkable in this regard: his work made up the whole history of his existence and provided its real content. It unfolded without setback or pause until the day death caught him by surprise as he was revising the first pages of the *Phenomenology* for a new edition: the end of his life had carried him back to his beginnings. Of the three great encylopædists the history of philosophy has known, Hegel alone confined himself to pursuing his written work and oral teaching. Aristotle travelled the length and breadth of the world, and meddled in the teaching of politics. Leibniz simultaneously immersed himself in administration, political counselling, diplomacy, polemics, and reflection. Hegel simply developed his thinking, and drew sustenance from it. He appears in his thought as if it were his real existence: it was the realm in which he was free, because nothing in it was alien to him, because he was 'at home' in it, *bei sich*. If he explained that the fulfilment of any content was freedom, he first demonstrated what he meant in the way he conducted himself vis-à-vis his thought: through it, he assimilated everything, stayed abreast of everything, kept pace with history as it moved towards fulfilment. The divine service known as philosophy did not estrange him from the world, but, on the contrary, trained his attention on events and made him an inhabitant of the present.[4] This 'journalist-metaphysician'[5] appropriated history and the world by means of thought, seized and assimilated them in an act he did not hesitate to compare to chewing and swallowing; indeed, he called on that simile to construct an astonishing variety of images. Here we might perhaps be permitted to suggest that this mastery through thought was, for Hegel, a means of conjuring away the fate history tells us befell his classmate Hölderlin – a means of escaping the extreme solitude of a system of thought stalked by madness, as if madness were its natural culmination or standing temptation.[6]

Yet if Hegel was saved from the isolation of absolute subjectivity by the richness of his work, he also used that work, to some extent, to conjure away everything his situation as a professor made it impossible for him to engage in personally. Prior to Nietzsche, Hegel was the severest judge of all who ever passed sentence on professors, those 'intellectual animals' evoked in the chapter of the *Phenomenology* about the spiritual animal kingdom and deceit. In the encounter with men of action, the professor's consciousness 'interferes ... in the action and work of others, and, if it can no longer take the work out of their hands, it at least shows an interest in it by passing judgement on it.'[7] To be sure, Hegel surpasses the judging consciousness. However, to the extent that he reaches the level of the consciousness that acknowledges the other and is capable of recognizing itself in its opposite, the content of his consciousness becomes, because that content is his own and yet other, the living mediation between himself and the other. Better still, it becomes the reconciliation between the active consciousness and the consciousness that offers recognition:

> the reconciling *Yea*, in which the two 'I's let go their antithetical *existence*, is the *existence* of the 'I' which has expanded into a duality, and therein remains identical with itself, and, in its complete externalization and opposite, possesses the certainty of itself: it is God manifested in the midst of those who know themselves in the form of pure knowledge.[8]

We need to decipher this passage, which closes the dialectic of the Beautiful Soul, in order to understand that Hegel is here describing himself vis-à-vis Napoleon, as an 'I' matured by discourse confronting an 'I' matured by action; and to understand as well that the reconciliation of the professor and the emperor, or, in other words, the reconciliation of Hegel with the demiurge he would never become, comes about through mutual recognition. The professor reveals to the emperor the meaning of his own actions. Napoleon has forged the unity of Europe without knowing it; because Hegel *does* know it, he gives the man of action his own truth back, is reconciled with him, and, in this way, gives rise to the manifestation of God. Thus Hegel's work represents not only the fulfilment of its author's existence, but is also presented as the fulfilment of a destiny more extraordinary than any a Prussian civil-servant could have dreamt of in 1806, amidst the defeats and in the schools. Not only did it fulfil the existence of G. W. F. Hegel, but it also brought history to fulfilment by conferring its meaning upon it. It was thus truly the living revelation among men, *der erscheinende Gott*. This excess of plenitude is for Hegel, if not for men in general, the revelation of himself in and by his work – an extravagant attempt at self-justification, which, in its extremity, may well bear witness to the temptation to madness that haunts any solitary individual, even a thinker.

In a well-known phrase, Marx called Hegel 'the thinker alienated from his being', who was acquainted with 'ennui, the longing for a content'.[9] Remarkably, this idea of *ennui* occurs in Hegel himself, in a curious passage about the Stoics, whose 'general terms', because they 'cannot in fact produce any expansion of the content ... soon become tedious'.[10] The similarity between the two ideas would seem to indicate that the reason for such *ennui* is to be sought in the vacuity of a certain abstract mode of thought: *ennui* appears to consciousness, negatively, as the desire for content, so that the movement by which the philosopher 'plunges into the content' is, in some sort, a reconciliation with the very source of his desire, i.e., with his alienation.[11] Taken as a whole, Hegel's work may accordingly be regarded as his reconciliation with his own destiny, now understood as a mission of divine revelation. Consciousness of alienation, however obscure, can be borne only with the help of a mediation that justifies this alienation: Hegel has to paint a dignified portrait of himself if he is to bear looking himself straight in his professorial face. This maker of revelations makes revelations not only about the world, but also about himself. It is in this capacity, and thus in his work, that Hegel can think his own alienation, and it is thanks to the mediation of his work that he comes to accept it – because, so conceived, it appears to him to be the very opposite of alienation. Here language has the same magical function in Hegel's work which Hegel shows it has in the *Phenomenology* – that of inverting and then negating the forms of immediate experience. But we have come back round to Hegel's work, which, detached from the context of what it meant for him personally, will now come before us in its own right – to begin with, in the pure universality of thought.

B. Hegel's Times

It was not the particular but the universal individual Hegel who discovered the import of his work. He did so at the very moment when his work was about to crystallize, not only in him, but also in the historical context of the late eighteenth century. Remarkably enough, Hegel took cognizance of this historical moment, on the religious, political and philosophical plane, as the moment of vacuity.

This void had a name: the Enlightenment. Hegel experienced it before coming to understand it and then going on to give the extraordinary description of it found in the *Phenomenology of Spirit*. In his early works, this void had not yet become an object for him; it was the element in which his consciousness was immersed, and in which the young generations of Romantics felt they had no place. 'I discovered within me an inexplicable void that nothing could fill,' wrote Rousseau.[12] Not only did Hegel's contemporaries discover this void within themselves; it loomed up before them and hemmed them in on all sides – a world without content or depth. In one of his *Xenien*,[13] Goethe makes Nicolai a luckless fisher for knowledge who catches nothing because he fishes *on the surface*. Such is the *Aufklärer*. Novalis puts the same indefatigable (*unverdrossen*) *Schreiber* before us in a curious passage of Heinrich von Ofterdingen.[14] Interminably, the *Schreiber* covers sheets of paper with notes, then hands them to a divine lady (Wisdom); she bends over an altar on which stands a basin of pure water (Truth). What the *Schreiber* writes cannot, however, withstand the test of Truth: only blank pages emerge from the developing bath. How, indeed, could the Enlightenment accept this trial, since it claims to be in sole possession of the truth, and, at the same time, regards it as non-existent?

> It is the same opposition as that which existed in the decadence of Roman public and political life under Augustus, and subsequently when Epicurean-

ism and indifference set themselves up against Philosophy. Under this influence, when Christ said, 'I came into the world that I should bear witness unto the Truth,' Pilate answered, 'What is Truth?' That was said in a superior way, and signifies that this idea of truth is an expedient which is obsolete: we have got further, we know that there is no longer any question about knowing the Truth, seeing that we have gone beyond.[15]

In this world emptied of its truth, the young Hegel and his friends in Tübingen, Hölderlin and Schelling, longed to reconquer plenitude. But the perfect richness they sought was not to be had in a period that reduced reality to an exercise in pure intellection, a pure extension of all-devouring light, and that worshipped, in the form of the Supreme Being, the very void to which it had reduced the world. This tension between two conflicting terms, each of which was simultaneously the complement and truth of the other, and, because it was alien to the other, ultimately appeared to be alien to itself, this fundamental insight of Hegel's maturity had already begun to take shape in the analyses and reflections of his youth. When he turned toward the world the Enlightenment held out to him, what he found was a figure of pure utility: everything was external to itself and subordinate to the other, in an endless series that spirit ran through to the sole end of negating it. Such criticism robbed every individual thing of its meaning, reducing it to its relationship to another thing, and annulled even relationship in a movement in which spirit turned back upon itself in the satisfaction of the void: 'the Enlightenment . . . is satisfied.'[16] When Hegel turned toward faith, as if toward the truth of this world divested of its truth, he discovered that the Enlightenment had emptied faith of all content, reducing its significance to that of immediate sense-certainty (bread is bread, stone is stone), and leaving only an abstraction in its place, the Supreme Being of contemporary Deism, which the *Phenomenology* calls 'empty', a 'vacuum',[17] 'stale gas'.[18] The Hegel of Tübingen and Bern has not yet grasped the essential relation between Deism and the understanding in the Enlightenment, but he 'lives' it insofar as he rejects or refuses this satisfaction, seeking, after his own fashion, to recover a lost Paradise and original plenitude.

Germany's political disarray made, perhaps, as deep an impression on the young Hegel as did the formalism of its religious life; interestingly, it is only with difficulty that we can distinguish his political from his religious thought amongst the concerns of his early years. In a letter to Schelling, dated from Bern, as well as in the 1802 essay 'On the German Constitution', Hegel paints a picture of contemporary political society. Two contradictions in particular preoccupy him: first, the political fragmentation of Germany; and, second, the contradictions of the law, torn between an unrestrained absolutism and egoistic individual interests. In the separate existence of a multitude of states, absorbed in quarrels as petty as their rulers and bent on destroying the larger state that alone could confer authentic cohesion and stability upon them, Hegel sees nothing but the absence of a state: 'As a result of contemplating this pitiful reality, of living in patience or despair, of accepting a crushing destiny, souls turn toward dreams and pure longing with such ardour as is left them.'[19] Political unity cannot simply be represented in dreams or conceived in thought; cannot, that is, be conceived in its absence. What is to be expected of such political atomism, if not the anarchy that ensues when the parts all try to escape their truth, i.e., the whole?

> What the German Empire does as such is never an act of the whole but only of an association with a greater or lesser scope. . . . Associations of this sort are like a heap of round stones which are piled together to form a pyramid. But they are perfectly round and have to remain so without any dovetailing, and so, as soon as the pyramid begins to move towards the end for which it has been built, it rolls apart.[20]

An implicit reality is already beginning to come into view here, which alone makes it possible to conceive absence as absence, the void as void – the reality of a plenitude that resides in the totality. It is this intuition which inspires the critique of the absolutism of these petty German states. Absolute power stolidly confronts the citizens of the state as an alien force that imposes its alien will on men and creates 'an unbridgeable gulf between reality and men's minds'.[21] They therefore seek to outwit it; they live in dependence upon it, and in the hope of escaping it by its own consent; they wrest rights from the state that are the very negation of Right, and elevate them into privileges, instituting injustice where justice should hold sway. And, just as the petty states decimate their truth, so the citizens demolish their own polity:* empty power stands over against a social life emptied of its meaning, dead legality confronts illegal life. The contemplation of this spectacle guides Hegel toward the intuition of an organic totality exemplified, for him, by the Greek city-state. This fundamental intuition, which here manifests itself negatively, is a constant in Hegel's thought: we shall encounter it again in his reflections on religion. Here it finds confused expression in something like nostalgia for a primordial age when the City actually embodied the law, when public life and the life of civil society were made of the same substance. This unity has, however, been lost, and consciousness knows it only in its loss; it does not yet experience it as present in its very loss.

Hegel's examination of the religious problem enabled him to develop these initial considerations. He began by taking a position on the Enlightenment. There are doubtless passages in the texts of his Tübingen

---

* *Cité*, which means both 'city' and 'body politic'.

period in which he seems to echo the Enlightenment's criticism of the positivity of religion – i.e., the content of revelation – which one of his professors, the theologian Storr, had presented as inaccessible to the understanding, in an argument inspired by Kant.[22] This can only be seen as one of the features of the early work that anticipates Hegel's mature thought: content, religious content included, is even at this early stage felt to be something other than a mere given. Yet the negation of the given is not conflated with the negation of its content: even as he criticizes a conception of faith as irrational, the young Hegel rejects a religion that would separate man from God, a religion that would not be life. Therein lies the basic problem of the *Theologische Jugendschriften*. We can trace it through a number of different forms, especially the notion of good positivity, that of *Volksgeist*, and the conception of mediation through love.

Those three subjects of reflection simply make explicit a certain intuition of religious plenitude in the midst of fragmentation; this is one of the profoundest thoughts in all Hegel. At stake is an attempt to recover the meaning of authentic positivity, to recover, that is, the practical uses of the content of revelation and its concrete implications for the conduct of action. This meaning has been lost with the passage of time, which has transformed maxims into dogmas and so walled truth off from life. Also involved here is an attempt to think this true positivity as a concrete historical reality, i.e., as bound up with the organic totality known as the *Volksgeist*. This notion of a total religion embodied in the people must be understood as the transposition of an image of Greece that haunted Hegel and his friends; we find its poetic translation in Hölderlin. The Greeks knew nothing of the transcendence of an alien God; no revelation rose up before them; they had no morality outside themselves. Religion was simply the exercise of life itself; the gods came and went in a familiar world, as men among men. Men themselves were worthy of the gods; with a pang, Hegel recalled the time *wo jeder die Erde streifte wie ein Gott*[23] as a time of lost intimacy and harmony. It is noteworthy that this idea, which recurs constantly in the early writings,[24] should recall a time now dead and gone or a lost original unity: this only exposes the more cruelly the void left by its disappearance. Greece is present as a potentiality [*est en creux*] in Hegel; its place in his soul would always be that of a void to be filled.[25]

Hegel was not, then, duped by history; he was not unaware that this form of religious plenitude had itself disappeared under the blows of Christianity. This development explains the ambiguity of his judgement of Christ. On the one hand, Christ appears as the destroyer of the happy unity of the Greeks. Unlike Socrates, who lives on a friendly footing with men, revealing them to themselves, Christ is at once the separated and the separator: he descends from on high, bearing a transcendent truth;

he is not of this world and must leave it; thus he sows the seeds of division in the world of men, putting an end to its spontaneous freedom and social instinct in order to preach the pernicious virtues of suffering and weakness (which Hegel denounces before Nietzsche).[26] The Christian is like an exile in this world; 'he finds relief in every tear shed, in every mortification. He is urged on by the thought, "here Christ walked, here he was crucified for me", a thought from which he gains renewed strength.'[27]

Yet, if Christ destroyed Greek harmony, he brought reconciliation to another fragmented world, that of the Jewish people. Here there reappears, obliquely, as it were, the concrete historical reality Hegel observed with love and yearning in pagan religion: Christ restores plenitude to a particular people, amidst the greatest imaginable fragmentation. Admirable analyses of the condition of the Jews and the unhappiness of consciousness are to be found here. This arid consciousness is represented by Abraham, who follows his herds beneath an empty sky, under the eye of a hostile God; his consciousness is itself the other of this absolute other, which crushes it beneath the weight of its alien power. Thus man's relationship to God, experienced as the greatest possible separation (that between the Almighty and man's nothingness), in fact turns out to be a relationship of affinity between man's nothingness and God's. (God, as He is Almighty, no longer represents anything more than the sheer, absolute other for man.) This is why Judaism ultimately evolves into an empty legalism. Christ's mission is precisely to reconcile man with the Law, to infuse the Law with a living content: Christ comes to *fulfil* the Law, he is himself the Law fulfilled; he reconciles God with his people, and the people with its destiny, by means of Love.

Here the notion of a totality informed by love comes into play; the totality is, however, no longer represented as a given, but as something gained through effort. It is essential to note this point in the development of Hegel's thinking. Whereas the organic totality of Greek religion has, in some sort, no past, and is reflected less as a result than as an origin which takes its place within a pre-reflexive immediacy, Love is the end result of a process, the overcoming of dismemberment. It is, as Plato would have it, at once very young and very old; it has a history – and its past is no stranger to it (if it were, we would once again find ourselves amidst dismemberment), but rather rests within it, in division and appeasement. Love is *Aufhebung*,[28] a supersession which embraces contraries and expresses their truth. Here it appears to Hegel for the first time that the totality is not primary, but ultimate; that it cannot be in the beginning, but must be at the end; and that it is therefore necessary to pass beyond consciousness of the void as the mere consciousness of a lost content, in order to attain to the consciousness of the void as a content that must be conquered.

At this point, the perspective is inverted in Hegel's meditation itself. There is a negativity of the void known to guilty consciousness, which mourns innocence and Paradise lost. Such consciousness is pessimistic and despairing, experiencing its condition as the very opposite of life: Hölderlin singing of a Greece that is dead and gone. But there also exists, in some sort, a positive side to the void; it teaches us that fulfilment lies in the future, that nothingness is the Advent of being, that dismemberment is the anticipation and coming of totality. In these inward stirrings of a consciousness in quest of itself, we can already detect the emergence of the idea that dismemberment is necessary to ultimate fulfilment; we can discern something like a *necessity of the void*. After experiencing the void as, simply, the immediate context of his existence, and then as the painful loss of an original plenitude, Hegel, in his dialectic of love, anticipates the idea that the void is the promise of a fulfilment, the moment requisite to this fulfilment. The consciousness of the void is enriched; it can already discern a certain content in the emptiness it feels. Once Hegel has understood this transfiguration, which comes about in his own thinking without his being aware of it, insensibly transforming the void into fullness and nothingness into being, he utters the great, profound cry of joy of the *Phenomenology* about the spirit's tarrying with death: 'This tarrying with the negative is the magical power that converts it into being.'[29] Even *for us*, who know that this discovery lies ahead, it comes as an astonishing revelation to see the dynamic of the consciousness of the void as it develops in Hegel's thought – to watch this consciousness as it gradually works out the meaning and, in a sense, the content of vacuity, at a time when Hegel does not yet say 'for us'; when, in other words, he is still unaware of the significance of his own intellectual quest.

But love is not the endpoint of his religious reflections. Hegel cannot separate the advent of love from the concrete historical context; he regards it as something that has come into being, but disappeared as well. The totality disintegrated in Christianity as it did in pagan times. The plenitude of fulfilment in the Christian sense is therefore conceived as something now past or annulled; its absence even from consciousness simply bespeaks the destiny of modern Christianity. With this, Hegel has returned to the starting point of his reflections, the state of contemporary Christianity, but by way of a development that has transformed this starting point into a culmination, the origin into a result. It is, indeed, the fate of Christianity to bear within itself a defect inherited from Christ himself, who failed to accomplish in history the reconciliation he had announced. In *The Spirit of Christianity and Its Fate*, Hegel dwells on this failure of Jesus' destiny, which was the failure of the first Christian community as well; it explains the emergence of the bad kind of positivity. Instead of accepting his destiny for himself – as, at the end of

his days, in pain, his eyes destroyed, Oedipus accepts his human portion
– Christ accepts death and the Cross as his divine portion: the Father's
will be done. This choice transfigures his destiny, but also sets it apart
from the common lot of mankind. Christ's return to the Father is also his
disappearance from the world of men, and a refusal to share his people's
future:

> The fate of Jesus was that he had to suffer from the fate of his people; either
> he had to make that fate his own, to bear its necessity and share its joy, to
> unite his spirit with his people's, but to sacrifice his own beauty, his connection
> with the divine, or else he had to repel his nation's fate from himself, but
> submit to a life undeveloped and without pleasure in itself. In neither event
> would his nature be fulfilled . . .[30]

Christ's purity, his sense of his divine filiation, and the significance of
his mission ultimately mattered more to him than actually reconciling
his people with God. Thus he did not consent to share the fate of his
people as a people, but simply to submit to the fate his people subjected
him to; this cut him off from them. In a sense, Christ found, in death, the
separation he had come to abolish.

Here, however, the positive aspect of his failure appears: this is not the
same separation as before. If Christ cannot re-establish the familiarity in
which Abraham originally lived with the divine, before being charged
with his mission by Yahweh, if he cannot establish an all-embracing,
organic religion among the Jewish people through the mediation of love,
he does at least teach that a form of reconciliation is possible within
historical division – the reconciliation of subjectivity. With the discovery
of this depth, he transforms the purely objective dismemberment of
Jewish consciousness into subjective dismemberment.

Hegel traces this development through the evolution of the first
Christian community: confronted with the empty tomb, it internalized
Christ, living on his love[31] as if in pure interiority amidst a hostile world.
But, with the passing of time, this memory itself was inevitably objectified and set over against Christian consciousness as a content alien to
love; it mediated love itself, inasmuch as it precipitated its emergence.
This marked the return to the bad kind of positivity, the return, that is,
to an element which now lost its concrete quality, to be transformed into
a given posed before religious consciousness. The life of Christ became a
transmitted story: it was situated in a remote past, assigned a fixed,
determinate form, and recomposed in a manner unrelated to the life of
the believer. Revelation, codified in dogmatic form, took the place of
Abraham's alien God; it stood over against love, which took refuge in
subjectivity. This internal alienation once again sundered the terms that
were to be joined. It had its historical counterpart in an objective
phenomenon, the disintegration of what had once been a total religion:

subjectivity now found itself counterposed not only to the given of revelation, but also to the concrete history of peoples. At this point, Hegel again takes up the thread of his criticism of Christianity – that it is the religion of a sect, a small group of people who live in an isolation imposed by a rule, without seeing that this rule, if applied to society as a whole, would destroy it; without seeing, again, that the society Christians take their distance from is the very condition of their isolation. We find an echo, here, of the bitter language of *The Life of Jesus*, and of this astounding running commentary on the Lord's Prayer: '"Thy kingdom come, hallowed be Thy Name": this is the wish of an isolated individual; a people cannot form such a wish. "Thy Will be done": a people conscious of its honour and strength executes its own will and regards any other as an enemy ... "Forgive us": this too is the prayer of an isolated individual.'[32] The further development of Christianity manifests this twofold contradiction between subjectivity and the content of revelation, and between subjectivity and concrete history; Hegel could observe it in the society of his day, in the form of the division between Church and state, world and God, virtue and sensibility. Religion had become formalistic, had been emptied of its life and content. This development would seem to lead us back to our point of departure; certain formulae Hegel uses to describe the servile nature of Jewish legalism and Christian formalism tend to confirm the idea that we have come full circle.

However, the opposition no longer has the same form: whereas the Jews had conceived their solitude as that of an object confronted by another object, so that *they existed, in some sort, over against themselves*, as nothingness in the face of God's omnipotence, Christians would henceforth internalize one of the terms, and conceive division in the form of subjectivity. In other words, the Christians experienced and conceived their own inner selves as one of the terms of the division, and their religious consciousness was simultaneously separation and the consciousness of separation, the void and consciousness of the void; the unhappiness of consciousness had become the unhappy consciousness, and the object of consciousness was now no longer the void, but the void as constitutive of consciousness, or empty consciousness. Or, if one prefers, consciousness would henceforth be its own object.

This kind of phenomenological development of the religious meditations of Hegel's youth thus leads up to a sort of transition from consciousness to self-consciousness; it prefigures the analyses of the *Phenomenology*. We set out from the void of consciousness that manifested itself first as a lost plenitude, and subsequently as the engendering of plenitude; it has finally revealed itself to be the essence of consciousness. This new-found consciousness of subjectivity as such has a name in contemporary thought: Kantianism.

C. Hegel and Kant

At this point, there occurs an event of the first importance: Hegel encounters Kant. The significance of this encounter emerges from the obscure evolution of Hegel's earlier investigations. Hegel encounters Kant in the latter half of the eighteenth century, not as a stranger who was accidentally born a German and a philosopher, but as the truth of his own malaise. Ἀλήθεια, the truth is what is unveiled; for Hegel, Kant is the Enlightenment without veils,[33] and, simultaneously, the truth that unveils for him the meaning of his own reflections. What seemed, for us, to emerge from Hegel's meditations on Christianity – the idea that *the void* is *the very essence of consciousness* – is a conclusion Hegel, for his part, finds expressed in Kant. Having acquired this truth by dint of personal experience, Hegel now finds it put before him. Indeed, these two movements – that through which Hegel discovers the truth of his consciousness in Kant, and that through which Kant is invested with his truth – are one and the same. This encounter affords us the opportunity to come to grips with one of the profoundest reactions in the *Phenomenology*, one that attests to its authenticity. At the point to which, as we have just seen, the development of Hegel's consciousness has brought it, it grasps itself in Kant as if in itself, discovering its truth in him. It beholds itself in Kant as if beholding its own self in the other, and, cognizing the other as itself, sets about bringing itself forth out of its cognition of Kant. The cognition [*connaissance*] of Kant is the birth [*naissance*] of Hegel.[34]

The importance of the critique of Kant lies wholly in this phenomenon of the generation of the self in the other. Accordingly, this critique will, as it unfolds, reveal itself to us as an *Aufhebung*: what is negated in Kant is also preserved and restored to its proper place. Thus Kant's chief merit, in Hegel's eyes, is to have represented the moment of subjectivity; Kant invested thought with a new dimension, which overturned the relations between things, transformed the reflexive relations of being into reflexive relations of the subject, and replaced a philosophy of the world with a philosophy of the self – in short, Kant revealed the depth of the inner self. But (it is here that the negative aspect comes into play) Kant did not conceive this dimension in its truth; he described it in purely formalistic terms, as an identity without plenitude. Kant discovered depth, but his was an empty depth, because he simply transcribed in terms of the inner self, as if transferring them to a form prepared in advance, the reflexive schemes of the classical philosophical systems. This discovery of the emptiness of depth is already, in Hegel, the cognition of a depth without emptiness; its reflexive emptiness and visible depth are merely its manifestations. Truth suddenly passes over into its error, which just as suddenly passes over into its truth. It is in the critique of Kant that this *Umschlagen* [sharp reversal] is first presented to us as the very process by which nothingness is converted into being and the thought that negates itself in fact constitutes itself. Thus Hegel's critique is, in the very process of its unfolding, a cognition becoming cognizant and taking possession of the truth.

This is perhaps one of Hegel's most un-Kantian ideas, for Kant conceives critique as purely negative. For Hegel, Kant is the philosopher who wants to acquire knowledge of his knowledge before knowing, and who assumes that, by acquiring knowledge of his knowledge, he will come to know its limits. This retreat before knowledge provokes biting sarcasm on Hegel's part: it is, he says, quite as if one needed a theory of digestion before risking a meal, or had to learn how to swim before diving into the water.[35] Reflection on knowledge is itself a kind of knowledge: if the mind is not already in knowledge when it begins to question knowledge, it will never attain it. Critique that takes the form of prolegomena is, in some sense, the very act whereby the mind refuses to acknowledge that it is already in the element of truth; it is the mind's ignorance *in actu* constituted as, or raised to the rank of, a system – a written, published confession that spirit has gone looking for itself where it is not, and failed to find itself where it is. The critical philosopher falls victim to the same misadventure as the Jewish people: *God is amongst his people and his people knows him not.*[36] But it is also because he does not recognize the truth that he invents it, converting his ignorance into truth. The truth of critique is its ignorance, which it worships as truth. This reflection reveals one of the key conceptions informing Hegel's relationship to Kant – namely, the notion that there is no need to seek the truth about Kant outside Kant, that Kant's thought is the essence of Kantianism, i.e., already contained its own truth for Kant himself. The whole of Hegel's reflection on Kant consists in showing that the Kantian system reveals itself, unbeknownst to its author, as contradiction actualized or objectified in a philosophical system. This is the very theme of alienation: Kant thinks within contradiction, and because he does not know that he is in contradiction, his thought, once formed, is contradiction given form; it reflects his own image, his essence, his truth back to him.[37] Thus God dwells in* his people in a double sense; not only is he amongst his people, he also hovers before them, like a phantom. Truth is the very element of Kant's meditations – but he knows it not. Yet it also hovers before him; he encounters, in his system, his own truth: but he recognizes it not. Kant looks at himself without seeing himself. His thought thereby becomes the very essence of non-recognition.

Thus the mistrust characteristic of the thought that seeks to put itself to the test before cognizing anything is contradictory from the outset. 'If

* *Habite*, which also means 'haunts'.

the fear of falling into error sets up a mistrust of Science, which in the absence of such scruples gets on with the work itself, and actually cognizes something, it is hard to see why we should not turn round and mistrust this very mistrust. Should we not be concerned as to whether this fear of error is not just the error itself?'[38] This formal contradiction, which leads to an infinite regress, merely shows that there is an unresolved contradiction in the content of the thought. This fear is not its own *raison d'être*, but rather presupposes a certain conception of both truth and cognition. 'It takes for granted certain ideas about cognition as an *instrument* and as a *medium*, and assumes that there is a *difference between ourselves and this cognition*. Above all, it presupposes that the Absolute stands on one side and cognition on the other, independent and separated from it, and yet is something real.'[39] The formalism of the Kantian conception consists, for Hegel, in this absolute separation or basic dualism. Kantianism is merely a vain attempt to think the unity of two terms originally posited as entirely alien to one another: it is the impossible wish to *evacuate the void*.

1. Although Kant discovered the moment of subjectivity and went beyond consciousness to attain self-consciousness, he did no more than internalize the old reflexive opposition between form and content: 'The *Ich* transforms the finitude of the earlier objective dogmatism into the absolute finitude of subjective dogmatism.'[40] Rather than conceiving the world as a relation between terms which, posed before thought, refer to one another, he conceived knowledge as a relation between two counter-posed terms: the form of transcendental apperception and the given of sensibility; or, rather, he posited as absolutely separate two terms he should have conceived in relation. 'Concepts without intuition are empty; intuitions without concepts are blind.' This short sentence, cited by Hegel in *Faith and Knowledge*, is the closest Kant comes to conceiving that relation; but the connection is immediately severed, inasmuch as thought and being, the I of apperception and the thing-in-itself, are posited as antagonistic. Unity is banished; conceived outside unity, the two opposed terms reveal themselves for what they are: empty, estranged, hostile.

The artificiality of Kant's description resides entirely in the operation by means of which he thinks the separation of these terms. Whereas the subject is in fact revealed by the object, form by content, the constitutive by the constituted; whereas the given relates to the I of apperception, and the manifold to unity, as the conditioned to its condition – that is, in virtue of a reflexive operation which is meaningless in the absence of the reflected term – Kant conceives the two terms outside the relationship constituting them: he conceives the condition without the conditioned, and the conditioned without the condition, in a pre-reflexive state. This 'without' becomes an *in-itself* that is supposed to pre-exist the operation which justifies conceiving it as an in-itself. The *thing-in-itself* and the *I*, although they are given in cognition, are nevertheless assumed to pre-exist it as if they were two separate *in-itself*s. On the one hand, we have the form, and on the other, the content, waiting to come together in a reflexive relation as if they were not the very products of reflection. Thus Hegel describes Kantian time and space, comically, as forms patiently awaiting their *Erfüllung* [fulfilment]; they pre-exist it, much as 'the mouth and teeth, &c., as conditions necessary for eating', wait for their food.[41] Yet they are *already there*, *a priori*, given outside of all experience. This ambiguity, by which the reflexive product of experience is described as if it existed *a priori*, outside of all experience, is the essential feature of abstraction. It thus appears that the essence of these abstractions is the void. The I is a pure form, and, as Hegel profoundly says, 'pure unity is not an original unity',[42] is not a pre-reflexive unity, but merely the abstraction of the act by which the I purges itself, emptying itself of all it is not. By Kant's own admission, the I conceived separately is, accordingly, an empty unity abstracted from its content; it knows its content only as the other, as an alien entity which, in cognition, comes to inhabit it [*vient l'habiter*] as the result of an incomprehensible operation.

But the abstraction which isolates the subject from the object also isolates the object from the subject. In its abstraction, the given, present outside any and all determination by thought – this unformed content or transcendental matter, in a word, the thing-in-itself – is an image projected by the I: 'This caput mortuum is still only a product of thought, such as accrues when thought is carried on to abstraction unalloyed ... it is the work of the empty "Ego", which makes an object out of this empty self-identity of its own.'[43] The thing-in-itself and the I are consequently posited as estranged[44] from one another, although each is, in reality, the other's truth; and, precisely because they are nothing but this emptiness, even their opposition is an empty one. At the point of abstraction it has reached, Kantian consciousness is still phenomenological, and fails to recognize itself in the object with which it provides itself. It conceives the I and the thing-in-itself as empty, without realizing that it thinks *itself* in the emptiness of its object. At every turn in his reflections, Kant butts up against the truth. He postulates it unawares, and moves on without recognizing it. In so doing, he merely gives expression to the alienation of the Enlightenment, which fails to recognize, in the content of faith reduced to the emptiness of its Supreme Being, the essence of the impulse of spirit that subordinates all reality to purely utilitarian considerations.

This alienation also appears in the form in which Kant conceives the subject/object opposition: in terms of master and slave, i.e., dependence. Kant simply internalizes the conflict of Jewish religious consciousness, positing content in its dependence on form: *Begreifen ist Beherrschen* [to understand is to dominate]. But this dependence is reversed. Just as the *Phenomenology* shows that the master's truth resides in the slave, so Kantian philosophy reveals, upon analysis, that the dominated is the truth of that which dominates; i.e., it shows that that which dominates is dominated by the dominated. The same reversal occurs in Fichte's philosophy. Fichte too can conceive content only in terms of domination: but the self that dominates the non-self is in fact dominated by it, inasmuch as this non-self is the very condition on which the power of the self is exercised. To remain within the relationship of master and slave is to inhabit the contradiction without thinking it – and hence to be subjected to it. Purity is an unwitting form of servitude. Thus the Kantian moral subject, who opposes duty to the senses and the law to the manifold of concrete experience, is in fact the slave of the content which he has banished from his mind and which yet dominates its master. Thus content is the truth of form. It yields up its truth when examined apart from all relation to form; yet the truth thus liberated is simply that of the form which has been separated from it. Hence the truth of the content actually lies outside the content; content is therefore defined, in the realm of Kantian abstraction, by its externality to itself. However, in Kant this externality is merely postulated, not thought as the essence of content. Accordingly, Kant's thought is situated in externality; it is not externality thought. It thinks content in terms of externality while refusing to think the content of externality. It is itself dominated by its object, trapped in a relation of servitude of which it is merely the phenomenological description. Hence Hegel repeatedly says that Kant has produced a philosophy of perception,[45] and that he limits himself to analysing contradictions without thinking them; or, again, that he has produced a phenomenology[46] which discovers only the truth of self-consciousness – the abstraction of the void.

2. This weakness in Kant's position commands his thought as a whole, especially his conception of cognition. Thus far, we have considered only the two poles of cognition, which we have treated as separate essences. On the one hand, Kant postulates that they exist in absolute isolation from one another. On the other, he wants to think them as linked. Yet, for him, this does not involve going back to the original connection in which the two poles were given before all abstraction; it does not lead to an attempt to grasp the pre-reflexive state or original unity that provided the point of departure for the differentiation of the poles; it does not involve thinking the very element of the contradiction. Kant grasps the connection only as reflected, that is, from within separation itself. The unity thus reconstituted is far from being the element in which separation comes about; rather, this unity comes about in the element of separation.

To put it in Hegelian terms, it is the separation which is the truth of the unity, not the unity which is the truth of the separation.[47] This reversal has a very concrete meaning for Hegel: quite simply, it signifies that separation (or contradiction) is the truth of all the middle terms Kant uses to represent cognition, that is, to think unity within division. Nothing is more striking in this regard than the role and destiny of the transcendental imagination, to which Hegel devotes several remarkable pages in *Faith and Knowledge*. The transcendental imagination is, he says, reason itself; it is the positing of the contraries in their original state, a fundamental unity which undergoes an internal division into subject and object, only to discover, in aesthetic and 'organic' endeavour, that it is reconciliation *in actu*. 'For the root judgement, or duality, is in it as well, and hence the very possibility of *a posteriority*, which in this way ceases to be absolutely opposed to the *a priori*, while the *a priori*, for this reason, also ceases to be formal identity.'[48] The imagination is the truth of an arid system: failing to recognize this, Kant conceives imagination as an ordinary faculty, a human faculty he locates within the psychological subject. Here imagination is no more than a middle term dependent on its extremes, a μεταξύ between the understanding and the sensibility,[49] a mediation of the void by the void.

Similarly, when Kant sets out to think objectivity, he counterposes it, certainly, to the subjectivity of opinion, conceiving it as the universal and necessary; but these qualities belong to it only to the extent that they are ours, and ours alone. Mediation here is simply the mediation of one of the terms taken as the middle term between itself and its opposite. The I and the thing-in-itself are 'identical only as sun and stone are in respect to warmth when the sun warms the stone. The absolute identity of the subject and the object has passed into this formal identity, and transcendental idealism into this formal or more properly, psychological idealism.'[50] This explains the insubstantiality of the objective, which is a pseudo-middle term: not a synthetic unity in which two extremes are posited, but rather the simple recurrence of these extremes at a point between them. 'If the subjective is point, then the objective is point; and if the subjective is line, then the objective is line. The same thing is regarded, first as idea, then as existing thing: the tree as my idea and as thing ... and the category, similarly, is posited once as a relation of my thinking and then again as a relation of the things.'[51] The substantiality of a *Mittelding* of this sort depends entirely on the extremes; it is a dummy, a third figure which mimes two figures that unwittingly mime one another.[52] It reminds Hegel of an episode in Goethe's *Das Märchen*; he appropriates the passage, down to its very language,[53] in order to compare objectivity to a composite being whose substantiality derives solely from its neighbours, so that it collapses when they withdraw, just as objectivity collapses when the categories are withdrawn. All that is left after its collapse is an inchoate, unspeakable mass: 'The world is, inherently, something that falls apart.'

But it is in connection with reason that contradiction appears in all its innocence – without, however, being recognized for what it is. Reason is either marked by the empirical character that presides over the choice of categories in the table of judgement ('Kant rummages in the bag of the soul and finds reason there', as if it were a faculty among other faculties in a purely psychological ego); or else it is quite simply an abstract version of the understanding ('reason ... is in reality no better than empty understanding'),[54] a unifying, regulatory power alien to its contents, as is demonstrated by the antinomies. In Hegel's eyes, the discovery of the antinomies was one of Kant's merits; but, as with everything else Kant achieved, the fact is that he did not recognize his discovery for what it was: he did not accept the idea that contradiction constitutes the very being of the content. His tender regard for humankind led him to displace contradiction onto the mind; he thus transformed it into a kind of misunderstanding, the fruit of an illegitimate use of reason. The consequence is that reason, in the antinomies, is obviously sundered from its object: in taking this division upon itself, it merely takes back what belonged to it in the first place. Within this division, the fundamental dualism of the I and the in-itself can only come up against insubstantial middle terms, or else division itself. The abstract cannot escape its essence, which is posited within separation, whatever the power one might think one has assigned it. Hegel's analysis shows that what is here divided in two cannot escape its fate, because its fate is simply division actualized. Thus in the *Critique of Practical Reason* reason may well come forward as absolute autonomy (clearing a path for Fichte), as unconditioned infinity; but the fact remains that this verbal travesty cannot restore its original independence: 'This infinitude, strictly conditioned as it is by its abstraction from its opposite, and being strictly nothing outside of this antithesis, is yet at the same time held to be absolute spontaneity and autonomy.'[55] Whence the paradoxes of legalistic morality, in which spontaneity, incapable of attaining being, survives as duty.

3. With this, we reach the most profound point in Hegel's reflections. The original unity of subject and object, though destroyed by Kantian abstraction and the absolute opposition of these two poles, nonetheless subsists as the unity within which division took place. But this unity is not thought. All that is thought in Kant is the unity that exists within division. Analysis reveals, however, that it is contradictory, a pseudo-unity that is not coextensive with the original unity in which dismemberment occurs. Thus Kant must contend with a paradox: he does not think the unity that actually exists, whilst the unity he does think is not true

unity. Therein lies the import of the *sollen* and the axioms of practical reason: they express the unity that *should* be achieved in the form of a unity that has *not* been. In other words, they cast the very essence of Kantian contradiction before thought in the form of a beyond.[56] So far, we have seen that each of the two counterposed terms assigns its own truth to the other, and have observed the self-destruction of the connection thought establishes within this division. Now we are at the endpoint of Kant's endeavour, the point at which it produces its own truth, conceiving itself, in the form of the *sollen* and the axioms, as nothingness: 'The supreme effort of this formal thought is the acknowledgement of its own Nothing and that of the Ought.'[57] Such is the significance of the Faith founded on the ruins of knowledge. The unity Kant was unable to establish within division finds itself projected outwards, into a beyond – not into something that is, but into something that should be, i.e., into a notion devoid of content: '[The content of] faith . . . is empty because the antithesis which as absolute identity could be its content has to remain outside it; expressed positively, the content of this faith would be Reasonlessness because it is an absolutely unthought, unknown and incomprehensible Beyond.'[58] Thus we are here confronted with the contradiction in its completely developed form; Faith thinks it as a contradiction, but does not make this contradiction its body and soul, because it conceives it as something beyond itself. Hence the contradiction remains purely formal. The void of what-should-be thus expresses the essence of the relationship between the absolute terms that are counterposed in Kantian cognition. We have come full circle: neither at the beginning nor the end of his philosophy did Kant possess the plenitude of the content; he conceived self-consciousness only abstractly, and discovered in it nothing more than the sheer void of its abstractness.

One sees, then, what it meant for Hegel to grasp the formalism of Kantian thought. For him, Kant's thinking captured the very element in which his own phenomenological consciousness had developed: Kant was the Enlightenment's vacuity translated into thought, and thought as void. In Kant, Hegel encountered the truth of the element in which his own consciousness had developed; retrospectively, Kant lent meaning to the confused aspirations of the young theologian who had rejected the religion of his day, and of the young political thinker who had turned his back on the modern polity. In Kantian and Fichtean formalism, Hegel encountered the principle that animated the obscure impulses of his early consciousness. The void which he had initially apprehended as a lost plenitude, and then as a plenitude to be reconquered, but which lay, in some sort, *in front of him*, as if it were other – as if, that is, it were invested with the externality of consciousness – this void emerged for him, in Kantian philosophy, as the truth of self-consciousness: not an *in front of*, but an *inside*; that is, not as an object of his thought, but as his thought as such.

For Hegel, this discovery could no more be detached from its historical context than its context could be detached from it. The vacuity he had observed in the world, the inner vertigo of the years of his youth also found expression in Kantian philosophy, which was their truth. This inner dynamic of Hegel's developing thought was also a moment of historical development. What Kant showed Hegel was thus simultaneously Hegel's truth and the truth of his times. In taking cognizance of Kant, Hegel simply appropriated and explained the historical moment in which, by thinking the void, human thought had already become the desire for a plenitude it could not conceive, yet longed for. *Nach dem Gehalte der Wahrheit war mithin eine Sehnsucht vorhanden* ['hence there existed a yearning for the content of the truth']. Incontestably, Hegel had detected in Kant the ambiguous point at which satisfaction with the void had become unbearable and demanded to be transcended. One is reminded here of the astonishing passage in the *Wissenschaft der Logik* [*Science of Logic*] in which Hegel shows that philosophy is 'the need of the already satisfied need'.[59] It is perhaps not illegitimate to imagine that, in taking cognizance of the satisfied Enlightenment, Hegel precisely took cognizance of the need to transcend this satisfaction, do away with it *as* satisfaction, and derive from dissatisfaction the truth it required to attain fulfilment – namely, the content of the truth. From the nothingness of the formal thinking it had tarried with, Hegelian spirit drew forth the plenitude of being; it abided in Kant as in death, and this 'abiding' was indeed 'the magical power which converts the negative into being'.

Here again, then, we find the remark that opened this chapter: Hegelian thought can be the thought of the content only if it fills the void it exposes, and can overcome the fundamental dissatisfaction it reveals only by becoming the thought of the content. We have now described the first – phenomenological – aspect of this operation. We need to go on to describe the second aspect as it unfolds, that is, the constitution of Hegelian philosophy as a philosophy of content.

II

COGNITION OF THE CONCEPT

Elle est retrouvée,
Quoi? L'éternité.
C'est la mer mêlée au soleil.

A. Rimbaud

Philosophy, according to Hegel, is not a rhetorical art that treats of all and sundry by proxy, reproducing, in language, everything that exists. Nor is it the endless chatter of a conversation that floats with detachment over the subjects of its choice, and, thinking to preserve its freedom, in fact destroys it. The power to dominate by means of language is, first of all, a cultural inheritance of which one can have the use without realizing its significance: this accounts for the prejudice, pervasive at all times, that philosophy is within anyone's reach, that it is not something to be learned, that it is not a science:

> There seems to be a currently prevailing prejudice to the effect that, although not everyone who has eyes and fingers, and is given leather and a last, is at once in a position to make shoes, everyone nevertheless immediately understands how to philosophize, and how to evaluate philosophy, since he possesses the criterion for doing so in his natural reason – as if he did not likewise possess the measure for a shoe in his own foot.[60]

In fact, such instant philosophy is to philosophy proper what 'chicory is [to] coffee'.[61] Still more deceptive would be the pretension, on philosophy's part, to be what its name suggests it is, a love of knowledge content to desire knowledge without attaining it, remaining outside it as, in Platonism, understanding remains outside the idea of the Good: *a science on the threshold*. Hegel, for his part, claims to fulfil this unsatisfied love, closing the distance between philosophy and scientific form, so that 'it can lay aside the title "love of knowing" and be *actual* knowing'.[62] For Hegel, thought must not remain on the threshold, but should rather step into the house; it has to dwell 'at home', *bei sich*, that is, in its object, its own content: 'Philosophy is the thought of the content.'[63]

There nevertheless exist a good many types of knowledge that fail to create this intimacy of subject and object. Analysing them makes it easier to understand the specificity of the philosophical method by way of contrast. The mathematical method, though highly esteemed by a great many philosophers, cannot legitimately claim, on Hegel's view, to be philosophically useful. Hegel offers a hostile description of it in the Preface to the *Phenomenology*: the geometer knows his proofs from the outside, *auswendig*, not *inwendig*, inwardly, in a manner reflecting their own genesis. If, in hope of defending himself against this charge, the geometer sets out his proofs, there appears a curious phenomenon of mechanical disjunction between the mathematical object and its transformations: certainty in mathematics is a personal relation between the mathematician and his object. This relation is, however, such that it seems to produce the truth of its object rather than emerging from it: 'the movement of the mathematical proof does not belong to the object, but rather is an activity external to the matter in hand.'[64] Consider the mathematician: his knowledge stems from his own activity, by means of which he takes the entire truth of the object into himself; the object is little more than a pretext in his hands. Consider the mathematical object: before our very eyes, it undergoes a series of amputations, sutures, and dislocations that alter it beyond recognition. One is reminded of *Gestalt* psychology's analyses of mathematical proof: Hegel's remarks are direct anticipations of them. 'The triangle is dismembered and its parts are consigned to other figures, whose origin is allowed by the construction upon the triangle.'[65] The original object is ultimately reconstituted, the same triangle appears before us; yet it is another triangle that has materialized from God knows where, inasmuch as the first triangle has disappeared in the course of the proof. 'Insight is an activity external to the thing; it follows that the true thing is altered by it.'[66] If we turn back to the person who works out the proof, we observe the same external relation between necessity and content in him. The proof is carried out in obedience to an idea external to it:

> As regards [the cognitive process], we do not, in the first place, see any necessity in the construction. Such necessity does not arise from the notion of the theorem; it is rather imposed, and the instruction to draw precisely these lines when infinitely many others could be drawn must be blindly obeyed, without our knowing anything ... except that we believe that this will be to the purpose in carrying out the proof.[67]

We understand why we have made certain moves only in retrospect, just as someone who has fallen into an ambush discovers the trap only after the fact. A mathematical proof is thus a ruse in a twofold sense: a ruse as far as the object it destroys and reconstitutes is concerned; and a ruse with regard to the truth it establishes by detours that are not dictated by any law. The necessity of the matter resides solely in the subject who knows where he is going, lays out his course of action, and transforms the object so as to achieve his goal. The content merely bears witness to his adventure.

If philosophy does not consist in simply applying a method, neither does it consist in mechanically imposing a schema on the rich plenitude of an external content. Yet this is precisely the fate Kantian triplicity suffers in Schelling's philosophy, where it has become 'a lifeless schema'.[68] Kant's profound anticipation of the truth has been transformed into 'a mere parlour trick'[69] in the universe of identity; all it has to recommend it is that it can be performed time and again. But this very advantage grows tiresome: 'once familiar, the repetition of it becomes as insufferable as the repetition of a conjuring trick already seen through'. The procedure involved consists in dressing up every difference discovered in the real world in a pair of determinations inspired by polar magnetism – in literally pasting this schema onto everything the way one pastes labels on tins or cardboard tags on a skeleton.[70] But Schelling's monotonous formalism can no more be expected to generate the diversity of the content than bones can be counted on to generate flesh and blood. To be so christened, the content must be ready and waiting: otherwise, its reality itself would vanish into the 'emptiness of the absolute' in which all differences fade, like cows into the German night. Thus conceived, necessity does not inhere in the content, whilst necessity has no grasp on the content from the moment it is pure necessity. If necessity is only an outer covering, the content 'cannot escape the fate of being thus deprived of life and Spirit, of being flayed and then seeing its skin wrapped around a lifeless knowledge'.[71]

To this 'superficial' knowledge, to this method alien to its object, to Schelling's mechanical schematism, Hegel counterposes a vision of philosophy deeply immersed in the life of its object. 'Scientific cognition, on the contrary, demands surrender to the life of the object. ... Thus, absorbed in its object, scientific cognition forgets about that general survey, which is merely the reflection of the cognitive process away from the content and back into itself.'[72] True knowledge must 'tarry with [the object], and lose itself in it',[73] abandoning itself to it rather than to itself. The only way for thought 'to be reconciled with the solid content [confronting it]'[74] is to overcome this opposition, sacrifice the pseudo-freedom of distance, and renounce itself in order to find itself again in the other. Thought must 'sink this freedom in the content, letting it move spontaneously of its own nature, by the self as its own self';[75] in this way, the operations of knowledge, 'absorbed in the content', can become the very movement of the content, its own development, 'the immanent self of the content'.[76] But the very movement that reconciles thought with its object, enabling it to tarry with the richness of the content, also reconciles that object with necessity, which is thus no longer a form external to the object, but the object's self-transformation. It follows that the necessity which surrenders itself to the content thereby surrenders itself to necessity; it witnesses its own birth in the generation of the content and provides the developed content with the assurance that its necessity is not its enemy, but is rather indistinguishable from its own freedom. It is this genesis of the content that we would now like to trace, by way of an examination of three moments: the given, reflection, and the Self.

A. The Content As Given

When the naive consciousness attempts to imagine the content, it conceives it as a *given*. Thought is naturally inclined to picture its own operation as an encounter or a reaching-out-towards [*geste*]. What I come upon was already there; the continent whose shores I land on was waiting for me from the beginning of time. What I seize in an action (*Handlung*), or, simply, with my hand (*Hand*), was *already there*, even if my act revealed its presence and detached it from its usual context. The fact that it was to hand (its *Handgreiflichkeit*, to use the nice expression of the Preface to the *Wissenschaft der Logik*) implies a certain priority. In a sense, the apple I grasp is older than my hand; even if it was picked last October, it is πρεσβύτερον, more ancient in years, more respectable by virtue of its condition, inasmuch as it was already present when I started to stretch my hand out towards it. Similarly, the food I eat or the meat a dog devours, even if it can be said to 'be devoured' only in the belly of the hungry one, nevertheless possesses a dignity his voracity does not. It was there before his hunger; if it were not for this *presence*, the act of eating could only feed on itself. Thus the given is loaded, and, indeed, overloaded with significance, since an *already* is superadded to a simple *in front of*, and since the *before* belongs not only to the order of time, but also to the order of being, designating the very origin of what is.

We can sense the depth of the content in this naive representation of the given; this explains the benefits reaped from it by canny philosophies that set out from the evidence of intuition and the obvious, i.e., pure receptivity. Thought need only open, like an eye, and look at what is put before it, whether directly, in the world, or, still more directly, in God. Thus, for Descartes – if we put aside everything in his method involving merely psychological preparation, intended to train the attention – intuition is plainly a state of mind in which truth is *given* to the mind in its purity, in which the simple natures are offered to it in their original discreteness, in which mind takes action only to prevent itself from acting, and prejudges only its own prejudices. Here Descartes merely falls back on the old idea that reason is contemplative, as simple and passive as the gaze; that it is Plato's 'eye of the soul', open to a world of eternal verities. This notion of the possibility of direct access to the eternal is also the defect of the Romantic thought of Hegel's day, the illuminism or *Schwärmerei* which claimed to replace scientific conceptions with mystic intuitions, thereby absolving itself of the obligation to make any conceptual effort whatever. Finally, the deductive and analytical philosophies are also elaborations of an initial given: they need only hold fast to a first principle, given in intuition, in order to establish the ordered body of their propositions. Somewhat as Spinoza begins with God and simply develops an already given content, or as Descartes begins with intuition and goes on to construct his chains of proofs, dogmatism too sets out from a first principle. As this principle has not been deduced, it can only be given; as it has not been posed, it can only be presupposed. Here again we find the philosophical expression of the priority of the given, always conceived, more or less straightforwardly, as an origin. Reinhold wanted to perfect Kantianism by seeking, like Archimedes and Descartes, a fixed point to which to anchor the deduction of the categories;[77] Fichte too began, in a certain sense, with a primordial intuition, I = I, from which all the rest followed; as for Schelling, the intellectual intuition of the aesthetic totality is not only the origin, but also the very subject-matter of his thought. We can see, then, what is at stake in the naive notion of the content-as-given, as well as the multiple prospects it opens up. We need to keep them in mind if we are to grasp the import of Hegel's analysis.

The myth of the Fall is at the heart of Hegel's thinking on this subject;[78] it may serve as an illustration here. The innocence of thought's experience of the given is that of the first people in the first garden. It is also that of animals, who simply come upon their lives and unquestioningly accept them: paradise is joyous animality. In Eden, Adam and Eve could eat of the tree of life, but were forbidden to touch the tree of knowledge. Then Eve sinned. The act of reaching out to take the apple, which was, like all apples, *handgreiflich* (to hand), was also the act by which she acquired knowledge of the apple, and, with it, of everything that had been *given* until then. This revelation brought the end of innocence, the end of the happy meaningfulness of things, and the discovery of the true essence of the immediacy of life: once it had become an object of cognition, the given revealed itself to be divided from itself and different from itself. Its truth now appeared in its destruction, and scission came into the world.[79]

This profound figure re-emerges in ordinary perceptual knowledge. What transpires when naive consciousness pictures its own way of apprehending an object in sensory intuition? The perceptual content is transformed into its opposite through a sudden leap. I believe that I have grasped what is given to the senses in its infinite variety, I direct my attention to it as it is, and it eludes me: thus I direct my attention toward a tree or a house or the sun at high noon, but all I come away with is a here and now. 'Our "*Meinung*" [opinion], for which the true content of sense-certainty is *not* the universal, is all that is left over in the face of this empty or indifferent Now or Here.'[80] I expected to attain fullness and being, but came away with no more than nothingness and the void. With this begins the long detour that cognition must make in order to take possession, in truth, of what eludes its certainty. For what I direct my attention to and miss at the outset is nevertheless there, is already there; but this already-there is also experienced as something not yet there: being is immediately nothingness, and yet my attention was directed, not to nothingness, but to the concrete entity that will only be given to me at the end.

Such is the lesson of the *Phenomenology*: the given content is destroyed in the very act by which I seek to take possession of it, but it does not elude me *qua* content, it eludes me only *qua* given. And the very act by which I destroy what is given in the content is the initial moment of a dialectic at the end of which the content I aimed at will be restored to cognition – not, this time, as an original given, but as a mediated result. That is why the origin appears as the end; even in the humble experience of sense-certainty, we can discern the outlines of Hegelian circularity. This circularity has as its sole basis the twofold paradox of an original content that is destroyed as original content, yet subsists amidst its destruction, and has therefore to be conquered, developed, and revealed before being possessed in its own result. However, if the content had not been, in a sense, *already present* at the beginning of its adventure, it would not be there at the end; in truth, it is already contained in the movement by which it destroys the form of immediacy in itself and undertakes its self-conquest, as the man is already in the child who has to destroy the child in himself to be worthy of the man. Again, the result in which it conquers its plenitude can only be the original content itself, though divested of the innocence that enabled it naively to coincide with the form of the given, and developed to the point of becoming for itself what it is in itself. It is for this reason that the end is the beginning and the beginning the end. The content is thus a circle; it is the discovery of the self in the other extreme, now recognized as the self's very essence. Whence the Hegelian images which depict the content as youth and maturity at once, somewhat as Plato depicted love: 'the content is always young' because what it sets out in quest of is its own innocence, because it destroys its given nature only in order to make it yield up its truth. Yet this stubborn youth is at the same time indistinguishable from the essence of its given nature, a dignity which already makes it older than itself, and which, in its youth, already reveals that its maturity is its truth. That is why the content also resembles an old man who, in his old age, truly knows the child he once was, and who therefore possesses his true youth precisely because he has lost it. Such are the meanings that emerge on a preliminary examination; further analysis of the given will enable us to expand upon them.

For Hegel, the philosophical experience of the sudden destruction of the given was that of empiricism. 'From Empiricism came the cry: "Stop roaming in empty abstractions, keep your eyes open, lay hold on man and nature as they are here before you, enjoy the present moment...".'[81] This profound cry of emancipation, whose only equivalent in the history of thought is Husserl's appeal 'to things themselves', rang out in the silence and then faded away. Doubtless the principle underlying empiricism's intuition was a fruitful one: 'The everyday world, what is here and now, was a good exchange for the futile other-world – for the mirages and the chimeras of the abstract understanding. And thus was acquired an infinite principle, that solid footing so much missed in the old metaphysic.'[82] But, on closer examination, it appears that the infinite determination of the concrete passes over into its opposite as soon as we try to apprehend it. If we do not wish to destroy it, we have to abandon the attempt to cognize it; we have, that is, to contradict our own act. I can, of course, refrain from performing that act; but then what I had taken as my object no longer means anything for me, and disappears from my universe. The given of empiricism is transformed into my cognition of it from the moment I take cognizance of it: perception dissolves the concrete, reducing it to properties that are no longer givens, but abstract universals. Perception tries to discover the truth contained in the given by operating an analytical reduction; it peels the object 'like ... an onion',[83] and fails to notice that that object disappears into its properties as an onion does into its peeled layers: 'Analysis starts from the concrete ... it establishes the differences in things, and this is very important; but these very differences are nothing after all but abstract attributes, i.e. thoughts.'[84] The consequence is that empiricism cannot overcome the twofold temptation besetting it: this form of thinking either allows itself to be benumbed by matter, subjected to the given, in which case it is nothing more than a form of *bondage*; or else it falsifies the given by presenting as a given what is precisely destroyed *qua* given when it is apprehended, in which case empiricism sinks back into abstraction. The lesson empiricism teaches is thus the same as that offered by perceptual knowledge. To grasp the content as a given *is to destroy it as given*. It is, therefore, to reveal the nothingness within it as its very essence, to define it in terms of what it is not, and to relegate it to externality. But this also shows us the positive significance of such destruction, which is not mere annihilation without a sequel, but an *Aufhebung* – a supersession by which the object negated is also preserved. The end, here, is not an absolute end; it is the true beginning. In its own end, the object begins to be what it is.

However, this end is not the true end, in which the object will be actualized as that which it is now just beginning to be; it is merely the end of immediacy, the annihilation of the given. It is thus also an end cast in the form of immediacy, in the form of the beginning itself. At this point we know only that the given is nothingness. Not until the moment of reflection will we see the being of this nothingness emerge; only then will the original void, experienced in the given, endow itself with its own content.

The abolition of all presuppositions, which the phenomenological dialectic shows us in the fate of empiricism, nevertheless poses the problem of the place of presuppositions in Hegel's thinking. Does Hegel not re-establish, in his Logic, the ontological anteriority he goes to such lengths to suppress in his concrete analyses? If he eliminates the given from cognition in the process of emerging, does he not reinstate it in the Logic? Hegel accuses Plato of having treated the Ideas as if they were objects set before the mind that contemplates them in the divine understanding, where they exist prior to any vision. But did he himself not claim to have made the Logic *die Darstellung Gottes*, a representation of God's understanding 'as he is in his eternal essence before the creation of nature'?[85] Is his Logic not, on his own description, what the ἀλήθεια of Greek dogmatism was – *die Wahrheit ohne Hülle*[86] in its eternal truth?

Passages suggesting this abound. They authorize a theological inter-pretation of the Logic: it is itself the original, primordial content out of which all truth, nature or spirit, has proceeded, just as, in Platonism, all that exists emanates from the world of the Ideas, or, in Leibnizian dogmatism, every event originates in the mind of God. The Logic is a third Testament[87] in which we can read not only the Word of God, but also his calculations, his thinking, his manifestations. It might therefore be argued that Hegel only gives us an elaborate transposition of the attitude of the first dogmatists, who set out from some primary term – water, fire, earth – or of the attitude of religious thought, subject to a revelation whose content it merely develops and clarifies. Approached by way of the *Phenomenology*, no doubt the Logic too appears as a result, and this result is doubtless 'nothing apart from its becoming'; otherwise it would be a carcass left lying on the ground. But this result is the crowning stage of its emergence, which shows that it is its *raison d'être*: at the end of the *Phenomenology*, in Absolute Knowledge, consciousness discovers that it is not its own truth and law, but rather the manifestation of absolute Spirit; it thus discovers that its truth stands outside it, pre-exists it and manifests itself in it, and that the highest point it can attain is to contemplate and cognize Spirit's law. The *Phenomenology* too is its own undoing; it destroys itself *qua* form, and, after abolishing the difference between consciousness and its object, considers only *its truth* in its eternal content. This content is that of the Logic in which Spirit contemplates itself. Are we not thus brought back round to a contempla-tive, innocent philosophy in which the object is given in the very element in which it is given, in which its being and meaning coincide, in which the eye need no longer question itself in order to see, and the hand no longer fear what it grasps? This seems all the more plausible in that Hegel eventually stopped thinking of the *Phenomenology* as the first part of the system of knowledge and simply made it a chapter of the *Philosophy of Spirit* [of the *Encyclopædia*]; he thus put manifestation back in its place as manifestation, subordinating it to the *Logos*, which is clearly, as in the Gospel of St. John, 'in the beginning', and constitutes that from which everything else proceeds. It could even be shown that Hegel's conception of things, which breaks with traditional formal logic, reinforces this interpretation. For, in Hegel, the *Logos* is not divided into an objective and a subjective *Logos*, and the truth is not torn between the given and that which confers its necessity upon the given, i.e., the forms of unifying thought; if it were, we would be dealing with a reflexive essence of logic, analogous to the essence of the laws derived from the ordinary objects of science (Kant never got beyond this conception). In that case, the Logic would itself be conditioned, its content presupposing another that would act as its foundation. Hegel, however, conceives the Logic as the unity of form and content, in the profound sense of classical metaphysics, for which the *Logos* was simultaneously the substance that manifests itself and the form that reveals it. He is happy to cite Anaxagoras, for whom the voῦς is the principle that governs the world: thought refers to nothing but itself when it thinks the world. The Logic, it would follow, is clearly an ontology, an absolutely constituted content, the original Kingdom of Truth.

Yet, if this were indeed the case, it would be hard to understand the development of this content. If everything were already given, what internal necessity would oblige the 'already' to go forth from itself and manifest itself? If the *Logos* is the whole and the whole is present from the beginning, how are we to explain the emergence of the parts, nature and spirit? If Hegelianism were a variety of dogmatism, we would find in it the impotence of every dogmatic philosophy which posits the *whole* at the outset, presupposes it, and then finds itself unable to deduce its differences. Hegel, however, relentlessly attacked dogmatism; to assume that he reconstituted in the Logic the presupposition it was the mission of his thought to abolish would embroil us in a fundamental, unthinkable contradiction. If, for him, the given is nothingness, if the beginning is its own end, then the Logic must itself be its own negation, and must manifest, in the beginning, less the content than its absence. This is indeed what occurs, if we bear in mind not only the place of the Logic in Hegel's system, but also the way the Logic itself begins. The movement by which Logic becomes Nature and Spirit is not an act of creation that would presuppose, in its turn, a subject who plays the role of creator; nor is it an analytic operation, an inventory. It is rather the process by which the logical Idea conquers its own content.

Discussing the Kantian categories, Hegel remarks that, in a sense, Kant was right to regard them as empty, adding that their emptiness is precisely the reason they evolve:

> [the categories] and the logical Idea, of which they are the members, do not constitute the whole of philosophy, but necessarily lead onwards in due progress to the real departments of Nature and Mind. Only let the progress not be misunderstood. The logical Idea does not thereby come into possession of a content originally foreign to it: but by its own native action is specialized and developed to Nature and Mind.[88]

Taken by itself, then, the sphere of logic is abstract; it is not a given, but the primordial void that exists only by virtue of the content with which it endows itself. In the Logic, as in perceptual knowledge, the *given* falls prisoner to the void: 'The nothing,' Hegel says in *Differenz*, 'is the first out of which all being, all the manifoldness of the finite has emerged.'[89] And he recalls the theory put forward by certain ancient thinkers, who conceived the *void as motor*. This notion that the logical void generates its own contents explains why Hegelian logic is not a form counterposed to a given content, why the necessity of this generation is also the necessity of the content generated – and why the method is 'the soul immanent in the content'. It also explains the reversal which relegates the totality to the end, instead of positing it at the beginning. If he is to rule out every possible presupposition, Hegel cannot start from anything other than nothingness. We can see this at the beginning of the *Logic*: Hegel begins with being as the most abstract determination, one that is *inhaltlos*, without content; he goes on to locate the truth of being in non-being. 'All that is wanted is to realize that these beginnings are nothing but these empty abstractions, one as empty as the other. The instinct that induces us to attach a settled import to Being, or to both, is the very necessity which leads us to the onward movement of Being and Nothing, and gives them a true or concrete significance.'[90] Finally, taking scrupulousness to an extreme, Hegel entertains the possibility, in Book 1 of the *Science of Logic*, that being itself might be considered a presupposition or original given; this would make it necessary to elucidate the notion of origin as such, in order to determine what the act one was beginning with signifies: 'As yet there is nothing and there is to become something. The beginning is nothing, but a nothing from which something is to proceed.'[91] Or, as Hegel even more explicitly says: 'That which constitutes the beginning, the beginning itself, is to be taken as something unanalysable, taken in its simple, unfilled immediacy, and therefore *as being*, as the completely empty being.'[92]

Hegel thus destroys the old notion of the *in-itself*, whether it be taken at the level of perceptual knowledge, founding principle, or the logical notion of origin. Before Hegel, the *in-itself*, in the form of ideas or the empirical, was the posing, in thought, of a constituted totality or original world which comprehended the whole of reality. The Platonic Idea was an in-itself, as was the Epicurean atom, for both comprehended all possible meanings, enfolding them within themselves, in the form of exemplarity, participation, or mechanical causality. This notion of truth as a world is also to be found in Descartes' substance, and, especially, in Spinoza's notion of God. Substance is posited as *ens per se*, that is, as a constituted totality which contains its own necessity within itself, but is unmarked by internal development, so that the substance is always *already present*, is itself the origin, and always precedes itself in its modes. Let us note that this in-itself can be either an *a priori* or an *a posteriori*, [depending on] whether one takes the world serving as reference point in its ideal or empirical totality. This notion of the in-itself had maintained its ontological primacy in Kant; but Hegel showed that this in-itself can be conceived as a fully realized totality in Kant only on condition that it be conceived as inaccessible, with the result that the in-itself is transformed into an inaccessible point of reference, an entity devoid of determination or content, pure nothingness: the plenitude of the in-itself is here the void. *But it is a purely negative void*: it plays a purely restrictive role with respect to the phenomenon, and does not even succeed in constituting itself as an authentic totality in the ideas of reason, which play a regulatory role and are a *sollen*. This failure of the in-itself once again reveals its pure negativity. Hegel's merit is to have conceived the positivity of the void, or, if one prefers, the positivity of the negative, which enabled him to rule out every 'substantialist' [*mondaine*] conception of the in-itself, and to attend to its emergence.

Hegelianism is often characterized as a philosophy that regards the world *sub specie aeternitatis*, as an *a priori* system of reference. We shall see later in what sense this judgement is valid. Here, however, it must be understood that Hegel's aim is to abolish every system of reference, to do away with every *pure given*, whether *a priori* or *a posteriori*, by exposing its abstract nature. The in-itself is not, for Hegel, a constituted whole: it is an original void which, through its own movement, constitutes itself as a whole. If one can speak of a totality here – and we shall see in what sense this is possible further on – the totality can be said to exist only at the end, which means that the in-itself is assigned the characteristics it produces in the course of its development only by anticipation. Hence one may say that it is merely something *hidden*, a germ, something non-existent which will emerge as something existent, something immediate, something yet-to-come [*à-venir*]; one discerns the promise of the Whole in the in-itself as one discerns the promise of the man in the child, or, in the acorn, the promise of the boughs of the oak. But this very anticipation accentuates the Hegelian reversal, in which the in-itself is no longer an *already-there*, but is rather a *not-yet*; it is its own absence, is contained within itself only latently [*en creux*]; and, let us note, it is not latent within something else, which would thus be the in-itself of reference,[93] it is *latent within itself*, constituting itself only by way of the dialectical discovery of itself in its own nothingness. The in-itself has to conquer its own Self. We shall see that this in-itself, once conquered, is by virtue of that very conquest no longer an in-itself but a *for itself*; that the substance is no longer substance but Subject; and that the in-itself thus conquered is not – at any rate, Hegel does not intend it to be – the reconstitution of the original in-itself, but the annihilation of the fulfilled in-itself, and its elevation to Freedom.

B. The Content As Reflection

If the content is not a pure given, the 'self-enclosed' entity the *Encyclopædia* speaks of, if the content negates itself *qua* given, it nevertheless does not abolish itself *qua* content. The void Hegel expressly sets out to eliminate is not its own truth; if it were, thought would never succeed in emerging from nothingness; indeed, nothingness itself would be inconceivable. The truth of the void is the very being of the void; it is the content of what is negated. Hegel inverts the Spinozist axiom which says that every determination is a negation; for him, every negation is a determination.[94] In other words, negation itself has a content, it is *negation of*, and so contains the term it negates. This is not the place to insist on the profundity of that insight, which expresses the revelation Hegelian consciousness anticipated in its meditations on the void: like Nature in classical philosophy, Hegelian thought abhors a vacuum, and delights in the discovery that the nature of the vacuum is to abhor itself, to recoil from itself, and to do away with itself upon discovering that it contains its own plenitude.[95] Whence the cry of joy in *Faith and Knowledge* over the death of God, which is the beginning of life, over the meaning of the negative, which is life itself, and over the silent labour of nothingness in being.[96]

This positivity of the negative explains how the content can be preserved even as it is annulled. And, with that, we pass from the content as given to the content as reflection. The given points to its negation as to its truth; it thus ceases to be self-enclosed, opening onto the outside and the other that is its true nature. Here we have the transition of the *in-itself* to its own negation, which is not pure nothingness, but the opposite of the *in-itself* – literally, the *outside-itself*. The content attempts to find, in the given, its truth in itself, but in itself it discovers only its own nothingness. It is thus, in itself, something other than what it is; hence the truth of the given in Hegel's sense, according to which truth is the revelation of what is hidden, is *externality*. The truth of the inside must be sought in the outside, the truth of the child in the grown man, the truth of the seed in the tree laden with fruit, the truth of Logic in Nature.

Here we discover the positive aspect of the myth of Eve (initially, we noted only its negative aspect): it signifies the division attendant upon the destruction of unmediated innocence. Paradise lost is not a return to the chaos that preceded creation, nor is it the establishment of the reign of nothingness on earth; it is the passage to the outside. In the intimacy of the beginnings, act and object coincided. Eve discovered the truth of this intimacy the moment she lost it: the truth of Paradise lies in the losing of it [la vérité du Paradis est d'être perdu]. The flight of the first human beings was merely the geographical emblem of this trial, as it were: henceforth, truth would be exile, would dwell outside, would itself be the outside. Hegel serenely adds that this misfortune was not a punishment, but rather an entirely natural discovery, inasmuch as it was the truth of what it destroyed. From this moment on, then, truth was not the inside, but the outside the first human beings were driven towards; it was, indeed, the outside of this outside, since it had to be conquered in the face of adversity, cold, and thorns, in travail and the sweat of man's brow, and in the struggle in which man learned that he was not merely Nature's other, but his own as well. It is this notion of the content as externality that we now wish to trace in the logical, natural, and human orders.

1. (Logic). The word 'content' itself helps us define the logical nature of the content. The German word In-halt unequivocally indicates what this nature is, via both the accessory preposition and the passive form of the root: the content is something 'held', and what is held is 'in' – in a relation of dependence to something else which holds it.[97] Content points to a master, and bears the traces of this in its very name. It does not refer to itself, and is therefore not something that is given in the form of immediacy; it refers to another, indicating that this other makes it what it is. Thus it has no subsistence in and of itself; it is not Parmenides' One, solid and self-sufficient, but has its subsistence and truth in the other.

In this sense, the content reveals that it is inessential, taken by itself, and recognizes the other as being essential for it. This 'for it' provides the measure of its mediated character. Its being does not belong to it, is not per se; rather, its essential being lies outside it, so that it is what it is only in relation to this other, external being – only by its mediation or detour. The being of the inessential is a being only through the mediation of the essential. But what is the nature of the essential that confers its meaning upon it? Is the essential ens per se? If it were, it would be both an absolute reference point and ens per se; the straightforward conjunction of these two definitions is, however, unthinkable. 'Reference point' implies the existence of external terms that are reflected in it, whereas the *ens per se* has no outside. But what is inessential does not, as such, disappear in its confrontation with the essential, because it subsists, and because the essential is, from the standpoint of the inessential, the detour that endows it with subsistence. The essential does not, then, absorb the external terms in reflecting them; it is therefore not *ens per se*. At least to a certain extent, it is itself what it is *by virtue of the other*; its nature too is conferred upon it from the outside. Its status as essential is not its birthright, but rather accrues to it by the detour of the inessential. It is in reflecting itself in the inessential that it becomes aware that it is essential; thus it is through the mediation of the inessential that the essential finds inner confirmation. Whence a certain weakness of the essential, which in fact depends on the inessential, owing precisely to the relation through which it exercises its domination over it.

This dependence is, however, odious, from whichever end one regards it. The mediation required to reduce the alterity of the two poles simply reduces them to their own antagonism; such mediation is nothing more than the consciousness of their bitter hostility and dependence, and can only lead to utter exasperation. From the standpoint of the reflexive relation, mediation is not mediation with the other, but rather mediation with oneself via the other. Accordingly, it presupposes the antagonism and devouring domination of the other, whose presence is not acknowledged for its own sake, but put up with, under duress, as a hateful necessity. In order to reflect itself in itself, in order, that is, to discover itself as it actually is, the inessential has to endure servitude to the other, while the essential has to endure the humiliation of dependence. In the one case as in the other, then, the mediation (which is here immediate) is pure servitude, and alterity becomes an exercise in sheer constraint and impurity. The mediating relation appears in its truth, which is to be a *non-relation*; it annuls itself, leaving only the poles of the reflection to subsist in the ordeal of contradiction.

Such, in bare outline, is the schema of the dialectic of the content as reflection. As we can see, the other is not always equally harsh: initially, it is simple otherness, i.e., *difference*, as perceived by the pole in which the content is reflected. This position of the second pole becomes *mediation* when each of the two poles confers its nature upon the other and experiences the mutual dependence of itself and the other. The ordeal is, however, unbearable, for this mediate bond is merely the reflection of the reflection upon itself; and, as the element of reflection is externality, the reflection which reflects itself upon itself actually reflects itself outside itself, annulling itself (or degenerates into a middle term, a *Mittelding* that collapses in upon itself). The two poles of the content are thus left face to face in *contradiction*, which is pure non-relation in relation and conflict in the absence of mediation, for mediation through conflict has not yet been recognized. Thus contradiction here is the developed content of the reflection, the truth of the reflection. And contradiction remains its truth to the extent that it is considered to be simply the truth of the content, not what the content actually is – this for as long as contradiction continues to be the fate of the content without becoming its very nature.

The dialectic of form and content provides a good example of the nature of reflection. Once again, Hegel's aim here is to banish any material substratum presumed to exist prior to its form, as the marble exists prior to the bust – even if this substratum is regarded only as a purely logical possibility. The form–matter relation involves two distended terms; at its two poles, one can admit the existence of raw material without form and of an ultimate form without matter. Too loose a statement of the problem of form and content permits the surreptitious return of the in-itself as reference point; Hegel formulates the problem rigorously, giving it appropriate expression in the dialectic of form and content, which is a dialectic of dependence.

The content has no subsistence apart from its form: 'Content and matter are distinguished by this circumstance, that matter, though implicitly not without form, still in its existence manifests a disregard of form, whereas the content, as such, is what it is only because the matured form is included in it.'[98] Similarly, it must be said that the form does not, for its part, have any consistency apart from its content, and that it is not possible to conceive a pure form without simultaneously imagining a certain content inside it. In short, Hegel's treatment of the problem puts the accent on the dialectical relation between the terms involved, highlighting the sudden shift which brings about the transition from form to content and content to form: he calls this an *Umschlagen*. Thus the essence turns into the phenomenon when we focus our attention on it, the whole dissolves into its parts, the inside becomes the outside, force becomes the manifestation of force. Conversely, the same *Umschlagen* transforms the phenomenon into essence, the parts into the whole, the outside into the inside, the manifestation into force: 'We are here in presence, implicitly, of the absolute correlation of content and form: viz. their reciprocal revulsion [reversal], so that content is nothing but the revulsion of form into content, and form nothing but the revulsion of content into form.'[99]

What we will here call the dialectic of the sandglass seems to us to bear a very close resemblance to the dialectical contaminations *Gestalt-theorie* has drawn attention to. The relations established between form and content, at the level of essence, are much the same as those that are established between figure and background in *Gestalt* psychology: when the mind ceases to concentrate on the figure as figure, it becomes the background, at least in certain ambiguous cases, whilst the background becomes a figure. Such, for example, is the case with force: when I try to determine what the content of force is, I find I must look to its manifestations, whereupon that in which I was seeking the content, i.e., force, becomes the form and is separated from its content. Similarly, if I examine the whole, I discover that it resides in its parts; the minute the accent is thus shifted from one term to the other, the term I wish to zero in on is transformed, becoming external to itself. Thus the whole that discovers its truth in its parts is henceforth mere form, an external bond that maintains the parts in their cohesiveness. Yet if, after reaching this point of division, I ask what the content of the parts is, I see straightaway that it can be found nowhere but in the whole, in which it once again seeks refuge as if this were where it belonged, eluding my gaze and leaving me confronting the parts in their isolation.

We can see, then, the basic ambiguity of the content *qua* reflection: this dialectic of the sandglass, this *Umschlagen* of form into content and content into form is not experienced as the very essence of the content, which discovers itself only in the externality that is one moment of this process. The content is here expelled, driven out of itself; but while it is plainly the same content that is simultaneously in- and outside itself, simultaneously inside and outside, it does not perceive itself as such. From the standpoint of reflection, the content encounters its truth in the other, but does not realize that it is this other. Whence the relations which spring up on the basis of this misunderstanding: the content struggles amidst indifference, alterity, and hostility, without understanding that it is merely struggling against itself. 'Destiny,' as Hegel profoundly says, 'is consciousness of oneself as an enemy.' The content cannot get the better of this enemy which it encounters in the process of reflection onto its other, unless it recognizes itself in it and ceases to tear itself to pieces. Yet it is in this conflict that it becomes cognizant of its own dependence and of the need to pass by way of an other – and thus of the need to contain mediation: 'The content carries a mediation with it.'[100] Here it discovers that this other is an alien force which has coercive power over it – which is what the slave discovers about the master, or the phenomenon about the essence.

It is in otherness that we can observe the profound dismemberment characteristic of the understanding: the supreme example is provided by the philosophy of Kant, in which form and content, the given and necessity, the particular and the universal condition one another amidst mutual hostility. The result is an inability to reconcile, in conflict, adversaries sustained by the conflict itself: hence reflexive philosophy poses necessity over against content or the universal over against the concrete, while the only relations it succeeds in establishing between the terms it has thus torn asunder are those of the very reflection that engendered them. Even the problem that inspired Hume's investigations – how to reconcile necessity with the content – could find only one issue, which again consisted in ranging the terms over against one another, in the very position in which the philosopher's reflection had initially placed them: content without necessity over against a necessity that was nothing more than custom. Similarly, Kant, as we have noted, merely maintained the basic opposition within which his thought evolved, under cover of various intermediate artifices. With Fichte, Hume's problem was inverted: but if the question was no longer to deduce the form of necessity from the content, the challenge was to introduce the form itself into the content. The result of this attempt, which remained in the domain of the *sollen*, proves that the antagonism between these terms cannot be overcome within their division; and that for as long as it does not recognize itself as itself in the other, the content cannot free itself of domination and dependence. The free man, according to Fichte, is in reality merely unaware that he is a slave, whereas, for Hegel, the slave begins to be free as soon as he becomes conscious of his servitude. Finally, this antagonism reaches its highest pitch in the contradiction in which content no longer confronts an indifferent form, a contingent externality, and encounters itself in its opposite instead.

Such is the paradox of Hegelian contradiction: it constitutes the highest form of relation at the heart of non-relation. In a well-known phrase, the young Hegel serves notice of his ambition to think 'the relation between relation and non-relation'. The concept of contradiction is the point where relation is conceived within non-relation, and this so intensely that, if matters were taken just a little further, non-relation would appear as the limit of relation, and be conceived as relation in its turn. Kant stopped short of this: in the antinomies, he encountered contradiction in the content, but chose not to maintain it there. He had come face-to-face with contradiction, but saw in it only a defect of reason, whereas it is in fact the very essence of the content. A great many texts treat this point: there is nothing in heaven or on earth that does not contain contradiction – such is the truth which the 1801 dissertation on the planets presented in the form of the *contradictio regula veri*, and which we find again in all of Hegel's mature works: 'everything is inherently contradictory.'[101] We have come a long way, even from the merely logical standpoint, from the solid content that perceptual knowledge, in its innocence, assumed was its object. Negation, mediation, and contradiction have drawn the content out of itself and fixed it so firmly in externality that it ultimately fails to recognize externality as the sphere in which it exists: the content now literally *contra-dicts* itself [*se contre-dit*], i.e., declares what it is by repulsing its opposite.

2. (Nature). However, this logical analysis is an abstraction too, as the ana-lysis of the given has shown. Even reconciled with itself, logical extern-ality makes sense only with the fulfilment of the Logic. Paradoxically,

the analysis of reflection is still an in-itself, in that it remains confined within the element of pure thought. The for-itself of this in-itself cannot be reflection within the in-itself; it must rather be the outside, precisely, of the in-itself, i.e., Nature. Hegel here takes up the old idea of a Nature whose externality is its essence in a twofold sense: it is because Nature is external to the *Logos* that it is external to itself, and that it continues to be *partes extra partes*: 'Nature has yielded itself as the Idea in the form of *otherness*. Since the *Idea* is therefore the negative of itself, or *external to itself*, nature is not merely external relative to this Idea [...] but is embodied as nature in the determination of *externality*.'[102] It is this self-externality of the content which Hegel reconstitutes in the *Philosophy of Nature*, moving from the great dispersion of mechanics through the reflexive externality of physics to the relative concentration of the organism.

It is not hard to grasp this externality in space, in which the content is, in some sort, juxtaposed to itself,[103] so that universality is here a sheer abstraction. It is, however, perhaps more difficult to understand the externality of the organism, at the other extreme of the dialectic of nature. What is actualized in the organism, as various passages in the *Phenomenology* indicate, is a living totality in which each part subsists only in virtue of the whole, and the whole, in its turn, only in virtue of the parts. A part in isolation loses its significance: a hand that has been cut off, says Hegel, is no longer a hand. But the organism considered as a totality itself stands in a twofold relation to externality. To begin with, the organism subsists on its own only in a formal sense, inasmuch as it draws its substance from the 'inorganic'; thus the organic totality points to an exterior which conditions it. If we regard living creatures from this angle, we can say either that they contain their objective within themselves – in which case the means lie outside them – or else that they possess these means, in which case their objective is outside them. The living creature is external to itself in another sense as well: it does not contain universality within itself. The developing individual produces *another* individual as its result, and effaces itself before its product. Commenting on the fact that, among certain primitive peoples, it is customary to kill one's aged parents, Hegel observes that this is the very meaning of life: a child is, literally, the death of its parents. In other words – and this is no less true of plants than of animals – the genus manifests its externality in that it destroys its individual members so as to actualize itself as genus.

> The *original disease* of the animal, and the in-born *germ of death*, is its being inadequate to universality. The annulment of this inadequacy is in itself the full maturing of this germ, and it is by imagining the universality of its singularity, that the individual effects this annulment. By this, however, and in so far as the universality is abstract and immediate, the individual only

achieves an *abstract objectivity* ... devoid of process, the individual having therefore put an end to itself of its own accord.[104]

This inability on the part of living creatures to acquire universality in the course of their individual development, and to preserve it even as they perish, means that they cannot become true totalities: the cycle undergone by the seed, which grows, acquires branches and leaves, and puts forth blossoms and fruit, terminates in a falling seed. This seed has no memory; it contains nothing more than the seed which enabled it to sprout and mature; it is not a history, but an adventure that repeats itself. Hegel here recurs to the old Aristotelian idea of a cyclical nature in which universality is an organic circle that produces its own point of departure at its point of arrival: 'Nature is what it is; and so its alterations are therefore only repetitions, its movement is only circular.'[105]

This phenomenon of repetition, in which development cuts itself off from itself and naively resumes its course, as if, at every instant, the past were swallowed up in the void – in a word, this phenomenon in which development is juxtaposed – makes it impossible to regard Nature as an authentic totality. We are here at a point at which totality is still, at least in some measure, extensible, in which the parts have not been perfectly internalized, but are rather combined through a process of dispersion and repetition. Nature attains its highest degree of concentration in the reality of organic cycles, in which Hegel finds the same fundamental externality of the *partes extra partes* that is so obvious in space. The natural totality is external to itself; hence Hegel cannot be satisfied with the conception, inherited from Hellenism, of Nature as a Whole that includes all meanings within itself and realizes the reflexive unity of their differences. Here again we encounter the temptation to conceive the content as a whole, not original, this time, but reflexive, and yet so constituted that reflection is, as it were, annulled in it by an optical distortion which makes reflection appear as self-repetition. Earlier we noted the significance of the *Umschlagen* of the whole into its parts and the parts into the whole: the same phenomenon makes itself felt in the notion of *natura naturans* and *natura naturata*, or in the thought of a Giordano Bruno, which Schelling turned back to in his later works. Whether we represent Nature as an extensive totality, a vast living whole, or indifference, we posit the totality in its externality, with the parts outside the whole, and life outside the living creature; we restate in the one term what we posit in the other, since the terms make no sense apart from their reflection. Thus life is simply a universal standing over against individuals; it is, however, a destructive universal:

[Nature] falls from its universal, from life, directly into the singleness of existence, and the moments of simple determinateness, and the single organic life united in this actuality, produce the process of Becoming merely as a

> contingent movement, in which each is active in its own part and the whole is
> preserved; but this activity is restricted, so far as *itself* is concerned, merely to
> its centre, because the whole is not present in it, and is not present in it
> because here it is not *qua* whole *for itself*.[106]

Here, then, we can see the deficiency of the reflexive totality of Nature:
Nature refers us, by default, to a totality which would be neither
immediate nor reflected, neither a given nor a cosmos, but an interiority.
'Organic Nature has no history . . .',[107] i.e., it does not possess the internal
dimension thanks to which content ceases to be a reflection into another
and becomes reflection into itself.

3. (Man). The same reflexive externality characterizes every anthropology founded at this level – that of the Renaissance or the Enlightenment,
for example. In such an anthropology, man is no longer defined in and
of himself: his nature is rather to be a reflexive determination of Nature,
to depend on Nature even as he differs from it. *Qua* living creature, man
is an organism who consumes an 'inorganic' Nature and converts it into
his own nature; *qua* man, he negates his own nature. This negation also
implies the negation of 'inorganic' nature, but the negation is not
conceived as one which, turning back upon itself, absorbs its own
precondition; it is a determinate negation, subordinate to the Nature
which serves as its reference point, with the result that it is conceived as
determined by Nature itself. Thus established within a determinate
context and located within a constituted universe, human negativity
returns to the state of nature, becomes an element of Nature: there are
laws of human nature as there are laws of Nature *tout court*. Aristotle
discerned, in human politics, the same circularity he found in Nature;
the philosophers of the Renaissance conceived man as a little world. For
its part, post-Cartesian science strove to show that man was a living
clockwork machine which functioned in accordance with the laws
governing bodies. Finally, the philosophers and jurists of the eighteenth
century (from Montesquieu to Grotius [*sic*]) established the role of Nature
in the direction of all human endeavour, and founded the theory of
natural law.

Thus, when we consider man, we find ourselves referred to Nature.
But, when we consider Nature, we discover only the contrary of man.
Discussing Gall's phrenology, Hegel points out the absurdity of any
judgement that would reduce man to a skull-bone – 'the spirit is not a
bone' – or, more generally, to any natural determination whatsoever.
Curiously, the philosophers of the Renaissance had already envisioned
this reversion of man to Nature and of Nature to man: confronting the
little world with the big one, they sought, by turns, the meaning of man
in the universe and the meaning of the universe in man. They thus

revived the traditional Judeo-Christian notion of Adam's pre-eminence[108] and human negativity; we can find in some of them the idea that the significance of the world is exhausted by man,[109] and that the universe exists only in order to be assumed, appropriated, and invested with its dignity and truth by human thought. This idea of the paramountcy of man found a place in the thinking of the seventeenth century, which held, with Pascal, that 'the dignity of man resides entirely in thought.' However, the non-natural nature of thought was soon reduced to the Cartesians' substance, which was, although independent of extension, something of which thought was only an attribute. Hence the dialectic of the *Umschlagen* was internalized in the obscure notion of the unity of body and soul: the reversion from passion to will, natural determinism to freedom of action occurred in man himself. The Kantian antinomy of freedom and necessity was the truth of this conception of man, which pitted him, in the form of a wholly external negativity – that is, in the domination of servitude – against the universe and his own nature. It was the same external negativity which made it possible to conceive man's negation of nature through labour on the model of organic transformation – as the modification of one common, universal substance, or even as the extension of biological and mechanical laws. Nature was subject to man, who ranged freely through it, tamed the animals, ploughed the fields and furrowed the seas, and 'ensnared the birds in his nets'.[110] But man was a king subject to the domination of dust. Animal nature was the ruse that triumphed over reason and took man to itself again in the decay of death – 'and the fields sprout again in silence.' The only escape available to this living contradiction, unaware that contradiction was the essence of his being, was to conceive the actualization of his negativity in the mode of the Beyond, just as Kant projects the resolution of the reflective contradictions onto the *sollen*, that is to say, God. At this level, man's reflexivity prevents him from constituting himself as a totality; or, rather, the totalities he attempts to create are deficient and still-born.

The first of them is love, a totality in which the lovers exist only by way of each other, reflect back each other's image, and attempt to fill the lack in their own nature through the nature of the other. The old theory of sex as division is implicit in this conception of love, which sees man as cut in two; the two halves strive to come together again, and are ordained to meet by virtue of their very division. But this totality in the form of externality does not, in natural love, rise above the level of animality: totality is achieved only outside it, in the child, the 'beyond' of love. This process merely serves to bring out the domination of the species, which utilizes love to perpetuate the genus: the universality engendered by man is not the universality of love, but that of the genus, which limits him and presides over his death. Here again, the mediation is immediate in that it destroys without preserving, and the negativity is external: death is, in the form of the corpse and the child, the truth of love, while the universal is brought back under the sway of natural law. The human race is an inhuman race*.

The second still-born totality is that of political life. In the present perspective, it displays the same inversion of human particularity into inhuman universality – the universality of the state, whose essence is law. Here again, man is not reconciled with the universal, but submits to its domination. The sole reflexive bond established here is the transfer represented by the abrupt dialectical shift: man's nature attests that law is his essence, but the law's externality to man literally subjects him to his truth as to a form of servitude. Man's truth is not his reality, because it is outside him; the law is not flesh of his flesh, but an alien force that destroys his flesh in his flesh. The Fichtean state actualizes the essence of this domination, in which a multitude of human atoms endure the dictatorship of the universal,[111] which is literally intolerable, because it is the truth of man, and, at the same time, crushes him.

Finally, man's attempt to recreate in his mind the totality he does not experience in reality culminates in failure. The developed consciousness of this failure takes the forms of realism and idealism: that is, universality passes from one extreme to the other. Sometimes the object is posited as universal, and the subject is subjected to it as if it were a particular content suddenly confronted with an external truth. Sometimes the ego, the abstract universal, posits universality over against all particular content; but the object can no more definitively free itself of the subject than the subject can free itself of the object. The alternating extremes are prisoners of their hostility; brothers, yet enemies, they are locked in perpetual struggle.[112] This heterogeneity of form and content admits of only two 'ideological' resolutions – which are, in reality, merely simulacra of totality.

The first attempt, reflecting on reflection, leads to the progressive disappearance of reflection into the substance: here that negativity which is external to itself is reduced either to false difference (Spinoza), or to indifference (Schelling). Whether the substance involved is conceived as mind or matter, it is merely a compact, reconstituted universality which absorbs even the reflexivity that constituted it – with the result that the ideology thus constituted becomes a world which forcibly absorbs the world. Commenting on Spinoza's system, Hegel says it is a form, not of atheism, but of a-cosmism; that in a system in which the world vanishes, man too is fated to disappear; and that, inasmuch as neither man nor the world disappear in reality (thus Spinoza is not really absorbed by the *Ethics*, which remains external to him; this constitutes *de facto* recognition

---

* *Espèce*, which also means 'species'.

of externality), 'ideology' in fact remains reflexive in its very desire to do away with reflection.

The impossibility of reducing reflection to substance inspires the second attempt. Rather than conceiving the reality of the totality as substance, it contents itself with noting that the totality is aborted by reflection, conceiving it as not realized. But the non-realization of the totality is itself a reflexive determination that refers us to the totality, conceived, simultaneously, as real and non-realized, or, in other words, as realized in a realm beyond natural reality. The Whole is accordingly a beyond in which all contradictions subside: 'God is the stream into which all contraries flow,' says Hegel; in him, the universal and particular are brothers, and the totality triumphs at last. But this mode of thought (classical philosophy down to Hegel – the religions) in fact establishes a new contradiction between this world and its beyond: the reality of this world becomes a term in this new reflection, in which real contradiction points to a fictive totality. On the one hand, we have reality without totality; on the other, totality without reality. In neither case is dependence surmounted, since the beyond remains the slave of this world, which conditions it, while this world finds itself dominated, in religion and thought, by a beyond that is its truth but not its reality. There is no such thing as happy nature.*

Yet its very unhappiness is the presentiment of a totality that would no longer be a simulacrum, but a reality. In reflection, content looks towards a beyond which is its truth: content must be reconciled with its truth and supersede external reflection. The truth such reflection announces is reflection's own beyond: no other totality is possible, and it is the profound nature of reflection to abolish itself in its truth,[113] or, rather, to bring the expression of its truth to the point of disequilibrium at which reflection tolerates only the image of its truth, or annuls itself in the actualization of its truth. Reflection holds its truth at a distance, contemplating it in painted images. It has a confused sense of the fact that this distance and these images are the margin of grace in which it subsists. If its truth were to be actualized or its images made flesh, reflection would be emptied out and reduced to an insubstantial form. This is the sense of the transition from religion to absolute knowledge in Hegel; in absolute knowledge, the content is internal to itself. God is the truth in which the contradiction of the content subsides; however, this truth is not actual in reflexive ideologies. Yet God is posited as being the beyond of reflection. This remark has a triple significance. To begin with, the truth of reflection, properly speaking, transcends and abolishes reflection. Secondly, the end† of reflection is the actualization of its

---

* Il n'y a pas de nature heureuse, echo of a poem by Louis Aragon, Il n'y a pas d'amour heureux.

† Fin, which means both 'end' and 'goal'.

truth, that is, in the proper sense of the word, *God made man*, Christian Revelation become a world. Finally, this actualization merely abolishes the externality of the form in which truth was given to reflection – as to the content, it is reflexive truth's own content, but freed of its externality and restored to itself. With that, we have come to the end of this process: now the content is not reflected in the other, but in itself; it no longer endures the servitude of externality, but is free, and henceforth has to do only with itself: it is *Self*.

C. The Content As Self

The conception of the content as Self articulates a profound intuition of Hegelian thought, which sees in contradiction the advent of unity and in servitude the gestation of freedom. After abolishing the immediacy of the given in the otherness of reflection, the content realizes the truth of reflection in the Self, attaining peace and the totality. The nothingness of the beginnings at last conquers the element of truth and actuality, the authentic unity in which the totality finally coalesces, in which it ceases to be divided against itself and to look beyond itself for its own truth. The Self is itself in the other; it exists in virtue of itself and the other simultaneously, and, overcoming contradiction, recognizes itself in its adversary. The contrary is no longer merely the flesh of its contrary, but flesh of its own flesh, and the battle, once ended, becomes the meditation of brotherhood. The necessity thus revealed is not, however, a new form of servitude, but the exercise of freedom: the content is its own content, it is everywhere, like God, and everywhere at home *with itself*, that is to say, free. Free of external alienation, free of internal alienation, the content is the *Absolute*.

The *concept* (*Begriff*) is for Hegel both the instrument that serves to liberate the content, and also its very nature. What are the defining features of the Hegelian concept?

It is distinguished not only from intuition, but also from the concept in the ordinary sense of the word. If, very schematically, we discriminate between philosophies of intuition and philosophies of the concept, then Hegel's philosophy resolutely intends to be a philosophy of the concept. Thus it denies the primacy of intuition and the obvious, the Cartesian virtues thanks to which the mind gains direct access to the universal. Intuition in Descartes is a divine gift; the sole human contribution to it consists in severe self-discipline: we have only to clear away prejudices and impure images through doubt in order to reach, in intuition, the *terra firma* of truth. We reach it, in some sort, by right;[114] in Descartes as in Plato, the whole problem consists in approaching the truth by a kind of creeping or climbing of the mind, until we arrive at the point at which the face of the Eternal emerges. At that point, doubtless, sensory intuition is no longer any more than an occasion for the intellectual intuition which is its model – yet both are conceived on the same pattern, as a vision in which we behold truth without distance or detour. It is this direct apprehension of thé universal that Hegel combats in the *Schwär-merei* of his contemporaries or the religious philosophy of Jacobi. Indeed, the philosophies of intuition are always more or less knowingly religious, in that man participates in the truth only negatively; he is entirely submissive and passive before Revelation ('in intuition we can become unfree in the highest degree'),[115] before the content it unveils. Thus intuition in Descartes, as in St. Augustine, delivers the imperfect up to the perfect, putting creation in God's hands: the universality attained without detour is a universality that brooks no appeal. Hence the ambiguity of intuition, which turns the intransigent purity of man's gaze against him: the truth is literally blinding, like the sun when we look at it with open eyes. To philosophize with open eyes is to philosophize in the dark. Only the blind can look straight at the sun.[116]

Since Aristotle, the philosophies of the concept have developed in opposition to this tendency. They hold that there can be no direct revelation of the truth, that it is the detour, rather, which is rewarded with the universal. They observe that the path laboriously carved out by thought is the price of its vision, that the goal has no meaning apart from the path leading to it, or, better, that the mediation of the path is the condition of universality – that the truth offers itself less in the content of what is grasped than in the very act of grasping, considered as the content at last seized and repossessed in its absolute truth. 'Concept'[117] and *Begriff* both express this idea of *capturing* the truth: truth is seizure – but in the concept, it seizes itself. The ambiguity of the concept comes into view here: for the difference and unity of the concept are posited simultaneously, and the conflict between them is not clearly resolved. Any capture wears a double aspect: it presupposes the taker and the taken. The concept rises above intuition in that it recognizes and respects this duality, betrayed without qualms in intuition. But that respect is the tragedy of the concept, which is unable to think the unity of this real duality. This explains the fact that the concept was, before Hegel, an imperfect mediation which did not succeed in overcoming the externality of the truth to its content, of the act of seizing to the seized. The concept was the other of its content, an abstract universal which negated the content, or preserved it in fact while negating it in the *word*; it was negated in its turn in yet other words, without preserving for itself this preservation of the content in its very negation. Ultimately, the pre-Hegelian concept posits a truth that is universal but emptied of its content, over against a content that is full but contingent. Such is the *genus*, the Aristotelian concept, an external universality without inner mediation, which plunges directly into the opposite extreme, the particular; such is the Kantian concept, an empty category dependent on an external content that is a pure given: 'Concepts without intuition are empty.' The general idea cut off from its origins and the content cut off from its truth confront each other as if they were strangers. This is the image we encountered in discussing the moment of reflection. This is the contradiction the Hegelian concept internalizes and thus transcends.

The Hegelian concept can be reduced neither to one absolute term (intuition), nor to two contradictory terms (general, formal ideas/concrete content). Rather, it is accomplished in the third term. This is the famous triplicity or triadic structure, generally conceived in terms of the thesis/antithesis/synthesis schema, a concatenation of words which has no real meaning. There are not three terms, for Hegel, but one: the concept. The two terms reflection posits as external to one another are not suddenly flanked by a third that acts as their intermediary (like the demiurge in Plato, or the transcendental imagination in Kant). We know that the intermediary is a provisional entity which disappears once its mediation has been achieved; the demiurge is a discreet accessory; the third term of an Aristotelian syllogism is nowhere to be found in the conclusion, just as the constructions used in mathematical demonstrations or the unknown quantity in a solved equation disappear from the result. Before Hegel, triplicity was a game, and, in the end, the third term clearly showed itself for what it was: a *nonentity* [*non-être*] *that had been reabsorbed*. Having accomplished his task, the god ascended again into heaven in his *machina*; one sought him in vain on earth.[118] Hegel completely overturns this schematism: his third term is not a nonentity and does not disappear,[119] for a good reason: it is its own stage, it does not find itself by anyone's side because it is the whole, it is the only entity endowed with being [*le seul à être*]. The Hegelian concept is not 'third' at all, because three presupposes one and two; or, rather, this three is a three without one or two, it is an *absolute three*. Thus nonexistence descends upon the two previous terms: the one and the two do not exist in the true sense of the word, but are ambiguous entities which receive their truth – that is, nothingness – from the three. Thus far the reversal clearly seems to be a simple for-or-against, except that nothingness now affects two terms instead of one. And, upon examination, these two terms clearly seem to play the same discreet role vis-à-vis the third that the third plays with regard to them in the dialectic of mediation discussed above. Are they not temporary, twin demiurges? Do they too not vanish in their result? It is here that the paradox appears: the gods do not ascend again into heaven, they remain on earth; the two terms continue to dwell within their result, they are abiding gods. Such is Hegel's solution;[120] it shows that the three is the truth of the one and the two, shows the three to be the only place where the one and the two are *at home*. This is the true resolution of the problem of the externality of the concept, the resolution which finally leads to totality, since there is nothing outside the three: the concept is the Absolute Whole. That is why the concept is the 'kingdom of subjectivity' for Hegel, negativity in positivity, content in truth. We now need to develop the significance of this perfected totality.

The Hegelian concept is pure interiority. This feature of the concept has a twofold significance. It implies, to begin with, that the concept is the totality in the absolute sense, which not only leaves no determinate term outside itself, of course, but also reabsorbs externality itself *qua* element. In other words, this whole is not a cosmos, a clearly delineated figure suspended in the void, a compact entity standing out against nothingness. Here the totality does not emerge against any background whatever, or draw its substance from any 'inorganic' nature foreign to it. It is a figure that serves as its own background: the concept is its own element.[121] Secondly, the concept's intimate relation with itself implies that even the element in which we might be tempted to situate it can in fact only be the concept itself – externality and the void, in particular, are the stuff of which the intimacy of the Self is constituted. The concept reaches out to draw everything within its embrace: any grasping of the concept in whatever form is nothing but the grasping of the Self by itself. 'The Self has no outside' means, then, that the outside is the inside of the Self.

To put it differently, externality is not annulled, but is internalized. Kroner[122] points out that, in Hegel, 'reflection' becomes *Selbstreflexion* [self-reflection]. Here we may recall what we said about triplicity: the two and the one are present in the result; reflection is internal reflection; and, as the Self is omnipresent, reflection in the Self is reflection of the Self into itself. Such is the significance of the *Selbst* – of the *Self* which, linguistically, designates pure movement back towards the subject. This reflection is not abolished, but is rather *aufgehoben*, that is, preserved but subjected to its own truth. Thus the unity of the Self is not the undifferentiated solidity of an entity which is simply given; it is a unity wrested from division through the reciprocal conversion of opposing terms. Contraries subsist in the content *qua* Self; they are, indeed, its reality, because they have recognized one another in it and found their truth there. They are not forced to accept a dictated peace or outside arbitration; nor are they reconciled *pro forma* or in a certain form: rather, they find their truth by being converted to their truth.

Conversion must be understood in the sense it has in Plato, who says, in a lovely phrase, that the warring elements of the content turn toward their true nature σύν ὅλῃ τῇ ψυχῇ, with all their soul, with all their substance, for it is there that they acquire their soul and their substance. Thus the Self recaptures reconciled enemies by means of this internal reflection: the speculative syllogism represents, in Hegel's thought, the inwardly directed gaze that enables the Self to make the circuit of its own diversity and reappropriate it, without going forth from itself. We have an example in the cosmological syllogism according to which the existence of God follows from the existence of the world even as it explains it. Prior to the revelation of the concept, what was proven necessarily depended on the proof: God was the world's royal slave. But then how was God's reflexive nature to be reconciled with the other attributes conferred upon him by thought: omnipotence and freedom? The Hegelian concept is the movement through which the result recovers its origins by internalizing them, by revealing itself to be the origin of the origin. This process of envelopment implies that the initial term and the reflected term are *aufgehoben* in the result:

> The demonstration of reason no doubt starts from something which is not God. But, as it advances, it does not leave the starting-point a mere unexplained fact, which is what it was. On the contrary it exhibits that point as derivative and called into being, and then God is seen to be primary, truly immediate, and self-subsisting, with the means of derivation wrapped up and absorbed in himself.[123]

Similarly, Hegel shows that the concept is the true infinity, that it absorbs and posits the pseudo–infinity which emerges from simple reflection on the finite. In general, everything is a syllogism and the Self is the Absolute Syllogism in which the reflexive moments of particularity and universality are absorbed and founded in an individuality that is no longer an external middle term, but rather a totality resulting from its own mediation by itself. Externality as such is thus the mediation of interiority in the content considered as Self.

Externality inevitably brings us to negation. To say that the Self is its own mediation comes down to showing that negativity is the soul of the whole. Indeed, the totality constitutes itself by means of negativity, which is supersession of the supersession, that is, negation of the negation. It is impossible to miss the creative, positive role of [negativity] in the process that preserves the annulled content in the form of negation, and re-establishes it in its authentic truth in the negation of the negation. It is tautological to say that the essential being of the Self is contradiction and that the essential being of the Self is negativity. But this leads to an important idea: if the totality is in fact the mediated *recuperation* [*reprise*] of the original content, and if this content has, for us,[124] revealed itself to be nothingness, then, in a certain way, this recuperation can only be the *recuperation of nothingness* in the totality, that is, the recuperation of the totality by itself in the form of nothingness. In a sense that we shall have to pin down, we have here reached the point at which the Self reveals itself to be a substantialization of the void.

In any case, this reflection unambiguously clears up two points: the Self is no longer external negativity defined in opposition to a second term. It can only be internal negativity – and the positivity of nothingness is finally evident in this totality, which has come about as a result of the 'tarrying with death' and the 'silent labour of the negative' that mark the course of its development.

Our analysis of the Self thus brings us to a third point: the totality is neither given nor reflexive; it is the syllogism of the given and reflection in the Self. It is, then, a result. 'The True is the whole ... the true [is] a result. ... The result [is] the result together with the process through which it came about.'[125] These sentences from the *Phenomenology* deline- ate the problem and show clearly that conceptual truth is, for Hegel, capture, not grace. Yet this capture is not forgetful; the truth is not ungrateful. A result which was not the memory of its becoming would be a carcass left lying on the ground,[126] a lifeless concept. Thus the content is not only its own inside, it is also its own internalization, *Er- innerung*, whose other name is, in French, *souvenir*. The concept is the memory of itself – it is in this sense that, in man, it is history – but it is a strange memory which remembers itself only in the strangest forms, and conquers the truth of its childhood only at the end of its history: the most astonishing thing is surely that the remotest memory surges up only at the end, so that, in this sense, childhood is a gift of maturity. This is how that profound remark of Hegel's, 'the content is always young', must be understood; for the Self finds the truth again, that is, the revealed reality of its beginnings, only in its end. The end is the meaning of the beginning, while the beginning, considered in isolation from the ultimate, meaning- ful totality, is mere nothingness – yet the beginning is the reality of the end, or, in other words, the reality of the content is won back in the end (by virtue of the double negation); far from being expelled from the result, it is its soul and body: the Self is nothing other than this reality in the movement of its own mediation. That is why Hegel says that the Self is something immediate; but it is such in the element of the concept, not, as before, in the element of reflection or of a posited absolute. The circularity of the concept is its own youth set free; it is, literally, a 'second childhood'.[127] This circularity is the sign that the concrete has been redeemed and transfigured: it invests the totality of the preceding moments with their truth.

At the end of the dialectic of the content, then, we see the generosity of the immediate, and even the grace of intuition, re-emerging in the liberty of the self. But the immediate is simultaneously a universal here; the given is charged with all the meaning it has acquired throughout its history, and intuition is now no longer the fruit of blindness. '[T]he eyes of the Spirit and the eyes of the body completely coincide' – or again, as Hegel puts it, just as 'the husband sees flesh of his flesh in the wife', the

Self henceforth contemplates 'the Spirit of his Spirit' in simple being.[128] This connaturality at the level of substance, this profound homogeneity of universality conquered at last, this substance become Self, and this domain pervaded by negativity are, for Hegel, freedom.

The conversion of the content into its truth – freedom – explains why Hegel simultaneously defines the concept as the *kingdom of subjectivity* and the truth as the *substance become subject*. For the Self never has to do with anything other than itself in the guise of the other. Not only is I an other, but, in the element of the concept, the other is I: the Self recognizes itself in the other. The content is *bei sich*, truth at last dwells in its own abode, God, descended from Heaven, dwells amongst men; this is no longer the Jewish God, whom his people do not recognize,[129] 'a stranger in his own land',[130] but the truth become man in a human world that has become truth, a native land reconquered, the profound unity of the Self and the totality. In this sense, freedom is no longer conceived in terms of domination and servitude, that is, as simple external negation. Freedom is not purity, for the pure individual is only a blind slave; nor is it deliberate impurity, for impurity is Night's empire. Freedom in Hegel is neither the rejection of necessity nor its acceptance, neither a straightforward no nor a straightforward yes – it is rather the no of the no and the yes wrested back from the no. Freedom is circular, and this circularity is the advent of the subject. In a reflexive dialectic, the subject is not at home amidst his attributes, but subjected to them. Not only is the slave a slave; the master is too. Thus the God of the old metaphysics was merely a desolate solitude waiting for the metaphysician to restore him his nature, with the attributes of being, power, and freedom. This God was a Subject-King,[131] which is to say, a Slave-King. Hegelian freedom precisely delivers the subject from his subjection, and converts his servitude into a kingdom. The concept is the kingdom of subjectivity, that is, the realm of the subject become king. The slave-subject and the Subject-King find, in the King-Subject, the fulfilment of their truth, in which the attribute is no longer domination by truth; the attribute is the tribute of truth, the recognition [*reconnaissance*] of the truth by itself and a denunciation of its ingratitude (in Hegel, recognition is always a phenomenon of gratitude). Such is the circularity of freedom in the concept: it is the transformation of servitude, the transformation of the subject into his reign.

The meaning of the transformation of the substance into subject thus becomes clear. The substance is the whole, but it is the reign of necessity, and freedom at the level of the substance is merely consciousness[132] of this necessity – that is, resignation to servitude. Hegelian freedom is a circle only because the substance is liberated: the subject cannot freely consent to the necessity of the substance unless this necessity is of its own devising; unless, that is, it commands it, and the substance is merely its own essence become substance; unless, by commanding the substance, it at last commands itself. This brotherhood in truth is accordingly the movement by which the substance becomes subject; but this movement is not a pure *Umschlagen* that simply puts someone new in command, placing the slave on the throne and banishing the monarch to the galleys; it is also the movement by which the subject becomes substance, that is, appropriates its own truth and makes it its own kingdom: '...*this movement* of the Self which empties itself of itself and sinks itself into its substance, and also, as Subject, has gone out of that substance into itself, making the substance into an object and a content'.[133] The totality of the Self is, then, this twofold movement by which the substantiality of the subject and the subjectivity of the substance are constituted as a 'resultant identity'.[134] For Hegel, this dialectical totality is *Spirit*, or Absolute Totality.

All the totalities we have reviewed thus far have confessed their insufficiency and come undone by themselves. The in-itself revealed that it was nothingness; the reflexive totality of nature showed itself to be a two-dimensional totality lacking totalizing mediation, and obscurely solicited the concrete mediation of the Self. Doubtless it would be possible to find, in organic life, processes that are a kind of first approximation of the actualized concept; Kant was not wrong – although he attributed the reality of the concept to 'transcendental accident' – to focus on the purposefulness of the living organism. The spectacle of the germ, in the form of the egg or seed, has always fascinated the human mind. Today's acorn is tomorrow's tree, a *future* of leaves and branches, an accumulated necessity, waiting to be born and to provide its own content, wood and sap – and, ultimately, to produce its own beginning in the acorns of autumn. The acorn is a little concept that develops and reproduces itself unaided: 'The germ of the plant, this sensuously present Notion, closes its development with an actuality like itself, with the production of the seed. The same is true of mind; its development, too, has achieved its goal when the Notion of mind has completely actualized itself.'[135]

But the resemblance is imperfect, for three reasons: first, because the seed is in externality, drawing sustenance from an earth which is foreign to it; second, because 'the seed produced is not identical with the seed from which it came';[136] finally, because this ovular schema is simple repetition: the seed has no memory, and the content it internalizes is its own past, which, since it repeats itself, is, rather, a present. Nature has no future because it has no history. There is literally nothing new under the sun; the oak is old before it sprouts, whereas the content of Spirit is 'always young'. Biological circularity is one eternity juxtaposed to another; it *reproduces* itself because the content is subject to an unmastered necessity. The circularity of the Spirit, in contrast, is a memory that cannot reproduce itself, because it transforms its own law as it gains mastery over it: the developed in-itself produces, not the in-itself pure and simple, but an undecaying totality which absorbs the initial in-itself in its ultimate movement, and does not repeat itself. Spirit is an acorn that produces, not another acorn, but the very tree it fell from a moment ago. This circle is infinite inasmuch as it endlessly completes its own circuit,[137] but it produces itself unaided, and is a circle because the truth is revealed only at the end – when the seed (the in-itself) discovers it is the fruit of the tree which emerges from it. The tree of truth has only ever produced a single seed, the one it sprang from – and the seed learns this only when the tree is full-grown. It is in this sense that the Spirit is Self, that is, auto-development, creation of self by self; and it is in this sense that it is an absolute totality, inasmuch as it is a whole which depends on nothing, and itself posits the origin it springs from.[138] In this sense, if Spirit presupposes Nature (just as self-reflection presupposes reflection *tout court*), one cannot say that it is *engendered* by Nature, for it is 'rather ... Nature which is posited by mind, and the latter is the absolute *prius*.'[139] Thus 'Mind which exists in and for itself is not ... mere result ... but is in truth its own result; it brings forth itself from the presuppositions which it makes for itself.'[140]

This, in turn, explains the nature of those presuppositions themselves. Spirit is the *concrete* totality, the absolute content, the signifying totality. Logic and Nature, and all the separate elements that presuppose Spirit, are merely parts of it, i.e., moments or constituent elements which have no *raison d'être* outside it. To the extent that the totality has not yet been revealed to the constituent elements, these moments are posited by themselves in pseudo-independence: they merely represent the abstraction that has given rise to them, but, because the totality does not exist for them, they experience it only negatively, in insubstantiality and suffering. The anticipated totalities of the *Logos* and Nature are suffering, unhappy totalities, because they give obscure expression to their limitations and the depth of their solitude. Yet, for that very reason, they supersede themselves in their very effort to constitute themselves as totalities, for it is precisely when they reach their limit and seek to grasp it that they actualize the infinity within them: consciousness of the limit is the advent of the limitless.[141] Hence the ambiguity of the isolated moments of the totality – in themselves they are deficient: Logic is the 'kingdom of shadows' and Nature a 'fallen Spirit'; they subsist, not by themselves, but solely by virtue of Spirit. However, Spirit restores the solidity of these moments; they become the body and substance of the Spirit which arises from their development.

If one considers these moments in isolation, then Spirit may be said to transcend them; it is the God of the old metaphysics, the Absolute Other which casts them out into nothingness. But if one considers Spirit, then it appears to bear them within itself as if they were what gave it birth. Such is the paradox of Hegelian Logic and the Hegelian Philosophy of Nature: if we do not treat them as abstract moments whose truth is Spirit, if we seek their truth or the absolute truth in them, we fall into the classical errors of post-Hegelian interpretation and make Hegel's philosophy over into a form of panlogism or naturalism. But there is a paradox to Hegelian Spirit as well: if we treat it as a term external to the *Logos* and Nature, if we regard it as something transcendent, without noticing that it is the very content of the *Logos* and Nature, which engender their truth within it, such that the *Logos* and Nature are its very substance and reality, then we misunderstand Hegelianism as a mystico-theological, creationist philosophy. Hegel's absolute is not the restitution of a transcendent in-itself which, whether in the form of the Word, Nature, or Spirit, produces and presides over the world; it is the concrete, immanent totality in which the content of its moments attains its truth; it is the absolute content born and brought to fulfilment in its own history. If we view this totality as the development and, simultaneously, internalization of the Self, Spirit is History. Let us examine this point a bit more closely.

With Hegel, history becomes the kingdom of the absolute and its manifestation, that is, a theodicy in the true sense. The expression is ambiguous, and might incline one to think that Hegel merely reworks the notion of a history directed from on high by a Providence which manifests itself in history for the good of men and its own glory; or of a history that simply reveals an inner law established from all eternity, just as canine exploits disclose the essence of the species dog; or, finally, of a history that manifests a linear development through the play of an evolutionary causality operating on a given content. But Hegelian history is neither biological nor providential nor mechanistic, for these three schemas all entail externality. The negative dimension by virtue of which history constitutes itself through and for itself (projected onto Providence from the outside, this distance becomes God, or the pure, watching eye) does not lie outside history, but within the self: the nothingness by means of which history is engendered and then takes possession of itself as it evolves is in history. This nothingness is man.

In the *Philosophy of Nature*, Hegel strikingly describes the advent of man as the *birth of death*. In nature the universal exists in itself only in the individual, but the individual is not the universal for itself: the concept is external to itself, and death is the price exacted by this contradiction. The universal is undying (the genus is eternal), but it attains itself only through the death of individuals. Conversely, from the standpoint of the individual, any attempt to seize the universal (by way of the coupling that produces the child – 'the death of his parents' – or through disease, or the struggle of species for survival) is resolved in death. In death, contradiction *in actu*, universality erects itself upon a corpse:[142] the advent of the universal is the death of the individual. This servitude can be overcome only if the individual does not disappear in his death, but lives on and 'tarries with death', since, for the individual, death is the fatherland of universality. Disease – 'an anticipation of death' – represents the animal's supreme effort to possess death even while alive, and to actualize universality for itself. That is why Hegel sees it as the birth of Spirit. But disease is a living contradiction; it can be no more than an anticipated universality, since it is only an anticipated death that persists in being. True universality does not suffer antici-pation, which is why the sick individual gets better or dies. In reality, the individual can only attain and possess the universal by tarrying with the universal *in actu*, that is, with death *in actu*. From a natural point of view, man is a living death.

Hegel was not the first to conceive the essence of man as death. Platonism had early come forward as a meditation on death; but it made death an object. Hegel, recurring to the Christian tradition, treated it as a subject. If, however, Christianity placed human death against the back-ground of divine life, claiming that the old Adam had died and that the new man had been born in the image of Christ – if, that is, it seized on the negativity and mediating capacity of death – Hegel was above all concerned with the positive function of death, with, that is, the positivity of the universality preserved in death. For Hegel, life stands out against a background of death, as the particular stands out against the back-ground of the universal – and it is clearly because of the absence of death that nature is insufficient. The Kingdom of God is, for Hegel, the kingdom of death; what he announces in the birth of man is the advent of death, the making of nothingness into a kingdom – in a word, the death of God (not as event, but as substance: death is henceforth God's essential being). For Hegel, the Spirit is nothingness that has become being, or, in his romantic language, 'night become day'.[143] This night is the universal *in actu* in man: 'the human being is this Night, this empty nothing',[144] an empty nothing posited as not-being in its very being. 'We see this Night when we look a human being in the eye',[145] this death which affects the very nature of man. Man is the one creature who can deliberately choose his own life,[146] and, in the form of suicide, his own death. This will *in actu* is man standing on his own two feet, upright in a world bent earthwards. This nothingness is not in itself an external negativity brought to bear on a pre-existent something; its human desire is not desire for a thing, but desire for a desire. We see this in love, where the lover seeks his own night in the eyes of the beloved; in struggle, where man wants the other to accord him recognition of his irreplaceable individuality; in knowledge, where consciousness sets out to rediscover the universality of the *I think* in the object. History is nothing other than this profound struggle for the recognition of nothingness by self, that is, of the universal individual by the totality of individuals. In other words, history is the realization of that human essence which is the Self. This realization implies that the universal, which is, in itself, the human individual in his negativity, must become the reality of the whole. That is, it must become the substance, not only of the individual as such, but of the very element in which he exists, so that man may be not only the desire of nothingness, but its actualization, consubstantial with the world of fulfilled Spirit. Spirit desires its own freedom; Spirit is freedom realized, not a vague desire for it.

This is the first movement of the Self in the absolute syllogism through which the subject becomes substance: history is the realization, through struggle and labour, of the universal individual or concrete universal. This is a long and painful process; it is 'the labour of the negative ... seriousness ... suffering ... patience'.[147] For man, who seeks to compel direct recognition of himself in struggle, confronts the depth of his own negativity. If he joins the struggle, he must accept the risk of death and control his trembling body, which shows that his arms and heart are not of the same temper he is; if he kills the adversary from whom he seeks recognition, he kills his own will, and remains alone, as before – from which he understands, confusedly, that he himself is the other; if he vanquishes and subjugates the adversary, forcing him to work for his own pleasure, he subjugates himself, for he is none other than the slave who grants him recognition, and even his pleasure is in the slave's hands. If he himself is vanquished, then he is compelled, because he preferred his body to his death, to work in voluntary submission – but he gradually discovers that the master is the slave of his own work, which feeds him, and that the nature he kneads, forges, and ploughs becomes his freedom *in actu*, his kingdom, and the means of his emancipation. The subject becomes substance through the mediation of his labour: first, because he thereby negates nature and reconstitutes it in the image of man; second, because the slave's labour is his emancipation: it permits him to dominate, not the master, but the master's domination, realizing human totality in the truth of its contents. The history of the transformation by which the unmediated, contradictory totality that man creates in struggle becomes the self is the history of the development of the state into the universal state, in which the citizen realizes the truth of master and slave. In the total state, which is Spirit *in actu*, the individual is 'immediately universal', and his universality is universally recognized. The universal, which 'repossesses' itself in death, has imposed its law: negativity is the very substance of the homogeneous state. The Spirit triumphant is indeed the triumph of death.[148]

Yet this fully accomplished totality can only engender itself in the circle of Spirit. Man as 'sick animal' or 'living death' makes sense only in contrast with the nature he stands out against, even when he posits himself as his own negation. One can only triumph over an adversary; the triumph of death implies the adversity of natural life, which is merely one moment of Spirit. In fact, Spirit triumphs over nothing but itself in death, and the production of the Self as substance in real history, the revolutions and wars, are simply the production of the totality by itself. All the moments of universal history take the form of 'free contingent happening[s]'[149] when considered in isolation; as far as their content is concerned, however, they are simply moments of the fully accomplished totality. In this sense, history is a ruse that yields up its secret only at the end; it dupes the individuals who make it amidst toil and suffering. It is truly the triumph of Night and Death, for it is in the night that men die uncomprehendingly. It would be pure deception if it were nothing more than this brutal, unrevealed totality, this self-contained, silent divinity, a blind galley human slaves propel only God knows where. This totality would be a monstrosity if to make it were not also to reveal it, if the movement by which Spirit constitutes itself were not also that by which it apprehends itself. With this, we approach the second aspect of absolute content, in virtue of which 'Substance [is] *equally* Subject,'[150] in virtue of which, in other words, Spirit takes cognizance of itself in history.

'Spirit is *self-knowing* Spirit.'[151] And, from this standpoint, history is nothing but the phenomenology of Spirit, the development of the forms of self-consciousness in which Spirit grasps itself: 'The movement of carrying forward the form of its self-knowledge is the labour which it accomplishes as actual History.' Considered from this angle, history becomes the production of the for-itself of Spirit in the various concrete forms (*Gestalten*) of consciousness, all the way up to Absolute Knowledge, the ultimate Science whose content is pure self-knowledge, a *sich wissen* without internal distantiation. This conquest is possible only if the contradiction that is the essence of knowledge is resolved: all knowledge takes the form of consciousness, and first presents itself as the content of consciousness. The emergence of the self-consciousness of Spirit therefore involves converting the form of consciousness into its content and this content into consciousness, so that this 'education' ultimately issues in the connaturality of consciousness and its objects, so that consciousness is not only *bei sich* in its object, but also knows it is, discovering that the spiritual totality can be fully accomplished only through this act by which the whole becomes conscious of itself.

Again we see Hegel's desire to 'reveal' depth and hold it *captive*. 'The goal [of the historical succession of 'Spirits'] is the revelation of the depth of Spirit.'[152] The spiritual totality would be stolid and dull if it did not recognize the presence of its own depth, which is self-consciousness; it would be a totality for someone absent, that is, a totality for an outsider, whether God, Hegel, or nobody at all – i.e., for someone who was purely and simply a witness for the other side [*pur témoin contradictoire*]. It would, in that case, be absurd even to speak of spiritual totality. Discourse is in itself this triumphant depth, because it is the realm of speaking consciousness, but it represents only a partial conquest: Spirit must overcome its own distance from itself in the process of becoming victorious discourse, must speak, that is, of itself and not of something else. It must, then, be *for itself*, must lead the totality toward self-consciousness, releasing the individual from the stifling world of primitive Morality in which he finds himself enmeshed in a dense network of unexplained obligations (the constraint of the universal, the human law of the polity – and the demands of mute particularity, the divine law of the family). It must lead the subject toward the new awareness constituted by the abstract self-consciousness of the Stoics' freedom, toward the revolutionary demands of Christianity by way of the lived contradiction of the unhappy consciousness, i.e., of a subject who knows he is universal in himself, but is crushed by a hostile world; alienation, in that case, is the domain of the self-consciousness of Spirit. The Spirit which speaks of the alienated world in the philosophies and religion is unaware that it is speaking of nothing but itself, for it has not yet overcome the contradiction between consciousness and its content: the totality is here conceived as unrealized, and the new awareness of alienation is not yet alienation conscious of itself, inasmuch as its truth is its beyond. The content of the truth is, without doubt, the totality of Spirit (that is, resolution: Spirit is plainly the resolution the historical totality is pregnant with), but this content is not yet *for itself*; Spirit is still trapped in the form of external consciousness, up to the moment when self-consciousness reappropriates this absolute content as its own essence. This final stage is the transition from Religion to Absolute Knowledge, in which Spirit contemplates God in itself, freedom takes the form of freedom,[153] and self-consciousness is at last realized.

Viewed from this angle, then (substance becoming subject), history is the progressive development of the forms of self-consciousness; it is the history of the various 'ideologies'. These abortive attempts at the emancipation of self-consciousness make up the history of doctrines; we can thus see why Hegel proclaims that history ultimately boils down to the history of philosophy. This formulation would be shocking if considered in isolation. It is, however, only the second aspect of the absolute totality, for Spirit is not only the becoming-subject of substance, but also, as we have seen, the becoming-substance of subject: it is not only 'ideological' History, but also real history – and the totality is the encounter between these two movements, in which subject and substance are transformed into one another in the absolute content. History is the concrete third term, the place where this transformation is actually brought about. It is nothing other than this transformation, and it is this transformation which is its motor, down to the smallest details: the circularity of history is real in the sense that self-consciousness (that is, ideological history) is the effect of the contradictions of the totality and the driving force behind the revolutions of real history. Truth is merely reality revealed, but it is truth that haunts reality, that prevents it from sleeping, and that spurs it on until reality has conquered its due. Truth is the remorse of the real;[154] forgiveness is simply remorse realized. One closed circle is another open circle which the contradictions between the real and the true close in their turn, until the advent of the absolute circle, in which the extremes are at home, actually dwell in their own truth, are at last transformed into their eternal content. In this divine kingdom, freedom is at once reality (substance) and self-consciousness (subject); the state is homogeneous, inhabited not by masters and slaves, but by citizens who grant one another recognition. This real freedom is also freedom realized: if the essence of self-consciousness is freedom, freedom sees before it the freedom it wills;[155] object and subject are homogeneous, and thought, having reached the end of its Calvary, at last finds itself in its own element. Ideology has found its truth in *Absolute Knowledge* – and concrete development has conquered its truth in the *Absolute Content* of the universal state. Absolute Knowledge is no longer a form opposed to Absolute Content, but is Absolute Content conscious of itself; and Absolute Content is no longer dependent upon Knowledge, but contains its own self-consciousness in itself. History is well and truly the conquest of the total content by itself, fulfilled and revealed by itself, contemplating itself in its endlessness.[156]

III

MISCOGNITION OF THE CONCEPT

Il en est de l'histoire des hommes comme du blé ... Malheur à qui ne sera pas broyé.

Vincent Van Gogh

The profound necessity of the content, a necessity that emerges before our very eyes in Hegel's text and is transformed into freedom there – this eternal kingdom in which man is God for man, this real church inhabited by God-become-man, this God Himself, at once Father and Son of man, this fully realized *plenitudo temporum*, this Advent whose prophet is Hegel – all this is presented so compellingly and with such rigour that the possibility of its falling apart would be unthinkable, if history did not offer us the spectacle of its disintegration. Yet, from another stand-point, this uncompromising rigour shocks the sensibilities, and the extravagance of the culminating moment is all but unbearable. The mind does not easily grasp this *Parousia*, suddenly unveiled before it as one unveils a statue; it reacts to the compelling obviousness of the outcome as to an act of violence. The 'sunburst which, in one flash, illuminates the features of the new world'[157] is of such brillance that it burns the eyes. Ever since Plato, man has known that the face of the Truth is blinding; in Hegel's presence, the old reflex is reactivated, and, despite itself, spirit draws back into its night, in which it can, at all events, save its open eyes. Having the sun within arm's reach is, like the Promised Land, a childish dream: the adult believes in the childhood he goes looking for, but fails to recognize the one he finds. Thus the story in which the sun falls to pieces dispels his anxiety and assures him he was right. It is, however, a taciturn event, a decisive but mute phenomenon. Hence another sort of fear wells up amidst the silence of history: the fear of night. Spirit seeks a ray of light in the shadows it has regained, wishing to preserve the rigour of this rigour that has come undone. Garrulous, man talks, because history says nothing: he devises a dis-course in which his fear is allayed by the reasons he finds for the captive event. If Hegel is a misadventure, let this misadventure be, at least, a rigorous one. Such is the meaning of the post-Hegelian projects that aim to replace Hegel with an inevitability as compelling as his own. We shall see that this reduction is not unproblematic; that Hegelian truth often draws its masters back into its grip; and that, in the new slave of modern times, what is coming into being is, perhaps, freedom.

A. The Sins of the Form

The Hegelian totality as such cannot come undone: if it collapses, its parts lose all relation to its necessity, its content becomes a stranger to its form. Proving the necessity of its decomposition comes down, then, to demonstrating the mutual alienation of its content and form – to showing either the inadequacy of the form or the inadequacy of the content. So tightly-knit is this content that one is initially tempted to look outside the totality as given for the form that mediates it. Here, asserting its right to assume the obvious, the artisan's way of looking at things exacts its revenge: unwilling to assimilate the producer to his product, it conceives the idea on the model of a piece of handwork, and sets out to find the worker. The search for the form thus becomes a quest for what created it, variously identified, as we shall see, with Hegel himself, his language, and the dialectic.

1. Hegel's mediation

The first attack on Hegel was indirect. As it was not possible to launch a frontal assault on the system, its creator was subjected to an attack that took the naive form of the Kierkegaardian aporia of the account and the accountant. The system was said to have only one defect, its author. Its perfection was factitious, in the noblest sense of the term: 'perfect' and 'factitious' have the same root [il y a fait dans parfait]. But the making of something reveals the maker, however discreet the latter is – and the maker is always outside what he makes. The circle the geometer traces does not drag him in by the heels, and when the day's totals have been tallied, the accountant goes home: he is nowhere to be found in his accounts. Such, then, is Hegel's artifice. We thought he had broken with the tradition of the Aristotelian third term, but, in reality, the break was merely verbal: Hegel shows us an absolute totality emerging before our very eyes, and the power of his discourse is such that one eventually forgets that it is he who is uttering it. He is himself the living third term which disappears in the conclusion; his silence is simply the discretion that attends rigour. The true mediator is, accordingly, outside; his genius consists in quietly taking upon himself the whole of the mediation, which, in the system, is nothing more than a shadow.

This paradox of the whole points to the classical conception of God: a totality exists only for a third party, as, even in Descartes, the rainbow exists only for the man out on a walk, or, in modern physics, a system of reference exists only for an observer.[158] The absolute Third of classical philosophy is God, in whom all meanings converge. Hegel is an Evil Genius who hides his God; or, rather, he is this 'hidden God', and imitates, in his work, the divine Creation: 'On the seventh day He saw that everything he had made was very good, and he rested.' This creator's rest is in his courses and students. And yet Hegel was not always able to contain himself. Indeed, he hardly could have: the total revelation he imparted betrayed the presence of the God within him. Even if he did not confess that the whole was his work, he surely had to allow the dignity of the Prophet [*Révélateur*] to shine through – as may be seen in the *Phenomenology*, in which he describes the thinker who comprehends the work of the unifier as *der Erscheinende Gott* [God manifesting Himself]; or in the *Philosophy of History*, in which he so thoroughly initiates us into God's secrets that we can dispense with God. Here, then, we see the demiurge in God's dwelling-place and on his throne; is it not the height of imposture – and skill – to pass off as God everything of the artisan's that does not go unperceived? Is God not an alibi for Hegel, who hides behind him in his own house – so as not to be discovered outside it? Hegel cries 'God!' the way others cry 'Stop thief!' to avoid capture. But this time we have him.

The problem with these arguments is that they are to be found in Hegel himself, and are transcended simply by virtue of that fact. Hegel openly declares that he stands, not outside the totality, but in it, as, simultaneously, philosopher, child of his age shaped by his own time, and particular individual. Let us examine these three points.

1. Hegel is the first to have thought the thinker in the truth thought, by dint of a prodigious effort to turn thought back upon itself. This *Umbiegen* [turning-back-upon] is, properly speaking, Self, i.e., self-reflection, by means of which the subject attains himself in the object he thinks. This undertaking may seem excessive; but it is the basis of the Hegelian revelation, and irrevocably sunders Hegel's enterprise from those of all his predecessors.

Before Hegel, philosophy had not succeeded in including the philosopher in its field of reflection; it only rarely considered that possibility, and, when it did, was simply confused by it. Either it resolutely ignored the problem, as in the case of Parmenides and Spinoza, with their seamless totalities; or else it tried to come to grips with it, and ended up doing away with the whole. Thus Plato, reacting against Parmenides, destroys the Sphere from which the manifold, time, and thought have been excluded, and then attempts to find a place for the philosopher within the universe he reconstitutes. But he runs up against the insurmountable enigma of time, through which the totality escapes: the philosopher contemplates the truth he reveals, but he is a man subject to change, whose discourse passes away. Plato's position is untenable: the philosopher is not of the world he aspires to, while his ideas are not of the world he respires in. He has access only to the in-between realm Plato calls μεταξύ, but this externality is even more inadequate than it seems, for the status of the philosopher in Plato is not the status of Plato vis-à-vis his own philosophy. This ambiguity does not dominate Plato's thinking; it is dominated by it. It is not hard to understand the reason for that *coup d'état*. Without it, we would be trapped in an infinite regress; silence saves us from the argument of the Third Man. In reality, Plato too is a discreet demiurge who simply conceived a pseudo-demiurge in a totality he himself dismantled.

Spinoza falls victim to the same mischance. The writing of the *Ethics*, and thus the contingency (or necessity) of the circumstance that Spinozism as a doctrine made its appearance in history by way of a lens-grinder, leave no trace in any of the master's books. Put more simply, truth is all-devouring in his system and burns an indestructible author in effigy. The consubstantiality of thought and extension (or subject and object) is a *coup d'état* which ensures that the thinking of this consubstantiality disappears without hope of recall from Spinoza's philosophy. Kant, unlike Spinoza, was at pains to think his own act of thinking; but he got only as far as the abstraction of the transcendental I in a reflexive philosophy; this thought of the regression of thought involved him in an infinite regress, of which progression toward the *sollen* was merely the inverted image. Thus pre-Hegelian philosophers had only two alternatives: to think the totality and ignore the thinker, or to think the thinker and destroy the totality. That either-or speaks volumes, for it points up the reflexivity of the thinker and his thought, while revealing the negativity of the thinker before whom the totality breaks down. Hegel was the first to take cognizance of reflexivity *qua* totality and, simultaneously, of the thinker's negativity; and he was the first to resolve this contradiction by extending negativity to the totality. He literally put the philosopher to the question, and did not rest until he had thought the significance of the question itself in the truth he announced.

He thereby revealed, to begin with, the significance of his question, by showing that the question (or the negativity of the thinker) is not something detached from the truth, but is rather bound to it by ties of blood and birth, since the negativity of thought is what generates truth. Second, he showed that developed truth, far from implying a rejection of the thinker, is in fact his fulfilment. 'The whole includes the negative' means that it includes the thinker. Subject and object are transformed into their truth, which is the freedom of Spirit. This truth is reality revealed, the ἀλήθεια of the Greeks, in which the α- ceases to be merely privative in order to become emancipatory negativity: it not only leaves its mark on the object emancipated, as one finds the mark of the potter's thumb under the handle of the pitcher, but is transformed into and embodied in the object. In Hegel the phenomenology and the history of philosophy are thus literally the history of the metamorphosis of philosophy into truth. This is the reason that Hegel is the last philosopher, in whom the race of philosophers attains its entelechy, and the first to be on intimate terms with the Truth. He does not stand poised on the threshold, ἐν προθυροῖς τοῦ ἀγάθου, living on desire alone; nor does he disappear into the substance as the painter in the Chinese tale disappears into the landscape he has painted: he circulates among the divine brotherhood, and, dwelling in the whole, dwells in his true kingdom.

2. Let us further note that the thinker in this case is not, as in all pre-Hegelian philosophies, the thinker in the abstract, someone belonging to no particular historical period, but rather concrete, historical man, who dwells in eternity in his own time and his own time in eternity. Here Hegel breaks sharply with Plato, who withdraws his philosopher from the world and casts him in a suspended time. There is no ἐποχή in Hegel, as there is for Descartes, enveloped in the warmth of his thought, his windows all shut tight to the winter and the war, or for Rembrandt's deaf old man, lost in the contemplation of his stairwells. In Hegel, Jena rushes in through the open window, along with the roar of battle, the defeat, Napoleon draped in his victory, and the distant reunification of a reawakened Europe. Neither barricades nor brackets can hold up under history's onslaught: the child who shuts his eyes thinks he has brought on universal night, like the philosopher who does not think the noonday of history, does not plunge into it and make himself at home in it. This idea kept its grip on Hegel to the end: he never abandoned the intention, which took shape, as we saw, in the early stages of his thought [conscience],[159] to seek in his time the traces of the lost truth, and to discover in the truth the splendours of his own, redeemed time. More precisely, the moment of the Enlightenment, in which he lived his alienated youth, did not simply take its place in the system; it acquired meaning and substance there. Within the system, the void which we saw crystallizing and then yielding up its essence in consciousness found not only satisfaction in the plenitude of the final totality, but also its justification, since it was owing to this void that the world of the Ancien Régime was able to transform itself in the Revolution.

Here there appears another dimension of the vacuity of Hegel's adolescence; this dimension could only make itself felt at the end, since it represents the reappropriation of the world of the Enlightenment by its truth. The Enlightenment was brute fact for Hegel, who laboured painfully under the burden of an historical situation that was not his by choice: his youthful analyses, like his critique of religious, political, and philosophical life, were the consciousness of this servitude, which might well have seemed irrevocable. But, as we saw, Hegel did not content himself with clarifying his sense of oppression. He acquired the knowledge of his servitude in the void of consciousness, whose theoretical expression was Kant. He still had no more than a presentiment of the positive aspect of this void; he had not yet come to understand it as the reappropriation, by the truth of the age of maturity, of its historical youth. It was only in the *Phenomenology* – observed, that is, from the high ground of the hard-won truth – that the path was invested with its meaning by the goal, and, by the same token, that the servitude of the beginnings and the historical origins of the philosopher found their true explanation. These presuppositions had constituted neither an irremediable absolute, nor the *Dasein* of a void, but rather the mediation of freedom in the process of emerging. Thus history is not servitude: Hegel is not a deaf-mute become suddenly voluble, he does not pass from scorn to servility, he is not won to a conception of historical relativism – rather, he emancipates history, and emancipates himself in history in the fulfilled totality.

3. At this point, however, it is not only the philosopher or the child of his age who is emancipated, but also the concrete individual Hegel, in the guise of the sage-citizen-writer. For Hegel is the last of the philosophers in that, attaining Absolute Knowledge, he replaces the love of knowledge with knowledge; he is thus the Savant or Sage – the first and last – because those who come after him can only retrace the contents of the System of Knowledge (in 1806, Hegel thought of the *Phenomenology* as Part I of this System).[160] But Hegel can be this Sage only if Spirit has overcome all opposition, if history is ripe, if Spirit contemplates itself in the world; if, that is, the world is freedom, the universal state homogeneous, and the Sage a *citizen*. Once these conditions have been met, the individual is no longer excluded from the true world, because he is simultaneously particular and universal, a living syllogism in whom the universal is finally united with the individual, mediated by his particularity. In a word, the particular is no longer alien, and this mediation occurs in the element of mediation, i.e., the immediacy of the Self. This means that the particular individual no longer needs to sacrifice his particularity, as ascetics do, and annul all determinability in himself in order to reach the Truth; without self-contempt or shame (over his body, size, character, race, etc.), he can go out to meet a friendly world in which others directly recognize, in his very particularity, the universality of man. 'It is "I", that is *this* and no other "I", and which is no less immediately a *mediated* or superseded *universal* "I".'[161]

By way of the Sage Hegel, then, the individual Hegel is reunited in the totality with Hegel the child of his age. But we have yet to determine with precision the difficult point where the circle closes upon itself. We know all of this thanks to Hegel's written work; but what place does this writing have in the totality? Why did the individual – the sage – Hegel feel the need to publish the Good News? Was it pure caprice, or did he merely fulfil a design of Spirit's? And what gap did he thereby fill in this faultless Whole? Hegel answers by pointing out that the freedom which does not know itself is not true freedom, and that only the consciousness of the whole brings the whole to perfection. Well and good; but why this declaration? There is only one legitimate reason for it; it seems inconceivable to Hegel that the consciousness of the actualized whole should be unshakeable in one man and dormant in his brothers, who are 'he himself'. Hegel's written work is thus consciousness in its extended form, the universal *Sich wissen* [self-knowledge] in which Everyman recognizes himself. The printing press, Hegel pointed out, is the expansion of Spirit: his books are universality in written form, which everyone can read. In this respect, the book is also an event, like the different figures of consciousness in history, and it is a decisive event that is, for Spirit, the other face of the Spirit forged in war. Like Hegel, then, we can only regard it as miraculous that Napoleon should have completed the construction of Europe right under the philosopher's windows, just as Hegel was completing, in his notebooks, the Absolute Knowledge of the *Phenomenology of Spirit*.

2. The mediation of language

What has just been said opens up a new perspective. If Hegel and the significance of his work are reabsorbed by the whole, it is due to the force of his arguments. But, before being *meanings*, those arguments are written down; they are aggregations of *signs*. We looked for the mediator in the person of Hegel; he vanished into the signifying totality he himself presents in words. For us, he nevertheless continues to be a mediator thanks to whom meaning comes into being and persists: the reality of the Word. At this point, the objections begin to proliferate; they run from verbalism to panlogism. When the Hegel of the *Philosophy of Spirit* offers us a description of the Americas as a syllogism 'with a quite narrow middle between the two extremes',[162] or logically deduces the necessity of firearms[163] and races,[164] we certainly do have the impression that he has transformed a real problem into a verbal one. Again, when he proclaims the kingdom of the truly universal, and then looks back on the merely verbal universality that characterized the beginnings of the Revolution, criticizing its empty formulae and 'paper achievements', one wonders by what aberration he managed not to notice that he was falling into the very error he had denounced. Marx, as we shall see, did not fail to throw the accusation of logomachy back at him. More profoundly, questions of wordplay aside, one can regard Hegel's work as a meditation upon the unity of all things in the word – as a philosophy of the *Logos* or Word. So considered, mediation would indeed take on its full meaning – an Hegelian meaning – in the sense that this revelation through language would be not only the Word that announces God, but God become the Word that makes all things plain. The religious implications of such a position are not hard to see; they are by no means absent from Hegel. For him, Christ or the Word is the fully accomplished totality that reconciles God and man. But, by the same token, this revelation is its own origin: the Word that finds fulfilment existed before all things, and, as St. John says, was with God, and was God. Thus the Word already was what it was to become; it was, potentially, the totality and ratio of all things, *Logos* in the double sense of the Greek term – Word and Reason. Is this not exactly what Hegel sets out to show in the *Logic*, in which he proffers us 'the exposition of God as he is in his eternal essence before the creation of nature ... [and] the truth as it is without veil'?[165] Is the totality not the unfolding of the *Logos*? Such, in broad outline, is the basic argument of those who interpret Hegel's philosophy as a form of panlogism, a misreading of Hegel that developed over the course of the nineteenth century, especially in France. We examined the negative aspects of this misinterpretation in chapter II. Let us go straight to the heart of the question, and try to grasp the nature of this mediation by the Word in terms of the nature of the word itself.

We need only read Hegel to discover the philosophy of language that answers our purposes. The first chapter of the *Phenomenology* puts before us the spectacle of our fundamental experience of the word. If it is night-time, says Hegel, and I am asked, what is 'now'?, I answer, 'now' is night, and I write down this truth. 'A truth cannot lose anything by being written down, any more than it can lose anything through our preserving it. If *now, this noon*, we look again at the written truth we shall have to say that it has become stale.'[166] In this miracle, we grasp the power of the word, which changes day into night; through it, the particular thing I have in mind turns into the universal I utter: 'In [language], we ourselves directly refute what we *mean* to say.'[167] For the word 'has the divine nature of directly reversing the meaning of what is said, of making it into ... a universal'.[168] And, within this universal, I encounter nothing but the stubborn universality of words: 'When I say: "a single thing", I am really saying what it is from a wholly universal point of view.'[169] What, then, is this extraordinary power that abolishes the particular and engenders the universal?

It is, says Hegel, the 'negative';[170] and we learn at every turn in Hegel that maintaining a firm grip on it 'is the most difficult thing of all'. But here, in the case of the word, we are precisely in the presence of a *nothingness* that persists; we would like to capture this nothingness in other words which are, in their turn, persistent nothingness. This is why, of all reflections on language, Hegel's, perhaps, affects us the most nearly: it puts the inner self to the test, and everything we are is called into question by it, down to the very words we write. The word, then, is a nothingness that persists: this life after death is what is universal about it. The convergence may remind us that we have already seen this alliance of the universal with death – in man. Man is the being through whose agency the universal known as death is firmly maintained within life; the essence of man is, consequently, the word. Hegel notes that animals give vent to cries which express their reactions of the moment, such as rage or joy, but that they do not live on after themselves and do not elevate themselves above time. The song of the birds is immediate bliss, nothing more; it involves neither knowledge nor distantiation, and is literally lost, as is Spirit when it becomes Nature. Man, then, is a speaking animal. But the spectacle offered by the animal world reveals something more: birds do not know that they sing, nor dogs that they growl; man, in contrast, knows that he speaks, for the word creates the distance that allows him to maintain contact with everything in himself that has ceased to be. Thus, by means of the word, man reappropriates himself; that is, he reappropriates what he was in a word that is not what he is, and that he is nonetheless. Man, says Hegel, is *that which reappropriates itself*; he is the sole creature to say *I*, and to reflect, in the word, the universal he is.[171]

This double appropriation clarifies the nature of language. By means of the Word, man apprehends, in the word-concept, the nothingness of being, i.e., universality; by means of the word, he apprehends himself as reflected universality, i.e., as *subject*. In the Self, language refers only to itself; Hegel therefore says that beings without language cannot be free, since, without the nothingness of discourse, they can neither emancipate themselves from nature, nor *seize* their own nature. Hence freedom is a *capture*, a grasping of the self; it is, in other words, a *Begriff*, or concept, in which the identity of the *Logos* with freedom comes into view. The Stoics had already announced this encounter of the *Logos* and freedom, but, for them, the *Logos* was merely the law immanent in the living totality, not negativity *in actu*. '[Language] is the *real existence* of the pure self as self.'[172]

This *Dasein* of language is thus the body of the universal Self in its *purity*, that is, in its element as such, which is the immediacy of the universal. Even when it becomes the middle term in which two consciousnesses acknowledge one another, it does not designate this or that particular I, but the universality of self-consciousness. 'The "I" is this particular "I" – but equally the *universal* "I"; its manifesting is also at once the externalization and vanishing of *this* particular "I", and as a result the "I" remains in its universality.'[173] Matters become clear once we identify thought with this universal. 'While the brute cannot say "I", man can, because it is his nature to think.'[174] Language is therefore the empirical existence of thought in the immediacy of its universality. That is why the contradiction between language and reality bulks large for as long as the universality of self-consciousness remains an abstraction and is not actualized in the world; that is why the philosophers talk and the caravans pass, the beautiful soul protests and the prayers go up to heaven – when flattery does not assail the throne. Such is the limit inherent in every philosophical discourse, and the contradiction marking pre-Hegelian 'ideologies': discourse treats of a world that is not discourse actualized; the universality proper to the word is not the concrete stuff of the universe; discourse is not, in short, *bei sich* in the alienation of the still unaccomplished world. Hence the word seeks a resolution in itself; it seeks the mediation between itself and the world in itself, yet never produces anything more than a demiurge of words, because it only makes its way out of itself in verbal fictions. Hegel avoids this pitfall, because his discourse is at one with the fully accomplished world he describes. There substance is subject; or, to put it differently, there thought is in its own element, the word, which is freedom; it is in harmony with the world in which it rings out. There the world has literally become discourse; every term contained in it is immediately universal, as in language. In this world, men behave like words: they sustain one another, and receive their essential being and significance from others. The world, a poorly constructed language, has been transformed into Science – a well-constructed language. This provides the key to the culminating phase of Hegel's thought: language is not a third instance between us and the world, because it is the empirical existence of universality made over into a world. Hegel's discourse is the Speech [*Parole*] of the world.

But with this we have also cleared up the second point. If language does not have a mediating role, can we not say that it absorbs the world in its totality? Here Hegel falls back on the Greek insight into the circularity and negativity of words. Plato clearly perceived the bond between the word and the Idea: it is their complicity that defies time. Aristotle codified this complicity in an ontological grammar. In the face of a world caught up in a process of becoming, language creates a stable second world, a true universe, eternal and articulated, which exhausts the totality of meanings. Doubtless this insight undergoes modification: Plato later tends to look for the essence of the logical universe in a universe of geometrical relationships. But the fact remains that this silent *Logos* is itself the origin and end of all things, and that it is *articulated*, καθ' ἄρθρα, as all language is. Is Hegelian Logic too not this articulated Whole that is the essence and structure of the World? Does the world not deliver up its secret in the guise of the Logic?

Here it is the nature of language that calls for attention. Language is merely the existence [*l'être-là*] of thought *qua* abstract universality, that is, the actual presence of thought for thought, the for-itself of abstract universality, 'the I in its purity'; it is not the substance, and the world develops 'behind its back'. The first man to speak prophesies the universal, because he pro-nounces it (this is the reason that the Word is in the beginning), but he does not know he is anticipating history; indeed, he cannot, for universality pronounced is not the actual. Or, rather, its actuality is an actuality of the *word*. Remarkably, Hegel maintained that languages [*langues*] cannot truly be said to undergo development. This implies that language [*langage*] as such is eternal: a language, however simple, is an organic totality, that is, a fraternal, circular world. The republic of words thus precedes that of men from all (its) eternity; the language [*langage*] that enters the universal state by the royal road of Science is the unvarying structure of the languages men speak [*le corps immobile de la langue*]. Language is simply the empirical existence of the universal as such, that is, the universal in its purity and abstraction, the other face of universality being the empirical existence of its impurity in the concrete. The true mediation of the universal is the speaking individual as a concrete figure of consciousness; Hegel is the foremost example. His discourse, *qua* act, is thus clearly the foundation of things; it is universality, in its freedom, speaking of itself for itself, an incantation – but this act is the living syllogism by means of which the totality completes the circuit of its own moments. Outside this syllogism, the body of words falls back into the circle of language, which is simply the existence of the universal in its *purity*.

The deepest meaning of the classical play on words emerges here: σῶμα / σῆμα, the sign is a tomb, words are death, language is a spectre. Hegel said neither more nor less when he proclaimed that 'the science of the pure Idea ... is the abstract medium of Thought' or 'the system of logic is the realm of shadows'.[175] Hegelian logic is cavernous: it is Plato stood on his head, the world turned topsy turvy. No longer is the *Logos* the body of the truth, and the world its shadow on the wall; now it is the inner shadow of the true world. Plato proceeds from the shadow to the body, Hegel from the body to the shadow, which is not recognized as a shadow until the end.[176] Thus the negativity of the logic, [which] we grasped in our opening analyses, acquires, in the end, its *being*. For the reality of words is empirical; they are the nothingness to be found within a certain being. If logic is abstracted from everything that confers meaning upon it, we can see in what its being consists: namely, in the being of language, i.e., the articulated body of the universal in its purity. We can see, too, the nature of the anticipation constituted by language. This 'exposition of God as He is ... before the creation of nature' is simply the universality of words soliciting the creative transformation of the world into a concrete universal. This 'before' is simply the in-itself of the universal in the man-who-speaks, and does not yet know that he is announcing the *end* of the world in his discourse. It is also creation, inasmuch as the concrete figure of language, which is man speaking, is historical man, who, by dint of labour and struggle, creates a world in conformity with his discourse, fully realizing the ultimate world whose Word is the Promised Land. The totality is an in-itself that has kept its word; the fulfilled world, when it speaks, is self-celebration. The promise has become a holy mass.* Philosophy, said Hegel, is a *'divine service'*.[177]

Thus we have been driven out from amongst words; they are merely the purity of the world outside the total syllogism of the absolute content. The *Logos* as abstract whole has its truth outside itself; Hegel clearly demonstrates the ambiguity of language, which, although it is a circle, nevertheless annuls itself as totality in Nature and Spirit. Panlogism is a contradiction in terms, because, if the *Logos* is in the beginning, the whole in Hegel is at the end; and, while it is indeed the case that Spirit precedes itself in words, words, as a constituted reality, have no meaning outside Spirit.

3. *The mediation of the dialectic*

We need, however, to address a point left in abeyance. If the *body* of language is reabsorbed by the whole, and is not a form external to it, its *movement* clearly seems to play a decisive part in the elaboration of the content. There would be nothing to add here, if the eternal nature of language did not also affect its movement in such a way that the *Logos*, not as substance but as *law*, appears to govern the totality. The being of language has been reabsorbed, but its inner structure persists as a silent, absolute movement that holds sway over the world. What is the relationship between this law and the world? Are we not here in the presence of a new externality of form to content? And if we call this law dialectic, is the Hegelian dialectic formal or real?

1. As far as Hegel is concerned, this debate is complicated by the tradition that sees in dialectic nothing more than the activity of the dialectician, that is, of discourse actively at work. 'Dialectic is commonly regarded as an external, negative activity which does not pertain to the subject matter itself, having its ground in mere conceit as a subjective itch for unsettling and destroying what is fixed and substantial.'[178] Such was, at least as his contemporaries saw it, the caustic power of Socrates, that acidulous, assiduous *flâneur*, who challenged received ideas and did not rest until he had left his adversary befuddled by his own vacuity.

* The pun is harder to miss in French: *la pro-messe est devenue messe.*

The Athenian burghers of the fifth century understood well enough that they were faced with a question of life and death, but were too dimwitted to grasp the fecundity of this verbal death: they kept life for themselves and condemned Socrates to his truth. That is why the death of Socrates became the life of Plato, who was haunted by this indestructible spectre. In his dialogues, the other, positive side of the dialectic appears: Socratic discourse destroys only in order to build; it rejects only out of a desire to seek truth and refute shadows. Platonic dialectic is transformation and ascension, a rooting out of error and steady advance towards truth amidst the clash of conflicting opinions. Hence its ambiguity; for truth is also the end result of well-marshalled discourse, that is, of victorious discourse. Socratic polemic is not a luxury; Plato is an ongoing battle whose form is dialogue, and in which truth is inseparable from artfulness. The dialectician is triumphant eloquence and *savoir-faire*: like a good butcher, he finds the right joint [*articulation vraie*] straightaway. But this similarity is problematic, for we need to consider whether the articulation he finds is merely a rhetorical one, the point in language at which opinions are thrown reeling, or whether it is also a matter of truth – which would imply that Socrates, Callicles and the Stranger are simply personae through whom the truth speaks exclusively about itself, and that the dialogic structure is simply an epiphany of the structure of the absolute.

2. Hegel invests this transition, obscure in Plato, with self-consciousness.[179] Simply, dialectic triumphs as discourse because it is the law triumphant: 'This dialectic, then, is not an external activity of subjective thought, but the *very soul* of the content . . . This development of the Idea as the activity of its own rationality is something which Thought, since it is subjective, merely observes, without for its part adding anything extra to it' [*Elements of the Philosophy of Right*, p. 60]. Only now do we come to the real problem, which has become a focal point of the attacks on Hegel: what is the nature of this *soul* and *inner activity*? Is not the dialectic the soul of the content in the sense in which gravitation is the soul of the stones and stars? Is it not an evolving law, or even, simply, a recurrent one?

It must be admitted that nothing in the outward appearance of Hegelian thought contradicts this interpretation. If we consider the *Phenomenology* itself, Hegel's most concrete and densest work, we see that, in it, consciousness is subject to a necessity which directs and shapes it 'behind its back'.[180] This necessity, comparable to Spinoza's,[181] is doubtless the necessity of the 'for us', and one may grant Hegel, come to the end of the process, that the ultimate consciousness is the 'back' of consciousness in its earliest stages. Yet it does not follow from this *point of view* that the 'dorsal' character of the *Phenomenology* is synonymous with its necessity. Indeed, this is ruled out if the manifestation of Spirit through the different forms of consciousness is not the manifestation of an eternal law, which can preside over the birth of consciousness only if it is *already present* and active. As has been very nicely said, the *Phenomenology* is a noumenology;[182] there is an in-itself of the Hegelian dialectic, and, if we pay close attention to the avatars of consciousness, this law will ultimately reveal itself, emerging from its body as Newton's law of gravity emerges from the apples and the stars. The *Encyclopædia* tells us that this law is the law of triplicity. Dialectical necessity is the law of the transformation of thesis into antithesis and antithesis into synthesis; in this schematic form, the development of the law is nothing more than its recurrence. The third term becomes the first in another set, from which there emerges a third term that generates another set in its turn. The systematic utilization of this schema, particularly in the *Philosophy of Nature* or the *Philosophy of History*, creates the impression that Hegel has reverted to a philosophy of laws, to formalism, and that he 'manipulate[es] [the content] from outside'.[183] If Hegel fell into discredit in the course of the nineteenth century, it was in large part because of the ternary formalism of the *Philosophy of Nature*, which did a good deal to give him a reputation for panlogism. Finally, the ambiguous formulations concerning the absolute method that Hegel puts forward in the last chapter of the *Greater Logic*, in which the essence of the ternary law is painstakingly spelled out, have, because they have been misunderstood, only heightened the confusion. Must we concede that Hegel lapsed into the formalism he denounced more strenuously than anyone else?

'Formalism has, it is true, also taken possession of triplicity and adhered to its empty *schema*.'[184] This caustic remark in the *Greater Logic* echoes the attack unleashed in the *Phenomenology* ten years before. That attack – and a very sharp one it was – was directed at Schelling. Since 'what results from this method . . . [is] labelling all that is in heaven and earth with the few determinations of the general schema',[185] Hegel is moved to draw the most unflattering comparisons, involving cooks, painters, furriers, white-washers, prestidigitators, bonesetters, butchers, packers, grocers, and card sharks. It is hard to believe that he could have mustered such rhetorical resources against formalism only to restore it to full honours later. He harbours a deep aversion for this superficial knowledge, which attains only to a semblance of the concept, in the form of a law external to the content. In his view, 'the determinateness, which is taken from the schema and externally attached to an existent thing, is, in Science, the self-moving soul of the realized content.'[186] By 'content', we should understand, not abstraction from all empirical diversity, but the object itself, with its own characteristic determinations: 'Scientific cognition, on the contrary, demands surrender to the life of the object . . . expressing its inner necessity [and] immersed in its content, [it] advance[s] with its movement.'[187] More: the fact is that the *only* truly scientific method is the one which 'is not something distinct from its object and content; for it is the inwardness of the content, *the dialectic which it possesses within itself*, which is the mainspring of its advance.'[188] This text is of the first importance, for it states the profoundest requirement of Hegel's thought, and identifies the dialectic with the content. This point bears closer examination.

Hartmann's penetrating analyses have drawn attention to the 'selfless devotion' (*Hingegebenheit*) of the Hegelian dialectic. 'This *dialectical* movement which consciousness exercises in itself and which affects both its knowledge and its object, such that the new, veritable object emerges from this dialectic before consciousness, is precisely what is called *experience*.'[189] Citing this text, Hartmann shows that the dialectic, which is a deductive schema in Fichte, is, in Hegel, the form devotion to the object takes. More precisely, he shows that the dialectic is neither a rule nor fixed laws, because the object and its *Maßstab* [measure] vary over the course of the process.[190] It cannot be a matter, then, of deducing the content or imposing a foreign schema on it; rather, the dialectic must emerge with its object. This experience will accordingly be, in Claudel's apt formulation, a 'co-birth' [*co-naissance*], in which spirit's role is the attentive self-effacement it brings to the effort of conception, *die Anstrengung des Begriffs*. This capture by spirit is simply the capture of the content by itself: i.e., the concept as such. Hartmann therefore quite rightly maintains 'that we can unhesitatingly range dialectical intuition in Hegel under the rubric intuition of essence (*Wesenschau*)',[191] and that, *pace* Husserl, Hegel's phenomenological description is Husserl's pure description of essence.

Hartmann concentrates all his energies on bringing out this purity of the object: if the dialectic is the movement specific to it, then there is no universal dialectic: rather, every content possesses its own dialectic, and, since real objects are not repeated, the same dialectic never occurs twice in Hegel.[192] All resemblance is superficial, like that between the eyes and ears of different faces. Neither the content nor the form permits us to transpose the dialectic of perception into that of master and slave, no more than we can transpose the dialectic of lordship and bondage into that of the unhappy consciousness. There is, then, a certain discreteness to objects, which finds its correlative in a discreteness of the dialectic. If the dialectic is not a law, the reason is that it does not apprehend itself as such; it lacks, says Hartmann, the moment of the for-itself. Hegel's aberration lay in wanting to find a formula for this for-itself, a law of the dialectic; he failed to see that no rule could be laid down prior to experience, because, in experience, the content makes good its right to transform the rule itself. Hence there can be no for-itself of the dialectic for anyone but God, who causes movements in us whose law he alone knows, and who *thinks himself* in the experience we have abandoned.

Hartmann's general conclusion thus re-establishes a philosophy of intuition in Hegel, with its theological implications, and does so quite seductively. But we know that Hegel is poles apart from this kind of thinking, which he himself denounced in Jacobi. Moreover, Hartmann's difficulties are significant: as he cannot blame the dialectic for what goes awry, he affirms that there are good and bad objects in Hegel's analyses. Thus[193] the descriptions of crime or servitude are good, that of becoming is bad. Hegel must be sifted, and Hartmann makes no attempt to hide the fact that a great deal more time will be required before everything is fully clarified. This reservation is surprising, whatever the degree of genius one attributes to Hegel, for we can at least follow his argument, after all, and judge his 'analyses of essence' along with him. Hartmann's uneasiness masks another problem: the nature of these essences themselves. They are not sufficiently discrete not to depend upon one another, and the mind is not free to draw them out in any direction it chooses. They strain in one particular direction, tending towards an irreducible whole, with the result that the content of intuition is unstable: it is an entity in motion. Hartmann cannot satisfactorily resolve this ambiguity. For if he acknowledges that the movement is an [Ab]hängen and not an Aufbau [a building up], that it is teleological and not summative, he fails to extricate himself from this movement to think the fully realized totality. 'Truth is the whole interpreted from this standpoint: consciousness is neither the beginning nor the end of the process, but the process itself.'[194] The totality, he says, is present in the movement, but by proxy, since the movement realizes it without reaching it.

We can, then, see the problems the two extremes lead us toward. On his own express admission, Hegel's dialectic is not a pure form, nor can it be the content grasped in the purity of an analysis of essence; for, advancing toward its goal, the real dialectic soon eludes intuition. How, then, are we to understand the Hegelian thesis that identifies the dialectic with the content? If the content is pure movement, then either it is governed by its law, and we fall back into formalism; or else its law is internal to it, but 'behind its back', so that, as Hartmann says, there is no for-itself of the dialectic. There is, indeed, no extricating ourselves from this contradiction, unless we assume that, for Hegel, the content has attained to Selfhood, i.e., that the movement has been accomplished and the totality realized – and if we forget that the problem of the dialectic can only be posed with reference to the absolute content. This is not taken into account by Hartmann, who identifies the totality with the process in its unfolding, because he wants to maintain both the intuitive character of dialectical experience and its teleological incompleteness – i.e., to posit the content as both total and non-total. His hesitations stem entirely from this omission. In Absolute Knowledge, where Hegel sits in state, it is correct to say that experience rules, in a purely Husserlian sense: in the form of a pure intuition of a content that is a law unto itself. At this point, it is possible to say that the dialectic is the 'soul of the content', or even to declare that there is no dialectic at all,[195] inasmuch as this absolute inside has no outside. But we already know that the outside of this inside is its now-mastered depth, and that the for-itself of this content is not 'behind its back', but at its very centre; that intuition is the concept at last arrived in its kingdom; and that the totality contains its own history. Put differently, the dialectic is not blind; it apprehends and appropriates itself in the absolute concept even as it disentitles itself there in an intuition of the absolute content.

We have, here, the two aspects of the Hegelian totality before us. *In the substance*, the solid, homogeneous aspect of the content and the obscurity of its soul are paramount – and in this sense there is no dialectic. *In the subject*, in contrast, it is the soul which triumphs, in other words, the conscious process, though still in the form of externality – and in this sense there is a dialectic, though it is a formal one. The totality is constituted through the development, accomplishment, and mutual recognition of these two aspects: in the totality, intuition and concept, substance and subject, content and form, dialectic and non-dialectic profoundly coincide. At this stage, dialecticity is the depth of non-dialecticity, the 'soul of the content', i.e., its own concept. 'The method has emerged as the *self-knowing Notion that has itself . . . for its subject matter.*'[196] Moreover, we know that negativity is the soul of the concept. It can therefore be said that the Hegelian dialectic is the concept of negativity, that is, negativity's own cognition of itself; accordingly, the dialectic attains to the for-itself only in the form of human negativity, once it has acquired self-consciousness – in Hegel, who was the first to apprehend 'this self-determination and self-realizing movement'.[197] The famous triplicity is merely the self-appropriation of negativity, i.e., the negation of the negation in the third term, which emancipates and completes the first. That is why the whole of the Hegelian dialectic is contained in Hegelian negativity – which attains to the for-itself only when it has negated itself, when, that is, the concept has succeeded in apprehending itself in the final totality. Thus Hartmann did well to say that the dialectic does not rise to the level of the for-itself, given that he refused to accept the idea that the Whole might be realized. But it has to be said as well that this concept of the concept is conditioned by the homogeneity of the concept and its element, in other words, that the dialectic apprehends itself as such (= negativity *for itself*), once it has realized the homogeneity of its self-consciousness and its being, once the subject has become substance.

This summit once attained, the omnipotence of the 'method' bursts into view. For the method was the obscure law of the substance, the blind movement which propelled it toward its goal. It did not know itself; 'the blind soul of the content', it backed toward the light. But the method was also the negativity of the for-itself in the process of creating a totality in its own image, a totality in which the for-itself would be able to grasp itself as an internal, not an external, negativity; it wanted to see light transformed into a world. Absolute method is this method encountering itself and recognizing in itself 'the absolutely infinite force'[198] that governs the world, which has reached the plane of absolute content. This method is thus nothing but negativity which has come to itself in the totality of absolute content.

B. The Sins of the Content

If Hegel's conception of things cannot be attacked for its form, except on the basis of a misunderstanding, the only remaining alternative is to seek the source of our critical uneasiness in the content – to attempt to determine whether this content is in fact worthy of its form, and whether it attains, in Hegel himself, the concrete universality that is its goal. We have just seen that the formal mediations adduced were factitious; in reality, these mediations are part of the inner content. It follows that the only way to explain and justify one's reservations is to attack the accomplished content. The preceding analyses should at least have established the validity of the formal aspect of Hegel's system by showing that its form is in no wise alien to its content. Let us now try to see if the empirical existence of the totality is indeed the fully realized form, negativity *in actu*, real freedom, and if the concrete is genuinely universal: if, that is, the content conforms to its concept.

There is no better way of determining this than to examine the realm in which the Idea exists in its empirical reality, in which universality endows itself with a concrete body: namely, the state. Now it is the Hegelian conception of the state that has elicited the sharpest criticisms. The Prussian bureaucracy held up to the world of the Holy Alliance as the actualization of the divine Idea! Whatever the importance of this regime and the force of the *fait accompli*, no-one who approached matters honestly could approve Hegel's benediction without feeling ill at ease. The very rigour of his thought made this brainchild of Hegel's appear all the more ridiculous. The memorable phrases in this text [*The Philosophy of Right*], astonishingly profound when taken out of context, ring very hollow indeed when confronted with history: it is only possible to describe what exists, the philosopher is the child of his time and cannot leap over it, the old owl that, like wisdom, takes flight at dusk – these phrases barely conceal a forced resignation. To his credit, Marx clearly articulated this feeling of ill-ease; he arraigned the content, and, in the name of Hegel himself, went to the heart of Hegel's contradictions. Let us see where this leads.

1. The error

Marx's critique is contained in a manuscript that dates from 1841–42. Only the preface was published during Marx's lifetime. The critique takes the form of a running commentary on the *Elements of the Philosophy of Right*, which Hegel wrote to clarify the chapter of the *Encyclopædia* devoted to the state, and published in Berlin in 1821.[199] We propose to assemble and review Marx's arguments here.

1. It must first of all be understood that Marx does not criticize Hegel for depicting 'what is', since the primacy of the actual is, and for the same reasons, an imperative for both Hegel and Marx. The young Marx seeks 'the idea in reality itself',[200] seeks God on earth and not in Heaven, just as Hegel himself rejected any sort of Beyond and any Idea that had not been actualized: the Idea is either concrete or else it simply does not exist. Thus 'Hegel is not to be blamed for depicting the nature of the modern state as it is, but rather for presenting what is as the essence of the state. The claim that the rational is actual is contradicted precisely by an irrational actuality, which everywhere is the contrary of what it asserts and asserts the contrary of what it is.'[201] Hegel's imposture consists, not in having described the actual Prussian state, but in having represented it as the actualized Idea, that is, in having attributed to an irrational content the prestige and legitimizing rationality of the Idea.

It is worth recalling here that the state is, for Hegel, the apex and glorified body of history, whose appointed end is to realize freedom. The state (Hegel hails its beginnings in Napoleon's unifying cavalcades) is the emancipation of the concrete and realization of the universal: in it, the antinomy of the universal and the particular and the contradiction between lordship and bondage are not only laid to rest, but dissolved in the profound peace of the harmonious polity. In the state, man is at last *at home* with himself; he is neither master nor slave, but citizen; he is no longer a 'stranger in his own land', but finds full satisfaction in universal recognition; his essential being finds its justification in human freedom, his true native country. The state at last actualizes the essence of Spirit: '"I" that is "We" and "We" that is "I"'.[202] Thus the universality of the homogeneous state lies, not outside man, but in his empirical existence itself: the citizen is immediately universal, in that he no longer needs to beware of [*se garder de*] a master and no longer holds [*garde*] his powers in reserve inside himself. He is elevated to a new dignity, and his body, gestures, and talents belong, in the exercise, to all men. Yet his freedom does not circulate in the polity the way the blood circulates in the body or the wind through the trees: it is freedom for-itself, conscious of itself and rejoicing in the knowledge of its own silent movements, the 'spiritual daylight of the present'.[203] In the state, universality is not only concrete, it is also for-itself. What is more, this transparency explains why the state is truly universal, as Hegel anticipated it would be with the coming of a united Europe, i.e., why the state alone is the unique, ultimate totality. There is only one God, and the state is the divine Idea actualized.

Let us see what remains of this vision of the state in the *Philosophy of Right*, and whether the empirical reality of the Prussian state is consistent with the state's rational essence. But it is all too obvious that in the state Hegel describes, the concrete is not universal, nor the universal concrete.

The very structure of that state betrays the fact that the concrete is not universal in it. Instead of offering us a circular totality, outside which there can be no freedom, whether nascent or accomplished,[204] Hegel presents us with the Prussian pyramid. Instead of equality, he gives us the hierarchy of power and command; instead of the real circulation of the Idea, the barriers represented by corporations, offices, and police forces. This structure is disturbing in itself, since, in view of the rigidity of their established positions, the high and the low cannot pretend to meet, except by reflection: the high is not the low, but is high only because there is a low. We are now sufficiently familiar with the matter to detect in this reflexivity a harbinger of alienation and servitude. The details make it abundantly clear that this is indeed what is involved: this hierarchy is, to begin with, that of the spheres of the family, civil society, and the state, which exist in close proximity and literally regard one another as strangers. There would be nothing remarkable about these differences as such if their alienation were not precisely the raw material of their hierarchization, for we know that the absolute content 'contains its own differences within itself', and that the absolute state cannot be inert substance or Parmenides' monolithic mass; however, the differences must, if they are to throw off their bonds, conquer their truth in their own freedom and be posited in the totality as immediately universal. Yet, though obvious, this is not what Hegel's opening words show us: 'From one point of view the state is contrasted with the spheres of family and civil society as an external necessity, an authority, relative to which the laws and interests of family and civil society are subordinate and dependent.' This dependence did not escape Marx, who notes: This 'necessity . . . relates by opposition to the inner being of the thing.'[205]

Here we encounter the ambiguity that commands all else. If the polity has a pyramidal structure, what we will find in it is, at best, that movement from one extreme to the other is also movement back in the other direction; yet the extremes will not meet, except perhaps figuratively, i.e., as the result of a disfiguration. In other words, the movement that begins at the top and reaches the bottom does not touch the top again as soon as it starts back out from the bottom, but rather reaches it only after once again passing through all that lies in between. In contrast, it is the essential nature of the circle to be free of external mediation: something that goes all the way around it reaches the beginning when it comes to the end. The circle remains in itself throughout its unfolding, for it is always all it should be: hence it is a worthy representation of immediately universal individuality, the only possible figure of Hegelian freedom. The whole paradox of the Berlin philosophy of the state is contained, then, in the following problem: how is one to transform a pyramid into a circle, bend the Prussian back-and-forth into the circularity of universality, or, in a word, invest a given content with a meaning it lacks? Hegel adopted the only possible solution, contraband; but he failed to reckon with the customs-officer Marx, who caught him in the act of smuggling in false contents.

The externality of the structure of the state is extremely concrete. If we leave aside the sphere of the family, which Marx deliberately ignores, the Prussian polity consists of two extremes, the state and civil society, along with their middle terms, the government, civil servants, and the Chamber of Peers and Chamber of Deputies. The state is for Hegel the body and soul of the universal, but this universal, in and for itself, is not the totality: it is merely one of its moments. Over against the state stand the world of the workers and that of money, organized in the corporations and associations [les communes] of civil society. 'Particular interests which are common to everyone fall within civil society and lie outside the absolutely universal interest of the state proper. The administration of these is in the hands of corporations.'[206] This sentence of Hegel's, cited by Marx, unambiguously expresses the essential idea: civil society finds the universal outside itself. As to the reason for this alienation, we have to strain to make it out: it has to do, first of all, with the brute fact of the Prussian state; but it is not unrelated to the very nature of civil society, which Hegel describes as a System of Needs, the unleashing of egoistic instincts, and the constantly fluctuating system of economic atomism – the very opposite, that is, of organicism. Civil society is a living contradiction, because, in civil society, universality is not an Idea, but the sum total of a number of particular needs, and, again, because universality is not *for itself* there, since no-one in civil society pursues anything but the small change of egoistic goals. Hegel does not acknowledge this contradiction, as Marx was later to do; he does not identify it as the essence of the content and proceed to derive the truth of the content from it. The sole conclusion he draws is that civil society is a pseudo-content incapable of finding its truth in itself; he therefore approves its attempts to find this truth outside itself, in the universality of the state. Or, if one prefers, civil society is a content that does not succeed in reaching, in-and-for-itself, the universality of its truth; it finds this universality outside itself, in the institutions of government. 'Hegel does not see,' says Marx, 'that with this third moment, the "absolute universality", he obliterates the first two, or vice versa.'[207] Either the truth does indeed lie outside civil society, which is, in that case, a pseudo-content, or else it is to be found in civil society, in which case the state is a pseudo-universality. 'In a rational organism the head cannot be iron and the body flesh. In order to preserve themselves the members must be equally of one flesh and blood.'[208] This profound remark takes up the very terms employed by Hegel, who intended Spirit to be consubstantial with everything, and wanted man to find in the body politic [organisme politique], as in the first woman, 'flesh of his flesh and spirit of his spirit'.

The falsity of the civil sphere does, however, transpire in another of Hegel's remarks, in which he affirms that the people is not capable of attaining to the for-itself of universality. One might think that 'the many' would be able, if not to actualize, then at least to imagine universality and commend it to the sovereign's attention. But this is not at all the case. 'To know what one wills,' says Hegel, 'and still more to know what the absolute will, Reason, wills, is the fruit of profound apprehension . . . and insight, precisely the things which are not popular.'[209]

This double alienation from the in-itself and for-itself of universality in the people spells the end of freedom for the individual members of civil society. The individual is, in fact, alienated in his direct economic activity. To be sure, the economic sphere is a product of human labour, but it is one that men have neither sought out nor appropriated for themselves. The concept is absent from civil society; or, rather, the circle of the concept is closed behind civil society's back. The individual who works and sells what he makes is impelled to do so by hunger alone; he merely seeks to satisfy his desires and needs. He does not know that the ruse of reason erects these needs into a system, forming a circular world: the products made by one person match the needs of another, and, in this exchange, in which each sees only what he himself possesses, unconscious egoisms are brought into profound harmony. This system is thus a universal by its nature, but it lacks the for-itself and does not attain the truth. Taking up this idea, Marx was to work out the truth of this basic, mutually compensatory interaction characteristic of economic relations by showing that the concept, i.e., the appropriation of this relation, could only consist in the revolutionary transformation of the social order. As developed by Hegel, this universal not only lacks the for-itself; its in-itself too is annulled by the mere presence of the monarch and his government. The sphere of civil society is reduced to merely serving as material for a universality imposed upon it.

That demotion is the second alienation of the individual in the Prussian state. The first, we recall, affected the individual's *for-itself*, above all.

Here the demotion affects man's very *being*, separating the citizen in a man from the member of civil society. The artisan was not conscious that he was already, by dint of the economic activity he performed in society, engendering the universal. Consciousness of universality came to him from the state, but it affected the individual in him without attaining the artisan. The citizen of the Prussian state is not the whole man, but man self-divided, the man who puts his concrete activity aside and is endowed with a hollow attribute. 'Consequently the citizen of the state and the member of civil society are also separated. . . . Thus, in order to behave as actual citizen of the state, to acquire political significance and efficacy, he must abandon his civil actuality, abstract from it.'[210] Accordingly, if the individual manages to enter the sphere of political activity (but this is merely an activity of delegation), and to penetrate to the heart of this new order, in which, says Hegel, the self finds total satisfaction, he learns that he has paid for his truth with his very being. He sees himself cut in two, like an apple, and discovers that there are two beings inside him. Shoemaking and the concrete existence of the shoemaker have nothing to do with the citizen-shoemaker. The truth of the citizen is emptied of its reality. The individual finds, in the state [*État*], not fulfilment and emancipation, but official acknowledgement of his servitude and alienation. 'In general, the significance of the estate [*État, Stand*] is that it makes for difference, separation, subsistence, things pertaining to the individual as such. His manner of life, activity, etc. is his privilege, and instead of making him a functional member of society, it makes him an exception from society.'[211] But, if real men find their truth only outside themselves, this truth can only be unreal, that is, can only be alienation *in actu*. The reality of this truth must not be its own. That is precisely what we see at the other extreme.

2. Here we come to the universal in-and-for-itself constituted by the state. And, to begin with, we encounter the Monarch. But is the Monarch not finally the Idea we are pursuing? We apprehend it in his person: he is free, because he knows no constraint apart from reason. He is, indeed, excessively free, because, possessing the right to pardon, he holds even the life of his fellow men in his hands; he is active, because he chooses his ministers and agents, and rules; he is universal, because he is recognized by all, and, since he is not made of wood, is aware of his own majesty: he is a universal for-itself. But it is precisely this which is disturbing; we make the tally of all his attributes to find that there is finally only one, the for-itself. The Monarch suffers from hypertrophy of the for-itself, and for good reason: he has no in-itself. Or, rather, he is endowed with a derisory in-itself. Marx is merciless: what is this king's nature? Is he king because he has been recognized as such by common consent? Or is he recognized as such because he is a king by nature? By

nature: granted. But then all the fine reasons stated at the beginning were bogus – they were attributes of the king, not of the individual on the throne, of the persona, not the person. This brings us to the heart of the misunderstanding about the individual who is king: nothing appertains to the individual, everything is the king's, including even the individual, who constantly 'hears the king coming', as Frederick used to say whenever he let himself be human. The king, then, is cut in two like the ordinary man; this explains the sense in which there is a slave in the Monarch.

Let us go further: if it is not the king's human capacities that make him king, if his virtues come from wearing the crown, his crown comes from elsewhere. Hegel says: it is the king's by birth. We have at last come to the point. The in-itself of the king is to be born a king. Amazing, says Marx; all of us are born. 'Just as the horse is born a horse so the king is born a king.'[212] This, then, is the last refuge of the immediacy of the universal: the irrationality of natural determination. One thinks bitterly of the *Phenomenology*, which shows that Spirit is not a bone. Here the highest expression of Spirit is the birth of a skull. This can only be a mistake – or else it is the crown that makes it possible to smuggle the skull in under it. The Monarch is contraband. As to universality, the man decked out in it has been chosen at random: universality's content is not worthy of it. Or, to look at the matter from the opposite extreme, this content has to pretend to be what it is not, is a universal despite itself. Therein lies the profound reason for man's self-division: at the top as well as at the bottom, the state forces him, against his nature, to play the role of a character who swallows him up. Or, rather, what swallows Hegel up is that which, at the top, he rejects in the bottom: because he does not maintain the almost animal nature of the system of needs, but sacrifices it for the sake of an empty universality, natural brutality once again takes possession of the king. 'In its highest functions the state acquires an animal actuality. Nature takes revenge on Hegel for the disdain he showed it. If matter is supposed to constitute no longer anything for itself over against the human will, the human will no longer retains anything for itself except the matter.'[213]

3. Between the two extremes represented by the Monarch and civil society is posed, then, the problem of mediation. The mediation that proceeds from the top downwards is realized by the government (ministers, civil servants); in the other direction, it is the work of the estates. But what kind of middle terms can these be, caught as they are between a real world incapable of distilling its own truth and a truth incapable of legitimating its reality? 'The middle term,' says Marx, 'is the wooden sword, the concealed opposition between universality and singularity.'[214] This clearly holds for the estates, which Marx gleefully

takes to task. Where did they originate? They are simply a delegation dispatched by civil society, representatives of the corporations; they therefore defend private interests alien to the universality embodied by the state. What more are they than civil society constituted as a delegation which settles accounts with the state as one does with an adversary? In reality, this concentration in a parliament does not do away with the world of the economy. The Chamber is merely 'the nation *en miniature*'[215] gone forth to meet the enemy. But this reduction* is not a surrender. The middle term simply reproduces the contradiction: 'The Estates are the established contradiction of the state and civil society within the state.'[216] The government, however, which regards them as a middle term, also accommodates them, utilizing them to reach the people. In this sense, the estates are 'the amplified executive',[217] and, as Marx puts it, 'are themselves a part of the executive over against the people, but in such a way that they simultaneously have the significance of representing the people over against the executive'.[218]

We can see the ambiguity of this middle term, which is not a true mediation, because it merely reproduces the opposition it set out to overcome: the antagonism is posited as factitious in its very reality. 'This is a society pugnacious at heart but too afraid of bruises to ever really fight.'[219] This fight, which Hegel will have none of, is that of the truth which fails to appear in this imaginary mediation. The Hegelian third term, the concrete totality, is here a pitiful compromise between two hostile forces lacking the courage to fight; rather than serving as a vehicle for the extremes and bringing about their accomplishment, the third term interposes itself between them, and, as it only half succeeds, remains trapped there, stuck fast in the conclusion or, rather, the debate. Hegel's entire effort consists in presenting this juxtaposition as if it were a circle, this fictitious mediation as if it were an authentic ideal mediation. Marx exposes the fraud, and, against Hegel himself, goes back to the true Hegelian conception of the third term: the true mediation is the totality, and if 'the Estates are the ... contradiction ... at the same time they are the demand for the dissolution of this contradiction.'[220] The solution can only emerge from the very essence of the contradiction; the totality can only be constituted at the level of mediation. This authentic third term is, for Marx, the constitutive and legislative body representing the people, the sovereign popular assembly, the circularity of power and the masses, concrete universality animating a body worthy of it – that is, genuine democracy. The Prussian form of mediation is, to borrow a phrase from the *Phenomenology*, no more than a bit of wood tied onto a leg with a string.

* *Réduction*, which also means 'submission', 'surrender'.

2. The necessity of the error

Marx's critique thus lays bare an astonishingly perverse situation. For the Prussian state is described for us in all its empirical brutality, and it is quite obvious that this constitutional monarchy, with its hierarchical structure, is not the circular totality of the truth. The content is not the reality of its concept; the content is false. Yet this perversion is presented to us as if it were the truth. A derivative meaning is superimposed on the concrete reality of the content, which has failed to achieve harmony with itself. What is universal in Prussia is not a mediation internal to the content, but rather a concept which, from the outside, invests its institutions with a meaning other than themselves, one that transcends and legitimizes them. 'Thus empirical actuality is admitted just as it is and is also said to be rational; but not rational because of its own reason, but because the empirical fact in its empirical existence has a significance which is other than it itself.'[221]

But there is more to Hegel's Prussian state than a simple juxtaposition of meanings; it also shows us the meaning of this juxtaposition in the obscure necessity for juxtaposition. Monarch and people coexist in pseudo-indifference, and the connection Hegel seeks to establish between them is not so alien to them that they cannot each find it in their own essential natures. It is because the people does not contain its own truth that it contemplates it in the king; it is because the king is not a real human being that he seeks his *raison d'être* in the people. The 'significance which is other than itself' that Marx exposes in this hoax is, in contrast, painfully internal: it is this significance that haunts the actual, aspires to fulfilment in the actual, and, in its very failure, anticipates its actualization. Because the people has failed to liberate the universality that lies dormant within it, and has also failed to reappropriate, as something willed by itself, the economic sphere whose law it is subject to, it experiences this universal will as a lack and projects it onto the Monarch, venerating it in him unawares. Significance is a form of compensation; such is the profound bond of Prussian alienation, which is reminiscent of Hegel's analyses of Kantian reflexivity. God dwells amongst his Prussian people as he dwelt among the Jews – but his people knows him not. This other significance, this Heaven, is the truth of the content, which, since it does not know it, renounces the thought of reappropriating it and making it over in its own image.

It nevertheless seems as if Hegel has repudiated the force of his thought, and that, far from working towards the people's conversion to its truth, he tries to project another meaning onto the contradiction. For, once recognized for what it is, compensation becomes a subversive, revolutionary force. It is as if Hegel had become the accomplice of the night and were trying to hide the people's own God from it, while justifying the fact that God is hidden. Thus he hides the content's total significance from it by perverting its real significance. He says that the state is the truth of the people, but does not show that the truth dwells amongst a people ignorant of it; instead, he affirms that the people cannot know the truth. The reason he gives is not to be lightly dismissed: how can the truth come into being amidst the economic anarchy and intellectual poverty of the worlds of artisan and burgher – how can the truth be born in a manger? And if the truth is not in the people, is it any wonder that the people has too lowly a spirit to grasp it? Hegel accordingly declares that the truth has a completely different significance. Far from emerging out of the reality of the parts themselves, far from fulfilling their own truth by revealing it to them and enabling them to recognize it at a glance, as one recognizes a father or a brother, it abruptly transforms their reality into an alien truth – one they are most unlikely ever to recognize, for now it takes great philosophical patience to make out the truth, and long preparation and training to recognize one's brother. One cannot even say that the people trails its truth behind it, as do phenomenological consciousness or Plato's prisoner, so that it would only have to turn around – be converted body and soul – to find itself facing the sun and the truth. The king, minister, and civil servant are always standing in front of it; moreover, their being too is consumed by a meaning that exhausts them: the king's blood is not the meaning of the king.* Thus it is that the significance of the Prussian state remains unaffected by the power of compensation, and that people and king are stripped of their concrete reflexive meaning and invested with the 'crown and robes of the universal'.[222] The reason for the state is simply *la raison d'état*, a reason derived from another world which conceals the unreason [*déraison*] of this one.

This other world is the Idea, which, paradoxically, becomes the truth of the content's untruth. Thus we arrive at a conception of things in which depth emerges as an evasive dimension of the concept. The meaning of the Prussian state does not lie in its essential contradiction; this meaning is not at the same level, but rather stands above it. Hegel thus reverts to the verticality of truth despite his unrelenting efforts to make truth something immanent:

> Hegel's chief mistake consists in the fact that he conceives of the contradiction in appearance as being a unity in essence, i.e., in the Idea; whereas it certainly has something more profound in its essence, namely, an essential contradiction. For example here, the contradiction in the legislature itself is nothing other than the contradiction of the political state, and thus also the self-contradiction of civil society.[223]

---

* *Le sang du roi n'est pas le sens du roi.* In an older pronunciation, *sang* (blood) and *sens* (meaning) were homonyms.

Hence Hegel's appeal to the Idea is inseparable from his rejection of reflexive compensation. Hegel does not develop the content of the people, because, to do so, he would need only the king, not the Idea, which, for him, provides the foundation for the twofold *fait accompli* of people and king:

> True philosophical criticism of the present state constitution [says Marx] not only shows the contradictions as existing, but explains them, grasps their essence and necessity. It comprehends their own inherent significance. However, this comprehension does not, as Hegel thinks, consist in everywhere recognizing the determinations of the logical concept, but rather in grasping the particular logic of the particular object.[224]

The last criticism brings the difference between the two positions into clearer focus. Hegel inverts order and value; he can assign a given content a truth that is alien to it only if he invests this content with a meaning different from its own, by making the real over into a phenomenon of the Idea.

This inversion is not only apparent in the details of Hegel's description of the state, which is where Marx finds it, although that spectacle is by itself highly instructive: it shows us real beings emptied of their being and dressed up in a ridiculous universality, false beings loaded down with a borrowed nature that crushes them under its weight. For the disguise becomes nature, and the enduring Prussian state is nothing but this perversion stabilized: in the end, the crown makes the king, the portfolio the minister, the ballot the citizen. Disguise, then, has an essence and a meaning that are not simply the properties of masks. We can understand the perversion in its entirety only if we consider its essence, which is, on Marx's view, Hegelian logic.

Because Hegel refers to the logic throughout, he constantly rewrites real beings in terms of their ideal-logical significance and incarnates moments of the logical Idea in beings borrowed for the purpose. The reflexive toing and froing characteristic of·the level of contradiction is here replaced by uninterrupted movement between the real and the Idea, by a permanent redemption and incarnation. For Marx, the essence of this imposture lies in Hegel's conversion of subjects into predicates. The veritable subject is concrete; Hegel transposes it into a predicate, which is only ideal. Thus universality is not a predicate of the concrete individuals of this particular historical people, their basic element and daily bread; they themselves are, rather, mere instruments of an ideal necessity that dupes and crushes them. They are not real people who are really free, but rather vassals of the freedom of the Idea, whose ways are unfathomable. The state does not belong to them, is not a *Tun aller und jeder*; rather, it is they who belong to the state, and owe it service, taxes, and respect. More precisely, they belong to the Idea, of which constitutional monarchy is merely the visible body. For, if they really had to do with the concrete subject who dominates them, they might succeed in gaining satisfaction from him, in compelling him to restore not only their property, but also their dignity; they might succeed in deposing the Monarch and taking back their own predicates – power, universality, freedom. Here, however, Hegel clings so tightly to his aberration that it is impossible to destroy it with the weapons he himself provides. The Monarch is simply the body of an Idea one can neither kill nor overthrow; he is himself a subjected subject, a concrete individual like all the others, compelled by the Idea to pretend to exercise power, and, like them, in Its hands. The subject constituting the concrete individual in the king receives his own nature as a manifestation of the Idea from the moment of his birth. Thus it is that a text by Hegel reinstates the dualism of truth and reality that he had taken it upon himself to eliminate; the beyond once again emerges as a signifying totality opposed to the real. To be sure, this beyond is within arm's reach, since it is nothing other than the Idea which has yielded up its secrets in Hegel's logic. In the Philosophy of the State, says Marx, 'we have before us a chapter of the *Logic*'.[225]

Here Marx's analysis reaches a critical point. One can take the view that, in the system of the state, Hegel contradicts himself: 'Here, then,' says Marx, 'we find one of Hegel's inconsistencies within his own way of viewing things; and such an inconsistency is an accommodation.'[226] Such an attitude implies that Hegel's error is tacitly corrected in the thought of his critic, who judges Hegel in the name of his own vision of things. But it is also possible to yield to the fascination of the error and affirm that the system, even if it has been demolished, is as necessary to the error as the error itself. Such is the power of the content in Hegel that a perverted content overflows its limits and seeks a perverted form. The content has the form it deserves. The Prussian state is the incarnation of a logical idea worthy of it; if we reverse the terms of the proposition, we find ourselves but a short step from another, to the effect that the logical Idea could give rise to nothing but this bastard state. The perversion of the content is not happenstance or inconsistency, but rather the most consistent of phenomena: the false content emerges, in that case, as the truth of a falsified Idea. Thus it would be possible to speak of the necessity of error in Hegel; one needs to work one's way back to this necessity in order to understand how Hegel can, in the name of the highest reason, defend the basest of monarchies.

Marx dwells on this point with a kind of vindictive complacency; applying what he says of Hegel to Marx himself, we could even say that he takes 'pleasure in having demonstrated the irrational to be absolutely rational'.[227] In Marx's eyes, this Hegelian falsification was no accident, but a necessity:

This is the root of Hegel's *false* positivism ... reason [in Hegel] is at home in unreason as such. Man, who has recognized that he leads an alienated life in law, politics, etc., leads his true human life in this alienated life as such. Self-affirmation, in contradiction with itself ... is thus the true *knowledge* and *life*. There can no longer be any question about Hegel's compromise with religion, the state, etc., for this falsehood is the falsehood of his whole argument.[228]

Let us, then, go to the heart of the matter; to the heart, that is, not only of the logic – for the logic is only one part of the system – but of the movement by which the logic itself is posed and justified: namely, the circularity of the concept. This should bring out not only the essence of the logic, but also the reason Marx identifies it as the essence of the empirical reality of the state. The concept is characterized by its triplicity, that is, the movement by which it goes forth from itself, posits its differences, recognizes them as its own, and takes them back into itself. The differences of the concept hold a strange place in this movement: they are simultaneously posited as real and annulled as unreal. Thus their *raison d'être* is not to be found in them, but rather in the concept that posits them so as to reappropriate them. Considered in isolation, they are either substantial [*consistant*] but meaningless, or else insubstantial but replete with meaning, with the result that if the concept is allowed to operate, it has a curious effect upon them: it must annul even while preserving them. Yet, in the event, it is quite as if the concept annulled the non-meaning in the meaningless substantiality and the insubstantiality in the meaningful insubstantiality, leaving us, in the totality, with a meaningful substantiality. The substantiality is not, however, of the same nature as the meaning, which is why this pro-motion hardly affects it: it is quite simply confirmed, in its externality, by the meaning that crowns it. The solution is absolution.[229] The Prussian state can rest easy, if its conscience ever troubled it at all. 'The annulment of alienation becomes a confirmation of alienation.'[230]

But what possible reason can there be for this paradoxical security, other than the omnipotence of the concept which has quite simply produced these very differences? When we consider the question from the opposite standpoint, we see the concept affecting to externalize itself and posit differences which are, apart from its act of positing them, nothing at all, and which are therefore not real, but accidental. That is the key to the matter: one can grant absolution without a second thought, for, in the real, one only absolves shadows. Nature is annulled before it comes into being;[231] like the state, it has the substantiality of a phantom. At the level of the differences themselves, doubtless neither nature nor the state appear to be painted shadows. In order to grasp the insubstan-tiality of their substantiality, we need to look at things through the eyes of God, who sees the differences men seek desperately to experience disappear even before they have come about. To discover this reassuring perspective, we have to take up a position at the origin of the concept, with the help of our philosophy: 'Consequently, my true religious existence is my existence in the *philosophy of religion* ... my true natural existence is my existence in the *philosophy of nature,* my true artistic existence is my existence in the *philosophy of art.'*[232]

But what do we find at the origin of the concept? 'The pure act of positing', which the *Phenomenology of Spirit* describes in abstract terms in connection with self-consciousness. '"Thinghood",' says Marx, 'is totally lacking in *independence,* in *being, vis-à-vis* self-consciousness; it is a mere *construct* posited by self-consciousness. And what is posited is not self-confirming; it is the confirmation of the act of positing.'[233] This act is divine power in the true sense, which is why Marx brands Hegel's philosophy mystical, magical, creationist. Employing a new vocabulary, and proceeding with logical rigour, Hegel merely reprised the old theological myths of emanation, in which causality concentrated in the divine being radiates outwards in concrete attributes: the concept is *causa sui,* like God, and the world derives from it as the modes of substance do. Hegel's merit is to have thought the content of this mystification; his error is simply to have believed in it, without seeking to uncover its meaning.

Marx provides us with this meaning. 'The act of positing' is merely the abstract form, produced in thought, of a 'real living act',[234] human labour. In the concept (or the idea of divine creation), men project the essential outlines of their substantial activity. In labour, they externalize themselves, thereby positing real, abiding differences. This externality is substantial (the mason bumps up against his wall); but the fact that it owes its existence to something else (the wall existed in the mason's mind – as something insubstantial – before he bumped up against it) means that it is potentially reappropriated as soon as it is posited, before revolutionary appropriation actually restores the product to its producer. Such is the concrete origin of the concept, which merely thinks and apotheosizes labour. From this we can see why God is an architect, watchmaker, and gardener, and why he made the world in seven days. We can see as well why Hegel, if he correctly conceived the essence of man in labour, nevertheless conceived this essence as an act which is its own origin, whereas the labourer is a concrete being in a world that precedes and goes beyond him. Hence 'labour as Hegel understands and recognizes it is *abstract mental* labour',[235] that is, labour in the element of thought. It is a form of creativity severed from its origins, emancipated from the real by virtue of its abstraction and purity; it conflates this emancipation with freedom, ascribing to itself the independence it owes to the world which made that independence possible. This liberty of thought is merely a relationship that has gone unperceived. That is why Hegel, like all philosophers, thinks in alienation: he fails to think the reality of his own liberty of thought. That is why he is literally penned up in the limitless universe he circulates in: abstraction is indeed without limit. Yet Hegel has a merit Marx does not deny: he travelled the length and breadth of the kingdom of thought, catalogued its forms, established its circularity, and distilled its essence. Rather than proffering us the classical propositions of metaphysics without any explanation of their origins, 'Hegel substitutes the act of abstraction revolving within itself for these fixed abstractions.'[236] As we know, that act is the birth of the concept.

What has just been said enables us, in turn, to understand the perversity of the Hegelian necessity that operates top-down. When the philosopher wishes to quit the realm of the Idea and regain reality, to pass, that is, 'from *abstracting* to *intuiting*',[237] he tries to imitate, in reverse, the process that permitted him to take up a position in the abstract. He therefore leaves the realm of abstraction, yet, keeping up appearances, does not abandon his stake in it, as if an excess of liberty had induced him to consent to being. Thus the Idea 'deploys itself freely' in Nature; its fall is a graceful one, like that of a king voluntarily relinquishing the throne. But the philosopher only rewrites his own alienation in terms of being: because he is alienated from himself in his thought, his thought is the essence of alienation, and invests every being it lingers over with the inevitability of alienation. This explains why Marx exposes the necessity of Hegel's error and discovers the perversion of the Idea in the content as well: in Hegel, the Idea has the content it deserves. Thus Hegel's analysis of the state acquires, for us, a meaning that is both ridiculous and dramatic: Hegel needed Prussia so that he could seek and find his own image in it.

This brings us to a final point. The false content in Hegel points to a theoretical necessity: abstraction. But abstraction is merely the place where Hegelian alienation occurs. The various pseudo-contents sustain one another. The reason for Hegel's aberration is that Hegel was alienated in the abstraction of his thought. The philosopher thought, but did not think the fact that he thought; he did not reappropriate, in reality, the distance he took from the world, but rather withdrew into a feigned maturity without reclaiming his origins. His childhood regained was mere childishness. If he exalted truth, he did so the way a prisoner sang in the camps: in a condition of servitude that was not himself. And when he thought and described this condition, he depicted his own countenance. We are caught, here, in the toils of a pitiless system.

3. Necessity's revenge

Closer examination reveals, however, that we are already familiar with this system. Before Marx, Hegel had already defined the philosopher as an alienated being, a man who thought the alienation of his own situation by way of the totality – and who therefore thought, in the form of the Idea, the alienation of the world that sustained him. This is why the content of all philosophies is the contradiction of thought, which only belatedly attains self-consciousness in the thinking of contradiction. As a result, says Hegel, philosophy, which is the self-consciousness of Spirit in the various moments of its development, and thus in its alienation, is simply the reality of the world's contradictions translated into thought.

Accordingly, the necessity of philosophical alienation is as heavily stressed in the *Phenomenology* as in Marx: the contradiction of thought, which is the essence of each and every philosophy, points back to the fundamental contradiction between the philosopher and the historical world from which he abstracts himself in thinking it. This contradiction is ultimately nothing other than the self-contradiction of the world, which has not yet succeeded in overcoming its alienation; and the alienation of philosophical thinking is merely the alienated consciousness of this alienation. In the chapter entitled 'The Certainty and Truth of Reason', Hegel shows that, in idealism, we have the genesis of the alienation of the thinker, who withdraws from the world without saying so, and thinks it as if it were coming into being in his thought. The thinker neglects to think the *path* that leads up to his thought. But 'it is along that forgotten path that this immediately expressed assertion is comprehended.'[238] The defining feature of idealism is this refusal to think the genesis of the philosopher – therein resides the alienation of the thinker *qua* thinker. But this refusal is not without its reasons; it is simply a man's way of defending himself against his times. By refusing to acknowledge his concrete origins, the philosopher refuses to recognize the reality of the world that gave him birth. There is a necessity to this unconscious ill humour: the philosopher rejects the world as a place in which he cannot be in harmony with himself, and thereby reveals its alienation. It is because he is not at home in the alienated world that the philosopher takes refuge in the alienation of thought, where he attempts to fashion a friendly world. It is because the thinking slave had to bear the burden of the Roman world, in which only the emperor was, in a paradoxical sense, free (in truth, chained to his own role and the Empire), that he became a Stoic, seeking, in thought, the freedom the world denied him. It is because the individual in the medieval city did not know the profound peace of the universal reconciled with the particular, that he was a Christian, producing, in theology, a harmonious image of a strife-torn world. It is because the men of the eighteenth century did not feel at home in the decadent monarchy that they retreated into the Enlightenment, in which they reclaimed, with their encyclopædic knowledge, a world they could not master. Thus we have come back round to Marx: the philosopher's alienation is merely the spectacle of an alienated world.

Or, as Hegel puts it, in the philosophies and religions, Spirit (i.e., history) thinks its own alienation.

Yet Hegel clearly saw another point as well, one Marx neglects. How is one to think the essence of philosophy, that is, the alienation of thought, without becoming the prisoner of the essence of one's own thinking? Here the judge is judged by his own judgement; we are on a spinning wheel, caught in an infinite regress. This has been the fate of all thinkers who have tried to think their own place in their thought, as can be seen with Plato or Kant: they catch up with themselves only in God, the terminus of a race without end. Thinking alienation in the thinker can only lead to failure; the opposite would imply the negation of the essence of philosophy and the realization of the philosopher's secret desire. If thought could really reappropriate the alienation that spawned it, and repossess in reality what it endeavours to apprehend in a figure, it would abolish the real alienation of the world and reconcile the world with itself through the power of its discourse. This childish aspiration lies at the heart of every philosophy; Marx denounced it as a kind of magic. Hegel's grandeur lies in the fact that he consciously renounced this aspiration (at least in the *Phenomenology*), and demonstrated the necessity of that renunciation; he showed, in other words, that alienation can neither be eliminated in a figure, nor even simply thought as the essence of thought, before being concretely overcome in history. It is because the time is ripe, because history has been accomplished and Spirit has finally emerged as a homogeneous totality, that the thought of eliminating alienation is the elimination of alienation, that thinking about alienation is no longer alienated thinking. Hegel, says Marx, lived in an alienated world, which is why he was unable to 'leap over his own time'; his thought is simply the alienation, translated into thought, of his alienated existence in the world. But Hegel did not claim to be exempt from the law he discovered. He merely affirmed that, in the accomplished totality, the revolutionary world had won back its alienated being, and that this advent of the Truth marked the end of philosophy, i.e., of alienated thought. Thus Hegel does not lay claim to the title of philosopher in the *Phenomenology*: the philosopher cannot survive the reappropriation of his alienation. The death of the philosopher is the birth of the Sage, who is the concrete figure of Absolute Knowledge. Knowledge of this sort is no longer on the spinning wheel; it not only knows its own essence, but also the essence of the truth which perishes in it, i.e., alienation – without, for all that, being caught in an infinite regress. For (as Descartes had suspected) what is imperfect cannot truly apprehend either itself or perfection; only that which is perfect knows the imperfect, because it knows itself.[239]

Thus Hegel not only thought the essence of the philosopher in alienation; he also posed, concretely, the condition for the non-alienation of this thought, that is, the way out that would truly enable thought to reach the firm ground on which it could be both thought and also the thought of truth in the element of truth. Finally, he did not conceive this condition as a thought – i.e., an idea to be realized, and hence something unreal; he broke out of the circle of alienation for good and all by describing the present reality of this condition. These are strong positions, and Marx, far from overrunning them, clearly seems to be captured in his turn. For if he is in agreement with Hegel, he does not seem, at least not explicitly, to have accorded the conditions of thought with thought in a concrete sense. Quite the contrary: having denounced the alienation of the bourgeois world he lived in, and having merely predicted the end of alienation in the coming revolution, he was no more able than Hegel to leap over his time, and his own truths were recaptured by what they denounced. As philosopher, Marx was thus a prisoner of his times and hence of Hegel, who had foreseen this captivity. In a sense, Marx succumbed to the necessity of the error he wished to retrace in Hegel, in that Hegel had exposed this necessity in the philosopher, while overcoming it in himself so as to engender the Sage. Marx's error lay in not being a sage.

Or, rather, it lay in being one without saying so. It is here that Hegel takes his most spectacular revenge, by silently reconquering Marx from within. Not only does Hegel take back what is his by way of Marx's definition of him; Hegel is the one who inspires it, and who thus inspires Marx's truth. If Marx brings the necessity of error to light in Hegel, it is only by virtue of the presence of Hegel himself, who has become, in Marx, the necessity of the truth. Hegel is Marx's silent rigour, the living truth of a body of thought which is too pressed by circumstances to apprehend itself in self-consciousness, but which betrays itself in the least of its movements. What Hartmann said about the Hegelian dialectic actually applies to Marx: Marxist thought lacks a for-itself. That is perhaps what Engels meant when he declared that what he had retained of Hegel was his dialectic, which is, in Hegel, merely negativity that has succeeded in reappropriating itself. He thus expressed, rather confusedly, an obscure sort of recognition: Hegel is Marx's conscience/consciousness [conscience], and in him Marx reappropriated himself as if Hegel's self were his own.

There can, indeed, be no mistake: as soon as we attempt to disengage the for-itself of Marxist arguments, we find Hegelian necessity again, in its most rigorous form – that of the concept.

Let us look, for example, at the content of history as Marx presents it. He begins by insisting on the given, in a way that would seem to be in contradiction with Hegel's method: 'the premises from which we begin are ... real premises. ... They are the real individuals, their activity and the material conditions under which they live, both those which they find already existing and those produced by their activity. These premises can thus be verified in a purely empirical way.'[240] Thus Marx makes, at the level of his own time, a phenomenological cut, and literally carries out an analysis of essence in which the content yields up its structure. In so doing, he by no means imposes a form on a content, but rather thinks out 'the particular logic of the particular object'.[241] The essence he describes, i.e., the socio-economic structure of the capitalist world of the nineteenth century, is a contradictory reality. It is given, but is not a being *through-itself*; rather, it is a result, which thus points to its development as its origin. Hence the given is literally externalized, and seeks its *raison d'être* outside itself, in the historical process. What is most remarkable here is the fact that this outside-itself is not an alien entity that miraculously confers a meaning on the content, a generous Providence that, in a sudden burst of illumination, reveals its origins. Rather, this outside-itself lies within it; the externality of the process is the inside of the content. The present displays the internalized memory of the past within itself, showing that the process has been internalized and is, therefore, the outside become the inside; the present inverts the relationship between wrapper and wrapped. Thanks to memory, the process is in the content; but, on the plane of meaning, the content is in the process. The wrapper is thus wrapped up in what it wraps up; the inside is the outside of the inside. Here Marx transforms the subject into the predicate, effecting what is properly speaking an inversion of the kind he criticizes in Hegel. The present-subject becomes the predicate of its own past-predicate; what is internal to the content is thus posited as its origin. History, *qua* real idea, thus reappropriates its own presuppositions; history is the true subject which endows each of its moments with meaning, impelling them to accomplish their truth, which is its truth. Thus men living in a concrete moment of history, like Marx himself in 1844, acquire knowledge of their truth only from history, that is, from the total process enveloping them, which contains both their servitude and their freedom.

Let us go further: in this form, history can be nothing more than an abstract Hegelian concept. But, for Marx, the concept of history implies a reference to the concept of labour: 'For socialist man, *the whole of what is called world history* is nothing but the creation of man by human labour.'[242] This is quite remarkable. We of course take it for granted that the subject/predicate inversion has been carried out, and accordingly find ourselves in the presence of labour, which is initially posited as the *unity of the worker and his product* (first moment); this unity is, however, still enveloped and, as it were, abstract. It is something implicit that needs to become explicit, an in-itself that must attain its for-itself, a concept that has to posit its differences outside itself and then reappropriate them. Doubtless this necessity is partially retrospective, but Marx posits it as a necessity which goes beyond the present content, anticipates its own future, and discovers its anticipatory character in, precisely, the future that it commands even before that future appears. Thus one is entitled to concentrate in the origin all the necessity that unfolds in history, and to speak, with Marx, of 'the necessary development of labour'.[243]

But the original unity of labour, that is, the original unity of man and his product, develops within *division or alienation* (second moment). The origin of this split is the division of labour. In the original unity, the product is not separated from its producer, who consumes what he produces and produces what he consumes (this is the stage of the domestic economy without exchange). With the emergence of the division of labour, the labourer, now specialized, no longer consumes everything he produces, and, *a fortiori*, no longer produces everything he consumes: he buys some of the things he consumes and sells some of those he produces (the stage of the industrial and commercial economy). Thus the product is separated from the labourer; the *for-itself* (product) escapes from the *in-itself* (producer) and stands over against it in alienation.

No longer under the labourer's control, the product acquires freedom through exchange, and the limits on this freedom are gradually pushed back until they take in the whole world: the product tends to constitute itself as a universal whose limit is the *world market*. It becomes an abstract totality whose essential being no longer consists in the material body of the product, but in the reflexive meaning or value condensed in money; the internal circulation of this abstract totality is free trade. This endpoint is reached only after a long period of historical development. Only under liberal capitalism does the product, separated from the labourer, finally attain the extreme form of separation in the abstract universality that is money. Marx insists on the necessity of this development. Speaking of capital, he writes, 'in the course of its formation [on a world scale] it must achieve its abstract, i.e. *pure* expression'.[244]

At the other pole, the labourer undergoes a similar adventure, which induces his further development. In the product that escapes his control, he loses his personality and possessions; even his bodily integrity is threatened. Little by little, he acquires the status of the proletarian, i.e., of the pure labourer who does not, as a rule, consume any part of what he produces, and who receives, in the form of his wages, nothing but the recognition of the necessity of his physical survival. In proportion as the for-itself of the product tends towards universality, the in-itself of the labourer tends toward the particular: vis-à-vis the law of money, the labourer is nothing but an anonymous body lost in an indifferent crowd. In the literal sense, he has nothing left but his body, that is, a purely natural determination of his particularity.

This moment is alienation, in the strictest sense. The in-itself and for-itself confront one another as strangers. The labourer's own force has become the brutal domination of money, that is, the power of a universal master who has him at his mercy and condemns him to hard labour. The human reality of the labourer has become a worn-out body struggling against death. '[In their case]', says Marx, 'labour has lost all semblance of self-activity and only sustains their life by stunting it.'[245] Yet it is not only the product of his labour which escapes the labourer's control; the reason for his degradation also escapes him. This is the height of alienation: the for-itself of necessity is absent from it, and men cannot think their own history without invoking fatality. They submit to the domination of economic laws and their own decline as if bowing to a blind and capricious destiny. The simple clarity of labour, in which the labourer sees an obedient product coming into existence in his hands, has become the dark night of unfathomable servitude and poverty. This result of history is an immediate reality for the worker, who daily performs, in an incomprehensible, inhuman world, the simple miracle of labour, and does not understand the monstrous perversion of his gestures.

Nonetheless, if we consider these two extremes in their totality, we can see that they are already straining to meet: the universality of the economic sphere is abstract, and its abstraction marks it out for death. It is not in possession of its own law, which is only a system of chance: the force driving it toward domination is merely the provisional necessity of a happy anarchy that does not outlive its order. (This universality is merely the abstract form of economic individualism.) At the other extreme, the division of labour has created the mass of proletarians, reduced to their bodies and stripped of their souls. But it has also bound these bodies together in close dependence on the assembly line, all in the same wretched situation: particularism is transformed into its opposite in the proletariat, which is already, de facto, the real body of a soulless universality. These opposing extremes are merely the developed forms of the labour process, which creates, in contradiction, the element of the unified totality.

This is the third moment of the concept: after the original unity and ensuing division, what emerges is unity reconquered, the in-and-for-itself, the concrete universal, the identity of subject and predicate, the free, human world. The process that culminates in this result is well known. It is precipitated when the contradiction becomes acute, amidst the crisis of capitalism and the coming to consciousness of the proletariat. The proletariat grasps the significance of its alienation, which it had earlier submitted to as if to its fate, reappropriates its own nature through revolutionary action, and abolishes 'the alien relation between men and what they themselves produce'.[246] As to the power of economic forces, it is now tamed: 'All-round dependence, this natural form of the world-

historical co-operation of individuals, will be transformed by this communist revolution into the control and conscious mastery of these powers.'[247] In short, the final historical totality, which marks the end of alienation, is nothing but the reconquered unity of the labourer and his product. This end is simply the restoration of the origin, the reconquest of the original harmony after a tragic adventure. The pre-eminence of the in-itself is thus restored.

Yet it is only in a formal sense that the final unity is the restoration of the original unity. The worker who reappropriates what he himself produces is no longer the primitive worker, and the product he reappropriates is no longer the primitive product. Men do not return to the solitude of the domestic economy, and what they produce does not revert to being what it once was, the simple object of their needs. This *natural* unity is destroyed; the unity that replaces it is *human*. Socialist man does not raze the factories, scrap technology, or renounce civilization and physical mastery of the world, a mastery that would be unthinkable without the division of labour: he maintains, in the form of technology and industrial concentration, the *de facto* universality his products had realized against man under capitalism. But he transforms it in reappropriating it, converting an inhuman universality, whose law is impersonal anarchy, into a human universality subordinated to men's designs. As to the worker, he is no longer the worker of primitive times, and does not go back to 'cultivating his garden'. As a rule, he continues to work in his area of specialization, but the meaning of his existence has changed: he is no longer the lone individual of the domestic economy, or the slave of an irresponsible system, but has rather, from the depths of his poverty, conquered his true nature, which is to be a human being and not mere nature. In the implicit or developed proletariat, he fully realizes his essential being, which is human brotherhood: henceforth the human race is, for him, the concrete universal which gives his life and work their meaning. And this universality is neither fate nor an imaginary beyond: man is the end of man. Marx saw the emergence of this moving truth in the fraternity of the French socialists: 'For them, the brotherhood of man is no empty phrase but a reality, and the nobility of man shines forth upon us from their toil-worn bodies.'[248]

This transformation of natural into human unity is crucial, for it allows us a better understanding of the necessity of the concept. Necessity first manifests itself in details – for example, the necessity that generates a socialist humanity amidst the contradictions of capitalism: 'Communism,' says Marx, 'is for us not . . . an *ideal* to which society [will] have to adjust itself. We call communism the *real* movement which abolishes the present state of things. The conditions of this movement result from the premises now in existence.'[249] But this necessity is merely a consequence we can deduce from a given situation – without establishing the necessity of that situation itself. This is the deterministic side of Marxism, and the reason that Marx so often comes in for the kinds of reproach directed at every system of natural determinism. Yet Marxian determinism has nothing to do with natural determinism in an unqualified sense. For Marxism, necessity is something more profound. The nature of the reconstituted unity reveals the significance of this Marxian necessity. Necessity *in* alienation is effectively enveloped by the necessity *of* alienation as such. For Marx, there is a *positive* side to capitalism; this is not a paradox, but rather rigorous thinking. Without capitalism – without, that is, alienation in its extreme form – man would have succeeded neither in transforming his material powers into something universal, nor, above all, in reappropriating, through the brotherhood of man, the universality of his essential being. Without capitalism, man would not have known that he was man, and, most importantly, would not have become man: capitalist alienation is the birth of humanity.[250] We need not force the terms unduly in order to identify the fecundity of this division with the Passion of Hegelian Spirit, which does not go forth from itself by chance, but in order to appropriate its true nature, and which, in this fall, attains the revelation of a depth realized by the totality. The proletarian discovers the truth of humanity in the depths of human misery.

We may add something that follows directly from the preceding. The internal determinism or law of development of the present world is, for Marx, conditioned by another profound necessity, which teaches the present not only about its future, but also about what made it the present. Whence the ambiguity of the economic determinism in Marxism. On the one hand, *it is natural*, and thus brooks no appeal; one needs to know its law. At this level, [freedom] for Marx is exactly what it is for Spinoza: 'consciousness of necessity'.[251] On the other hand, *this determinism is human*. In other words, it is enveloped by the necessity that founds it, and has neither meaning nor existence apart from this necessity – the realization of human freedom. We cannot grasp this point, according to which natural necessity is once again assimilated by human necessity, unless we understand that this natural necessity is itself human, and that it appears to men as natural necessity because it is an alienated human necessity.

This metamorphosis occurs within labour itself. For Marx, nature is a fall: the product that falls from men's hands and escapes their control literally becomes nature from the instant it is separated from the producer.[252] At every moment, the worker accomplishes the miracle of the Hegelian Idea. The profound unity of the producer and his product gives way to division; this alienation gives birth to nature. In the alienated product, man externalizes himself, is transformed into a natural body, and, to the extent that he is unaware that the body of the product is nothing but his own body, treats what he himself has produced as if it were nature, that is, a substance that is simply given, matter in its own right, governed by natural laws and natural necessity. It is these objective laws which the theorists of the liberal economy have worked out. In the economic order, they have seen only the fatality of an inexorable determinism, one that is natural in the true sense of the word, and that reabsorbs its crises the way nature reabsorbs natural disease and deformity.

But there is a good deal more to be said here: since man endures the domination of what he himself produces, the initial relationship is inverted; man is subject to the power of natural law, which produces and dominates him. Thus the proletarian is the product of capital, which engenders him by the same natural necessity that engenders crises and then resolves them. This necessity establishes his standard of living and customs, furnishes him with his bread and his thoughts: it penetrates to his very heart, defining his essential nature in terms of his needs, and his moral code in terms of a calculus of pleasures. Ultimately, it even brings about his emancipation, since the capitalist order destroys itself and is transformed into a socialist economy by an inexorable necessity. Here alienation is carried to an extreme: the movement by which man at last attains human dignity is conceived as a purely natural necessity.

In Marx too, nature is, in truth, a ruse. Man is subjugated by what he himself produces; that is, he is governed by human forces whose ruse consists in appearing inhuman, material (in the mechanistic sense), and natural. In this sense, what Marx reveals is that the natural or purely material does not exist: nature is man in disguise, or, as Marx says, Marxian naturalism is a humanism. That is why this materialization of man has to be unmasked, why it is necessary to emancipate man, not by forcibly wresting him from the grip of natural necessity, but by inviting him to reappropriate, in nature, the obscure human freedom that has become nature.

Capitalism is man become nature: capitalism is a hidden humanity (Spirit) that must reappropriate itself. Just as Hegel's Nature naturally produces within itself, in the form of man, the natural being who has to reappropriate it; and just as Spirit, although it is the end of Nature, is nevertheless born of Nature and in it; so capitalism naturally produces within itself, in the proletariat, the natural being who has to reappropriate it, while the proletariat, although it is the end of capitalism, is nevertheless born of capitalism and in it. That is why human freedom seems to emerge from economic-natural determinism as Spirit emerges from Nature. That is why there is something like a necessity of freedom in Marx. Indeed, this freedom born of necessity would be inconceivable if freedom were not already the truth of necessity, and if freedom did not itself reappropriate itself in the alienated form of natural necessity. If, in

Hegel, Nature were not already Spirit in alienated form, Spirit would not be able to come forth from it to establish its Reign.

We could pursue these reflections. But the essential result would simply be to confirm that Marx is thoroughly informed by Hegelian truth. Moreover, Hegel is thereby illuminated from within in ways that are often unexpected, but that do him no disservice. Here is decisive proof: to return to the beginning of this debate, we have just seen that Hegelian necessity is so marked a presence at the heart of Marxist thought that Marx could not simply combat Hegel by occasionally turning his own weapons against him: he could not, in his critique of the *Philosophy of Right*, establish the inevitability of Hegelian error without finding himself the prisoner of Hegelian truth. This capture was not an unfortunate and, as it were, chance occurrence – it was substantial and profound. And Marx could not have consented to it as profoundly as he did if he had not taken this *seizure* for the truth.

We must, however, add the following: in proportion as Marx and Engels felt, cognized, and recognized the positive role of Hegel in their own thought, they accentuated the contradiction that runs through the *Philosophy of Right*. Of the dialectic, triplicity, alienation, or negativity, they claimed to have retained only the *form* of Hegelian truth. Its specific content (Philosophy of Nature, Philosophy of Law, Philosophy of Religion) they rejected. Engels' distinction between the good dialectic and the bad system affirmed nothing other than this contradiction between form and content. The distinction was not purely verbal, since the Prussia Hegel endorsed became the target of Marx's fiercest attacks, conducted with Hegel's own weapons. It is thus not the least of the paradoxes of Marxism, which has time and again accused Hegel of formalism, that it retains Hegelian form as valid, while condemning the perversion of the content.

Thus the criticism of the bad content once again directs our attention to the good form; but it is a solitary form, whose quality alienates it from the content imposed upon it. The only way to salvage this form is to abandon its carcass. Thus we find ourselves confronting Hegel's Prussia with increased embarrassment. What is the significance of this foreign body in Hegel? If we cannot admit the necessity of this error, might there be an error of necessity in Hegel, and something like a degeneration of the Truth?

C. Countenancing the Content*

It would seem that we have worked our way to the end of the critical undertaking by which the post-Hegelian mind attempted to dispel the

---

* The title of this section, *La bonne contenance*, is an untranslatable pun. *Bonne* means 'good'. *Contenance* means 'contents' in the sense of 'capacity', 'volume', but also 'countenance' in the sense of demeanour; whence *faire bonne contenance*, 'to put up a good front'.

vague malaise that Hegel's all-embracing enterprise inspired in it. To Hegel's claim to have revealed the absolute content of the accomplished totality, we opposed, to begin with, the arguments purporting to point up the defects of the form (A); proceeding point by point, we saw that Hegel's supposedly questionable mediations, those of the *Logos* and the dialectic, had been intended by Hegel himself as internal mediations, that they did not exist outside the totality, and, as a result, that they ultimately found their way back into the absolute content. This return led us to a consideration of one of the most contestable aspects of the content, which we conceived as defective (B). Marx's critique helped us grasp the perversity of the Hegelian state, but we saw that, far from succeeding in its attempt to extend the perversion of the content to the form, this critique was itself, down to its deepest levels, drawn back into the embrace of Hegelian necessity. Nevertheless, there was here no *return* analogous to that observed in connection with the first point: whereas the defective form made its way back into the content (A), the defective content failed to make its way back into the good form (B). Our analysis has thus enabled us to single out an apparently irreducible entity, which will henceforth present itself to us as a residual content. Here, then, is the point we need to focus on in order to cull the reasons for this malaise from Hegel himself, and finally dispel it.

1. What, then, is the necessity in Hegel of this residue which has proven alien to Hegelian necessity? That very contradiction defines it. Marx pronounced the word: 'here . . . we find one of Hegel's inconsistencies.'[253] We were unable to locate the reason for this inconsistency in the system; it must, then, lie outside it. This recourse to an outside, which presupposes that there is an outside which has not been reappropriated, is, paradoxically, the course of history as experienced by Hegel, which, according to his system of thought, is precisely the interiority of Spirit. Thus this reason would strike at the very essence of the Hegelian totality. Let us examine the point more closely.

Our analysis of the content (ch. II) was deliberately restricted to the level of the *Phenomenology of Spirit*, which presents us with a remarkably coherent body of thought: Hegel's thinking as it stood around 1806. The *Elements of the Philosophy of Right*, from which we have drawn Hegel's conception of the state, dates, in contrast, from 1821. The Hegelian perversion is difficult to understand if these dates are not taken into account. 1806 was the year of the Battle of Jena and the triumphant procession of Napoleon's armies across Europe. All enlightened minds saw the French victories as proof that the Revolution was sweeping the whole world before it. By contrast, 1821 was meditation over an illusion, or, rather, the day after the meditation. Europe had rid itself not only of the Emperor, but of the French and the Revolution as well. The rebellion of 1813 had unleashed nationalist forces which the traditional hierarchies had swiftly moved to bring under control, and which they then subjected to the reactionary order of the Holy Alliance. Just as, in 1806, the Revolution had captivated people's attention with its unforeseen grandeur and triumphant promises, so, in 1821, the disappointment felt by the best minds merely offered further proof that the Revolution had been crushed.

The civil servant Hegel probably had no shortage of reasons to teach the thinker Hegel the force of the *fait accompli*. The freedom of the professor in Jena was undoubtedly the youth of his thought, but it was also Napoleon just under his windows. The Berlin professor of 1821, in contrast, fed his freedom on memories alone, under the watchful eye of a well-informed police force and a well-entrenched sovereign whose rule he legitimized.[254] We would be ill-advised to interpret the power the present had over Hegel as primarily due to a lack of courage. It is better regarded as Hegel's acceptance of his concrete vocation, in the most rigorous sense: he would not have been faithful to himself if he had not thought the real present of history. Not being able to leap over one's own time is not, for the philosopher, a restrictive limitation: it is not only the condition of his existence, but also accords with his will, since philosophy 'is the thought of the real'. It is, furthermore, the site of his concrete freedom, given that the freedom which is not the freedom of the present content is merely flight to an imaginary beyond, or retreat into the void of subjectivity. Hence it is illegitimate to pit the philosopher of the *Phenomenology of Spirit* against the philosopher of the *Philosophy of Right* on this point, and to reproach the latter for the intention one endorses in the former. One cannot honestly say that the truth is deferred in the *Phenomenology* and comes due in the *Philosophy of Right*. This obvious fact, which becomes obvious in historical perspective, i.e., with the benefit of hindsight, is valid only for us. Yet such is Lukács's interpretation of this point. On his view, the *Phenomenology* is revolutionary by virtue of its very incompleteness: this explains why we can derive a philosophy of action from it. In 1806, everything was in motion, and the outcome unknown. By 1821, it was known how things had ended up; everything was over. Our works and days are ended when the owl takes flight. Truth is a lifeless totality, and wisdom, as Nietzsche would later say, is nothing more than 'crows on a corpse'. Thus there was no longer any question of hope or action; Hegel's thinking, revolutionary in 1806, had turned conservative by 1821. This due date brought only decline [*cette échéance est une déchéance*].

A retrospective reading of this sort presupposes that Hegel presented his thought of 1806 as anticipation, that its truth was still to come. Doubtless certain texts are ambiguous when taken in isolation from all the others; thus the new age, which constitutes the fulfilment of Spirit, is at first only a dawn and a presentiment of the sun. Yet this early morning is more than a promise, since the sun comes up all at once over a new world.[255] This glorious day is the Absolute Knowledge that closes the *Phenomenology*, together with its Absolute Content. Truth is in Hegel a sun that never sets – it is night abolished and the reign of light, or, better still, night become light.[256] Thus if Spirit in the *Phenomenology* resembles a dawn, this has strictly to do with the light's recovery of itself. The movement of things here, in the accomplished totality, is simply the content taking possession of its absolute element: 'But the actuality of this simple whole consists in those various shapes and forms which have become its moments, and which will now develop and take shape afresh, this time in their new element, in their newly acquired meaning.'[257] Hence this movement does not affect the totality as such. It is, rather, the apparent movement of the totality, which passes itself in review in the Logic: in Absolute Knowledge, the 'difference [of the moments of Spirit] is only the difference of content'.[258] At this point, knowledge [*connaissance*], is simply an inventory of absolute Truth. This is what permits us to say that, in the *Phenomenology*, the truth appears at dusk, since, in this sense, history has ended.[259] But this dusk is only a retrospective image, for the evening in which thought first takes wing is the noon of Absolute Knowledge. At all events, the *Phenomenology* is not an anticipation or premonition of the truth, but the good news itself: time has been fulfilled, God made man, absolute content attained. But if *both* the *Phenomenology* and the *Philosophy of Right* signal the Advent of the Absolute in present reality, and are therefore both *the truth* that has come to term, how is this dualism of the truth to be understood? What explains it? How are we to conceive this double identity of reality and the truth?

Let us turn first to the *Phenomenology*. There can be no doubt that a number of auspicious events helped Hegel articulate, in the *Phenomenology*, his profoundest idea: the identity of truth and reality. If he differs from classical philosophers, it is by virtue of his understanding of events; but it is also owing to these events themselves, which, for the first time in history, prove equal to their own truth. Hegel does not conceive himself as does the Platonic philosopher, who flees this world for the heaven of the ideas; he thinks his temporal condition, and sees the maturity he announces come to fulfilment in his own time. Prior to Hegel, truth was a recourse against the real, a refuge, hidden essence, or controlling law; the real was a falling off from the true, and took the form of process, accident, or mode. In this alienation (the true estranged from the real), philosophers merely thought the alienation of the historical totality. That is what leads Hegel to legitimize their dualism: in an historical world in which the truth is estranged from reality, philosophers could think their unity only as a beyond or a contradiction. This is so rigorous a conception that Hegel himself would have been unable to break free of it by virtue of his genius alone, if history had not brought about the reconciliation he announced. Such is the true meaning of the supposed complicity of history. Before being the philosopher of the courses in Berlin, who deciphered the mystery of events, and seemed to be privy to the secrets of a complaisant history, Hegel had been the citizen of an apocalyptic age in which contradictions were resolved and the veils torn away. He was a lucky man, the chance accomplice of the Advent of the Absolute. What is involved here is not modesty. Hegel was merely the last actor in a drama that the whole of humanity was bringing to a conclusion; he was simply the voice which announced the fulfilment of the Last Days. If the totality were not being realized before his eyes, if the Kingdom of God were not being established in his times, he could not have pretended to bring heaven down to earth in his work and to herald the hitherto always thwarted identity of truth and reality. If he escaped alienation in its classical form, put the philosopher in himself to death, and pronounced himself a Sage, it was simply because the object of his philosophical consciousness had made philosophical consciousness its proper element – because, *by means of* the prodigious labour of history, reality had at last conquered its own element in the truth and surmounted the dualism of alienation. Truth and reality were thus *brought into harmony* in the historical totality that Hegel experienced: 'The highest and final aim of philosophic science [is] to bring about, through the *ascertainment of this harmony*, a reconciliation of the self-conscious reason with the reason which is in the world.'[260]

This concrete harmony, thanks to which Hegel abolished philosophy and founded Science, is, then, fundamental, and is quite simply to be sought in the historical events of Hegel's day. The French Revolution realized the abstract universality of the Enlightenment, abolished the monarchy, which the literature of the eighteenth century had already set tottering in the mind of the age, killed the king (where Sade saw a simulacrum of parricide, Hegel saw the abolition of Lordship – an organic social structure – and thus a potential end to alienation), and established the very opposite of monarchy in the dictatorship of the law, which penetrated, in the Terror, to the innermost reaches of people's consciousness. Through this dramatic internalization, the Revolution at last brought about universal recognition. The revolutionary state Bonaparte seized control of was dominated by the symbolic dialectic of liberty, equality, and fraternity: fraternity was the totality in which the extreme form of subjectivity (liberty) was reconciled with the extreme form of objectivity (equality). The totality of the state was now organic, a *Tun aller und jeder*, was its own reason and substance. Not only was the moment of the master-slave duality annulled; so too was the abstract dictatorship of universality (Robespierre), and the very possibility of a conception of social contract like Rousseau's, in which individuals are supposed to agree to respect a conventional structure. The will was no longer that of an individual, but of a people, in which each was freely granted recognition of his essential being and devoted himself to the common good. The Revolution organizing its regime even as it mobilized it against the outside world, transforming subjects into citizens, both juridically and in actual fact – since the Frenchman worked and fought[261] – this prodigious spectacle represented, for Hegel, the Real Presence of the organic totality he had dreamt of in the Greece of his youth, and vainly sought in the historical and ideological universe of the Enlightenment. The last act of this miraculous advent was rung in when Napoleon spread the Revolution across Europe, transforming the world into concrete universality. 'This was,' Hegel said towards the end of his life, 'a glorious mental dawn. All thinking beings shared in the jubilation of this epoch. Emotions of a lofty character stirred men's minds at that time; a spiritual enthusiasm thrilled through the world, as if the reconciliation between the divine and the secular was now first accomplished.'[262] It is hard for us to imagine the profound repercussions these events had on the noblest minds, who literally seemed to have been struck by a revelation. One need only think of the aged Kant suddenly uneasy in his solitude, or of Goethe prophesying the birth of a new world in the twilight of the defeat at Valmy, in order to understand how Hegel could affirm that his voice added nothing to these prodigious events beyond the consciousness of their ultimate grandeur.

Such was the basis of Hegel's audacity. It was not the world he lived in that reflected Hegel's own audacity back to him; it was Hegel who held up the mirror to the world's audacity, that is, to the truth of the world. Hegelian truth is *bei sich* in the real, because it encounters itself in a world that has come to embody this truth. It is in this sense that Hegel supersedes idealism, as he himself says; and, if he founds absolute idealism, he necessarily founds it on absolute realism. This absolute is the third term in which absolute truth fuses with absolute reality. 'What is rational is actual; and what is actual is rational.'[263] This late pronouncement of Hegel's acquires its deepest meaning, like most of the aphorisms of his maturity, at the level of the concrete totality of 1806. It can even be said that the whole system was built up at this level, so that, if we ignore this shaping influence and the intuition of a totality which was simultaneously real and true, it becomes extremely difficult to grasp the structure of Hegel's thought, especially the Logic, the relation of Logic to Nature and Spirit, the dialectic, and the legitimacy of the system as form, that is, circularity. It was by invoking this profound identity between real and formal circularity that we were able to meet the objections to the effect that the form was defective. Hegel could not repudiate the idea of the identity of truth and reality, the absolute condition of the system's coherence; if he had, it would have fallen apart. Indeed, the fact that the idea of circularity was maintained right up to the final texts proves that this identity was not an idea of Hegel's youth that gradually fell by the wayside, but that he defended it to the end, even in the unfortunate passages of the *Philosophy of Right* and *Philosophy of History*.

2. But what had become of this identity by 1821? The fact that Napoleonic Europe had collapsed, that the universal state had disintegrated into a series of narrow nationalisms, that the promises of the revolution had been snuffed out, monarchy restored, and a universal alliance of police forces established, provides eloquent testimony. Nothing remained of the Napoleonic totality but traces of war amidst ruins and extreme poverty; but the peace had grown up over all that. Of the Revolution, there remained a few law codes and concessions granted by the monarchies concerning the constitutions and the conduct of the Parliaments, concessions made for appearance's sake, and to guarantee the security of Europe's thrones. If the universal state did not exist, universality could hardly exist in the state, which was a compromise that 'preserved the forms' and duped the people – a sham universality, as Marx clearly saw. Could the totality of 1806, that fraternal union of free and equal men in a unified Europe, recognize itself in this confused mass of cavilling, hierarchically organized states, barricaded behind their borders and guarantees, and feeding pampered aristocrats, *nouveaux-riches* bourgeois, and poverty-stricken workers on the illusion of a merely verbal equality and freedom? In other words, could Hegel, in 1821, still discern in this general decline the substantial union between reality and truth he had discovered in Jena?

The tragedy of his position lies here. To acknowledge the obvious facts about Prussia would not only have been to denounce the defective content of the Prussian state (here we will say nothing about the concrete possibility and the consequences of such a disavowal, which would have jeopardized not only the career of the individual Hegel, but perhaps even his freedom), but, above all, to undermine the system as a whole. For if there is no necessity of error in Hegel's thought, the necessity of truth brooks no appeal. Thinking the truth of the Prussian state, i.e., thinking the essence of the defective content in terms of contradiction, would have obliged Hegel to acknowledge the dereliction of the totality, that is, the alienation of absolute content. To see in the Prussian bureaucracy and constitution a species of political formalism alien to the real people, which was forced to do real work, preoccupied by real cares, and, moreover, internally riven by economic contradictions, would have been to revive the dualism of form and content and lapse back into reflection. Hegel's claim, however, was to have attained the subject. To admit that the worker, the bourgeois, or even the aristocrat were not citizens, that is, immediately universal and leading 'a world-historical existence', as Marx puts it,[264] because their lives were divided between an occasional or ceremonial political existence and a daily routine of cares, work, and pleasure – to admit this simple fact would have been tantamount to denying that the individual had acquired true freedom, that the universal had become concrete and recognition universal. To acknowledge this defective content would have forced Hegel to revert to a pre-Hegelian position. It would have brought him back to the state of Fichte and Kant, and, a few details aside, to the general structure of the political world that had been the despair of his youth.

Moreover, via the state, the whole system would have been undermined. Alienation would have become the element, not only of historical reality, but also of Hegelian thought. But the circularity of the truth was predicated on nothing other than the circularity of absolute Spirit, on, that is, the reabsorption of alienation. Thus circularity itself would have been affected, and, with it, the profound inner bond of the system in which Hegel claimed to grasp the historical and ideological totality of the world. Once that bond had come undone, the system would have fallen to pieces, or, rather, the pieces would have reconstituted themselves and resumed their separate existences in a history without end; Kant himself, whose territory Hegel had so thoroughly occupied, would have regained his independence. As for the internal bond, the dialectic, if it maintained its claim to truth, that truth could henceforth only be an external one. We would have found ourselves facing either a truth distinct from reality, an internal law, or a beyond. Science would have relapsed into mere philosophy, while Absolute Knowledge would once again have become the mere love of knowledge, humbly making use of a method, discrete middle terms, ruses and demonstrations. In this 'hunt for the truth', the thinker would again have played his role without thinking it, would have caught the hare while forgetting the course, or forgotten the hunter in announcing the hunt.

Could Hegel have thus repudiated his own thought, destroying it with his own hands? Should he have acknowledged the presence of his own truth in the very necessity of this destruction that would have driven him with relentless logic toward his death – the reason for which would at least have been his? Should he have been born again of this reason, and re-entered a race without end, in which, thinking to take possession of himself, he could only have clutched his own shadow while suffering the ordeal of a bad infinity? Such consistency would have forced him to adopt an idealism of the Kantian variety, to deny the reality of the Idea and proclaim the untruth of reality. He would have had either to abandon absolute circularity and bow to contemporary reality, or else abandon the contemporary content so as to save, at that price, the system of absolute truth. In Hegel's torn and divided world, it was no longer possible to keep a grip on the two extremes simultaneously.

Yet all indications are that Hegel set himself just this absurd task. He maintained, in alienation, the demand for unity; but, as alienation had once again become the element of his existence and thought, he encountered the limits, precisely, of the contradiction within which he was attempting to think unity; this unity was thus a prisoner of the contradiction it was meant to resolve. We observed an analogous process in Kant. The same thing happened to Hegel. He was unwilling to renounce his circular system and the absolute unity of reality and truth. He upheld, at all costs, the claim that this unity existed; and, as it was no longer real, it became the ideal unity, the insubstantial middle term, which Marx unmasks in the Philosophy of the State.

Hegel nevertheless clung to his original requirements. He persisted in thinking the truth at the level of the real, form at the level of content. Necessity accordingly became a *ruse*. In Hegel, the concept of the ruse is contradiction *in actu*, the necessity of non-necessity, unreason's revenge on reason. The ruse wants victims, perpetually: once seen through, it is no longer a ruse, but disarmed naiveté. The ruse's element is secrecy; in this sense, it is an absolute secret for its victims, and Hegel makes no bones about this when he shows that ordinary people are too limited by nature to grasp the reason at work in history. These blind men, whether bourgeois or workers, are in good company; there are others of their kind who are more illustrious, but just as obtuse. The Monarch and his officers, who are the ruse of the state, think they are privy to the secrets of the universal: their self-assurance is but one more ruse. They merely generate, by way of wars, a universality they themselves do not see, a universality that dupes them. The drama of the civil servant of 1806 had at least been a real one. The civil servant of Jena, who incarnated the universal that was Prussia, suddenly saw true universality emerging in the person of the enemy, and, recognizing it, was won over to it; the situation was perfectly clear, falsity was giving way before truth, the only conceivable debate involved questions of conscience or moral scruple; the universal was at least an honest universal. By 1821, the tragedy had turned to farce: the civil servant in Berlin could be quite sure he would never face such a crisis, and it did not so much as occur to him that, in this service, he was celebrating a mystery; his untroubled conscience was not pure complacency, but necessity, because it is in the clash between such universal causes that universal history develops its ruses. Spirit is literally hidden in History, as it is in Nature; it would be an enshrouded, buried Spirit, and absolutely Dead, if imposture had no for-itself.

Here we see the other pole of the contradiction, in which the ruse reveals itself for what it is. An absolute ruse that does not know itself to be a ruse is literally unthinkable. This is the monstrous temptation that Descartes had already rejected in rejecting the Evil Genius, in whom Hamelin rightly detected the hypothesis of the world's absolute irrationality. There is no universal imposture, for, if the impostor imposes on himself, he is, by that very fact, caught at his own game, and the rules of the game are transformed into the rules *tout court*: the universal ruse cancels itself out in universal necessity. To persist as ruse, it has to preserve the distance that permits it to posit and maintain itself as such. At the limit, this awareness of the ruse is nothing other than cunning [*rusé*] consciousness in the pure state; in other words, Providence is 'absolute cunning'.[265] The appeal to the notion of the ruse is, accordingly, an acknowledgement of the contradiction that springs up at the level of the defective content, that between reality and truth – and this evasive solution is merely the acknowledgement that that contradiction is irresolvable.

Thus, by way of the ruse, it appears that the truth is conceived as reality's secret, and this secret banished [*refoulé*] to the beyond. To be sure, Hegel, at least, is on familiar terms with God; this old-fashioned hermeticism contrasts strangely with the protestations of the *Phenomenology*. Hegel now asks for nothing more than good fortune, which he expects from the Monarch: let the mysteries be spread far and wide, let his philosophy become the state philosophy, since it is not possible to make the state philosophical. Hegel here follows in Plato's footsteps, but at a goodly distance: he uses the king not to realize the truth, but to preach it. But the king has no grounds for alarm: this truth is not dangerous, it legitimates state, king, and hierarchy, and even the squalor of the present. It makes out 'the rose in the cross of the present, and . . . delight[s] in the present'.[266] One has to put a good face on the defective content.* Yet, while the official philosopher is at pains to impose upon the world a truth that is not one, his own truth slips away, and, as it is not at home in the end result, takes refuge in its origins. Whereas, in the *Phenomenology*, the historical totality absorbs and inspires all possible meanings, the order is inverted in Hegel's last works; increasingly, it is Logic that plays the role of Spirit. The critical misunderstanding that sees Hegelianism as a panlogism has its origins in this inversion, which reproduces, within the system, truth's retreat before the world.

This retreat transforms Hegelian unity into a contradictory totality: the system becomes the absolute truth of a content that is external to it, and that experiences its externality in its contradictions. Circularity is driven back into the element of thought, whereas reality lies outside it: the Hegelian Idea becomes a Kantian idea again, i.e., an ideal. It is, however, an ideal that has discovered its own element and recovered its origins in it: at least in thought, it is a real circularity, whereas the Kantian idea is a beyond even for thought itself. That is why this concrete ideal cannot be surpassed philosophically, and can be proposed as a

---

* *Il faut faire bonne contenance au mauvais contenu.* See translator's note, p. 140.

guide to action. In this sense, Marx is right when he says that Hegel is the last philosopher – but he does not mean it the way Hegel did. Hegel is the last philosopher without being the Sage of the *Phenomenology*; he is the last philosopher because, in the form of the circularity of the concept, he wrests philosophy's own kingdom from philosophy. All that remains is to translate Hegelian circularity into reality, to transform philosophy into a world, and, to that end, to seek in the actually existing historical world the dialectical element that will enable man to overcome alienation and render history circular. This is the Marxist transition from contemplation to action, and the transformation of history into universal history,[267] i.e., the elevation of the content to the level of freedom.

But this very transition poses the problem of the circularity that exists in thought, revealing its ambiguity. For the realization of the truth is not possible if the truth is not a real anticipation, that is, an implicit universality developed by history and revolutionary action; if the realization of the truth is not, in some sort, the development of reality in its own truth. What is required, says Marx, is not to confer empirical existence upon the truth, but to lead empirical existence towards its own truth. This objective would simply seem to be the contrary of the advent of absolute content: it is up to history to conquer its own truth in concrete reality, a truth Hegel worked out only in the abstract element of thought. On this view, Hegel only reached the furthest extreme of self-consciousness in its own element; that circular extreme would thus be an allegory heralding the circular totality of the absolute content. For the empty Idea calls for a reality that is not the fruit of chance, but that, even as it realizes the Idea, legitimizes the Idea's own element (that of abstract thought). To this ambiguity of the truth there corresponds, in Marx, the ambiguity of the real. Marx concentrates on the empirical content of his times, and thus on the concrete – the real, signifying totality. But this totality has not reached fulfilment; its significations would consequently be suspended and indecipherable if they were not already, in this contradictory state, called upon, as it were, to come into their truth. They bear their own truth within them, in an obscure necessity that demands to be thought. Or, if one prefers, they have reached the point of maturity and disequilibrium in which the revolutionary future is already visible in the present. With a modicum of attention, humankind could discern within itself the implicit universality that is destined to mature and claim its kingdom. Speaking of the communist workers, Marx says: 'They have no ideals to realize, but to set free the elements of the new society with which old collapsing bourgeois society itself is *pregnant*.'[268] The proletariat is this implicit universality; in its present state, it contains the future and the freedom of all humankind. It is, potentially, the circularity of absolute content.

*

3.   This potential of the real poses, precisely, the fundamental problem of our time with regard to the revelation and decline of Hegelianism. As we said in the introduction to this study, we are all caught up in the decomposition of Hegel, in a double sense.

On the one hand, no philosophical undertaking can do much more than resume and develop, abstractly, one or another moment pried loose from the Hegelian totality. Thus both Kierkegaard and the modern existentialists have appropriated Hegelian negativity in its subjective form, and contemporary philosophy has, paradoxically, constituted itself as a system on the basis of this abstract element of the system. In so doing, it has neglected the other aspect of Hegel, namely, substance. Similarly, Marxist thought has a tendency to retain the substantialist side of Hegel – objective necessity and the law of the development of history, conceived as an objective totality – a tendency to preserve, 'at least on the ideological level', objective negativity, while neglecting the depth of subjective negativity. Again, contemporary phenomenology seems to draw its inspiration from the ideas of a dialectical totality and an 'abandoned' dialectic, both very close to Hegelian phenomenological 'experience' – without, however, attaining circularity. Whether or not it realizes its dependence, contemporary thought has been created out of Hegel's decay, and draws sustenance from it. Ideologically speaking, then, we are dominated by Hegel, who comes back into his own in modern philosophical endeavour; and this dependence is genuine, since it does not break free of the decay of Hegel, i.e., the transformation of Hegelian truth into ideology. Modern *ideologies* are reappropriated by Hegelian *ideology* – right down to their deliberate ingratitude – as if by their mother-truth.

This restitution would not modify the status of Hegelian truth, if the decomposition of Hegel had merely given rise to *ideologies*. But, to a certain extent, it has also engendered a *real world* in the form of workers' movements and revolutionary action. We said at the beginning of this work that Hegel had become our world. The whole of our present problem is that this world is not only an ideological, but also a real political world. Hegel is present amongst us not only as truth, but also as reality. Nevertheless, the decomposition of Hegel no longer permits us to conceive the relationship between this truth and reality in Hegelian terms: the part of Hegel which has become reality does not coincide with the Hegelian circularity that has been driven back into ideological truth. In other words, the Hegelian necessity we have described as the Marxian for-itself is compelled to beat the same retreat in Marx himself as it does in the world. That is why the status of this necessity is so obscure in Marxism, and why Marxism both adopts and rejects it, as the notion of turning the dialectic 'right side up' indicates: Marxist reality accepts Hegelian truth only if it is 'placed back on its feet' (what would circularity put back on its feet be?). One may say, then, that, in Marxism, the real status of Hegelian necessity does not coincide with its ideological status; or, in other words, that Marxist practice [*comportement*], which is both real and fruitful, has not yet grasped its own structure, because it has not yet clearly conceived the place Hegelian truth occupies within its own reality. This failure draws our attention back to our own time and, even if ideologically, poses for contemporary 'abstract' philosophies the problem of Hegel's status in our world. Indeed, we live in a world in which, on the one hand, Hegelian truth exceeds its purely ideological status, whilst, on the other, Hegelian reality refuses to recognize Hegelian ideology as its truth. This duality, this contradiction, invites reflection on the problem of the intellectual structure of our times.

This is not the place to examine the problem, for that would take us well beyond the bounds of our subject and competence. We would simply like to set out a number of elements that emerge from our study; they will allow us, perhaps, to adumbrate the general features of this structure.

The implications of the disintegration of Hegelianism and the contradictions of Hegel's posterity establish a first point: the total structure of this real world is not circular, or, at least, inasmuch as the totality has not been fully realized, its circularity is not *in actu*: it is possible to conceive of it as truth, but it is not a presently existing reality. We are therefore condemned to a certain dualism between truth and reality.

And, with that, we find ourselves back in an intellectual structure which is in certain respects analogous to that of the immediate pre-Hegelian period, i.e., transcendentalism. Marxist practice can teach us something about this point, because of the fundamental importance which revolutionary action attaches to conditions; more generally, it can teach us about the pre-eminence of the concrete historical totality, which literally becomes the *a priori* condition of any undertaking whatsoever. It is one of the major themes of revolutionary *praxis* that it is not possible to attempt just anything at any given moment, that revolution is not to be confused with revolt, that if the 'existing conditions' are not favourable, any immediate action is merely dangerous agitation. The same structure emerges from scientific practice, which has a conception of a kind of necessity of discovery. Research is no longer a matter of happy discoveries that depend solely on the genius of the researcher. Rather, research and its results are subordinate to the pre-existent scientific totality as their *a priori* condition; they are subordinate, that is, to the organic set of hypotheses, theories, instruments and results in existence at a given point in the history of science. It is this conditioning totality that lends both revolutionary activity and scientific research their meaning; thus it appears, at any given moment, as the condition and *a priori* form in which every political and scientific content is cast.

However, this structure only distantly resembles Kantian transcendentalism, or, rather, sheds light on it by going beyond it. The transcendental in the political or scientific sense is at once *a priori*, inasmuch as it is the condition for any event, and also *a posteriori*, inasmuch as it is not deduced, but discovered. The necessity of the objective structure of the scientific or Marxist *a priori* is of the order of what modern phenomenologists call a '*de facto* necessity'. This remark will remind us of the paradox of the Kantian categories, which did not escape Hegel's notice. The categories of transcendental logic are derived from the table of judgements; hence they are *found*. Thus Kant was limited by the empirical nature of the content of transcendental logic; but he did not think it. He was unwilling to recognize that the *a priori* was *a posteriori*. Had he acknowledged this, he would have been obliged to conceive the existence of an empirical transcendental, the *a priori* character of the *a posteriori*, i.e., literally, at the level of his abstraction, Hegelian circularity. He would thus have been led to abandon the notion, not of the structure of the transcendental, but of its absolute nature, that is, the idea that it is eternal. Hence he would have had to conceive time not simply as an *a priori* form, but as the element of all form: he would have had to think history.

That is a major advance, and we are indebted to Hegel for it. Interpreting his thought freely, we may say that history (or Spirit) becomes the absolute totality that absorbs all possible meaning. If we abandon the idea of the end of history and the eternal nature of meanings, i.e., the absolute circularity of reality, then history becomes the general *element* in which we move and live; it becomes the concrete transcendental, the only place in which the entities and meanings that condition and determine us come into being. But since history is not over, there is no eternal transcendental logic, but rather, at every instant, an articulated historical structure which dominates the world in the manner of an *a priori*, and conditions it. The reality of history resides, from this standpoint, in the dialectical nature of the structure that conditions events, but is also transformed by them in its turn. The historical totality is a concrete, dialectical transcendental, a condition modified by what it conditions. Thus scientific discovery, shaped by the totality of theories and instruments, modifies them in its turn; over the course of history, the 'transcendental logic' of the sciences changes as a result of the advances science makes. Similarly, the economic and political structure that conditions revolutionary action is in turn modified by it.

But one point still requires clarification. Our examples display analogous structures, but do not tell us whether the essence of the historical totality coincides with the structure of transcendental reason; whether, in other words, the historical totality and reason are homogeneous. Here too Hegel paves the way. Today we know, thanks to him, the fundamental truth that there is no reason outside the community of consciousnesses that come face-to-face in struggle for mutual recognition. In this sense, Hegel took up and thought the positive content of the Kantian reservation, which identified reason as 'our reason'; he worked out the full meaning of that 'our', eschewing both solipsism and abstract idealism, by showing that reason is itself subject to the domination of the human totality, of the universe of consciousnesses in their concrete relations with one another. If Plato's slave ultimately discovers reason in the depths of his soul, if Descartes sought reason in his solitude and yet recognized that it is something shared, it is because the nature of reason is subject to that of human interdependence, or rather because reason, in the broad sense, is the concrete structure of human interdependence. That is why knowledge of history is not a knowledge external to history; that is why temporality is not a category or a form; that is why any system of thought that would depict the I as a transcendental form, without conceiving the concrete totality conditioning all rational discourse, can only be abstract. If we must always conceive the transcendental as reason, it cannot be anything other than the organic reason of the given historical totality, that is, an element of the human structure of the world.

Thus we are brought back round to our thesis. The disintegration of Hegelianism thrusts us back into transcendentalism. But the transcendental which conditions the *a priori* activity (theoretical or practical) of man has, now, conquered its nature: it is the concrete historical totality. We owe this conception of history as basic element and signifying totality to Hegel. It is likewise owing to him that we are able to identify the rational nature of this totality with the nature of the human totality. But this is a truth touched on in passing and buried in the *Phenomenology*; Hegel himself failed to draw its major inference. To say that the historical human totality is the totality to which all else must be referred, and the *a priori* condition of all human activity, is a truth as abstract and empty as the domination of the transcendental I would be in Kant, in the absence of the table of categories. In the fundamental structure of the human totality, Marx gives us the table of human categories that govern our time. *Capital* is our transcendental analytic. Such would seem to be the significance of Marx's work: the discovery and appropriation of the human categories in the socio-economic structure of our day.

This undertaking has to be understood in a very broad sense: because reason is the self-consciousness of the human totality, this determinate social structure is the *a priori* condition of all human activity – aesthetic, scientific, political, etc. Thus the present period throws into clear relief the condition of science, which, by way of the vast collective enterprises indispensable to modern research, is discovering its dependence on the industrial capacity, i.e., the economic totality, of the world. Modern 'scientific categories' are extremely concrete: contemporary science is dominated by the production of its instruments (the cyclotron), or the substances it experiments with (uranium, heavy water, etc.), which remind us of the effort humanity expends on work, and of its structure. Marx merely sketched these perspectives; a vast amount of epistemological research will have to be carried out to establish the table of modern scientific categories. Yet it will not be enough to produce this inventory, if we do not simultaneously attempt to determine the relation of these epistemological categories to the socio-economic categories that command them. Here, what Marxism has put forward is still embryonic. Yet it seems to lead to a conception of science dominated by the human character of scientific appropriation. When discussing experience, Kant always insisted that experience was *ours*; but he did not specify the nature of this *ours*. Contemporary science, in the Marxist conception, is marked by the tendency to seize on this *ours* and think it as the dominant characteristic of science. Accordingly, the essence of science would be historical, not natural, and the very object of science would be subject to the domination of historical categories. In Marxist statements about nature, the Kantian ambiguity vis-à-vis the given of sense experience reappears. Nature does not exist in a pure state; it is given only in human apprehension, which is historical (only the atolls that have surged up out of the sea, remarks Engels ironically, are purely natural). Yet the categories of science do not exhaust what is given in nature, because, without it, they would be of small use. What appears in this ambiguity is merely the contradiction between reality and truth that we observe in the disintegration of Hegelianism.

If the world of science has not been well explored, the world of politics is, thanks to Marx, infinitely clearer; and, as it is in this domain that we gain access to the basic structure of the human totality, it is there that the destiny of our times will be played out. If our information is not too inaccurate, it is at this level that we should try to define the structure of Marxist practice. Marx understood that the transcendental was history, but he did not consider it possible to think history in general, apart from the *concrete content* of the dominant historical totality. He therefore determined the socio-economic structure of capitalist society, positing this world as a contradictory totality in which economic categories dominated the sheer diversity of human matter. Yet he did not posit the categorial totality as eternal (as did Kant, and also Hegel, unbeknownst to himself, when he proclaimed the end of history or the validity of the Prussian state in an ongoing history). He conceived this totality as dialectical, that is, as modified by the very manifold that it conditioned. Finally, he maintained, within contradiction itself, the obvious fact of the concrete unity of the categories with the manifold in concrete labour. Kant did the same in his discussion of the transcendental imagination.

But, in Kant, the totality is not dialectical. That is why this median unity is, in Kant, a mediate unity. In Marx, by contrast, the categorial dialectic makes possible the immediate unity of the labourer and his product, forged at the level of the manifold. Thus the revolutionary effort can be considered, in its entirety, as the reappropriation of the economic categories by the manifold of human matter, that is, as the appropriation of the transcendental by the empirical, the appropriation of the form by the content. That is why the Marxist movement is a materialism, arguing, as it does, the domination of matter; but also a humanism, since this matter is human matter, struggling against inhuman forms. That is why this struggle can be imagined as something other than the 'infinite task' of the Kantian Idea, and why the socialist state can be conceived as something other than a 'transcendental accident'. Revolutionary action can, at least formally, conceive of the day when the human totality will be reconciled with its own structure.

These significations are nevertheless not reducible to pure determinations within the element of thought. We do not find ourselves in the transparent circularity of Hegelian truth, but in a concrete world whose significations are enveloped by concrete realities. The Marxist movement *is* its own signification; it is not necessarily the one it gives out as its own. The disintegration of Hegelianism is tangible even in the difficulty reality has in conceiving its own truth. If we attempt to determine the intellectual structure of this post-Hegelian world, our objective cannot be to re-establish a definitive schema. For us, the future is in the secret movements of the present content; we are caught up in a still obscure totality which we must bring into the light.

Notes

In these notes, we have kept the system of abbreviations Althusser used for certain of Hegel's works in French translation. Below is a list of the works they stand for, together with the corresponding English translations cited here. Where appropriate, references have also been provided to Hegel, *Werke in zwanzig Bänden*, Suhrkamp, Frankfurt, 1970, and to Marx and Engels, *Werke*, Dietz, Berlin, 1983, abbreviated W and MEW, respectively.

Phn: *Phénoménologie de l'esprit*, 2 vols, trans. Jean Hyppolite, Aubier, Paris, 1939–41; *Hegel's Phenomenology of Spirit*, trans. A. V. Miller, Oxford, 1977.

Ph. D.: *Principes de la philosophie du droit*, trans. André Kaan, Gallimard, Paris, 1940; *Elements of the Philosophy of Right*, ed. Allen Wood, trans. H. B. Nisbet, Cambridge University Press, Cambridge, 1991.

Log. Véra: *Logique*, 2 vols, trans. Auguste Véra, 2nd edn, Germer Baillère, Paris, 1874; *The Logic of Hegel*, trans. William Wallace, Oxford, Clarendon, rev. A. V. Miller, 1975 (Part 1 of the *Encyclopædia*).

Ph. Esprit Véra: *Philosophie de l'esprit*, 2 vols, trans. Auguste Véra, Germer Baillère, Paris, 1867–69; *Hegel's Philosophy of Mind, together with the Zusätze*, trans. William Wallace and A. V. Miller, Oxford, Clarendon, 1971 (Part 3 of the *Encyclopædia*).

Nohl: *Theologische Jugendschriften*, Éditions Hermann Nohl, Tübingen, 1907; partially translated in *Hegel's Early Theological Writings*, trans. T. M. Knox and Richard Kroner, Chicago, University of Chicago, 1948, repr. Philadelphia, University of Pennsylvania, 1971, and *Three Essays, 1793–1795*, trans. Peter Fuss and John Dobbins, South Bend, Indiana, Notre Dame University Press, 1984.

1. Moses Hess, 'Die gegenwärtige Krise der deutschen Philosophie', cited in Bernard Groethuysen, 'Origines du Socialisme en Allemagne', *Revue philosophique de la France et de l'étranger*, 95, 1923, p. 382.
2. *Philosophy of Right*, Addendum to paragraph 21 [Nisbet, p. 53; W, 7:73–4].
3. *Encyclopædia*, §60 [Wallace, pp. 91–2; W, 8:144].
4. 'Philosophy is ... the comprehension of the present and the actual.' *Ph. D.*, p. 29 [Nisbet, p. 20; W, 7:24].
5. Bernard Groethuysen, 'La conception de l'État chez Hegel et la philosophie politique en Allemagne', *Revue philosophique de la France et de l'étranger*, 97, 1924, p. 180.
6. 'Insanity ... is nothing else but the extreme limit of sickness to which [the understanding] can succumb.' *Ph. Esprit Véra* I, 390 [Wallace, p. 130; W, 10:170].
7. *Phn.* I, 341 [Miller, p. 250; W, 3:309].
8. *Ibid.*, II, 200 [Miller, p. 409; W, 3:494].
9. Karl Marx, *Œuvres philosophiques*, trans. Jacques Molitor, Vol. VI, Costes, Paris, 1937, p. 91 ['Economic and Philosophical Manuscripts' {hereafter '1844 Manuscripts'}, in *Early Writings*, trans. and ed. T. B. Bottomore, McGraw-Hill, New York, 1963, p. 216; *MEW*, Supplementary Vol., Part 1, p. 586].
10. *Phn.* I, 171 [Miller, p. 122; W, 3:159].
11. A parallel can be drawn between this attitude and the way the contemporary philosophers of existence and *engagement* proceed. Philosophy, existence, commitment – these terms make strange bedfellows, and their conjunction would be merely ridiculous, if it did not point to a deep[er] cause than paradox: only the man who is uncommitted becomes the thinker of commitment, elevating commitment into a system. His discourse is primarily a way of acknowledging his alienation and an attempt to conjure it away with words – a magical verbal consecration and justification of the one who speaks, who thinks he has exorcized his affliction once he has named it.
12. Letter of 26 January 1762 to Malesherbes [Jean-Jacques Rousseau, *Œuvres*, Vol. 1, Gallimard, Pléiade, Paris, p. 1140].
13. *Xenia* 170 [Johann Wolfgang von Goethe, *Werke*, Christian Wegner Verlag, Hamburg, 1949, Vol. 1, p. 234].
14. Novalis, *Schriften*, Editions Kuckhohn, Leipzig, 1929, Vol. 1, p. 179.
15. Hegel, address of 22 October 1818 at the University of Berlin [*Lectures on the History of Philosophy*, Vol. 1, trans. Elisabeth S. Haldane, Kegan Paul, London, 1892, pp. 14–15; W, 18:32–3].
16. *Phn.* II, 121 [Miller, p. 349; W, 3:423].
17. *Ibid.*, 113 [Miller, p. 340; W, 3:413].
18. *Ibid.*, 133 [Miller, p. 358; W, 3:434].
19. Cited by Edmond Vermeil, 'La pensée philosophique de Hegel', *Revue de métaphysique et de morale*, 38, 1931, p. 447.
20. *Ibid.*, p. 449 ['The German Constitution', in *Hegel's Political Writings*, trans. Sir Malcolm Knox, Clarendon, Oxford, 1964, p. 180; W, 1:504].
21. *Ibid.*, p. 447.
22. Jean Hyppolite, *Genèse et structure de la Phénomenologie de l'Esprit de Hegel*, Aubier, Paris, 1946, p. 417 [*Genesis and Structure of Hegel's* Phenomenology of Spirit, trans. Samuel Cherniak and John Heckman, Northwestern University Press, Evanston, Ill., 1974, p. 430].
23. 'When every man swept lightly over the earth like a God': Hölderlin.
24. See *Nohl*, pp. 23 [Fuss and Dobbins, p. 51; W, 1:36], 47 [Fuss and Dobbins, pp. 77–8; W, 1:69], 207 [Knox and Kroner, p. 138; W, 1:182], 215 [Knox and Kroner, p. 146; W, 1:197–8], 358, 359, 375 [W, 1:242–3].
25. Hölderlin, in contrast, made it the subject-matter of his poetry; merely evoking its absence endowed it with real existence for him. So it was that he sought to *actualize*

his fundamental intuition, that is, actually to recreate the unity time had destroyed. But he eventually had to admit the obvious: the final unity could not be the unity of the origin.

26. *Nohl*, pp. 33 [Fuss and Dobbins, p. 62; *W*, 1:51–2], 57 [Fuss and Dobbins, pp. 88–9; *W*, 1:82–3].
27. *Ibid.*, p. 25, translated in Jean Wahl, *Le Malheur de la Conscience dans la philosophie de Hegel*, Rieder, Paris, 1929, p. 69 [Fuss and Dobbins, p. 54; *W*, 1:39].
28. This is how Hegel understands St. Paul's words about love being the fulfilment of the law; the term *Aufhebung* is the equivalent of the word πλήρωμα in the Greek text.
29. *Phn.* I, 29 [Miller, p. 19; *W*, 3:36].
30. *Nohl*, p. 328 [Knox and Kroner, pp. 285–6; *W*, 1:401].
31. *Ibid.*, p. 330 [Knox and Kroner, pp. 287–8: *W*, 1:403].
32. *Ibid.*, p. 399.
33. 'Theoretically the Kantian philosophy is the ... *Aufklärung* reduced to method.' *Geschichte der Philosophie* [*Lectures on the History of Philosophy*, trans. Elizabeth S. Haldane and Frances H. Simpson, Vol. 3, London 1896, p. 426; *W*, 20:333].
34. See Kroner, who takes this phrase from Windelband (Richard Kroner, *Von Kant bis Hegel*, Tübingen, 1921–24, II, Introduction): 'Kant verstehen heißt über ihn hinausgehen' ['to understand Kant is to supersede him']. We do not mean to suggest that Hegel's undertaking can simply be reduced (so to speak) to a logical development of Kantianism (this is Kroner's interpretation), even if Hegel's own approach in the *History of Philosophy* tends to re-establish the continuity of forms and systems. It seems to us that the role of Kantianism in Hegel's thought must be approached from two different angles. First, Kant represents the truth of a certain moment of Hegelian consciousness. This thesis does not deny the originality of Hegel's insight, to which most authoritative writers on the subject (Dilthey, Jean Wahl) have repeatedly drawn attention; but it does aim to allow us to grasp, in the development of that insight stimulated by religious meditations, the moment of the encounter with Kant as the moment at which Hegelian consciousness encounters its truth – encounters, that is, itself. This encounter is merely an encounter; it could be termed a result only if Kant's truth actually coincided with Kant's own certitudes; Hegel's analysis rejects the apparent coincidence as illusory. On examination, the encounter thus turns out to be a supersession. Here the second aspect of Hegel's position comes into play. We are inclined to say, with Kroner, that to understand Kant is to supersede him; yet this formulation is so vague as to accommodate every imaginable ambiguity. To understand is always to supersede; but to what extent, and in what sense, can one speak of supersession in the case of a system of thought which is treated as an object, and which, like every corpse, lives on even in death? This supersession holds another, more concrete meaning for Hegel: he treats Kant, not as an object, but literally as a subject. What Hegel understands in Kant is not Kant, it is Hegel. For Hegel, then, to understand Kant is to supersede *himself*, to develop his own truth in a number of successive moments, each of which turns out to be the truth of its predecessor, and which identify themselves as moments even as they unfold. Kant is one such moment: he is an internalized presence everywhere in Hegel's thought (references to him occur in the *Theologische Jugendschriften* and continue to crop up in the courses Hegel gave in Berlin). This absorption or ingestion of Kant, who is transformed into Hegel's flesh and blood, stands Windelband's terms on their head. For the Hegel who can look back over his development as a whole, what emerges from the encounter with Kant is less the aspect 'understanding' than the aspect 'supersession'. It is because he superseded Kant in superseding himself that Hegel could reveal Kant's significance. Thus, after representing the truth of Hegelian consciousness, Kant receives his truth from Hegel himself, along with his place in history. *To supersede Kant is to understand him.* This ambiguity in Kant's relationship to Hegel provides a concrete example of the twofold phenomenological dialectic of the in-itself and the for-us, and also of the circular relationship between means and ends. From an historical point of view, it is not possible to neglect this appropriation of Kant by Hegel, who consciously takes possession of Kant as if of himself, divests himself of himself in Kant, and thus unveils him in the nakedness of his truth. From an historical, and, simply, critical standpoint,

our understanding of Kant can no more be considered apart from what Hegel reveals about him than our pleasure in ancient music can be considered apart from what modern music reveals about it. What is more, this encounter has something to teach us about the basic procedures of Hegelian thought, which absorbs the object in the subject and contemplates itself in the other.

35. 'But to seek to know before we know is as absurd as the wise resolution of Scholasticus, not to venture into the water until he had learned to swim.' *Log. Véra* I, 193 [Wallace, p. 14; W, 8:54].

36. *Geschichte der Philosophie*, ed. Bolland, Leiden, 1908, p. 993 [*History of Philosophy*, Vol. 3, p. 429; W, 20:334].

37. For Hegel, there is no escaping the truth. When one does not know [*connaître*] it, one encounters it in the very act by which one fails to recognize [*reconnaître*] it: 'What calls itself fear of error reveals itself rather as fear of the truth.' *Phn.* I, 67 [Miller, p. 47; W, 3:70].

38. *Ibid.*, 66 [Miller, p. 47; W, 3:69].

39. *Ibid.*, 66–7 [Miller, p. 47; W, 3:70].

40. *Glauben und Wissen*. [Althusser's translation is inaccurate. A closer translation of the sentence he cites part of reads: 'Thus the Ego is changed from a soul-thing into a qualitative noumenal entity, a noumenal and abstract unit which, as such, is absolute; absolute finitude, which had formerly been a dogmatic object, becomes now a dogmatic subject.' {*Faith and Knowledge*, trans. by W. Cerf and H. S. Harris, State University of New York Press, Albany, 1977, p. 83; W, 2:319}].

41. *Geschichte der Philosophie*, p. 997 [*History of Philosophy*, Vol. 3, p. 435; W, 20:341].

42. *Glauben und Wissen*, p. 25. [Althusser's translation is inaccurate. A closer translation reads, '{Kant} turned the true *a priori* back into a pure unity, i.e., one that is not originally synthetic' {*Faith and Knowledge*, p. 73; W, 2:309}].

43. *Log. Véra* I, 301 [Wallace, p. 72; W, 8:121].

44. They are estranged from one another only because they are estranged from themselves; each term encounters its own alienation in the other.

45. *Ph. Esprit Véra*, II, 32 [Wallace, p. 161; W, 10:209].

46. *Ibid.*, p. 15 [Wallace, p. 156; W, 10:202].

47. Here there appears a central Hegelian concept, 'element', which must be taken very broadly to mean field or *milieu*. The 'element' envelops the distinct terms it contains and is thus the unity within which they are given; from the standpoint of the terms, this unity is their truth.

48. *Glauben und Wissen*, p. 33 [*Faith and Knowledge*, p. 80; W, 2:316].

49. Whereas it is in fact their in-itself (*Geschichte der Philosophie*, p. 1003) [*History of Philosophy*, Vol. 3, p. 441; W, 20:348].

50. *Glauben und Wissen*, p. 27 [*Faith and Knowledge*, p. 75; W, 2:310–11].

51. *Ibid.*, p. 28 [*Faith and Knowledge*, p. 76; W, 2:311–12].

52. One thinks of Picasso's three masks and three musicians.

53. *Glauben und Wissen*, p. 29 [*Faith and Knowledge*, p. 77; W, 2:312]. Goethe, *Werke*, Jubiläumsausgabe, Vol. 16, pp. 275, 298–9. Let us note that Hegel seems to get things confused when he speaks of a king of bronze. The insubstantial king was made of gold, silver, and bronze, the other three kings of metal; it was the king of bronze, the true king, who did not fall to pieces.

54. *Encyclopædia*, Addendum to §52 [Wallace, p. 86; W, 8:137].

55. *Glauben und Wissen*, p. 35 [*Faith and Knowledge*, p. 81; W, 2:318].

56. The unity of the *sollen* is at once nostalgic and prospective. Its prospective character mysteriously counterbalances the nostalgia, providing a sort of compensation for it: the inability to *express* an original reality which Kant is unable to think, although it exists, is displaced onto the *realization* of an ultimate unity which Kant thinks in the form of the *sollen*, but which does not exist and is unrealizable. The terms of the totality – unity, reality, concept – are plainly all present here, but they are *parcelled out* between the two extremes. On the one hand, we have unity and reality, but not the concept; on the other, unity and the concept, but not reality. Finally, on the middle ground occupied by Kantian thought, we have the concept and reality, but not unity. Two points appear here:

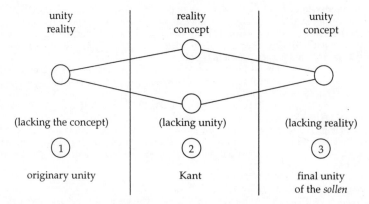

1. that the totality is always, if obscurely, present even in a system of thought limited to externality; it has to find a point of fixation (just as, in Freud, the totality of the libido persists forever, seeking an outlet in morbid or traumatic symptoms when it is not fully occupied and fully recognized) to make up for its mutilation and represent the spurned totality, if only symbolically (origin of myth and ideologies);

2. that, in Kant, this mythic reconciliation comes about at the price of a slippage [*glissement*]. Here we see the very origin of ideology in the suppression of the category of reality: in passing from 1 to 3, the totality loses reality and gains the concept. This is a classic ideology; it is conscious of itself, i.e., aware that it is a deferred reality, and presents itself as a *sollen*, a beyond, an 'endless task'. Kant's merit is to have provided ideology with an awareness of itself as ideology; Hegel's is to have worked out the meaning of ideology and assigned it its truth, i.e., to have destroyed ideology by perfecting it.

57. *Glauben und Wissen*, p. 126 [*Faith and Knowledge*, p. 165; W, 2:406].
58. *Ibid.*, p. 47 [*Faith and Knowledge*, p. 94; W, 2:330].
59. *Wissenschaft der Logik*, ed. Georg Lasson, Vol. I, p. 12, Preface to the Second Edition [*Hegel's Science of Logic*, trans. A. V. Miller, George Allen & Unwin, London, repr. Humanities Press International, Atlantic Highlands, New Jersey, 1969, p. 34; W, 5:23].
60. *Phn.* I, 58 [Miller, p. 41; W, 3: 63].
61. *Ibid.* [Miller, p. 42; W, 3: 63].
62. *Ibid.*, 8 [Miller, p. 3; W, 3:14].
63. *Log. Véra*, I, 184. [Althusser reproduces the spirit, not the letter, of Véra's translation. Cf. Wallace, p. 8; W, 8:47].
64. *Phn.* I, 36 [Miller, p. 24; W, 3:42. *Auswendig* is a common German adverb meaning 'by heart'; *inwendig*, which is rarely used, means 'internally', usually in a physical sense].
65. *Ibid.*, 37 [Miller, p. 25; W, 3:43].
66. *Ibid.*, 37 [Miller, p. 25; W, 3:43].
67. *Ibid.*, 37 [Miller, p. 25; W, 3:43–4].
68. *Ibid.*, 45 [Miller, p. 29; W, 3:48].
69. *Ibid.*, 44 [Miller, p. 29; W, 3:48].
70. *Ibid.*, 45 [Miller, p. 30; W, 3:50–51]. Hegel's position vis-à-vis Schelling was ambiguous, inasmuch as Schelling himself had an ambiguous position. *Differenz* seems to testify to Hegel's attraction to a philosopher who refused the *sollen* and discovered an aesthetic totality in Nature. Even late in life, Hegel acknowledged Schelling's contribution: Fichte had developed the Kantian dialectic in the direction of necessity, Schelling, in that of content (*Geschichte der Philosophie, op. cit.*, p. 1030 [*History of Philosophy*, Vol. 3, pp. 541–2; W, 20:453–4]). There can be no doubt that this intuition of a fully realized plenitude was something the young Hegel also aspired to; for him, it took aesthetic form in the Greek totality, which was at once religious and political. However, we have seen that this point of view is submerged, in Hegel's own reflections, by the discovery of the depth of subjectivity. Thus Schelling is in some sort a pre-Kantian, since

he has a conception of the objective totality (the idea of the universe as an organism in which Spirit is not the Whole, but a part of the Whole) which the Kantian critique of the antinomies had excluded from the realm of thought. Again, in the Preface to the *Phenomenology*, Hegel notes the formalism of Schelling's Absolute; it *does not think* the totality it posits and, by failing to envelop the content in the necessity of this very content, postulates a balance between content and necessity, which are placed on the scales of Indifference. Hence we need to explain the return to an earlier position apparent in both *Differenz* and the *System der Sittlichkeit* (the latter work, in M. Hyppolite's view, stands outside the development of Hegel's thought proper). With Kroner, we are inclined to the opinion that, linguistic similarities notwithstanding, *Differenz* already goes beyond Schelling, who plays the role of silent critic of Fichte. As to the *System der Sittlichkeit*, it seems to us to represent an abrupt return to the temptation of the totality. This throws up the question posed by Hegel's entire enterprise: can one think the totality in the dimension of subjectivity without destroying it *qua* totality? In other words, what sense does a totality claiming to absorb subjectivity still make?

71. *Phn.* I, 45 [Miller, p. 31; W, 3:51].
72. *Ibid.*, 47 [Miller, p. 32; W, 3:52].
73. *Ibid.*, 7 [Miller, p. 3; W, 3:13].
74. *Log. Véra* I, 172 [Preface to the Second Edition, *The Encyclopædia Logic*, trans. T. F. Seraets, W. A. Suchting and H. S. Harris, Hackett Publishing Company, Inc., Indianapolis, 1991, p. 17; W, 8:31].
75. *Phn.* I, 51 [Miller, p. 36; W, 3:56].
76. *Ibid.*, 48 [Miller, p. 33; W, 3:53].
77. Cf. Boutroux, *Les Post-Kantiens*.
78. *Log. Véra* I, 246 [Wallace, p. 44; W, 8:88]: 'The Mosaic legend of the Fall of Man ... treats of the origin and the bearings of ... knowledge.'
79. The 'revelation of depth' mentioned in ch. 8 of the *Phenomenology* commences with the Fall. It is Hegel's merit to have sensed this depth and grasped it in thought. This extraordinary accomplishment has, perhaps, no equivalent apart from the capture of depth in Cézanne's painting. The fisherman of the Enlightenment fished the way others paint, on the surface. Hegel fished the bottom – he took the whole sea, the depth of the sea, in his nets. The sense [*sens*, which means both 'meaning' and 'direction'] of the Fall also teaches us that there is no depth other than the one we fall into ourselves, and that truth is only given to those who grasp it and allow themselves to be taken in its grasp [the double sense of 'grasp' may give some idea of Althusser's pun here: *celui qui la prend*, which means 'he who takes it', is pronounced exactly like *celui qui l'apprend*, 'he who learns it']. Therein lies the lesson of the concept.
80. *Phn.* I, 85 [Miller, p. 61; W, 3:86].
81. *Log. Véra* I, 281 [Wallace, p. 62; W, 8:109].
82. *Ibid.*, 282 [Wallace, p. 62; W, 8:109].
83. *Ibid.*, 283 [Wallace, p. 62; W, 8:109].
84. *Ibid.*, 283 f. [Wallace, p. 63 f.; W, 8:110].
85. *Wissenschaft der Logik*, Vol. I, p. 31 [*Science of Logic*, p. 50; W, 5:44].
86. *Ibid.* [Truth without veils] [*Science of Logic*, p. 50; W, 5:44].
87. Nicolai Hartmann, *Die Philosophie des deutschen Idealismus*, Berlin-Leipzig, Vol. 2, p. 38.
88. *Log. Véra* I, 300 [Wallace, p. 71; W, 8:120].
89. *Differenz*, p. 41 [*The Difference between Fichte's and Schelling's System of Philosophy*, trans. H. S. Harris and Walter Cerf, Albany, New York, State University of New York Press, 1977, p. 93; W, 2:25]. See also *Wissenschaft der Logik*, Vol. I, p. 157 [*Science of Logic*, p. 166; W, 5:186]: 'The void ... contains the profounder thought that in the negative as such there lies the ground of becoming, of unrest, of self-movement.' [Althusser's translation is inaccurate; Hegel says that *the idea that the void is the ground of movement* contains the profounder thought that the negative is the ground of becoming, of the unrest *of* self-movement.]
90. *Log. Véra* I, 401 [Wallace, p. 127; W, 8:186–7].
91. *Wissenschaft der Logik*, Vol. I, p. 58 [*Science of Logic*, p. 73; W, 5:73]. [Althusser's translation is inaccurate; Hegel says 'the beginning *is not* pure nothing, but a nothing from which something is to proceed'.]

92. *Ibid.*, p. 60 [*Science of Logic*, p. 75; W, 5:75].
93. Or, rather, we should say that it is implicit in the final totality which, precisely, reveals its abstract nature. Here we catch a glimpse of the fact that Hegel destroys the original point of reference in order to create the final one; we see too that all meanings of whatever kind are, in Hegel, subordinated to the final totality. Let us also immediately note the strange proposition that follows from our remarks: nothingness and the whole are homogeneous. If the in-itself is *implicit within itself*, deriving its meaning only from the totality, then the totality must be precisely this *itself*, this *Selbst*, this Self (see *Phn.* I, 20 [Miller, p. 21], 'the negative is the self'), the very element in which it is engendered and in which its significance emerges. This implies that the Whole consists in the same substance as nothingness does; or, since the truth is the Whole (*das Wahre ist das Ganze*), that Truth is consubstantial with nothingness, that it is nothingness become substance. The scandal of Hegel resides in this paradox, which strikes at the heart of the entire philosophical tradition: rather than identifying being with truth, Hegel affirms that *the substance of truth is nothingness*. We shall attempt to determine the meaning of this astounding proposition.
94. James Baillie, *The Origin and Significance of Hegel's Logic*, London, 1901, p. 375.
95. Here we come up against an ambiguity: the positivity of the negative does not make sense in the absence of a certain externality. To be negated, a given content must be other than the nothingness which negates it, anterior to the act of negation, and external to it. Furthermore, it seems clear that, in Hegel, it is this act of negation or, in other words, the positivity of nothingness, which founds externality, since division comes into the world by way of nothingness. To put it another way, negativity constitutes every determination and thus every form of externality.

   We have here an index of two tendencies in Hegelian thought. 1. On the one hand, it is tempting to assume that the act of negation presupposes the existence of some primary matter, of a nature that came before nothingness or a given that came before and stands over against negativity. 2. On the other hand, what Hegel writes is unambiguous: 'Nothingness is primary, and all diversity proceeds from it.' Hegel's entire effort, as we have just summarized it, goes to show that he does not admit any system of original references, whether primary matter, nature, or substance; rather, he affords us a glimpse of the way nothingness develops into totality. 3. We need, then, to discover the significance of this contradiction: we have no choice in the matter. The only way to understand the idea that nothingness is both primary and secondary, condition and conditioned, is to posit that it is conditioned by itself alone; in other words, that the given which it presupposes (as eating presupposes the apple) is made of the same stuff as nothingness (if we may put it in those terms), is homogeneous with it – so that nothingness has to do only with itself in the form of externality, and, accordingly, unveils externality as such in unveiling itself, before going on to discover in this externality the fundamental identity it presupposes.

   Of course, this revelation is only possible at the end; only at the end does nothingness discover that the given it negates is connatural with itself. Moreover, the revelation is only possible from the vantage point of the totality, whose substance is nothingness; this totality contemplates its own emergence in the obscure movements of being and nothingness, those twins of the same blood, and flesh of its flesh.
96. The ramifications of Hegel's insight about the positivity of the negative are incalculable. Let us note in passing how the idea that the negated content is contained in its very negation reveals something about the Freudian dialectic: for example, it enables us to understand that the unconscious is a reality and yet also a rejected reality. The old arguments of classical psychology, which treat the negative as pure negativity, miss the fact that what is not can yet be, that the non-conscious can exist for consciousness. Thus they treat consciousness as a being and, simultaneously, the unconscious as a non-being, that is, as *things* bearing no dialectical relationship to one another. Freud himself seems to fall into this objectifying [*chosiste*] schematism when he attempts to make the unconscious an in-itself that can serve as a point of reference, even distinguishing 'geological' strata within it; or, again, when he wishes to think the relation between this in-itself and consciousness in causal terms. Hegel's reflections shed light on this debate by showing that negation, denial, and repression are not

pure nothingness, purely negative states we can say nothing about, but that they have a content, and that the form in which they are suppressed merely affects the *in-itself* of the unconscious, not the content itself, which subsists in negated form in denial and repression. Politzer's analyses of all these points in *Critique des fondements de la Psychologie* are evidently inspired by the Hegelian dialectic.

97. *Inhalt* must be distinguished from *Gehalt*, which Hegel uses rather rarely. *Gehalt* has a qualitative connotation in German, and designates the import of the content, or its value, rather than its nature. Hegel employed the term *Inhalt* with astonishing frequency: it occurs nearly three thousand times in the *Phenomenology*. [The second half of the sentence this note refers to reads, in French, *le contenu est un tenu, et ce tenu est* dans, *dans la dépendance d'un autre qui le tient.* 'To hold' is *halten* in German, *tenir* in French; the past participles, respectively *gehalten* and *tenu*, make themselves felt in *Inhalt* and *contenu*.]

98. *Log. Véra* II, p. 82 [Wallace, p. 189; *W*, 8:265].

99. *Ibid.*, 80 [Wallace, p. 189; *W*, 8: 265].

100. *Ibid.*, I, 361 [Wallace, p. 108; *W*, 8:164]; translation modified.

101. *Logik*, ed. Hermann Glockner, Vol. IV, p. 545 [*Science of Logic*, p. 439; *W*, 6:74].

102. *Encyclopædia*, Paragraph 247 [*Hegel's Philosophy of Nature*, trans. M. J. Petry, George Allen & Unwin, London, 1970, Vol. 1, p. 205; *W*, 9:24].

103. 'The primary or immediate determination of nature is the abstract *universality of its self-externality*, its unmediated indifference ... it is on account of its being self-externality, *collaterality* of a completely ideal nature.' *Ibid.*, Paragraph 254 [*Philosophy of Nature*, Vol. 1, p. 223; *W*, 9:41].

104. *Ibid.*, Paragraph 375 [*Philosophy of Nature*, Vol. 3, p. 209; *W*, 9:535].

105. *Geschichte der Philosophie*, p. 45 [*Introduction to the Lectures on the History of Philosophy*, trans. T. M. Knox and A. V. Miller, Clarendon, Oxford, 1985, p. 24; *W*, 18:51].

106. *Phn.*, ed. Georg Lasson, Leipzig 1928, pp. 219–20 [Miller, p. 178; *W*, 3:225. Althusser gives his own translation of this passage].

107. *Ibid.* [Miller, p. 178; *W*, 3:225].

108. In *Genesis*, the world is given to Adam, and it is Adam who gives the animals their names.

109. Carolus Bovillus. See Bernard Groethuysen, *Mythes et Portraits*, Paris, Gallimard, 1947, pp. 43–56.

110. Sophocles, *Antigone*: the ode [ll. 340–70].

111. 'The right which they receive will remain an external *fate* for them.' *Ph. D.*, 178 [Nisbet, p. 259; *W*, 7:381].

112. As to perpetual peace, it is, even in Kant, no more than a 'project'.

113. This production of the truth at the very heart of error – this, in some sort, compensation of myth by truth, or of truth by myth – is the positive reality of transition in Hegel. Lucien Herr used to say that, in Hegel, transition is feeling or sentiment. We would prefer to say that it is presentiment, while emphasizing the point that presentiment is unmistakably inscribed in the world caught up in a process of change. Such presentiment is the unrealized truth of the world under consideration, that is, its myth, or, if one likes, its ideology. On this point, we are in Hegel's debt for insights that go beyond Feuerbach's theses. Feuerbach saw little more than the negativity of ideologies; Hegel established the positivity of myth.

114. As can be seen in elementary Platonism or in Bergson, where intuition is, *de facto*, the form the vision of the truth naturally takes. I can therefore dispense with explanation, whereas non-intuition, error, perversion, and externality are scandals which need to be, if not justified, then at least explained and deplored.

115. *Ph. Esprit Véra* II, 146 [Wallace, p. 201; *W*, 10:256].

116. Cf. Kant: 'Intuition ... is blind.' And Hegel: 'Mere light is mere darkness.' *Log. Véra* I, 276 [Wallace, p. 58; *W*, 8:105].

117. To translate *Begriff* as *notion* is a pointless travesty that robs *Begriff* of its concrete, active meaning, and replaces it with a feeble, abstract word from which every positive connotation of 'grasping' has disappeared, leaving us with a neutral term dominated by the passive overtones of 'that which is known'. The use of 'notion' to translate *Begriff* was popularized by Véra and Noël; this makes it easier to understand the

usefulness of this unfaithful translation, which accommodated Véra's and Noël's interpretation of Hegelianism as a form of panlogism. M. Hyppolite has quite rightly restored the term 'concept' in his translations. Those wishing to bring out the concrete meaning of Hegel's thought need to begin by restoring the vigour of his language. [It will be noted that a number of the English translations of Hegel cited here translate *Begriff* as notion.]

118. The mediator's discretion is one of the major motifs of religious, philosophical, and literary imagery. In the *Iliad*, the gods swoop down from the sky, unleash a catastrophe, run the hero ragged, decide who will have the victory, and then vanish into thin air like a light fog. The same pattern underlies the revelations of the unhappy consciousness in Judaism: Yahweh speaks from within the flame or on the mountaintop, and then falls silent. Christ himself 'goeth back to the Father', leaving men standing before an empty tomb. It is true that he is resurrected and allows men to touch him, but he disappears again from their world, which the Holy Ghost alone continues to dwell in. The theme of the disappearance of the demiurge is a literary standby: the third thief disappears before the end, Jean Valjean puts the world to rights and melts into the night, Sherlock Holmes solves the mystery, unmasks the murderer, gives the lovers back their love, lights his pipe, and heads off: three's a crowd. Occasionally, one sees a demiurge emerge despite himself; he quits the scene only reluctantly, before learning that 'silence is golden'.

119. Hegel's third term has bad manners: it doesn't know when to leave. The fact that it has been brought up badly is the motor of the Hegelian dialectic: man is a perverted animal whom Nature fails to reabsorb, an ill-mannered child who insists on having his own way and forcibly transforms his perversion into a universal. Before being the measure of all things, he is the very principle of immoderation; and it is his obstinacy that transforms immoderation into measure. Truth is an *enfant terrible*.

120. It remains to be seen whether Hegel is not his own demiurge, and if the solution is not itself a middle term (see ch. III, A).

121. *Phn.* II, 309 [Miller, p. 491; W, 3:588–9].

122. Richard Kroner: *Von Kant bis Hegel*, Vol. I, pp. 143–4. Kroner takes his inspiration from Ebbinghaus. See Julius Ebbinghaus, *Relativer und Absoluter Idealismus*, Leipzig 1911, pp. 11ff.

123. *Log. Véra* I, 277 [Wallace, p. 58; W, 8:105–6].

124. See ch. II, A.

125. *Phn.* I, 18–19 [Miller, pp. 11–12, 6; W, 3:24–5, 13].

126. *Ibid.*, 7 [Miller, pp. 2–3; W, 3:13].

127. Which it can enjoy, Rimbaud adds, 'at will'. We shall see that the phrase is not inapt. Incidentally, one finds in Rimbaud astonishing images that help clarify Hegel's intuitions. It is well known that, for Hegel, the sea imaged freedom and the sun represented the truth. Compare Rimbaud: 'Eternity, the sea mingled with the sun'.

128. *System der Sittlichkeit*, ed. [Georg] Lasson, Vol. 7, p. 466 [*System of Ethical Life and First Philosophy of Spirit*, trans. H. S. Harris and T. M. Knox, State University of New York Press, Albany, 1979, p. 143].

129. See ch. I, C.

130. Aragon.

131. Hegel's language must always be taken in the most concrete, the strongest sense: this kingdom is the domain of a King, and this King is the Subject. This innocuous formulation is explosive.

132. Spinoza.

133. *Phn.* II, 308 [Miller, p. 490; W, 3:587–8].

134. *Ibid.*, I, 34 [Miller, p. 23; W, 3:40–1].

135. *Ph. Esprit Véra* I, 14 [Wallace, p. 6; W, 10:15].

136. *Ibid.*, p. 15 [Wallace, p. 6; W, 10:15].

137. In Absolute Knowledge.

138. Spirit is the act of plunging into itself – the acorn falls into itself. Cf. the anticipations of Hegelian circularity represented by the circularity of the Greeks' *ourobouros*, the quest for perpetual motion, or the images of art – such circularity is an operation that sets out from the self to reclaim its own origins. Cf. the child's fascination for the

circus, which, packing its animals, clowns, and sun back into its vans, is a travelling totality that spills out onto the public squares and 'has its own boats and trains' – or, again, the theatre, which puts up its stage-sets, hangs up its lights, and makes the boards over into a stage on which the drama, the tragedy, that 'insubstantial pageant', thickens and swells, then spirits itself away in its bags and trunks. There remains, however, an insurmountable externality: the theatre may be a travelling world, but this world is merely the dark stage on which one sets the scene in complicity with the night. The morning sun comes up over a deserted square.

139. *Ph. Esprit Véra* I, 38 [Wallace, p. 14; *W*, 10:24].
140. *Ibid.* [Wallace, p. 14; *W*, 10:24].
141. *Encyclopædia*, Paragraph 60 [Wallace, pp. 91–2; *W*, 8:144].
142. The universal is always 'the evening after a battle'.
143. Cited by Alain: *Idées*, Paris, Hartmann, 1939, p. 236.
144. *Hegels Sämtliche Werke*, ed. Georg Lasson, Vol. XX, p. 180, cited by Kojève, *Introduction à la lecture de Hegel* [Paris, Gallimard, 1947, p. 575; *Hegel and the Human Spirit: A Translation of the Jena Lectures on the Philosophy of Spirit*, trans. Leo Rauch, Wayne State University Press, Detroit, 1983, p. 87, translation modified]. The triumph of the universal individual is for Hegel the triumph of night. The Hegelian night is the night become light, 'night become midday' (*Differenz*), transparent, clear. In Schelling's night, the cows are black. Hegel, or the night of the white cows.
145. A sentence J.-P. Sartre should have used as the epigraph to his chapter on the *gaze* ...
146. *Ph. D.*, 65 [Nisbet, pp. 78–9; *W*, 7:110–1].
147. *Phn.* I, 18 [Miller, p. 10; *W*, 3:24].
148. *Ibid.*, II, 286 [Miller, p. 475; *W*, 3: 571]: 'Death becomes transfigured ... into the universality of the Spirit who dwells in His community.'
149. *Ibid.*, I, 311 [Miller, p. 492; *W*, 3:590].
150. *Ibid.*, 17 [Miller, p. 10; *W*, 3:23].
151. *Ibid.*, II, 288 [Miller, p. 476; *W*, 3:572].
152. *Ibid.*, 312 [Miller, p. 492; *W*, 3:591].
153. 'Thus everything depends upon the spirit's self-awareness; if the Spirit knows that it is free, it is altogether different from what it would be without this knowledge. For if it does not know that it is free, it is in the position of a slave...' *Geschichte der Philosophie*, Introduction [in fact *Lectures on the Philosophy of World History. Introduction: Reason in History*, trans. H. B. Nisbet, Cambridge, Cambridge University Press, Cambridge, 1980, p. 48].
154. The concept is, literally, biting; it is a capture, fictive murder. *Phn.*, ch. VII.
155. 'The will in its truth is such that what it wills, i.e. its content, is identical with the will itself, so that freedom is willed by freedom ...' *Ph. D.*, Paragraph 21 [Nisbet, p. 53; *W*, 7:74].
156. To this point, we have deliberately restricted our attention to the conception of the totality found in the *Phenomenology of Spirit*. The reason for this will be given in ch. III.
157. *Phn.* I, 12 [Miller, p. 7; *W*, 3:18–19].
158. This is the ideal of the 'universal tensor'.
159. See ch. I.
160. This point has been nicely brought out by Alexandre Kojève in his *Introduction à la lecture de Hegel*.
161. *Phn.* II, 303 [Miller, p. 486; *W*, 3:583].
162. *Ph. Esprit Véra* I, 123 [Wallace, p. 41; *W*, 10:58].
163. *Ph. D.* 261 [Nisbet, p. 365; *W*, 7:496].
164. *Ph. Esprit Véra*, I, 130 [Wallace, p. 44; *W*, 10:61].
165. *Wissenschaft der Logik*, p. 31 [*Science of Logic*, p. 50; *W*, 5:44].
166. *Phn.* I, 83 [Miller, p. 60; *W*, 3:84].
167. *Ibid.* [Miller, p. 60; *W*, 3:85].
168. *Ibid.*, 92 [Miller, p. 66; *W*, 3:92].
169. *Ibid.*, 91 [Miller, p. 66; *W*, 3:92].
170. *Ibid.*, 84 [Miller, p. 60; *W*, 3: 84].
171. 'Language ... contains [the I] in its purity.' *Phn.* II, 69 [Miller, p. 308; *W*, 3:376].
172. *Ibid.*, 70 [Miller, p. 308; *W*, 3:376].

173. *Ibid.*, 69 [Miller, pp. 308–309; W, 3:376].
174. *Encyclopædia*, Addendum to Paragraph 24 [Wallace, p. 38; W, 8:83].
175. *Ibid.*, Paragraph 19 [Wallace, p. 25; W, 8:67]; [*Science of Logic*, p. 58; W, 5:55].
176. This is why speculative logic was not discovered before Hegel. It is in this sense that the shadow of the Logic is the realm of the dead. It is the shadow of a living body after it has lived, that is, the shadow of a dead man, or the shadow of a living dead man. Here we find an echo of our reflections on the totality or the reign of death. If the whole is fulfilled, life (which creates and negates in externality) is suspended, nothing more happens, the substance is petrified, God is dead (= God is death). This death must be understood as the end of history Marx spoke of.
177. [Cf. *History of Philosophy*, Vol. 1, p. 63; W, 18:83.]
178. *Wissenschaft der Logik*, Vol. I, pp. 37–8 [*Science of Logic*, p. 56; W, 5:51].
179. Hegel credits Kant with being the first to have freed dialectic 'from the seeming arbitrariness which it possesses from the standpoint of ordinary thought and exhibited it as *a necessary function of reason*' (*Wissenschaft der Logik*, Vol. I, p. 38 [*Science of Logic*, p. 56; W, 5:52]). But we also know that Kantian Reason is a *sollen*, not the Reason of things Hegelian; thus Kant discovered the dialectic, but failed to recognize it. In this sense, he predates Plato, who is saved by his ambiguity.
180. *Phn.* I, 77 [Miller, p. 56; W, 3:79].
181. In Spinoza, consciousness is subject to a law it does not cognize until the end (see *Ethics*, Book V, theorems [*sic*] 31–3, Corollary), so that eternal knowledge is not the end but the beginning, making the development of consciousness into an illusion.
182. Hyppolite. [Althusser strikingly condenses a sentence of Jean Hyppolite's, which reads: 'The *Phenomenology* is not a noumenology or an ontology, but it remains nonetheless, a knowledge of the absolute.' Jean Hyppolite, *Genèse et structure de la Phénomenologie de l'Esprit de Hegel*, p. 10 {*Genesis and Structure of Hegel's Phenomenology of Spirit*, p. 4}].
183. *Phn.* I, 42 [Miller, 29; W, 3:48].
184. *Wissenschaft der Logik*, Vol. II, p. 498 [*Science of Logic*, p. 837; W, 6:565].
185. *Phn.* I, 44 [Miller, p. 31; W, 3:50].
186. *Ibid.*, 46 [Miller, pp. 31–2; W, 3:51].
187. *Ibid.*, 47 [Miller, p. 32; W, 3:52].
188. *Wissenschaft der Logik*, Vol. I, p. 36 [*Science of Logic*, p. 54; W, 5:50].
189. *Phn.* I, 75 [Miller, p. 55; W, 3:78].
190. Nicolai Hartmann, *Philosophie des deutschen Idealismus*, Vol. 2, p. 88.
191. *Ibid.*, p. 161.
192. *Ibid.*, p. 188.
193. See Hartmann's essay, 'Hegel et le problème de la dialectique du réel', *Revue de métaphysique et de morale* 38, 1931, pp. 285–316 [also in B. Croce, N. Hartmann, et al., *Études sur Hegel*, Publications de la *Revue de métaphysique et de morale*, Colin, Paris, 1931, pp. 41–90].
194. Nicolai Hartmann, *Philosophie des deutschen Idealismus*, Vol. 2, p. 89.
195. This paradox has been brilliantly argued by Alexandre Kojève, who seems, however, to have neglected the conceptual aspect of the dialectic. [Kojève, *Introduction à la lecture de Hegel*, Appendix I].
196. *Wissenschaft der Logik*, Vol. II, p. 486 [*Science of Logic*, p. 826; W, 6:551].
197. *Ibid.* [*Science of Logic*, p. 826; W, 6:551].
198. *Ibid.* [*Science of Logic*, p. 826; W, 6:551].
199. We will come back to the significance of this date. See ch. III, C.
200. Letter to his father. *Œuvres philosophiques*, trans. Jacques Molitor, Vol. IV, p. 10 [Marx and Engels, *Collected Works*, Vol. 1, Lawrence and Wishart, London, 1975, p. 18; *MEW*, Supplementary Vol., Part I, p. 8].
201. Karl Marx, *Œuvres philosophiques*, Vol. IV, p. 134 [*Critique of Hegel's Philosophy of Right*, trans. Annette Jolin and Joseph O'Malley, Cambridge University Press, Cambridge, 1970, p. 64; *MEW*, 1:266].
202. *Phn.* I, 154 [Miller, p. 110; W, 3:145].
203. *Ibid.* [Miller, p. 111; W, 3:145].
204. See ch. II, C.

205. Karl Marx, *Œuvres philosophiques*, Vol. IV, p. 19 [*Critique of Hegel's Philosophy of Right*, p. 6; *MEW*, 1:203].
206. *Ibid.*, pp. 89–90 [*Critique*, p. 41; *MEW*, 1:243].
207. *Ibid.*, p. 82 [*Critique*, p. 37; *MEW*, 1:239].
208. *Ibid.* [*Critique*, p. 37; *MEW*, 1:239].
209. *Ibid.*, p. 132 [*Critique*, p. 63; *MEW*, 1:265].
210. *Ibid.*, p. 161 [*Critique*, pp. 77–8; *MEW*, 1:281].
211. *Ibid.*, p. 169 [*Critique*, p. 82, translation modified; *MEW*, 1:285].
212. *Ibid.*, p. 196 [*Critique*, p. 95; *MEW*, 1:299].
213. *Ibid.*, p. 216 [*Critique*, pp. 105–6; *MEW*, 1:310].
214. *Ibid.*, p. 175 [*Critique*, p. 85; *MEW*, 1:288].
215. *Ibid.*, p. 145 [*Critique*, p. 69; *MEW*, 1:272].
216. *Ibid.*, p. 141 [*Critique*, p. 67; *MEW*, 1:270].
217. *Ibid.*, p. 145 [*Critique*, p. 69; *MEW*, 1:272].
218. *Ibid.* [*Critique*, p. 69; *MEW*, 1:272].
219. *Ibid.*, p. 182 [*Critique*, p. 88; *MEW*, 1:292].
220. *Ibid.*, p. 141 [*Critique*, p. 67; *MEW*, 1:270].
221. *Ibid.*, p. 25 f. [*Critique*, p. 9; *MEW*, 1:207 f.].
222. *Ibid.*, p. 136 [*Critique*, p. 65; *MEW*, 1:267].
223. *Ibid.*, p. 188 [*Critique*, pp. 91–2; *MEW*, 1:295–6].
224. *Ibid.*, p. 189 [*Critique*, p. 92; *MEW*, 1:296].
225. *Ibid.*, p. 43 [*Critique*, p. 18; *MEW*, 1:217].
226. *Ibid.*, p. 197 [*Critique*, p. 96; *MEW*, 1:300].
227. *Ibid.*, p. 74 [*Critique*, p. 33; *MEW*, 1:235].
228. Karl Marx, *Œuvres philosophiques*, Vol. VI, p. 82 ['1844 Manuscripts', p. 210; *MEW*, Suppl. Vol., Part 1, p. 581].
229. Jean Wahl.
230. Karl Marx, *Œuvres philosophiques*, Vol. VI, p. 87 ['1844 Manuscripts', p. 214; *MEW*, Suppl. Vol., Part 1, p. 584].
231. *Ibid.*, p. 95 ['1844 Manuscripts', p. 217; *MEW*, Suppl. Vol., Part 1, p. 587].
232. *Ibid.*, p. 84 ['1844 Manuscripts', p. 211; *MEW*, Suppl. Vol., Part 1, p. 582].
233. *Ibid.*, p. 75 ['1844 Manuscripts', p. 206; *MEW*, Suppl. Vol., Part 1, p. 577]. Translation modified.
234. *Ibid.*, p. 89 ['1844 Manuscripts', p. 215; *MEW*, Suppl. Vol., Part 1, p. 585]. Translation modified.
235. *Ibid.*, p. 70 ['1844 Manuscripts', p. 203; *MEW*, Suppl. Vol., Part 1, p. 574].
236. *Ibid.*, p. 91 ['1844 Manuscripts', p. 217; *MEW*, Suppl. Vol., Part 1, p. 586].
237. *Ibid.* ['1844 Manuscripts', p. 216; *MEW*, Suppl. Vol., Part 1, p. 586].
238. *Phn.* I, 198 [Miller, 141; *W*, 3:180].
239. 'Just as it was rightly said of the true that it is *index sui et falsi* [. . .] but that the true is not known by starting from the false, so the Concept is the understanding both of itself and of the shape without Concept, but the latter does not from its own inner truths understand the Concept.' [*The Encyclopædia Logic*, Preface to the Second Edition, p. 17; *W*, 8:31.]
240. Karl Marx, *Œuvres philosophiques*, Vol. VI, p. 154 [*The German Ideology*, Part 1, trans. S. Ryazanskaya, in Robert C. Tucker, ed., *The Marx-Engels Reader*, Norton, New York, 1972, p. 113; *MEW*, 3:20].
241. *Ibid.*, Vol. IV, p. 189 [*Critique*, p. 92; *MEW*, 1:296]. Translation modified.
242. *Ibid.*, Vol. VI, p. 40 ['1844 Manuscripts', p. 166; *MEW*, Suppl. Vol., Part 1, p. 546].
243. *Ibid.*, p. 120 ['1844 Manuscripts', p. 140; *MEW*, Suppl. Vol., Part 1, p. 526].
244. *Ibid.*, p. 125 ['1844 Manuscripts', p. 144; *MEW*, Suppl. Vol., Part 1, p. 529].
245. *Ibid.*, p. 241 [*German Ideology*, p. 155; *MEW*, 3:67].
246. *Ibid.*, p. 178 [*German Ideology*, p. 126; *MEW*, 3:35].
247. *Ibid.*, p. 182 [*German Ideology*, p. 128; *MEW*, 3:37].
248. *Ibid.*, p. 64 ['1844 Manuscripts', p. 176; *MEW*, Suppl. Vol., Part 1, p. 554].
249. *Ibid.*, p. 175 [*German Ideology*, p. 126; *MEW*, 3:35].
250. 'Big industry . . . produced world history for the first time, insofar as it made all civilized nations and every individual member of them dependent for the satisfaction

of their wants on the whole world, thus destroying the former natural exclusiveness of separate nations. . . . It destroyed natural growth in general.' *Ibid.*, p. 218 [*German Ideology*, p. 149; *MEW*, 3:60].

251. This unavailability of any alternative seems irrevocably to commit Marxism to iron necessity. This is generally the sticking point for those superficial critics who fail to get beyond the antinomy of necessity and freedom (for example, Sartre, in his recent article 'Matérialisme et Révolution' [*Les Temps modernes*, nos 9–10, June–July 1946; Eng. trans. in *Literary and Philosophical Essays*, Hutchinson, London, 1968, pp. 185–239]. For many people, Marxist freedom is merely, as Malraux says, 'the consciousness and organization of human inevitablity'.

252. This plunge of the product into Nature, which occurs as soon as the product escapes the producer's control and is no longer posited as being identical with him, gives us a better grasp of the creation myth. On the purest conception, God is the circularity of Love; he is sufficient unto himself and has no outside. The creation is literally a rupture in this circularity: God does not need the creation, so that it is, by definition, different from him. This non-identity of the Creator and his creature is the emergence of Nature. The product of the God-who-works escapes his control (because it is superfluous for him). This fall is Nature, or God's outside. In the creation, then, men unwittingly repress the essence of work. But they do still more: they try to eliminate the very origins of work, which, in its daily exercise, appears to them as a natural necessity (one has to work in order to live, work is a natural law entailed by the Fall – as appears in the myth of Eve: 'you will earn your bread by the sweat of your brow'). Moreover, work is inherently conditioned by nature, since the worker transforms a nature that is given. In the creation myth, this natural character of work disappears, because the Creator is not subject to any law, and creates the world *ex nihilo*. In God the Creator, men not only think the birth of nature, but attempt to overcome the natural character of this birth by demonstrating that the creation has no origin (since God creates without obligation or need); that the fall has no nature; and that the very nature which seems to dominate work is, fundamentally, only as necessary as the (produced) nature which results from work.

Developing and deepening this myth would perhaps enable us to anticipate what Marx means by 'the identity of man and nature in work'. Approached in this way, that identity would have two aspects. On the one hand, men are identical with nature in that they are identical with what they produce; their products become nature for them (this immediate identity through labour re-emerges in revolutionary action; one may therefore say that this alienation is already overcome in thought – men no longer need a myth to represent it, since it has become the object of economic science). On the other hand, men would also be identical with the nature that forces them to work, and which they transform through work; this second identity would be clarified through reflection of the first. Here, however, we would have only an embryonic anticipation, for, in the obvious, elementary sense, identity is still beyond men's grasp. Men see clearly enough that the natural world is given to them, and that they themselves exist because they exercise a measure of control over it, thanks to their knowledge and industry; however, they have not completely overcome natural alienation: they are subject to the elements, illness, and old age, and obliged to work in order to live. Moreover, if the work of scientific knowledge and of the transformation of the world is itself a recurrence of, and recovery from [*reprise*], natural alienation, the recovery is not complete: circularity is not re-established, and human circularity will no doubt be established before natural circularity (in a socialist world, say the Marxists, one will still have to overcome natural alienation). This deficiency explains why it is still necessary to revert to myth in order to conceive a totality which has not yet attained its concept; it is in the story of creation, on this view, that men contemplate the *reprise* of natural alienation.

253. Karl Marx, *Œuvres philosophiques*, Vol. IV, p. 134 [*Critique*, p. 96; *MEW*, 1:300].

254. Cf. the lecture of Hegel's placed at the beginning of the *Philosophy of History*. Hegel waits for the Monarch to authorize the broad dissemination of his thought; his thought is submissive.

255. *Phn.* I, 12 [Miller, p. 7; *W*, 3:18–19].

256. See ch. II C.
257. *Phn.* I, 13 [Miller, p. 7; *W*, 3:19].
258. *Ibid.*, 33 [Miller, p. 22; *W*, 3:39].
259. Alexandre Kojève has brilliantly argued this point in his *Introduction to the Reading of Hegel.*
260. *Logique Véra* I, 184 [Wallace, 8; *W*, 8:47].
261. That is, uniting in their persons the master's and the slave's attributes, but without the servility characteristic of both.
262. *Philosophie der Geschichte* [*Lectures on the Philosophy of History*, trans. J. Sibree, in Hegel, *The Philosophy of Right* and *The Philosophy of History*, Encyclopædia Britannica, Chicago and London, 1952, p. 364; *W*, 12:529].
263. *Ph. D.*, Preface, p. 30 [Nisbet, p. 20; *W*, 7:24].
264. Karl Marx, *Œuvres philosophiques*, Vol. VI, p. 178 [*German Ideology*, p. 126; *MEW*, 3:34].
265. *Logique Véra* II, 325 [Wallace, p. 273; *W*, 8:365].
266. *Ph. D.*, p. 31 [Nisbet, p. 22; *W*, 7:26–7].
267. Karl Marx, *Œuvres philosophiques*, Vol. VI, p. 181 [*German Ideology*, pp. 127–8; *MEW*, 3:35].
268. Karl Marx, *Sur la Guerre Civile en France*, p. 56 [*The Civil War in France*, in Marx and Engels, *Selected Works in One Volume*, Lawrence and Wishart, London, 1968, p. 295; *MEW*, 17:343].

Man, That Night[1]

(1947)

The profoundest themes of the Romantic nocturne haunt Hegel's thinking. Yet Night is not, in Hegel, the blind peace of the darkness through
which discrete entities make their solitary way, separated from one
another for all eternity. It is, by the grace of man, the birth of Light. Before
Nietzsche – and with what rigour – Hegel saw in man a sick animal who
neither dies nor recovers, but stubbornly insists on living on in a nature
terrified of him. The animal kingdom reabsorbs its monsters, the economy
its crises: man alone is a triumphant error who makes his aberration the
law of the world. At the level of nature, man is an absurdity, a gap in being,
an 'empty nothing', a 'Night'. 'We see this Night,' as Hegel profoundly
says, 'when we look a human being in the eye: a Night which turns
terrifying, the Night of the World that rises up before us. . . .' This passage,
which one would like to have seen Sartre choose as the epigraph for his
chapter on the gaze, dominates, from a commanding height, the whole of
contemporary anthropology. The birth of man is, in Hegel, the death of
nature. Animal desire – whether hunger, thirst, or sex – sates itself on
natural creatures. Man, in contrast, is born in a human void. This appears
in love, in which the lover seeks his own night in the eyes of his beloved;
in those struggles in which men do battle, not over territory or arms, but
to win recognition from their adversaries; in science, in which man seeks
his own traces in the world, so as to wrest from it proof that he exists;
and, finally, in labour, in which the artisan bends wood or clay to the
service of a fragile idea. History is simply the triumph and recognition of
man's nothingness, secured by dint of labour or force of arms. For, through
labour, man subjects nature to his will and makes it his place of abode;
through struggle, he wins recognition from his fellows and builds himself
a human abode. Hegelian Spirit, that mysterious third term, is nothing
other than the triumphant kingdom of humanity joined in a circle;[a] it is

[a] *L'humanité circulaire.* On the Hegelian circle, see pp. 88–9, 118–9 in the present
volume.

the Reign of Freedom, in which man, having overcome human alienation, regards his fellow men as his brothers, and sees, in the democracy of the universal state, 'flesh of his flesh and spirit of his spirit'. This third term is the Term as such, because, in the transparent totality, history contemplates its own end, and a joyous humanity revels in the victory of its own 'Night become Light'.

No-one has written on these themes as felicitously as Alexandre Kojève. His book is more than an *Introduction to the Reading of Hegel*: it is the resurrection of a corpse, or, rather, the revelation that Hegel, a thinker dismantled, torn to pieces, trampled underfoot, and betrayed, profoundly haunts and dominates an apostate age. Without Heidegger, as Kojève says somewhere, we would never have understood the *Phenomenology of Spirit*. It is not hard to turn the remark around, and to show that Hegel is the mother-truth of contemporary thought. Reading Kojève, one might conclude that this holds for Marx too – that Marx emerges from Hegel fully armed with the dialectic of master and slave, that he is the brother and spitting image of the modern existentialists – were it not that this paradox is an affront to common sense. It is here, perhaps, that Kojève's brilliant interpretation reaches its limits.

Kojève culls an anthropology from Hegel: he develops the subjective aspect of Hegelian negativity, deliberately neglecting its objective aspect. The partiality of his approach leads him to a dualistic position: he is left face to face with nature, the objective reality he neglects in Hegelian negativity. If error defines man, if man is a happy mistake, then we need to account rationally for the nature this aberration appears in. If man is a void in being who triumphs over being, then we need to determine the status of his unfortunate adversary. Hegel himself clearly felt this obscure imperative; that is why he showed that the totality was the Kingdom, not merely of nothingness (of the Subject), but also of being (of Substance). That is why nature is neither a shadow, nor the conjunction of human projects (as in Sartre, for example), nor the opposite of man, another world governed by laws of its own (as in Kojève). The Hegelian totality is the totality Substance-Subject. Kojève detaches the Subject (human negativity) from this totality, and ably demonstrates that history is merely the becoming-Substance of the Subject, who, in struggle and labour, makes his own nothingness the flesh of a human world, ceases to be a 'stranger in his own land',* and dwells, at last, *at home*, in freedom become a world. But this is only one aspect of the Hegelian totality. The other is the becoming-Subject of Substance, the production of Spirit by a concrete Nature, that is, the production of man by nature, and the objective working out of human freedom in the course of an exacting history. The triumph of freedom in Hegel is not the triumph of

* Aragon.

any freedom whatever: it is not the mightiest who prevails in the end;* history shows, rather, that human freedom is engendered by the slave. The reign of error is finally not that of a random error: Hegelian Nature exists in pre-established harmony with man, engendering, in the form of man, the sole error it is capable of acknowledging as its truth. This is why the truth reigns in error triumphant. Hegelian error is converted into truth only because it is, profoundly, already truth by nature; but it is an obscure, hidden truth that needs, in order to cognize and reappropriate itself, to construct a world in which it can at last contemplate its own presence.

This is the other aspect of the Hegelian totality, as critically important as the first. Hegel has been misunderstood for one hundred and fifty years because the two aspects of Hegelian necessity have not both been kept firmly in view. For a century, attention was focused on Hegelian Substance. Alexandre Kojève reminds us that this Substance is a *Subject*. But this is to cut Hegel in two, as one would an apple, and to give up any idea of putting the two halves back together. If we want to grasp the Hegelian totality, we must take Hegel to mean that 'the Substance is *also* a Subject' and that the totality is therefore the reconciliation of Substance and Subject, which coincide in the absolute truth.

That this is an extremely ambitious programme need not concern us here. We wish merely to point out that to disregard it is to cultivate brilliant but fragile paradoxes. Thus Kojève's existentialist Marx is a travesty in which Marxists will not recognize their own. It is difficult to understand Marx if we neglect, as Kojève does, the objective (or substantialist) aspect of Hegelian negativity. But one must read this aggressive, brilliant book, which depreciates contemporary thought only in order to restore part of Hegel's veritable grandeur.

Note

First published in the *Cahiers du Sud*, no. 286, in the latter half of 1947.

1. The title is a phrase drawn from a lecture Hegel delivered in 1805–06, cited in Alexandre Kojève, *Introduction à la lecture de Hegel*, Gallimard, Paris, 1947, p. 573 [*Hegel and the Human Spirit: A Translation of the Jena Lectures on the Philosophy of Spirit*, trans. Leo Rauch, Wayne State University Press, Detroit, 1983, p. 87, translation modified]: 'Man is that night, that empty nothing, which contains everything in its simplicity: a wealth of infinitely many representations, images, none of which occurs to it directly, and none of which is not present. This is Night, the interior of nature, existing here – pure *Self*. In certain phantasmagoric representations, it is night everywhere: here a bloody head suddenly shoots up and there another white shape, only to disappear as suddenly. We see this Night when we look a human being in the eye, looking into a Night that turns terrifying; it is the Night of the World that rises up before us.'

* As in Nietzsche or the various forms of fascism. The future does not belong 'to those who seize it', as a famous candidate naively says.

The Return To Hegel
The Latest Word in Academic Revisionism[1]
(1950)

My aim is, above all, to attempt to think the Marxian synthesis by taking Hegelian philosophy as a starting point. . . . We claim to have discovered a certain idealism in Marxist thought . . . Today it may be necessary to make revisions Marx never dreamt of.

> Hyppolite, *Bulletin de la Société française de Philosophie,* 1948, pp. 173, 179, 188.[2]

The Hegel question has long since been resolved.

> A. Zhdanov[3]

The fact that, for the last two decades, Hegel has had his place in French bourgeois philosophy is not a matter to be treated lightly. Before 1930, French bourgeois thought had displayed unexampled obstinacy in its disregard for, and ignorance of, Hegel. Véra's[4] old translations (the *Encyclopædia*), laced with delightful mistakes, slumbered in the bowels of the libraries. Only the socialists (such as Jaurès, in his Latin dissertation, Lucien Herr, or Andler[5]) took an interest in Hegel. Respectable French philosophy showered him with insults and nothing else. Hegel was a German, the bad German . . . of World War I, the spiritual father of Bismarck and Kaiser Wilhelm – might makes right, and so on. All the inanities of the chauvinism associated with the first imperialist war found an echo in the understanding of our Bergsons, Boutroux, and Brunschvicgs. The devil take that obscure philosophy, that 'violence done to reason', that horrid dialectic! Our philosophers had Descartes and self-evidence on their side, the simple act of the lucid mind and 'the great tradition of French spiritualism'. The whole was crowned with the old Brunschvicg's imprecations about Hegel's mental age, infantilism, and mythology.*

Yet today this dead god, covered with insults and buried a hundred times over, is rising from the grave.

The affair began in the France of the 1930s, timidly, with Jean Wahl's dissertation on *Le Malheur de la conscience*,[6] Alain's discussion of Hegel in *Idées* (1931), and the special issue of the *Revue de métaphysique* (1931, with articles by Hartmann and Croce). It found its continuation in Kojève's course at the École pratique des Hautes Études (1933–39), attended by a group that, semi-silent in those days, has become rather voluble since (Sartre, Merleau-Ponty, Raymond Aron, Father Fessard, Brice Parain, Caillois, etc.). Kojève spoke of Hegel's religious philosophy, the phenomenology of Spirit, master and slave, the struggle for prestige, the in-itself, the for-itself, nothingness, projects, the human essence as revealed in the struggle unto death and in the transformation of error into truth. Strange theses for a world beleaguered by fascism! Then came the war years, during which Hyppolite brought out his translations (*The Phenomenology of Spirit* in 1939 and 1941; *Introduction* to the *Philosophy of Right* in 1940), and the post-war period, which saw the appearance of Hyppolite's 1946 dissertation, *Genesis and Structure of Hegel's Phenomenology of Spirit*, Kojève's *Introduction to the Reading of Hegel* (1947), Father Niel's book on Hegel,[7] and Father Fessard's elucubrations in ten different journals.[8] The consecration followed: Hyppolite instated at the Sorbonne; Hegel recognized, via his commentator, as one of the masters of bourgeois thought; commentaries in the windows of all the book shops; the 'labour of the negative' in every term paper; master and slave in every academic talk; the struggle of one consciousness against another in Jean Lacroix;[9] our theologians discoursing on the 'lesser *Logic*';[10] and all the to-do connected with the academic and religious jubilation over a reviving corpse.

What is the meaning of all this fuss? To answer, we need to step back a bit in order to locate the event in the context of the history of bourgeois ideology. If we survey the one hundred and twenty years that have elapsed since Hegel's death, we can see that bourgeois thinkers have adopted two contradictory attitudes towards him: hostility, ignorance, and contempt down to the last decades of the nineteenth century; growing interest from the beginning of the twentieth century onwards. How is this volte-face to be understood?

Until the end of the nineteenth century, bourgeois philosophy showed no serious interest in Hegel. By its nature, indeed, Hegelian philosophy could not have satisfied the rising bourgeoisie of mid-century. From 1820

---

* See Brunschvicg, especially *Le Progrès de la conscience dans la philosophie occidentale*, Vol. 1, pp. 396 ff.

to 1848, Hegel's philosophy (especially the philosophy of Right and of religion) served as a warrant for the most reactionary elements in the Prussian monarchy, which was based on the squirearchy and the semi-feudal structures of a backward country that had not yet undergone its bourgeois revolution. The Hegelian system legitimized the king, aristo-cracy, large landholders, Church, and police; it legitimized the orders of the Ancien Régime and the submission of the third estate ('civil society', the economic activity of the bourgeoisie) to the other orders.

But, thanks to the rigour of its rational method, its conception of history as process, and its reflections on labour and the dialectic, Hegel's philosophy could also foster a 'critical and revolutionary philosophy' capable of calling into question, not only feudalism, but even the bourgeois order that had been established in France and England and was already silently sapping the foundations of the German feudal state. Marx and Engels acknowledged the important role Hegel had played in their development, and, though they subjected him to a thorough-going critique, revealed the extent to which his thought, stripped of its mystifications, had contributed to the creation of scientific socialism:

> In its mystified form, the dialectic became the fashion in Germany because it seemed to transfigure and glorify what exists [*a shot at the feudal reactionaries, ed.*]. In its rational form it is a scandal and an abomination to the bourgeoisie and its doctrinaire spokesmen, because it includes in its understanding of what exists a simultaneous recognition of its negation, its inevitable destruc-tion, because it regards every historically developed form as being in a fluid state, in motion, and therefore grasps its transient aspect as well; and because it doesn't let itself be impressed by anything, being in its very essence critical and revolutionary. (Marx, Preface to the second edition of *Capital*).[11]

The content of the system and the 'dialectical benediction' could be pressed into the service of the reactionary feudal state. The critical, revolutionary method could help spawn a scientific theory of history. But the bourgeoisie, for its part, had nothing to gain from Hegel. Allotted the meanest share and reduced to the level of the medieval corporations by the system, its future threatened by the method, the bourgeoisie failed to recognize itself in Hegel. It was rabid. It called him a 'dead dog'* (which is what Mendelssohn had called Spinoza), and sought other teachers.

The bourgeoisie's attitude toward Hegel was typical of the tendencies of a class already confident in itself, its economic power, and its future. The bourgeoisie did not find its concerns mirrored in a philosophy that

---

* This rejection of Hegel is evident in the *Works* of Haym, who condemned Hegel's thought as irrational and reactionary, and held out a liberal, neo-Kantian philosophy in opposition to it [Rudolf Haym, *Hegel und seine Zeit*, Berlin, 1857].

had reflected, always from a distance, but often profoundly, the terrible, concrete dialectic of the class struggle of the Revolutionary period and Empire. Or, rather, it did not want to find them mirrored there; it refused to inquire into the real origins of its power for fear of discovering portents of its fall. Hegel offered it either a defence of retrograde institutions (of the kind characteristic of feudal absolutism), or the threat of revolution. But the bourgeoisie of the period needed a *liberal* philosophy that would serve as ideological counterpoint to economic liberalism; it needed a philosophy of the wide-open future, of the harmony between its activity and the law.

It must be emphasized that *liberalism* constituted the ideology specific to the nascent and developing bourgeoisie, its 'pride', its ideal justification, its religion – and also that the bourgeoisie did not, to all intents and purposes, cease appealing to liberalism for self-justification until the great crisis of imperialism, whose last phase we are now living through.

The liberalism of *the philosophes of the eighteenth century*, the precursors of the revolution, constituted the first moment of this ideology, the critical and utopian moment when it was still engaged in pressing its claims. This was an abstract moment, in which moral and political demands provided cover for the economic and legal demands of the bourgeois class, hemmed in by the structures of the old feudal system. Once these structures had been smashed and the bourgeoisie had imposed the laws of its economic activity on society (freedom of industry, free trade, free labour), bourgeois liberalism took a new form. It had been critical, it became positive [*positif*]; it had been philosophical, it became economic. *The economists now became the philosophers of the bourgeoisie* (Smith, Say, and their disciples of the liberal school, the utilitarians, etc.); their optimism simply reflected the self-assurance of the bourgeoisie, which, through them, conceived the laws of its activity as providential, universal laws.

However, this triumphant liberalism did not long retain its original form: if it was to survive, it had to temper its ambitions and take refuge in disguise. After the workers had launched their first assault in 1848, after the first crises, the bourgeoisie had to renounce certain prerogatives in order to preserve others. It entrusted its fortunes to 'strongmen' (Napoleon III, Bismarck) and devoted itself to 'business'. Positivism was, in some sense, the philosophy 'descriptive' of this retreat. Turning its back on economics, positivism was at pains to link reflection on the most abstract forms of the rapidly progressing natural sciences to a legitimation of the bourgeois order. Liberalism by no means disappeared. Gradually driven from economic and political life by the inexorable development of capitalist concentration, crises, and increasingly violent forms of the class struggle (in France, the June days, the suppression of the Commune), *it took refuge in philosophy*. This is the underlying significance of the 'return to Kant' visible throughout Western Europe in the latter half of the nineteenth century.

But this *philosophical liberalism* no longer had the same positive meaning it had had in the eighteenth century. Eighteenth-century liberal philosophy had been utopian. It had translated the economic demands of the rising bourgeoisie into a *moral*, idealist philosophy (as can be seen in the Encyclopædists themselves, as well as in Rousseau and Kant), because the bourgeois forces of production were not sufficiently developed to appear as the driving force behind these demands. In the eighteenth century, then, liberal philosophy was merely the translation into ideal terms of the real (liberal) laws of nascent capitalism. The liberal bourgeois economists simply articulated the utopian demands of the eighteenth-century philosophers in the concrete language of the economy. In the second half of the nineteenth century, in contrast, liberalism abandoned the concrete terrain of the economy to seek refuge in philosophy. Its return to philosophy in this period took on a reactionary character in the world of the bourgeoisie. In the eighteenth century, philosophical liberalism had been the philosophy of visionaries; in the nineteenth, it became a philosophy of the blind. If, in the nineteenth century, the bourgeoisie conceived liberalism in moral terms, or in terms of the 'operations of the mind' (in neo-Kantianism), the reason was no longer its involuntary ignorance of the economy, but, quite simply, the fact that the economy was no longer liberal.

In this respect, neo-Kantian liberalism played a twofold role: it constituted a fallback position for the ideological legitimation of the bourgeoisie, and, at the same time, was the natural philosophy of petit-bourgeois intellectuals in their blindness. Hence this orderly ideological retreat had not only tactical significance, but also a precise social meaning. Having despaired of finding liberalism in the real world, the bourgeoisie was delighted to discover it in the unrealistic hopes of the petty bourgeoisie. Incapable of legitimizing itself in terms of what it actually was, it let those who were wooing it sing its praises, and, so that they might sing the better, lodged them in its Universities. The professors' liberalism no longer reflected concrete demands deriving from the economic and political activity of the ascendant bourgeoisie, but the aspirations of a petty bourgeoisie which the development of the bourgeois economy was crushing and thrusting back into the proletariat – and which yet aspired, in defiance of the facts, to join the ranks of the bourgeoisie. The history of this liberalism is simply the history of the operation that enabled the bourgeoisie to make its victims its apologists.

However, with the development of the monopoly economy, the growth and organization of the proletariat, the imperialist wars, the victory of the working class in the USSR, the deepening crisis of imperialism, the political dictatorship of the bourgeoisie, and the turn to fascism, the bourgeoisie had progressively to abandon the liberal ideology in which it had, until then, sought to legitimize itself at all costs. It did not take this step all at once, nor did the bourgeois 'philosophers' break all at once with their old loves.* But, little by little, new myths and masters emerged and gained prominence: they met the needs of a world plunged in crisis. *Grosso modo*, it can be said that the bourgeois philosophers changed masters when their world changed form, and that they made their transition from Kant to Hegel when capitalism made its from liberalism to imperialism. At this point, the bourgeoisie could no longer even afford to renounce certain prerogatives to keep others. From the end of the nineteenth century on, in the face of the menacing rise of the working class and amidst the fury of the world wars, it saw that it needed, to survive, not the pitiful hopes of the petty bourgeoisie, but compliant soldiers, policemen, civil servants, and judges, together with a tractable working class; not intellectuals still mired in classical liberalism, but philosophers of blindness capable of forging myths equal to the crisis, for consumption by the bourgeoisie's victims – capable of fashioning an ideology of servitude to bamboozle its victims and mobilize them in the defence of its most recent positions. The philosophy of liberalism, which had, despite all, maintained a certain optimism and confidence in science and history, now began gradually to disappear: there sprang up philosophies of 'experience', 'action', 'intuition', 'existence', 'life', the 'hero', and, soon enough, of 'blood'. The world was emptied of its reason and peopled with these myths.

Outside this context, it is hard to understand the way the 'return to Hegel' was carried out, and how Hegel was interpreted.

First, we need to note that this return took place throughout the Europe of the late nineteenth century and the half-century that has just elapsed. The discussions at the First Hegel Conference (1930)[12], which summed up the state of Hegel studies in Germany, Holland, Great Britain, Italy, and France, confirmed that this movement was an impressively harmonious one. Only France lagged behind, for reasons having to do with the extraordinary philosophical chauvinism spawned in our country by the imperialist conflicts of the late nineteenth and early twentieth centuries: the glorification of the 'great tradition of French spiritualism' as opposed to 'bad' German philosophy, the survival of 'liberal' philosophies of the Kantian or Cartesian type, the euphoria occasioned by the victory in 1918, the relative belatedness of the process

---

* They sought, sometimes desperately, to cloak their retreat and their abnegation in the vocabulary of the very philosophy they were repudiating: thus the reactionary philosophies of imperialism, whether Bergsonism, phenomenology, pragmatism, or *Lebensphilosophie* [see especially Dilthey's work], continued to invoke *liberty*, though they abjured *liberalism*. But this *liberty* no longer had anything to do with a *liberal, rational, and universal system* of the Kantian type; it consisted, rather, in the blind exercise of power and life, or their substitutes.

of concentration, the colonial safety-valve, etc. The fact that Italy and
Germany were the countries in which Hegel was most often invoked is
not irrelevant to our thesis. The 'advanced' state of Hegel studies in
those countries is obviously not unrelated to the 'advanced' state of the
crisis and the emergence of fascism there.

Second, it should be noted that, in this general picture, the interpretation of Hegel and the 'return' to Hegel are intimately interrelated. The
bourgeoisie did not turn back to Hegel in an attempt to understand the
real historical significance of his thought, or to seek out the promises of
a revolutionary method in the rational dialectic. Unlike the theoreticians
of scientific socialism, it did not undertake a critique of the system with
a view to extracting its rational, revolutionary kernel. It zeroed in on the
reactionary aspects of Hegel's philosophy, and, as it could no longer
sunder the master in two, it set out to show that the revolutionary in
Hegel was simply the reactionary in disguise. The result was a mass of
highly edifying exegesis. Dilthey, Haering, Kroner and Glockner were its
initiators in Germany; Jean Wahl and Hyppolite served as their teaching
assistants [répétiteurs] in France. The goal of the entire operation was to
show, as Dilthey put it in no uncertain terms, that the dialectic was not
scientific, that 'the dialectic [was] merely irrationalism built up into a
method', and that we must therefore seek the truth of the 'rational'
dialectic in a 'primitive irrationalism', or, again, the truth of Hegelian
'panlogism' in a fundamental 'pan-tragicism'.[13] As for the original
'irrationalism' or 'pan-tragicism', they had to be discovered somewhere,
and, if at all possible, *before* the 'rationalism' and 'logism'. If ever the
early Hegel was good for something, this brilliant manoeuvre was it.
This was therefore the golden age of Hegel's early works. They were
published (Nohl 1907, Lasson 1923, Hoffmeister 1931 and 1936, the works
of the Bern, Frankfurt, and Jena periods), and they were dissected. They
were obscure – so they were described as irrational; they spoke of
religion – so it was decided that they were religious;* they described
conflict – it was therefore proclaimed that they were the very picture of
dismemberment. One had only to strike up the familiar tune about the
'intuitions of Hegel's youth'[14] (it is a well known fact that a man in his
maturity never shakes them off, that he spends his days elaborating,
explaining, and translating them, just as we spend our whole lives
chasing after our first adolescent love), and declare that the whole of the
powerful dialectic of Hegel's maturity was only the small change of these
fundamental intuitions, of these religious, irrational, tragic intuitions –

* Lukács has brought this mystification to light in his book *The Young Hegel* (in German).
It seems likely that Althusser attended a lecture Lukács delivered at the Sorbonne on 29
January 1949, entitled 'New Problems in Hegel Studies'. A typed account of the lecture,
probably written by Althusser, was distributed by the Politzer Circle of the École normale
supérieure.]

and the trick was turned! We were straightfacedly told that, to understand the *Phenomenology* and the *Encylopædia*, we had to go back to Abraham, Isaac, and the desert. Today it is all too obvious that this sort of exegesis was merely a manoeuvre.

This interpretation makes it easier to understand the significance of the 'return'. To begin with, one is struck by the fact that the bourgeoisie has for half a century now been turning back to Hegel for reasons that, due allowance made, recall those that led it to turn away from him a century earlier. This is no accident. To take one example, the Hegelian philosophy of the state can, in its general political thrust, if not its actual content, serve the imperialist bourgeoisie much as it served Prussian feudalism a century earlier. The Hegelian theology of the state subordinated a young, expanding class (at that time, the bourgeoisie of 'civil society') to the will of a class which was all the more reactionary in that it was in its death throes (the Prussian feudal aristocracy). Today the roles have changed: it is the imperialist bourgeoisie, outstripped and condemned by the rising working class, which is in its death throes. No wonder that the moribund bourgeoisie should look fondly back toward the Hegelian version of a 'philosophy of the state' or a 'philosophy of history' that seeks to subjugate the ascendant class and put the world that is in the process of being born at the feet of the world that is breathing its last. It is no accident that the pro-imperialist German philosopher and historian Meinecke[15] should have identified Hegel as the inspired precursor of the reactionary politics of Wilhelm II, that doctrinaire Italian ideologues like Gentile and Costamagna should have refurbished the Hegelian philosophy of the state for fascism, that Mussolini should have gone to school to Sorel, who 'revised' Marx in the course of his return to Hegel, or that our moderns, such as Raymond Aron, Fessard,[16] & co., should find in Hegel what they need to pronounce a blessing on the projects of reaction in France.

Today, not only can we echo Marx's remark to the effect that 'in its mystified form the dialectic' is once again 'the fashion ... because it seem[s] to transfigure and glorify what exists', because it makes it possible to call servitude freedom, exploitation the common good, and police measures or war preparations defence of the human person; we must go even further, and recognize *in violence and war the true basis of this mystified dialectic.* Current developments are consonant with the bourgeois interpretation of Hegel and the true resonance of Hegel's Prussian philosophy. It is astounding to observe, today, that Marx had already gone to the heart of the problem, writing in his *Critique of Hegel's* Philosophy of Right that 'this ideality [*Hegel's idealism, ed.*] has its proper actuality only in the state's situation of war or exigency, such that here its essence is expressed as the actual, existent state's situation of war and exigency, while its "peaceful" situation is precisely the war and exigency of self-seeking'.[17]

The *belle époque* of *liberalism* – during which history was supposed to bring economic activity and the law into harmony – is dead and buried! With the generalized imperialist crisis, the bourgeoisie has entered the world of tragedy, in *the actual exigency of self-seeking*,[a] whose expression is war.

Precisely this 'mystified' dialectic furnishes the bourgeoisie with the 'tragic' concepts of the crisis in which it recognizes its own world, with the sole concepts that can justify the extreme forms of its dictatorship – violence and war. In particular, it is no accident if our modern Hegelians have put the Hegelian 'Robinsonade' of master and slave at the centre of their thinking, or if Fessard, Riquet,[18] Hyppolite, Kojève & co. delight in this myth. For they find in it the idea that the basis of the 'human condition' is anguish and violence, the 'struggle for prestige', the 'struggle unto death', a new 'will to power' which quite simply becomes the universal key to every human problem. They thus project onto the Hegelian myth the major themes of contemporary fascism, and conceive the condition of their own class, in its death agony, as the 'universal human condition'.

But this utilization of Hegel is not merely 'descriptive', nor is its sole purpose to produce concepts and references to shore up the good consciences of the policemen, mercenaries, and adventurers the bourgeoisie needs today. It has yet another aim: *the 'revision' of Marx*.[19]

However, Marx is not, this time, an author who can simply be dealt with by paraleipsis, as was done for decades. The working class has recognized in the thought of the founder of scientific socialism the theoretical weapon it needs for its liberation. Marxism is today the mode of thought of millions of human beings organized in Communist parties throughout the world, a mode of thought that is triumphing in the socialist countries, the Peoples' Democracies, and the daily struggles of the working class and colonized peoples still subject to capitalist exploitation. In this mode of thought, it is the 'rational' aspect of the dialectic that has been developed, together with authentic knowledge of the material content of history; this knowledge points – both in science and in the events inseparable from it – to the inevitable collapse of the bourgeoisie and the victory of the working class, which will emancipate the whole human race. In the face of this general assault, in this final battle, the bourgeoisie does not have a great many weapons to hand. That is why its philosophers, like its bosses and ministers, are now philosophical 'belligerents' who are trying out on the masters of scientific

---

[a] Althusser's translation reads *la détresse réelle de l'organisme*, 'the actual distress of the organism'.

socialism, preferably the oldest, the same diversionary tactics, if not 'provocations', that its police hope will succeed with the workers' movement. This language may seem excessive. But it is not in excess of the truth. The time has come *in which the overriding preoccupation of bourgeois philosophers and littérateurs is the following question:* 'What does the truth have to be for the Communists to be wrong? What does Marx have to be for the Communists to be wrong?' Thus it is that our bourgeois politicians and philosophers *fabricate* the truth and the events they need to condemn their adversary the more forcefully. This brings to mind the notorious derailment that occurred in the [*Département* of the] Nord during the 1948 miners' strike. The same demonstrative logic underlay it: '(so as to have deserved the troops and the bullets – this phrase was left between the lines), the strikers *must* be criminals – so as to be criminals, they *must* derail trains, for example. They don't? *Then let us do it for them.*' Thus it is that people are in the process of *fabricating a Marx-so-as-to....* Our bourgeois philosophers' Hegel is currently playing an important part in this operation, which has to show very plainly *what the real Marx must be for* (1) the Communists to be wrong, and for (2) the imperialist bourgeoisie to be right to treat them as it does, and to continue to pursue its violent policies.

Hegel, then, is the father of men and the gods, the father of us all – and the father of Marx, of course. Marx misunderstood him – of course. He tried to elude his grasp by founding a scientific, materialist theory of history. In fact, however, Marx did not succeed in eluding him. His truth is in Hegel; he is quite as much an idealist as Hegel is; he simply integrated into the movement of the Idea an economic content one has to grant – let us grant it, then.... But the fact remains that Marx was a utopian who wanted to realize the impossible *Idea* of communism, and who, to that end, used the proletariat as an 'instrument'[20] (here one strikes up an old song, which just happens to echo Trotskyist homilies: the poor proletariat, 'tricked', 'misled', 'exploited' by this utopian and his ruthless successors!). He threw it into the class struggle by promising it the World in the name of Science; but the misguided proletariat has not found a solution to economic and social problems in these struggles; it has only discovered the truth of the universal human condition: the tragic nature of violence and the struggle unto death, which one can already read about in Hegel – the tragic nature of this violence and this struggle unto death which are so intimately intertwined with the human condition that the bourgeoisie proves it every day on the backs of the strikers, Peace Activists, and Koreans! – so intimately intertwined with the human condition that fascism may be just one more expression of it, an expression nearer to perfection than the others, after all....

There we have the latest word in this bourgeois resurrection of Hegel. The themes that bourgeois philosophy 'finds' in Hegel are, 'coincidentally', the myths the bourgeoisie needs, in its desperate struggle, in order to arm and disarm people's consciousness. In 1931, Glockner said that what was at stake in the 'return' to Hegel was Kant. This was a half-truth, the only one he could admit to. Today we see that the question of Hegel is, for the bourgeoisie, merely a matter of impugning Marx. This Great Return to Hegel is simply a desperate attempt to combat Marx, cast in the specific form that revisionism takes in imperialism's final crisis: *a revisionism of a fascist type*.

Notes

First published in *La Nouvelle Critique*, no. 20, November 1950.

1. Althusser's typescript version of this article is entitled 'Hegel, Marx, and Hyppolite; or, Academic Revisionism's Latest Word'. It begins with the following paragraph, which was not published in *La Nouvelle Critique*: 'This article is intended above all for students of philosophy, Communist and non-Communist alike. By way of a discussion of the works of M. Hyppolite, we propose to address the problem of Hegel's apparition in bourgeois philosophy in France. We wish to show: (1) that the rediscovery or discovery of Hegel by bourgeois thought is specifically bound up with the bourgeois ideology of the imperialist period; (2) that bourgeois thinkers are obliged to distort Hegel's true historical significance in order to make him serve their own ends; (3) that this distortion is intended to fuel a critique and revision, a 'supersession' of Marxism, to divert intellectuals' attention from the class struggle in its most violent phase, and to provide arguments for an ideology of a fascist type; (4) that the Hegel problem has, for the working class, 'long since been resolved'.

2. Repr. in *Études sur Marx et Hegel*, Librairie Marcel Rivière et Cie, Paris, 1955 ['On the Structure and Philosophical Presuppositions of Marx's *Capital*', in Jean Hyppolite, *Studies on Marx and Hegel*, trans. John O'Neill, Basic Books, New York and London, 1969, pp. 126–49].

3. Andrei Zhdanov, 'Sur l'histoire de la philosophie', *Europe*, 23, November 1947 ['On Philosophy', in Zhdanov, *On Literature, Music and Philosophy*, Lawrence and Wishart, London, 1950, pp. 76–112]. Cf. p. 210 of the present volume.

4. Auguste Véra, who had published the only French translation of the *Encyclopædia* available at the time Althusser was writing, was also the author of *Le Hégélianisme et la philosophie*, Paris, 1863.

5. Jaurès' Latin dissertation was published in 1892. It has been translated into French: *Les Origines du socialisme allemand chez Luther, Kant, Fichte et Hegel*, repr. Paris, Maspero, 1960. Lucien Herr wrote the article on Hegel for the *Grande Encyclopédie*, Paris, 1885–1902, Vol. 29, pp. 997ff. Charles Andler was the author of 'Le fondement du savoir dans la *Phénoménologie de l'Esprit*', *Revue de métaphysique et de morale*, 1931, among other works.

6. *Le Malheur de la conscience dans la philosophie de Hegel*, Rieder, Paris, 1929.

7. Henri Niel, *De la médiation dans la philosophie de Hegel*, Aubier, Paris, 1945. Alexandre Kojève wrote a long review of this book: 'Hegel, Marx, et le christianisme', *Critique*, nos 3–4, August–September 1946.

8. The Jesuit theologian Gaston Fessard, who knew Hegel's work well, was the author, notably, of *France, prends garde de perdre ta liberté*, Éditions du Témoignage chrétien, 1946. In a review in other respects extremely critical of this anti-Communist pamphlet, Alexandre Kojève wrote that 'the author could be, if he so desired, by far the best Marxist theoretician in France' (*Critique*, nos 3–4, August–September 1946, p. 308). Reverend Father Fessard was also the author of a number of articles that appeared in the Jesuit review *Études*, among them 'Le communisme va-t-il dans le sens de l'Histoire?' (February 1948) and 'Le christianisme des chrétiens progressistes' (January

1949), a sharp attack on the 'Union des chrétiens progressistes', particularly André Mandouze, but also on *Esprit*. A heavily annotated copy of the latter article was discovered in Althusser's library; among the 'elucubrations' Althusser evokes, we find, for example, the following passage, which Althusser punctuated with a marginal gloss: 'Hegel-Marx and *Saint Ignatius!*' 'In order to sort out Mounier's confused comments, I have explicitly referred to St. Ignatius of Loyola's *Spiritual Exercises*, especially his famous 'Rules for Thinking with the Church'. I do not despair of one day being able to show that this book contains a technique of action, indeed, an historical dialectic, that is in no wise inferior to Marx's, or even Hegel's.'

9. Cf. the 'Letter to Jean Lacroix' in the present volume.
10. The 'Lesser Logic' is the Logic of the *Encyclopædia*, as opposed to the 'Greater Logic', i.e., *The Science of Logic*.
11. Postface to the Second Edition (1873), in *Capital*, Vol. I, trans. Ben Fowkes, Penguin/ NLR edn, Harmondsworth, 1976, p. 103.
12. See the *Verhandlungen des ersten Hegel Congresses*, Tübingen, 1931.
13. See Wilhelm Dilthey, *Die Jugendgeschichte Hegels*, Berlin, 1905, and *Introduction à l'étude des sciences humaines*, Presses Universitaires de France, Paris, 1942, the first volume of which Althusser annotated at length; Theodor Haering, *Hegel, sein Wollen und sein Werk*, Leipzig and Berlin, 1929–38, and *Hölderlin und Hegel in Frankfurt*, Tübingen, 1943; Richard Kroner, *Von Kant bis Hegel*, Tübingen, 1921–24; Hermann Glockner, *Der Begriff in Hegels Philosophie*, Tübingen, 1924, and *Hegel*, Stuttgart, 1929–40.
14. In his 1947 master's thesis [*mémoire de DES*], *Remarques sur la notion d'individu dans la philosophie de Hegel*, discovered in Althusser's library, Jacques Martin, the friend to whom *For Marx* is dedicated, makes a lengthy critique of this notion of an 'original intuition' that Hegel's philosophy supposedly developed. Martin takes issue, in particular, with the interpretations of Jean Wahl and Dilthey.
15. In French, see, for example, Friedrich Meinecke, *L'Idée de la raison d'État dans l'histoire des temps modernes*, Droz, 1973.
16. In the notes he took on his reading while preparing the present article, Althusser systematically associates the names of Raymond Aron and Father Fessard. The January 1949 issue of *Études* includes a highly laudatory review by Gaston Fessard of Raymond Aron's book *Le Grand Schisme*.
17. See Karl Marx, *Critique of Hegel's Philosophy of Right*, trans. Annette Jolin and Joseph O'Malley, Cambridge University Press, Cambridge, 1970, pp. 22–3.
18. See Father Michel Riquet, *Le Chrétien face aux athéismes*, Éditions Spes, Paris, 1950, a collection containing the 'Conférences de Notre Dame de Paris'. The two lectures entitled 'Prétextes scientistes à l'irréligion' and 'Une religion sans Dieu, le marxisme', were carefully annotated by Althusser. The June 1950 issue of *La Nouvelle Critique* includes a vehement article by Francis Cohen, 'Le Révérend Père Riquet, la théologie et le dernier stade du capitalisme'.
19. See Hyppolite, *Études sur Marx et Hegel*, p. 165.
20. See Hyppolite, 'La conception hégélienne de l'État et sa critique par Karl Marx', repr. in *Études sur Marx et Hegel*, pp. 140 ff. ['Marx's Critique of the Hegelian Concept of the State', in Hyppolite, *Studies on Marx and Hegel*, pp. 106–25]. 'What, then, is to be the instrument of the realization of this conception – the social man whom Marx, to repeat, does not fully describe – that is finally to end alienation? Marx gives this instrument a distinct name, that of the *proletariat*.... For Marx the proletariat is the subject that experiences to the extreme the contradiction of the human condition and is thereby capable of resolving it forever. But is such a resolution of all transcendence possible on the historical plane and not just at the level of thought? Does the human condition as a problem carry within it the solution to its problem?' (pp. 123–5).

A Matter Of Fact
(1949)

The only valid way to answer your question – 'Has the Good News been announced to the men of our time?' – is to consider the question itself, the meaning of the question, i.e., its real origins. Only those real origins can provide us with the elements of a response commensurate with the question.

Let me explain. The Church is like a sick man, who, using the most open-minded and concerned among the faithful[a] as go-betweens, asks his friends: 'Do I have a right to hope? Are people really turning away from me? Does anyone still listen to me?', and so on. When a sick man wonders when he will get up and walk again, if life will ever begin again, if he can ever again hope to take his place among the living, when he puts such questions to those around him, it is obvious that:

1. His illness has become a question for him *in a real sense*, he is really putting it to the question, and, from now on, he can experience the present and future only by way of this question.

2. The questions he puts to those around him are the method his illness uses to ask questions about itself, that is, about its outcome (which alone can bring the intolerable to an end), not about its origins.

3. The sick man's friends, taken unawares, will not have the heart to leave his questions unanswered, and, assuming they are not playacting, will treat them seriously; they will base their answers on the most valuable of their own experiences, which is to say, once again, on *results*, without going all the way back to the origins of their own lives, or, *a fortiori*, to the origins of the sick man's question. In matters of this sort, friendship is as poor a physician as love.

4. As for the doctor, he will not take the sick man's questions seriously; they do not mean to him what they do to his patient. They make up the

---

[a] *Ses fidèles*, which means both 'the faithful' in the religious sense, and those loyal to the sick man of Althusser's simile.

whole of the sick man's present life; they are merely signs for the doctor, the discourse of a man enslaved by illness, an unbearable sort of servitude that protests and longs to get things over with. The doctor knows that one restores a sick man to health, not by answering his questions, but by curing the disease that prompts them. The true answer is the one that simultaneously reduces the question to its real origins and really destroys them. In the man who has regained his health, the sick man falls silent; his existence has ceased to be problematic. The true answer renders the question superfluous.

This concrete 'reduction' comprises two moments:

1. The theoretical reduction of the question to its real origins;
2. The practical reduction of those origins as such.

I. Theoretical Reduction

What, then, are the real origins of your question?

To begin with, the question takes a universal form. It reflects the experience of a fundamental historical situation. On the one hand, the world no longer listens to the Church, whose words fail to reach the men of our day; the Church has become a virtual stranger for broad masses of people who are already the present and future of this world. On the other hand, when we consider the people faithful to the Church, the question arises as to whether their faithfulness is still religious. This historical situation is simultaneously the historical context Christians are living in, and a reality all men, Christians or not, meet at every turn. Just as, in an earlier age, all roads led to Rome, so, today, all roads lead to two obvious and interrelated facts: *the modern Church is no longer at home in our times, and the vast majority of the faithful are* in *the Church for reasons that are not really of the Church.*

That historical divorce reflects the kind of social, ideological, and political relations the Church maintains with structures alien to our times. The divorce is essentially social, ideological, and political. Although in 1789 in France, 1848 in Western Europe, 1917 in Russia, and quite recently in Central Europe, we have seen the abolition of *feudal structures* (economic, social, legal, and political); although the *capitalist bourgeoisie* – which has, generally speaking, been the successor to feudalism – has, in certain parts of the world, collapsed in its turn, and, in many countries, already senses that it is marked for death, even if it proclaims, as the American bourgeoisie does, that the century belongs to it; although our world is living on the ruins of feudalism and living through the ruination of the capitalist bourgeoisie, the contemporary Church is still very closely tied, by way of its social, ideological, and political positions, to feudal and capitalist structures.

The social situation of the Church

From a sociological standpoint, the body of the faithful is made up, broadly speaking, of:

(a) The peasant populations of 'young countries' in which feudal structures have not yet been eroded by industrial development (South America); of 'young countries' in which industrial development has taken the form of the mechanization of agriculture outside heavily populated regions (Canada); and of old countries that have stood apart from the trend toward industrialization (Ireland, Spain, Southern Italy, Hungary and Central Europe in general, until quite recently).

(b) The new bourgeoisie, which, after a period when its struggle against feudalism compelled it to oppose religion, has in general found it expedient to accept the official Church's decision to rally to its support, for reasons often having precious little to do with religion (France, Belgium, Italy, the United States).

We may estimate the mass of the faithful bound to the Church via surviving feudal structures at about fifty per cent of Church membership [*du corps de l'Église*]. Forty per cent of the mass of the faithful are linked to the Church by way of a capitalist bourgeoisie that has already been, or is in the process of being, expropriated. From a sociological standpoint, then, the Church is deeply enmeshed, as far as ninety per cent of its human resources [*son corps humain*] are concerned, in structures that are no longer those of our world. It must be added that the Church still finds itself, in certain countries, *directly* tied in to the economic structures of the feudal and capitalist world through its extensive land holdings. Generally speaking, it is only when we take these anachronistic structures into account that we can understand the Church, whether what is in question is its membership, audience, or role (e.g., its schools, and, in many cases, its hospital services and parish registry offices as well).

The ideological situation of the Church

From an ideological standpoint, the archaic nature of the Church's positions is even more obvious, if that is possible. Everything conspires to suggest that the Church – due to an inertia that reflects, in its fashion, its real ties to an outdated world – is incapable of renouncing the concepts to which that world gave rise. Broadly, it may be said that the conceptual systems the Church finds congenial are based on a philosophy (which can have variants) that is outmoded as far as both its form (*qua* philosophy), and the concrete content that originally provided its historical legitimation are concerned. Theology, be it Thomist or Augustinian, is based on a 'world-view' the Church finds so thoroughly congenial that it has knowingly or unknowingly assigned this philosophy, *qua* philosophy, the task of leading it to the final moment where it will again find Revelation – as if Christ had come into a world of concepts, not men. Whether God is 'in the beginning' or 'at the end', whether one takes him as one's starting point or claims gradually to be making one's way toward him, he is in classical theology one concept among others, the prisoner of a conceptual universe that no longer makes sense to the men of modern times.

In fact, the Church inhabits a conceptual universe that was established in the thirteenth century; it is based on the philosophies of Plato and Aristotle, 'adjusted' by the Augustinian tradition and St. Thomas Aquinas. From the thirteenth century on, the Church has consistently taken these central concepts as guidelines in its theology, politics, and ethics, 'adjusting' them whenever discrepancies became too flagrant. Far from calling Thomist or Augustinian concepts into question, however, this accommodation plays on their differences. Thus Malebranche, for whom God the Father, 'in his old age', became a Cartesian, in fact found his way back to the Platonic tradition via Descartes. The 'play' in Augustinian and Thomist concepts thus clears a path for opportunistic variations which, far from invalidating the content of the concepts employed or the traditions they implicitly refer to, and far from destroying, *a fortiori*, the philosophy that, *qua* philosophy, authorizes these operations, reinforces and legitimizes them on the practical level.

1. Despite the protestations of the theologians who claim to be investing old concepts with new meanings, the *content* of these concepts is still alive in a real sense, to the extent that these concepts are still intertwined with vestigial features of the worlds that spawned them. Doubtless, Aristotelian physics no longer exists, and there are no more Aristotelian physicists to defend Thomist concepts. But it should not be inferred that these concepts are today sustained by theology alone, as if theology were holding itself aloft unaided. This conceptual edifice has real foundations that implicitly legitimize its structure and guarantee its validity, while continuing to prevent the Church from giving way before the critique the modern world brings to bear on its outmoded ideas. We feel that this conceptual universe is ripe for demolition, but it lives on; it must plainly have moorings in life in order to persist even as an illusion. These moorings are quite complex, but they are real. In particular, it can be shown that the economic, political, moral, and educational conceptions of the Church can not only not provide their own legitimation, as goes without saying, but could not even be legitimized by theology itself (which is insufficient) if other real, unspoken motives did not, even in our own world, justify them in advance of all argument. It is no longer Aristotelian physics that saves Thomist concepts; it is rather the vestiges of the medieval world still present in our own. These concepts do not survive by the grace of God; they are sustained by the lives of men who, because they are subject to archaic structures, conceive and experience

their world and lives, politics and economy, practical morality and the education of their children, to say nothing of their naive theology, in terms of the concepts these structures engendered when they held sway. Thus the concept of natural law, which is at the heart of all the Church's morals and politics, is bound up, as a concept, with the conceptual universe of an historically superannuated world; this conceptual system thinks human activity, society, history, and morality as natural realities instituted by God, because it fails to grasp their real origins. But it is not from this conceptual universe alone that the concept of natural law draws such life as is left it. The concept of natural law and all the concepts it spawns are, rather, sustained by concrete structures that are still 'lived' by many of the men of our day, who need these concepts, precisely, in order to legitimize, defend, and perpetuate the structures in which they are born, grow up, and die.

We have to trace matters back to these concrete structures in order to understand the tenacity of obsolete concepts in religious ideology. Moreover, we have to expose these structures in order to help bring them to their appointed end, and to help the men who are brought up in them overcome them and become contemporary with their times. Finally, we have to convince ourselves that these economic, political, familial, and moral structures are bound up with the conceptual edifice of the theologians only to the extent that the Church is, on the whole, itself linked, by virtue of the economic positions it still maintains and the social situation of the great mass of the faithful, to worlds that our period has consigned irrevocably to the past.

2. One word more about the *form* of the 'philosophies' that undergird the Church's conceptual edifice. Through the uses to which it puts philosophy, the Church effectively defends it as the means *par excellence* of appropriating truth. Yet our time is in the process of translating Marx's dictum about 'doing away with philosophy' into reality. Let us not be frightened by the word: when he does away with philosophy, man does away with nothing more than illusions, but he does so in order to reclaim, in the very origin of these illusions, a portion of his real activity. Even if this prodigious event continues to escape the notice of many of our contemporaries, we have to recognize that our time has seen (thanks to the activity of the working class taking possession of itself) *the advent of a new form of human existence in which humanity's appropriation of the truth ceases to be carried out in philosophical form, that is, in the form of contemplation or reflection, in order to be carried out in the form of real activity.** Here, 'to appropriate' means concretely to reclaim possession

---

* This real activity concretely produces, in labour and history, the very life of men in its totality; it also produces the objects philosophy thinks it endows itself with, the contradictions philosophy thinks it resolves, and even philosophy itself – in order to manage, in thought, contradictions that get on all too well not to be hindrances.

of human activity and its products through human activity itself.
Philosophy is one such product: it must, then, be 'repossessed', but this
repossession must be accompanied by a critical reduction that will do
away with philosophy's philosophical form, i.e., the illusion that human
truth can be originally given to man in an act of contemplative or
reflexive appropriation. The Church, which makes use of, and, by that
very fact, sanctions philosophy as such, parts company with the men of
our day, who are in the process of concretely doing away with the form
of philosophy itself by doing away with the human structures that once
gave rise to, and still legitimize, it. Here too, the Church can, with some
semblance of plausibility, defend a mode of appropriating truth so alien
to our times only because it is itself subject, given its position and
membership, to the archaic structures that have engendered philosophy
and still assure it a paradoxical but tenacious lease on life.

The political situation of the Church

The imbrication of the membership and ideology of the Church in these
feudal and capitalist structures, or what is left of them, and the fact that,
nolens volens, the overwhelming majority of the faithful are concretely
tied to obsolete forms of civilization which are struggling against a world
that has condemned them to extinction, necessarily commits the Church
to the defence of reactionary political positions directed against the new
forces of emancipation. We cannot affirm *a priori* that religion is reactionary, but, *when we examine what actually transpires*, we cannot help
observing that, in the contemporary world, the economic positions
maintained by the Church in certain countries, together with the ties and
tendencies of the overwhelming majority of the faithful, determine the
policies the Church is currently implementing, overtly and covertly.

These policies are clearly reactionary, whatever the protestations and
rhetorical precautions of the most sincere or intellectually supple believ-
ers and priests. The most daring public positions of the Papacy, which
often anticipated or even offended the general opinion of the broad mass
of Catholics (for example, the *'ralliement'*, the 'social encyclicals',[1] etc.),
are merely reformist accommodations. The ostensible 'social doctrine of
the Church' in fact reflects the tacit pact which the Church, in the person
of its members and through its attachments, has concluded with faltering
structures. This compromise between medieval corporatism and liberal
reformism denounces the 'abuses' of economic liberalism, but ignores
their real causes, and, by its silence, ratifies them. To denounce the
scandalous effects without denouncing the real causes of the scandal is
plainly a scandalous diversion, for it diverts men's attention from the
real struggle. Just as the Red Cross is an endorsement of war and its

moral code, so the Church's social doctrine is simply the recognition of capitalism, and proof of the Church's *savoir-vivre*.

If the Church's most advanced proposals represent nothing more than a form of reactionary reformism, it is not hard to imagine what its 'non-advanced' policies look like. Through its hierarchy, its exhortations, and the faithful, the Church has recently lent support to fascist governments (at least by its silence, as in Germany, if not by its actions, as in Italy, Spain, and Vichy France), or to profoundly reactionary governments (Ireland, Canada, Latin America). In Central Europe, it is one of the chief counter-revolutionary forces; in Western Europe, where the religious crisis daily impels more and more of the faithful to call its traditional positions into question, the Church nonetheless persists in its support of the sterile, sanctimonious reformism of the Christian Democrats, who – as M. Hours* has recently clearly demonstrated – associate themselves with the German Centre and its nostalgia for the Middle Ages.

In sum, if we consider its policies on a global scale, we must admit that, apart from a few active but isolated small groups, the Church comprises, by virtue of its positions, ideology, membership, and the weight of the masses of the 'Western hemisphere', an objective, non-negligible force that maintains a deep, compromising commitment to world-wide reaction, and is struggling alongside international capitalism against the forces of the working class and the advent of socialism.

The Church is, then, objectively tied to archaic structures doomed to extinction.

On the one hand, these structures condition and determine the archaic, reactionary character of the Church's social, ideological, and political position in the world.

On the other hand, a large majority of the faithful gain access to religious life through the mediation of these structures, and the Church is so deeply implicated in them, they weigh so heavily on the concrete existence, orientation, and convictions of the men who live in them, that one is entitled to ask whether the mass of the faithful does not, on the whole, conceive and experience its religion as one of the major components of these structures, as their inner logic, legitimation, and theoretical expression.

If so, we are in a position to understand the origin of the twofold anxiety that *Jeunesse de l'Église*'s survey reveals.

1. To begin with, 'the Good News is no longer being announced to the men of our time' because the Church announces it in a language men no longer understand. A language cannot be reduced to a vocabulary; it is a

---

*See the May 1948 issue of *Vie intellectuelle*. [Joseph Hours had been Althusser's history professor in *khâgne*. See Preface, translator's note, p. 14]

totality of real meanings which are experienced and felt every day in life and its gestures, and which the spoken language evokes by allusion; these concrete meanings (social realities, structures, economic and political laws, everyday life, modes of behaviour, gestures) are the real content of the spoken language, which, without them, would be merely noise coming out of people's mouths. Yet the concrete meanings underpinning the language of the Church are precisely the archaic, isolated structures our age is struggling against, and which live on amongst us because they have, as it were, been granted a temporary reprieve. They have meaning only for those who still inhabit them; but even this meaning cannot be taken for granted, as it once was, and is further eroded with each passing day. The whole world has already laid siege to these structures, and is, little by little, carrying out their complete 'reduction'. *These structures no longer make immediate sense to the world they survive in*; they are alien to us. But it is these alien realities that sustain, with their unspoken meaning, the language of the Church! They are present in all the Church says or means to say, in the eloquence of its priests, the concepts of its theologians, and the advice proffered by its confessors, as well as the body of its ethics, social doctrine, and actual politics. When the Church wants to announce the Good News to the men of our day, it does not choose its language; it speaks the sole language it bears within it, or, rather, *what it is* continues to speak even in the best of those who would save it, whatever their intentions. The Good News speaks a language – in other words, reflects a world – that the men of our day do not understand because it is no longer theirs – when they are not actively combating it because it has become their enemy.

This basic condition narrowly limits the Church's capacity for 'adaptation'. It is not enough to borrow people's vocabulary to speak their language: the same words must refer to realities that coincide and are mutually recognizable. But, however sincere the most open-minded of the priests or the faithful, when they 'announce' the good news, even if they use the same words their brothers do, the Church speaks more loudly; it 'announces', in its nature and acts, a strange sort of news the men of our day do not recognize as relevant to them.

2. This state of affairs accounts for the other aspect of the contemporary alienation from religion: if the good news does not reach the men of our day because it finds expression in archaic structures, does it, at least, reach the men still under the sway of these structures? The fact is that the Church's social alienation explains not only the indifference or hostility of the proletariat, but also the religious alienation of the broad mass of those who have remained faithful to it. The Church is so deeply committed to certain determinate social structures, the access the faithful have to religion in their concrete lives is so thoroughly mediated by these structures, religion is, in their perception and their lives, so closely bound

up with them, that they experience and conceive it, at the *practical* level, as a determinant factor in their social universe. How many Christians have recognized the truth of Marx's analyses here, and have *met*, as abruptly as one meets a person, this alienation from religious life in an economic, social, or political form! When religion is in reality a social form that takes its place within feudal and capitalist structures, and holds the people in submission, forcing it to experience its submission to men as God's will; when, in its discourse, silences, or diversionary tactics, it shores up these structures and provides them with their theoretical justification; when it ensures their defence and 'compensation'; when the faithful experience religion, in reality, as the theory and legitimation of their social universe – one can no longer avoid the question: is this life of religion still a religious life, is it still the Good News that is being announced – even in the world of the Church?

This question brings us back to the heart of the problem. That the Church is like an alien presence in our world, and that the broad mass of the faithful are in the Church for reasons not really of the Church, is attributable to one and the same cause – the Church's profound historical commitment to those feudal and capitalist structures that are, today, the substance of human alienation.

II. Perspectives for a Practical Reduction

The very historical situation that conditions and poses the present problem indicates its real solution. If the Church is to speak to the men of our day, if it is to reconquer, at the price of an inner struggle, an authentic religious life, it must, to begin with, be freed of the domination of feudal and capitalist structures. Secondly, this social emancipation must be accompanied by a real reappropriation of religious life by the faithful themselves. Two tasks have to be accomplished simultaneously: social emancipation and the reconquest of religious life.

1. *The social liberation of the Church.* The nature and degree of the Church's alienation in feudal and capitalist structures – indeed, the very nature of those structures – condition the real means required for the Church's social emancipation. The 'theoretical reduction' of the present religious malaise has led us to identify religious alienation as its true origin. We need, then, to consider the means that can operate a practical 'reduction' of that origin by destroying it so as to transform it into its truth. The doctor too 'reduces' the cause of the sick man's illness, calling on means actually capable of modifying his patient's objective state, that is, capable of acting chemically or physically on the chemical or physical agents which condition the progress of the disease. The nature of these means is

itself determined by the nature of the disease to be fought. Broadly speaking, the same holds for our 'reduction': the social forces dominating the Church can only be reduced by social forces that are objectively capable of defeating them, and, indeed, that need to defeat them. These cannot be random forces; they must rather be the very forces whose advent threatens the destruction of the old structures, making them appear, precisely, as threatened, archaic, and outdated. These forces of reduction and combat are, today, those being marshalled by the organized proletariat. This problem and this struggle are not religious in nature; but, by virtue of the fact that the reduction of collective religious alienation presupposes this political and social struggle as the condition without which no emancipation, not even religious emancipation, is conceivable, no Christian sincerely concerned about the destiny of the Church can fail to conclude:

(a) that, in the present situation, only the organized proletariat (and its allies) is capable of combating, in a concrete sense, precisely those feudal and capitalist structures responsible for the Church's alienation;

(b) that the struggle for the social emancipation of the Church is inseparable from the proletariat's present struggle for human emancipation;

(c) that the Christian who truly wishes to put an end to the Church's social alienation has to play a *real* part, in the ranks of the proletariat, in the one struggle that can destroy feudal and capitalist structures: the political, social, and ideological struggle of the organized working class.

2. *The reconquest of religious life.* While participating in this political and social struggle, which alone can reduce collective alienation because it alone is commensurate with that alienation, the Christian must pursue, at the personal level, the 'reduction' of alienation and the reconquest of his religious life. Such reduction implies the destruction and critique, at the personal level, of all the alienated forms even an informed believer is obliged to pass through, in the present state of the Church, if he is to have access to religious life. This reduction must be brought to bear on the Church's conceptual universe, theology, and moral system, its theory of the family, of education, of Catholic action, of the parish, etc. It must engage and destroy, with a view to founding them in the truth, the modes of behaviour and human conduct, of living and being, that are suggested to, sustained by and reinforced in the Christian masses by those forces which are in the Church but not really of the Church. This 'purification' cannot be purely negative. It truly leads, when one lets events and facts freely confront one another and produce their own truth, to the revelation of their origins and the production of that truth, to the constitution of new, concrete modes of behaviour – familial, moral, educational, etc. – that are the truth of the alienated modes. If religion is

not, *a priori*, a form of alienation, this reduction should permit the Christian to reconquer an authentic religious life, whose conditions and limits he must already begin to define, in struggle.

We should not, however, gloss over the fact that, given the present state of affairs, this positive reconquest of religious life through real criticism cannot be the collective work of the Church, which is satisfied with its alienation. It will be undertaken, in the best of cases, by small groups of activists emerging in countries (such as France, Italy, and Belgium) and social milieux whose structures have evolved to the point where religious alienation can criticize itself, and this real criticism can manifest and reflect itself in the concerns and spiritual quest of the best-informed amongst the faithful.

But such groups are relatively small and terribly isolated in the immense world of the Church. They are active on its margins, in milieux that have themselves been severely shaken by the events of this century: they can hardly be active anywhere but there, in pockets of humanity that are already on the way to reducing capitalist alienation. Yet, even there, when they meet with men's silence, they question themselves, wondering why their voice is not heard, without realizing that, even if they pursued their self-criticism to the point of being able to offer men a truth they could recognize as truly theirs, they could not by themselves counter the collective might of the Church or its language, precepts, and alliances. They continue to feel that they are of little moment because they are on the fringes of the Church and cannot seriously expect to shake it up from within, without inducing it to threaten or repudiate them. *Although the objective conditions for a social emancipation of the Church through the proletarian struggle already exist, the conditions for a collective reconquest of religious life have not been created*. To create them, the Church as a whole would have to be capable of undertaking its self-criticism; but it is subject to the law of structures which defend themselves, and will not tolerate being questioned. It is necessary, then, to shatter these structures and struggle against the forces protecting them.

We are already engaged in this struggle. The future of the Church depends on the number and the courage of those Christians who, day by day, are developing an awareness of the necessity of the struggle and joining the ranks of the world proletariat. It also depends on the concrete reduction, by these same men, of their own religious alienation. The Church will live thanks to those who, through struggle and in struggle, are once again discovering that the Word was born among men and dwelt among them – and who are already preparing a humane place for it amongst men.

Note

First published in *Jeunesse de l'Église, Cahier X: L'Évangile Captif*, February 1949.

1. Allusion to the 'rallying' of France's Catholics to the Republic, advocated by Pope Leo XIII and publicly affirmed for the first time in a toast proposed by Cardinal Lavigerie in Algiers in 1890. See the encyclical *Au milieu des sollicitudes*. The 'social encyclicals' include *Rerum novarum*, about the condition of the working class (1891), *Il firmo proposito* (1905), *Singulari quadam*, on the trade unions (1912), *Urbi arcano* (1922), and *Quadragesimo anno* (1931). A 1947 edition of *Rerum novarum* was discovered in Althusser's library, with an abundance of critical comments. Althusser had originally planned to buttress his article with a number of quotations from *Rerum novarum* and *Quadragesimo anno*, but ultimately abandoned the idea.

Letter to Jean Lacroix
(1949–1950)

25.12.49

Dear Sir, Dear Friend,

I write amidst the silence of the École [normale supérieure], emptied of its students after the first term's work. This old institution counts amongst its ranks a good many young men who owe you a great deal and reserve a large place for you in their hearts because of all you have given them in the past. I am one of them, and I must say that I am still deeply touched by your affection. You have reaped an ample return for it, you know: an affection not only of the heart, but of the mind as well, which holds in high esteem the courage you displayed in Lyons through the long years of semi-solitude[1] – and who can tell just how much your struggle against countless difficulties costs you, the surcharge of work life imposes on you, to say nothing of the clamour of the children who are your delight, but also a burden in this society that does nothing to help men be fathers without giving up their work. I think of you often, and, incidentally, of M. Hours[2] as well, you who have a double posterity, the children of your flesh and of your spirit, and are equally fond of both, concerned about them and confident in them.

I would like to tell you in my turn, on behalf of all those you have helped become men, that they too have confidence in you and are concerned about you. We too know that, as a saying you like goes, the child is the idea and truth of his parents, and we know that, in us, you have helped your own truth develop and grow. That, moreover, is why you feel uneasy when it seems to you that you have grown apart from us, and that is why we feel uneasy when it seems to us that you have grown more distant from us. I think that that truth has enough to do with your letter[3] to warrant my mentioning it here. And I think that that truth is a fruitful one, because it calls the present into question and looks toward the future. You know well enough that we cannot live on memories, and that a friendship is doomed if it is based on memories alone, on keeping faith with memories. Memories, even of *khâgne*,[a] even of people, are not fruitful unless quickened by a present that prolongs them and a future that engages the man this past has helped bring into being. Before the war, you would often repeat Wilde's epigram for us: 'No-one who disregards his past deserves to have a future.'[b] I carried that epigram with me into captivity, and, in that time of betrayal, it was my source of strength. But I would also say, to bring out the full meaning of Wilde's phrase, that 'No-one who disregards his present and future still deserves to have a past'. I have read your book closely enough to feel certain that you will find nothing to object to in that sentence, which, I believe, echoes the essence of the closing sentences of your text.[4] And you are sufficiently close to us to have the same understanding of the idea that our life is truly not on deposit somewhere in heaven or the past, but rather resides in our present, in our present problems, housing and war and Descartes and Marx and religion, and also in our future, which is in the process of emerging, and has already emerged in our present problems and our present responses to them. That is our eternity, this present and the future that issues from it, and there is nothing I would change in that admirable text you cite on the last page of your book.[5] I would simply add this: if our friendship is sustained by that which *concretely* unites us today, and by that which creates, today, what will unite us tomorrow, you will grant that it is truly a friendship between men, and that age only plays the role of memories in it, with the difference that age is a memory one respects, and is truly a *present merit*, because our elders have had to seek out a path for us that is, thanks to their efforts and their pains, a good deal smoother for us than it was for them.

But you will agree with us when we say we are as old as the events we live through, and that since the world is always young, and, more profoundly, since it is possible today, for the first time perhaps, for men to be of the same age as a history they are making rather than enduring, then we are younger than ever, whatever our age, we are as young as the youth of this world that is taking shape through our efforts, we are younger than ever, you and I and Stalin and Cachin,[6] who laughs like a wrinkled and happy child. But this youth and joy in the same age have a very precise meaning: they mean being constantly, actively, lucidly engaged in and alive to [*présent à*] the real content of our time, the whole content of our time, the inner law of this human world that is the real basis for brotherhood and real friendship between men. I say being engaged in the *real content in its truth*, for one can be engaged in error

[a] See translator's note, Preface, p. 14.
[b] Doubtless a misquotation of Wilde's dictum, 'The man who regards his past deserves to have no future to look forward to.'

and crime; Hitler too was engaged and active and always in motion, and our sincere Hitlerites were ready to die for the sake of this engagement with crime, which they felt was an engagement with truth.

It may be that I have here taken up a theme of classical thought that you, perhaps, consider outmoded, but I say that there can be no friendship between men outside the truth; it is truth – not abstract, but real truth, the truth which is the life and the way (the way toward itself) – it is *the real, specific content* of this truth that makes for unity and friendship between men, not the spirit of truth (which is absolutely undefinable, and can therefore take in the true and the false, real values as well as crimes), but the truth in its *defined content*, a truth that depends, not on inspiration, but on the terrible and grand necessities of men's lives, and that can provide a basis for defining the spirit of truth as well, if you insist. I affirm that there can be no real friendship in crime and error; friendship in error only makes sense if it seeks, even in error, and unbeknownst to itself, the truth that will set it free, the truth that is already the reason for error and that makes it possible to speak of error and ferret it out. I would add too that this friendship implies that the friends should correct one another in the service of the truth they continue to live by, even if they have not always recognized and articulated it. I think that you acknowledge this law of friendship, the simplest, and that you will permit me to invoke it in all modesty in the interest of the truth we all live by, as I try to pay you back, on this occasion, a share of the truths that I owe you and that are the more fully developed, perhaps, for having been experienced in a part of the world in which I lived without you; to pay you back, as well, a share of the truths you have helped me discover, have helped dozens of men discover, in a world that today gives us reason to fear, a world that is our everyday lives, and our profoundest joy.

That said, I'm going to be hard on you, and so I would ask you to get ready to take a few knocks, even if it means paying me back in kind if I'm off the mark!

1. You *'do not set out to influence me in any way . . .'*, you do not think you have, 'in all good conscience, the right to criticize those who, in all good conscience and after carefully weighing up all the facts, are convinced that they must take a different course of action. *I merely affirm that my conscience does not permit me not to bear witness to what I believe in. That is all.'* I find this language absolutely unacceptable. For my part, I write to influence you, and I say so without making any attempt to hide the fact; or, rather, I write in order to help you recognize the truth, or, if you prefer, so that both of us can recognize the truth both of us live by, even when you declare that you do not think you have any right, etc. Have you *'carefully weighed up'* what you write? Is 'proceeding in all good

conscience' the criterion of truth? Your conscience does not permit you not to bear witness to what you *'believe in'*? What you believe in *tout court* or what you believe *to be true*? If it is truth which founds belief, it should be possible to demonstrate the truth, to account for it, λόγον δίδοναι; this truth once discovered and demonstrated, you can always say that it is not meant to 'influence', that it does not give you the right to 'criticize' anyone at all: yet, you know, the truth that is not under a bushel, but rather out in plain view, that truth is virulent; it does quite a job! It 'influences' and it 'criticizes', all your precautions notwithstanding! Why take all those precautions, then? Is it because you cannot *demonstrate* the truth you believe in? Because you prefer the spirit of truth to the content of truth? Because it seems to you *difficult to reconcile, in the realm of 'demonstrable' truth* (1) the crime of Rajk's condemnation, etc.;[7] (2) your good opinion of the Communists *as far as the rest is concerned*; (3) the denunciation of the 'crime' by *Esprit;*[8] (4) your concern to 'protect what you say from being used', etc.? Or is it because you ultimately think that this problem is basically ontological, that the truth, once *demonstrated*, would become an object, that truth is of the order of belief and the subject, etc.? Or is it quite simply out of friendship and respect for my convictions?

I cannot accept this last precept, not by whim or because I have simply decreed it to be so, but out of the very necessities of friendship, which is sustained only by an element held *in common*, and which must first identify this *common* element in order to discover its concrete, its veritable basis. It is as sure as sin that if we eat the same bread, we will be sustained by our life in common; if we feed on the same truth, we will be nourished by the truth we hold in *common*, which makes possible the simple exchange of *words* we call a letter, the exchange of *meanings* we call a conversation! We do not live on good conscience, but on that which makes up our lives, the common content of our lives, the *common* meaning of our lives; Malebranche already said, if you will pardon this classicism, that there was a *logos* among men, a truth, and that it was this truth that constituted their lives, their social lives, their communication, the fact that they could *talk to one another*, look at and understand one another, or even fail to understand one another! With your good conscience, we fall back into a subjectivism which is the counter-theory of *what we actually do, of what you do when you write me*! Or else we have to assign your good conscience another meaning: we have to demand that it submit to, that is, acknowledge the truth, that it utter it, show it, proclaim it, and work to ensure its victory!

If that seems too theoretical to you, I would answer, by what right would you have condemned a sincere Nazi? who 'in all good conscience . . .'? You say yourself, 'I do not think I have any right . . .'. Your theory of 'good conscience' is so vague and hollow that it might as easily serve as a theoretical justification for Nazism, Thibon,[9] or Guitton[10] as for Stalin's 'good conscience'! And that is serious, and in contradiction with your own actions! You will say, 'to good conscience, I add "after carefully weighing up all the facts"'; this would be perfect (1) if you defined 'careful weighing', if you constructed a *real* theory of what weighing was, that is, of what one weighs, what one weighs with, the result of the weighing, the reason for the weighing, etc., something that is not at all mysterious, but simply human, and real; (2) and if, secondly, you showed us how the 'good conscience' is connected with the weighing and what its dialectical relation with the weighing is, that is, if you constructed a *real* theory of historical judgement, which is meaningful only if it is the historical content of the situation under consideration that is *carefully weighed up*, and also a theory of the relationship between consciousness/ conscience [*conscience*] and historical judgement, that is, a theory of ideology. Otherwise, anyone at all can say 'my conscience does not allow me . . .', just as one says 'my concierge does not allow me to come home after midnight' – except that I can always go parley with your concierge, whereas you would have a hard time giving me the address of your conscience.

This is serious, because the ambiguity you leave the 'carefully weighed' in means that you pass insensibly from a theory of the truth to a theory of the conscience, from the truth which can be defined, to the conscience which is absolutely undefinable, arbitrary, and can encompass all sorts of things. What is serious, and what does not seem very honest to me, is that your theory precisely 'fails to account' for your own actions and concrete political conduct, that you assume infinitely more of the content of the truth in your own life than in your 'theory'. I do not mean honesty in the moral sense, but in a *material* sense, and I say that it is precisely the defining feature of honesty (intellectual honesty, if you like) to take responsibility in one's thinking for the content and meaning of one's conduct; I think you help us understand this requirement when you show that a man is not honest unless he 'takes upon himself' what he does.[11] One would like to see fuller recognition of your actual behaviour in your thought; one would like to love you as much for what you say as for what you do.

2. Second grievance: Rajk and Fejtö. I have not been at all 'galled', to tell you the truth, by the last two issues of *Esprit*.[12] *Esprit* no longer interests me at all. It should be ranged with the 'memories' that lead a merely 'historical' existence, in the bourgeois sense of history: history is what is *passé*, what is over and done with. *Esprit* offers me the small, mean satisfaction of showing me that I was not wrong, that *we have nothing to expect from Mounier, who is himself in the process of discovering 'his' truth, which is not a very pretty sight*. We will leave him standing in front of his

mirror, grappling with the problem of how someone can be a decent person, generous and courageous in private life, and a bastard in politics ... and move on to the question at hand. It is your reaction and your judgement that trouble me. Because it seems to me that you are close to us, and are making a real effort to understand us and to understand this truth that we are experiencing together with millions of others, yourself included, at the very moment you are subject to doubts. I will not take up the substance of this Rajk affair because you do not, either. I will take it as an example of something 'that has been *carefully weighed up*' and give you the benefit of the doubt: that is, I will assume that if you consider the trial to be a crime, you do so not on a flash of inspiration, but because you have 'carefully weighed up' the facts.

We have, then, a public trial involving precise accusations, full confessions,[13] and the testimony of a number of different people, testimony that counts (these witnesses are, if not cutting their own throats, at least putting themselves in the dock).[a] It has a political significance that is revealed by current events (the relations between Tito and the US!), and a great many historical precedents (Danton, Doriot, Gitton,[14] and the Moscow trials); one can even cite the theory of betrayal, based on class relations, that was put forward by Lenin and Stalin before the betrayals took place. If that is not 'carefully weighed up', I don't know what the word means. Over against this we have Fejtö; a long article with arguments about Rajk's past, a distant past, that are intended to cast doubt on his confession; and, finally, a spiel about Rajk, the willing martyr, with a hurrah for Koestler.[15] Mounier speaks of 'a valuable witness who has pursued his efforts to the point of suffocation'.[16] Here, the application of sound historical method suggests (ask M. Hours[17]) that we are confronted with a contradiction which is, let us say, disproportionate. Fejtö's arguments bear on only a few of Rajk's affirmations; thus his statements conflict with those of Rajk and cohorts only in a *narrowly circumscribed area*. Fejtö has not been hanged, etc.; I skip the rest. The whole problem consists in comparing the degree of validity of Rajk's and Fejtö's conflicting testimony,[18] that is, in subjecting their testimony to a critical examination, *on the basis of the information we have at our disposal* – namely, their testimony, the significance and consequences of that testimony, what history shows, etc. But you accept Fetjö's evidence *en bloc* and say that anyone who isn't troubled by it doesn't deserve to be part of the group around *Esprit*. That is an excellent way of defining *Esprit*, but a poor way of defining 'troubled'. Where is your 'careful weighing up' of the facts? What Fejtö's article contains is an accumulation of details that are, for him, so many proofs that Rajk had not been

[a] Allusion to Pascal, *Pensées* 593/822: 'I believe only the histories whose witnesses get their throats cut.'

'bought and sold' when he met him. This means he has to come to grips with the problem posed by Rajk's *confession*, and is obliged to resort to the hypothesis that Rajk is a 'martyr', when he could adopt the simpler hypothesis that a 'cop' who admitted he was a 'cop' to his friends or the first gendarme he came across, with a view to securing the esteem of the former and the right to the kind of treatment from the gendarme in which courtesy takes the place of a good pummelling, would not have much success either as a policeman or as a friend.

But all this presupposes that Fejtö's 'testimony' is acceptable. Where is your 'careful weighing up' of the external evidence? Do you know Fejtö? Since when have you been probing hearts and souls to assure yourself of the truthfulness of testimony that comes from someone who has been 'suffocated'? Fejtö, an odd sort of suffocation victim who has *never been a Communist*, who crawled on his belly before the Hungarian regime until the day he was given his walking papers,[19] a social democrat who had applied for membership of the Party six months before he was sacked, and who, in Paris, in liberty, that is, ensconced in a hotel room, wrote up an account of his life in which he beat his breast, accusing himself of having committed every imaginable political error in the past, which, as the Hungarian attaché said, was rather embarrassing, since many leading personalities in Hungary are former social democrats! Where is your 'careful weighing up'? I look at you, you look at me, looks don't deceive; to these revelations and all this 'decisive testimony' (perhaps it is decisive, but that needs to be *demonstrated*), I much prefer the caution of M. Hours, who, speaking of Mindszenty and drugs,[20] remarked to me that to explain the unknown in terms of the doubtful or the unknown was to explain nothing at all; if this principle is ignored, there is no point in engaging in historical criticism. Where is your 'careful weighing up'? Is substituting one's will for one's intelligence an honest way of going about things? Is it reasonable not only to refuse to place on the scales, along with this poorly weighed up Fejtö [*ce mal pesé de Fejtö*], everything that concrete history has carefully weighed up [*le bien pesé réel de l'histoire*] – the entire experience of the past and the concrete phenomena of the present historical process – but also to decree by means of a mental operation in which social democracy, Koestler, martyrs, and all sorts of 'good reasons' in ambush [*sic*], that Fejtö's evidence is valid, without subjecting it to either internal or external criticism?

Let me say frankly that it is only legitimate to be 'troubled' in this way on two conditions: (1) that one's uneasiness be *methodical*, i.e., that it be, as far as possible, a methodical *doubt* with suspension of judgement, including the very special sort of judgement that takes the form of an article published in *Esprit* with an introductory note by *Mounier*, in which, to do things up properly, one has to evoke Music and the Spirit of Truth, for lack of the truth *tout court*; (2) that one define the objective criteria which give this *methodical doubt* its meaning and prevent it from being transformed into an ontological intuition, or a revelation of truth in the form of doubt itself, something you are too inclined to do; in other words, on condition that one define the domain which, in the absence of a *radical internal critique* (doubtless impossible), *makes it possible to dispel doubt*. I have been told [. . .] that at the Congress of Peace Partisans, which denounced Tito six months ago,[21] Domenach said, 'I am not convinced by the Rajk trial, I cannot judge every aspect of it, I cannot, materially speaking, *decide* about those aspects of it that I do not understand, that are inaccessible to me or that seem doubtful to me. The matter will be decided by history, that is, by what happens between Tito and the US, the American agents and the People's Democracies; that is what will judge for me and dispel my doubts!!' Given Domenach's ignorance of the realities of the workers' movement and its problems, this seems to me to be the *only honest attitude possible*. Mounier violated this elementary honesty so crassly and basely as to beggar the imagination, and I am truly distressed that you did nothing to stop him from going about matters as ignobly as he did.

Read his introductory note again, 'L'Esprit de Vérité',[22] and you will see how emotionalistic it is! By way of argument, capital letters: the System (Koestler has truly won and Gabriel Marcel along with him!) and slanders: the Moscow trials marked the beginning of this *'dirty work'*, Communism produces *'crimes'*, and there will soon be only *'quaint little differences'* between anti-Communism and the System. Do you really find that acceptable? And the idea that the Communists are in the process of isolating the working class just as they left it isolated in the face of fascism before the war? Do you find that acceptable, Jean Lacroix? Do you find these lies and this blackmail acceptable? The blackmail consists in saying, 'We are saying all this for your own good, our Communist "friends", we are saying it in order to "liberate" you, and we are taking all the necessary precautions to prevent our articles from being "exploited".' But by what right does Mounier extend this protection to the Communists? In what capacity? It is doubtless ignorance of the Party and Marxism which confers such rights; it is doubtless the possession of a *truth* that has been so well *demonstrated* that it is necessary to summon the Spirit to descend upon it and cover it, just as Malebranche needed the Spirit of God to cover all his contradictions (I could supply you with the reference . . .), or as Bossuet and Leibniz needed Providence to cover all the dirty work of human history! As for those precautions, a lot of good they do! We, Mounier, in possession of the Truth, or, at any rate, the Spirit of the Truth, publish a text and an article, and take all the necessary precautions to prevent them from being exploited against our wishes. But exploited by whom? It's Mounier himself who exploits them, and with a vengeance! And as he sees fit, that is, against us. Otherwise the *Esprit* article would have been deposited in a no-man's land, hidden away somewhere like atomic energy, and we, we Mounier, would stand guard over it, over this sacred deposit, to make sure that it serves to fertilize the deserts and not to blow up the world! The damage has been done, you see, the exploitation has already taken place, and everything Mounier writes in the future has no other purpose than to excuse his bad conscience, to turn his hypocrisy and blackmail into evidence of truthfulness and generosity.

That is why I call Mounier a bastard; because he is betraying us, to be sure, but above all because he doesn't have the courage to think out what he is doing – or, rather, he does show a moment of courage in that introductory note, when he talks about Communism's 'crimes' and Communism's 'dirty work'. At that point we know whom we are [dealing with], an enemy, someone who declares *of his own volition* that he is our enemy; we always acknowledge the courage of our enemies when our enemies have the courage of their convictions and their acts, and our way of acknowledging them is to fight them, that is, to pay them back in kind.

I appeal to you, Jean Lacroix, from the profoundest depths of our friendship, and on behalf of all your former students – the dozens of them – who have become your friends, and who would sign this letter themselves if I were not reserving it for you alone as a letter that addresses a serious ongoing debate which is still a private matter between us, and which I do not believe I have the right to widen before hearing you out. I appeal to you, asking you to reread Mounier's introductory note and to carefully weigh up the arguments I am hastily submitting to you today; I appeal to you, I ask you: do you find all this disgraceful behaviour and blackmail acceptable? And this betrayal and these lies?

3. And now let us talk a bit about your book, and about philosophy, since you appeal to philosophy in defence of a number of attitudes and judgements. Let us begin with your book, and the article on Marxist man I once told you was a bit 'idealist' toward the end. The last part of that article, in which you said that Marxism produced remarkable men, but not saints, has disappeared;[23] you have replaced it with a critique I need to discuss with you. The pivotal passage is on page 42, where you pull out all the stops and speak on your own behalf after having lent your voice to the Marxists. I am not putting words in your mouth; it is you yourself who say 'that there is a certain intellectual dishonesty in speaking of Marxist man when one is not a Communist oneself, when one is not a militant in a party cell'.[24] That is a sentence which truly touches us, which says a great deal, and I thank you for it. What is even more touching is that, despite your isolation, you have, on a number of

very important points, on almost every point – with one exception – arrived at a profound understanding of Marxism that one looks for in vain in Mounier, or even in Desroches[25] (judging by a few texts of his I have looked at). But the truly extraordinary thing is this page 42 and what follows; what is extraordinary is to see how intelligently you go to the heart of the difficult points of Marxism, and how superficially you criticize it. Defending Marxist man so well, *understanding* him so well, requires an insight one cannot have if one does not endorse Marxism to a certain minimal extent, and the reader is astounded to see how carelessly you abandon arguments you seem virtually to have adopted yourself, so well do you defend them.

I will cite just one example, that of the *ideal* or *goal* [*la fin*], cf. page 21: 'for the Marxist as for the Christian, the goodness of the means is determined by the immanence of the end, and the presence of this end in the means.' This is an excellent definition; but it is immediately demolished by your note[26] and invalidated by your objection on page 45 as to the impossibility of making value judgements in history;[27] it is quite as if you had said nothing at all, or as if the patent truth of your definition had been borrowed. In any event, your refutation is subject to the very criticism of the idealism of values that you develop in your essay. It would seem, then, that you have developed Marx's arguments without endorsing them. But I do not think things are that simple: I really believe that you have endorsed them, and every time you return to Marx one feels that he matters to you a great deal, but one can clearly see that if you subscribed fully to Marx you would have to renounce a number of ideas that you value above all else and that seem to you to go by the board in Marx. Hence the entire problem came down to finding a weakness in Marx that would allow you to put by his rigour and patent truth, or, better, *a weakness in Marx's rigour that could allow you to put by his patent truth*. It is Hyppolite who, happily, produces this weakness for you, or rather (pardon) who confirms your view that it exists.

Here I put faith in the uses of friendship, and you will too, if I can show you that this weakness does not exist, that it has been invented, that it is everywhere and anywhere you like, only not in Marx and Marxism. Look at your note on page 23[28] and your critical remarks on pages 42ff., and you will see what I mean. (I take up this letter again in a little house in the Limousin region, where I've come for a few days' rest – amidst mud and drizzle – but let us get down to the matter in hand.) To see where the 'misunderstanding' lies, let us start out with Hyppolite's text, which is worth its weight in 'mistakes' (page 23)! The subject is the good old problem of the end of history and alienation. Marxism, says Hyppolite, wants to put an end to alienation. Once alienation has been eliminated, man will reclaim his 'social essence', and then there can no longer be any history, for history = dialectic = conflict

= alienation. You echo this idea (page 44): 'the disappearance of the various forms of alienation will bring the end of history in its wake.' The most curious thing is that Hyppolite explains his own blunder, but without realizing it! *'At a given moment in his development, Hegel, like Marx, looked forward to an end of history . . .'* (page 23). Let us, if you will, re-establish the plain facts of the matter:

(1) Marx never spoke of the *'end of history'* and *absolutely nothing* in his work justifies attributing that notion to him. *Neither the term nor the concept!* Quite the contrary: you are familiar with Marx and Engels' remark to the effect that, thanks to communism (and thus to the end of the various forms of alienation), humanity 'will pass from its pre-history to *real history'*.[29] A bit of rectification would seem to be in order here.

(2) In contrast, Hegel, in the *Phenomenology* at any rate (the period Hyppolite is alluding to), thinks constantly in terms of the *end of history*, and clearly says so in the chapter on absolute knowledge. And it is no accident that he finds himself brought up against this problem (to which Kojève has been particularly sensitive),[30] since, for him, history is the epiphany and flowering of Absolute Spirit, which cannot possess itself in its truth unless it is first entirely alienated, so as to be able to reappropriate itself in its entirety in the form of self-consciousness. This alienation of Absolute Spirit is a matter, then, of *going forth from itself*, of existing in *externality*; to find itself again, to reappropriate itself in the externality of alienation, is thus simultaneously the destiny and truth of Absolute Spirit, of the Absolute Subject, which, to be full, *vollkommen*, has to exist in the form of externality (alienation), but only in order to reappropriate, in the internality of absolute consciousness, its own alienated substance. Hence *alienation* has a precise meaning in Hegel: it is the existence, in *externality*, of *absolute Self-Consciousness*, the existence of absolute self-consciousness *outside itself*, in nature and in history, in Nature, things, empirical man, historical man, historical conflicts, historical development. And as the whole of nature exists for history (Spirit), *alienation is, consequently, history in its totality* (which includes nature too as an abstract moment). This plainly gives us *end of alienation* = end of history. (I do not mean to dwell on the absurdities of such a conception; I only wanted to demonstrate the content of this *alienation*. When Hyppolite says 'Hegel, like Marx, imagined an effective end to the alienation of man', he is using words improperly and ambiguously; alienation, according to Hegel, is the existence of absolute Self-Consciousness in externality, or the objectivity of History and Nature, it is not just any 'alienation' of man* – in other words, Hegel thinks alienation in relation to absolute self-consciousness, whereas Marx

---

* Historical and empirical man is himself a part or moment of this alienation of absolute self-consciousness.

speaks of the alienation of the proletarian of 1848. As for me, I will be happy to discuss the alienation of this absolute self-consciousness the day I can invite the consciousness in question out for a drink.)

(3) So: no end of history in Marx, but an end of history in Hegel in 1807, for reasons having to do with his conception of history as the Alienation of Absolute Self-Consciousness. A bit of legerdemain on Hyppolite's part: to show that there ultimately is an end of history in Marx, *one need only attribute to Marx the Hegelian conception of alienation!* Savour the delights of this little sentence: 'Hegel thought, as did Marx . . .'; what that really means is 'I, Hyppolite, think that Marx thought as Hegel did.' I don't believe we need long commentaries here to understand that, by *alienation* (when he uses this word, and he uses it less and less as he grows older, since it is a Feuerbachian and Hegelian term, and Marx himself says, see the Preface to *Capital*,[31] 'I . . . toyed with the use of Hegelian terminology when people were fond of calling Hegel . . . a "dead dog" – but what I say has nothing to do with Hegel'*), Marx intends something entirely different from the content of Hegelian aliena-tion. In Marx, history is not the *alienation* of God only knows what absolute self-consciousness (nor, *a fortiori*, of nature); history is the product of human activity, of the totality of human activity; whether or not men are 'alienated', history is always the product of their activity, it is their reality, their human truth. Thus history *is never the Alienation* of anything whatsoever: the air man breathes, the air in which man lives and moves is not Alienation (unless it is the alienation of God only knows what transcendent consciousness, which consents to alienate itself by becoming 'air', that is, consents to lose itself, to be other than itself, on who knows what whim! – and, *a fortiori*, air is not the alienation of man!), and history is even less the alienation of man, since it is his product, the theatre of his highest activities, what he lives on, what he lives in, what he lives by and for.

Thus, for Marx, history is neither the Alienation of God (or of some absolute Self-Consciousness), nor the alienation of man, but rather *the production by man of his own life* (in every sense of the word); if the realization of man through his labour and struggles and thought is his *alienation*, I'll be hanged, and you'll gladly be hanged along with me, but I want to hear, before they put the rope around my neck, who can possibly be alienated in this realization of man? Enough on that score. When Marx speaks of alienation, accordingly, he doesn't mean history, or historical existence, or 'contradiction', or 'tension', or anything else of

---

* You will appreciate what Laurent Casanova had to say on this score to a brilliant philosopher and member of the Party: 'Your alienation bores the sh.. out of us!' [A member of the Political Bureau of the PCF at the time, responsible for the intellectuals, Casanova played a very important part in propagating the theory of the 'two sciences' – bourgeois science/proletarian science.]

the sort – the tragic historicity of life & *tutti quanti*. Marx means *the part of history that, at a given moment, is wrested from the man who produces it*, from 'empirical' man, 'real' or, if you prefer, 'existing' man, who is thus actually *deprived by other men of what he actually produces, and, hence, of his own realization as a human being endowed with real capacities that have been diverted from their proper end [détournées]*. Alienation is an economic concept, in the broad sense; it is, if you like, a description of surplus-value in the broad sense, *of that part of what men concretely produce which is taken from them* (of their intellectual or material production, it being understood that it is their material production which is 'conditioning': nothing to be done about it, that's just the way it is, like being born, pissing, sleeping, having two arms and needing to eat); *and of that part of the real development of their personalities that is taken from those same men* in a given economic system (here, capitalism). These two aspects go hand in hand: the proletarian is alienated

a. in that the capitalist steals the better part of what he actually produces;

b. in that this theft deprives the proletarian of the right to the goods he and his brothers produce, material and intellectual goods, schooling, culture, leisure – in short, the development of his real talents in accordance with the technical possibilities of the science and culture of his day; to political activity, to the conduct and direction of affairs, to his dignity as a man, which has nothing metaphysical about it, to the *realization of his human nature*, which is not an abstract 'essence', but that which the men living in a given period could actually become, if society gave back to them what it took from them.

You see how far we are from the end of History! For *the end of alienation, according to Marx, consists in restoring to man, who makes history, all the history he makes, i.e., his concrete historical existence, i.e., the possibility of developing and freely making, of his own enlightened free will, the history that he earlier made in necessity and night.* If I have put things clearly, then I think we can read Hyppolite's short text together and laugh together over its 'profundity', and perhaps settle a certain debate about the problem of 'alienation' after the Revolution that you think you have discerned amongst the Marxists. When our doctor says, 'The Hegelian dialectic still preserves the tension of conflict at the very core of the mediation, whereas Marx's real dialectic works for the complete suppression of that tension',[32] we are truly in the night in which all cows are black! Words pitted against other words! As for the thing itself, not a prayer of finding it! What is this tension? For Hegel and Hyppolite, it is metaphysical, and one does not really know what one is talking about, if not that one *has* to speak of *tension* to make the lesson come off. *What 'complete suppression'?* Of course, Marx is for the complete suppression, not of the *tension* (?), but of the alienation of the proletarians, from whom the capitalists snatch what they produce along with their historical and social being, their humanity! Does this mean that, once the thieves have been eliminated, the man they have robbed will vanish into thin air? The emancipated proletarian will no longer have 'tension'? He will no longer have needs? He will no longer work? He will no longer love? He will no longer listen to music or try to compose it? What nonsense! I would go further: only then, in freedom, will authentic 'tension' be restored to the proletarian; to put it in clear French, let us say that only then will the proletarian go *straight to the heart* of the real *problems* of his life, the problems of the lives of his brothers and children, the problems of a history that will be his history; only then will men discover inside themselves a host of needs smothered by capitalism, the need for music, for snow, for the sea, for culture, invention, history, and who knows what else! Only then will emancipated man be nothing other than his *life*, directly and fully, only then will he be 'the very movement of Life' (thus Hyppolite), instead of the limited, asphyxiated, crushed being he is. Only then will he recover the profound unity that will confer meaning upon his natural activity and reconcile history and nature in man; there will no longer be a distance between labour (for the production of life) and history, and the pseudo-problem of 'natural alienation' will be put back in true perspective, that of a world in which man will no longer need to be exploited by man to wrest his life, by his natural and historical activity, from the nature that has given him birth.

Thus it is indeed the transition from pre-history to history that communism allows us to witness, the transition from a history made amidst brutishness and inhumanity to a history made in freedom and life. The dialectic – rest easy, all you Hegelians who still walk the earth – will not disappear, but it will be the heritage of all men *in its truth* and *in their truth*, rather than the property of an elusive Absolute Consciousness that has been incarnated, by the grace of God and to the proletarians' misfortune, in the meditations of tenured professors of philosophy. The dialectic will have a different content, its true content, the content of the lives of emancipated men. I will not surprise you when I say that it already has a true content in those proletarians who struggle and know why they are struggling in the Party; I may perhaps surprise you when I say that the Russian Communists have already given thought to this problem of the modification of, let us say, the 'dialectic' in their liberated society; you will find useful information on this point in Zhdanov's article on the history of philosophy (a text admirable in every respect, in *Europe*, November 1947).[33] I quote: 'In our Soviet society, where antagonistic classes have been eliminated, the struggle between the old and the new, and consequently the development from the lower to the higher, proceeds not in the form of struggle between antagonistic classes and of cataclysms, as is the case under capitalism, but in the form of criticism

and self-criticism, which is the real motive force of our development . . .'.
Zhdanov goes on to criticize the philosophers of the USSR who have not
taken up this question: '. . . our Party long ago discovered and placed at
the service of socialism that particular form [criticism and self-criticism]
of revealing and overcoming the contradictions of socialist society (such
contradictions exist, and philosophy cannot avoid dealing with them).'[34]
I give you these texts, which may reassure more than one Hegelian, and
from which it would be possible to cull quite a few remarks applicable
to a 'philosophy' of reflection that would nevertheless not be 'reflexive';
they show us, in living form, the truths that Marx succeeded in
discerning in his own time, and in predicting for the near future with
which his time was pregnant. And I believe we can close this chapter on
the end of history by rejoicing together over the fact that history goes on,
that Marx was not Hegel, and that Stalin and Thorez are not Hyppolite –
unless we are saddened by the fact that the argument has 'gone to smash'
in our hands and that we have to find others, less brilliant, but less
fragile.

4. True, you have one more argument against Marx, one that has to be
considered: the well-known problem of historical judgement and the
judging of history. Here again I am struck both by your deep understanding of Marx and by the superficiality of your criticisms. To refute your
reasoning, it is enough to counterpose to your own line of argument
what you expound in Marx. But if that is not obvious, let us approach
things from another angle.

The problem of the *judging of history* matters to you to the extent that
you accuse Marxists of falling into this error when they speak of the *end
of history*: but, as we have seen, they do not talk about that, so that you
cannot accuse them of playing Bossuet in their very conception of history.
You cannot accuse them of pronouncing Divine Judgement on history.
Rest easy: they leave Divine Judgement to the Divinity; all they ask is
that everyone, Marxist or not, yourself included, do the same. ('It is not
the judgement of history, but God's judgement – and, of course, with all
the risks of human error this entails', page 45. Thanks but no thanks!)

For you, then, there exist two types of judgement involving history:

1. Judgements *about history*, which take history to be finite, and (or)
judge in the name of a transcendent value: 'judgements about history,
that is, judgements that *transcend becoming*' (page 45).

2. '*Historical judgements that are immanent in becoming*' (page 44).
Example, the historical judgements of Marxists: 'judgements of fact that
are a matter of observing historical reality' and even judgements anticipating the immediate future. Fine – example: 'it can be said that the
French Revolution, democracy, Marxism, etc. have followed or are
following the direction of history' (page 44). This is excellent, for if you

are genuinely convinced that saying that 'the French Revolution followed the direction of history' – a statement many of our adversaries consider to be a value judgement – is a judgement of fact 'immanent in becoming', then we will soon be of the same mind.

But your text contains disagreeable surprises for us, two disagreeable surprises. Here they are:

a. on page 44, we find you criticizing Marxism because it is a 'theodicy', because it judges history in the name 'of a transhistorical ideal'. We say to ourselves, all this is excellent, because it follows that we must limit ourselves to judgements that are immanent in becoming, which is what Marxists do all the time – it follows too that every transhistorical judgement is to be avoided. But, on page 45, disappointment: we learn that one can pass judgements on history that are 'transcendent to becoming', which 'strive to be the judgement of God'. All our joy vanishes: this comes down to saying, in effect, that it is not illegitimate to bring a divine judgement to bear on history, that it is even to be recommended – and since Marxists were condemned for doing so (as you saw it), one can only conclude that they were not to be faulted for having made a divine judgement, but for having made the wrong divine judgement! This plunges us into unfathomable depths: *how can the judgement of God be wrong*? If it is wrong (but how can we know it is without being God?), then it is no longer God's, so that it returns to the level of history as an historical judgement, an historical error regarding the judgement of God. If it is wrong, then it follows that it could not have been a judgement of history: when Marxists wish to pronounce a divine judgement, *they go astray, but they do not realize it*! Put your mind at ease, they do realize it. – But I have perhaps twisted the meaning of your texts: the Marxists' mistake would seem to lie rather (page 44) in believing that *'history is the judgement of God'*. But you have to have it one way or the other. Either history is for them only the reality of history and the judgements 'immanent to becoming' that they bring to bear on it, so that history cannot be the judgement of God, since this judgement of history is not a transcendent judgement for them or for you; this would imply that Marxists sin by *omission*, in that they choose to make only historical judgements, not judgements which are 'transcendent to becoming' – a reproach that would not, I must say, unduly perturb them. Or else the 'history' they speak of is not an immanent, but a divine judgement, one 'transcendent to becoming', in which case they sin not by omission, thank God, or by making an error of attribution, but rather by virtue of the fact that the true divine judgement is not history (Bossuet and a long line of theologians, the greatest, beginning with St. Augustine, nevertheless believed that history is the judgement of God, and theodicy . . .); or because the substance of their historical judgement does not coincide with [*recouvre*] the judgement of God –

which is for its part swaddled [*recouvert*] in profound mystery. Let me assure you that I am not making fun of these 'holy matters' or of the direction of your research and thought, but am attempting to bring out the contradictions of your text, which, I hope, you fall into rather than intend.

b. *The second disagreeable surprise*, page 45. We learn that there are judgements 'transcendent to becoming', or divine judgements. We are given an example: value judgements, which can only be made with reference, not to a fact, but to a 'transcendent norm'. I do not think I am forcing things when I say that *value judgements are divine judgements* (you return to this point: there exist facts, which condition action, and values, which guide it), or, if you prefer, '*judgements about history that strive to be divine judgements*'. We will come back to that 'strive to be'. Your position is essentially untenable: everyone makes value judgements, every man who acts, indeed, every man who lives, inasmuch as men must anticipate what will happen in their lives if they wish to live; Hitler too made value judgements about the Czechs and the Jews and the Christians and the Communists: were they divine judgements? Did he 'strive to make' divine judgements? Bossuet would have said so, along with Leibniz and a good many others. But is this to do anything other than to make history a theodicy again, to make history in its entirety the judgement of God, which is the crime you accuse the Marxists of? Thus, when you go after Lukács,[35] the old man turns your argument against you. 'One can only judge a man's character to be "heroic or base" with reference to a transcendent norm', you write – but of course, and this transcendent norm is the movement of history, about which you say (page 44) that it can become the object of an 'historic' judgement. *The movement of history is real, is a fact, but transcends the 'character'* (this is not, incidentally, a very felicitous word, and I doubt that Lukács has been well translated here) of a man who has received his problems from history, derives his means of action and the conditions of his action from history, and is judged on his historic acts by history. It is history which lays down the rules of the game (I say game for the sake of clarity, for this is not a game but a terrible ordeal), and the player is judged by those rules. What do you reproach Lukács with? The judgement history passes on Hitler or Trotsky or Stalin is only an historical judgement; it is not a judgement of God, it is a judgement that does not go beyond its domain of validity – that is, for a Marxist, *history*. When we say that Hitler was a criminal, or that Trotsky or Pétain, etc., was a traitor, we pronounce an '*historical judgement*'; we do not say, Hitler, etc., *will be damned*, but that Hitler, etc., confronted history and tried to turn it against humanity by deflecting its course, that Hitler lied to his people, subjugated Europe, killed, etc. etc. The judgement we pass on him is the judgement history passes on him by way of the revolt of his victims, the subjugation of his people and ours, his defeat* and the freedom the subjugated peoples wrested back. We remain *within history*. Let God, if he exists and if he so desires, damn or save Hitler; that is not our affair. You will grant that it is not very honest to try to make one's adversaries – or one's friends – say what they do not in fact say, to try to make them say what they do not do, to use a technique of forced confession or forced conversion on them for the greater glory of the judgement of God, or a personalist theory of transcendence that is as vague and untenable as the theses of your friends are precise and rigorous. And if I have misunderstood you, please take me to task as unsparingly as I do you.

What is the positive content of the thinking that underpins your criticisms? Here is what you assert:

I. 'Without human duration, the history of the world would not exist; but, without divine eternity, the history of man would not exist' (page 74).

II. 'Man ... stands in relation with eternity; indeed, this is the definition of spirit in any form. ... When he tries to take the place of the eternal, he only produces a caricature of it that schematizes and betrays it. ... *The transcendent ... is not what comes after the immanent, but is, in some sort, what constitutes it, consolidates it from within and lends it its significance. For us, eternity does not represent an escape from time, but is rather that which judges history by giving it a meaning'* (pages 62–3).

III. '*Time* has meaning only by virtue of *the presence of the eternal in it*: if we understand time and are capable of mastering it even as we live in it, *the reason is that we transcend it.* ... *There would be no history for a purely historical being'* (pages 46–7).

There are a number of contradictions and obscurities here. Eternity is that without which there would be no human history. We know, or believe we know, what history is. As for eternity, no man hath seen it but the Son, as St. John says. But let us speak about it, let us use the word. What is the content of this word? Eternity is not *somewhere outside* time, but within it: (1) 'That which constitutes it ...' is its 'presence' in time, which ... (2) 'That which judges history by giving it a meaning'. If eternity is in time, if it constitutes it and is the 'prerequisite' for history, then every man who is in time and experiences history is subject to eternity; you yourself, the monk, the Marxist, and the Hitlerite. But this 'presence', although it is experienced by everyone, is perhaps not perceived by and known to everyone. This 'meaning,' this 'judgement of history' is, for everyone, the precondition of history, but not everyone, perhaps, arrives at it. Let us, then, try to determine this 'meaning' that is 'eternity's' last word. 'Time has meaning only by virtue of the presence

---

* His victory, had he won, would not have prevented him from being a *criminal* in our eyes and yours.

of the eternal in it: if we understand time and are capable of mastering it even as we live in it, the reason is that we transcend it . . . . '

What shall I say, all this is quite disappointing; if, for man, eternity consists in 'mastering time', in quite simply 'understanding' it, we are in eternity the way M. Jourdain is in prose; when he discovered he was in prose, M. Jourdain did not suddenly set to speaking verse. If, on the other hand, eternity means understanding time *in a certain way*, different from the way in which men ordinarily say 'tomorrow it will be nice out', or 'we face the threat of an American war', or 'I want either world empire via the Marshall plan, or else war', that is *something else again*, but *one needs to say so*!!* If eternity means grasping that every act of understanding or mastering time (or even of understanding a sentence, as you say) is the presence of eternity in time; if eternity means understanding that that is eternity, we are suspended in a void, caught in a revolving door, for, in order to understand the role (or significance) of eternity in our mastery of time, do we not have to master the significance of eternity, and so on? It's the story of Hitler and Mussolini in *The Great Dictator*: the one who wants to master the mastered ends up cracking his head against the ceiling – alas, there is no ceiling in our philosophical dwelling! It looks as if I am having an easy time of it here, but I believe this is a serious matter: as soon as you try to lodge eternity in time, that is, as soon as you try to assign it a concrete *content*, this content becomes universal and indistinguishable from an ordinary concept (here, *thought*, to keep things simple: man is a thinking being, and in that he is eternal). Does eternity add anything real to the concept? If history owes its *existence* to eternity, history as men 'understand' it, then eternity changes the meaning of history about as much as the amazement of Roberval – who discovered, after Torricelli, that men live 'crushed under a mass of air that bears down on their heads' – changed the respiration, sleep, or exchange of gases of his contemporaries. Someone who explained to the Nazis attacking Stalingrad, or the Communists defending it, that it was eternity which enabled them to be historical beings capable of history, would not thereby have changed anything in the attack or the defence . . .

To dub man's understanding of time 'eternity' is to change the name of a street without changing either its location or the people who live on it; it is a petty postal reform and a minor municipal ceremony. I am well aware that you have *something else* in mind, but you do not want to give up the idea that you can find eternity in time, or, still better, in the nature of man and of all men; that is, you do not want to give up what also make up your human nature – that which thinks – you *do not want to give up the idea of the universality and palpable obviousness of what you hold to be*

---

* One has to show this new content, to articulate it. Do you do that?

the truth. That is why you write, publish, write to me, and speak, and that is why you want to demonstrate that the truth you defend is present in what has already been *established* and is recognized as the truth by all men. You would perhaps do well to give some thought to this avatar of your eternity, which goes unnoticed when it fuses with men or concepts, which – and you are to blame for this – fuses so completely with them that we are unable to get a grip on it; it melts into them as water melts into water, or air into air. And you would perhaps do well to ask 'thanks to what presence' the man who thinks (who thinks thanks to the presence of eternity) wants eternity recognized at all costs as a universal truth in the very content of his life; and by virtue of what presence this eternity evaporates in the universality of the thought it conditions.

All this to say that *you do not break out of the circle.* (1) Either this transcendent entity is simply the meaning of what all men think, M. Jourdain's prose, a terribly modest 'prerequisite', in which case all this fuss over a cloudless day is likely to leave us unmoved. (2) Or this transcendent entity has a content you aspire to and cherish with all the force of your soul – and I am convinced you cherish it – but a content so 'transcendent' that, strictly speaking, you cannot but be ignorant of it; *not even your aspiration and your spiritual quest can be the sign and the guarantee of the content you aspire to* (no man hath seen God, says John, and Kierkegaard did not even want to call himself a *Christian*) – in this case, the judgement of God is in God's hands and we are not even at his feet, and *I do not see how you can speak of 'the risks of human error', since it makes no sense to speak of error when one cannot measure it against the truth –* so that one can see that *this aspiration is not even proof of itself and that this eternity is the annihilation of all meaning, beginning with its own,* and the condition of absolute absurdity (or, rather, not even that, for absurdity still has a meaning, whatever you say). (3) Or, again, this transcendent entity has an assignable content, i.e., you think there must exist values which explain history, which are history's inner law, at once present within it and governing it, but in that case say so, name them, and *confront them with the history* they are part of, seriously, honestly, without sheltering behind an eternity which is supposedly a *'presence'* in time, and that which 'constitutes' history; 'incarnate them' if need be, although, in your view, they are already 'incarnated' – but then you fall back into your (1), i.e., you fall back (but this is not a Fall) into the world of men, back into the history from which there is no escape, because, if the transcendent is not *at the end*, neither is it *off to one side*, like those little niches one sees in tunnels, carved out for the workers so that they can watch the train go by, when they are not in it, without being run over. (4) There remains the desperate attempt which consists in saying that eternity is not only a matter of having a meaning, but of having a determinate, particular, transcendent, 'spiritual' meaning, which is in history and the judgement of God – in history, where you, human beings, do not see it; in the judgement of God which I, Mounier, pronounce (with the proviso that I may err, and that this entails taking risks, but *this declaration of the risks annuls them*!!, it is my insurance policy; you know yourself that it is enough to be aware of 'conditioning' to 'liberate oneself from it', Jean Lacroix, page 77).

I am not joking: *a year ago, I heard* Mounier say at the École, in a public lecture[36] he must have delivered many times over, *that it was possible to write two histories of Munich*: an historical-history 'of the kind Marxists can produce' – and a 'much more important *spiritual-history*, on the spiritual significance of Munich'. Respect for the truth compels me to add that there was, among the – stupefied – listeners, a naive recruit[37] who spoke up, asking Mounier how he conceived this second history. Mounier was more than disconcerted, the answers he gave were as vague as can be imagined. That's exactly what he said: a spiritual history of Munich!!! That is what is lying in wait for you, and it pains me to think it, when you say about the Rajk issue of *Esprit*, 'What troubles me is that his testimony should have appeared in a context that seems – seen from the outside – to give it a political meaning (*and not a spiritual one*)' – my emphasis. You will surely understand that it is not possible to go on looking down on people this way. And when I say 'look down on people', I have in mind precisely the people who suffer, the millions of exploited, the millions of workers who make what we live on, you as well as I, who make history, who are *inside* it just as your eternity is, who are struggling for their lives and freedom, who experienced Munich and the war, and are experiencing the current betrayals and the difficult battle for their young democracy, who do not utter the judgement of God, but rather confront history with their ordinary lives, their ordinary experience, their unaided reflections, whom the struggle and their condition constantly compel to put their human truth and knowledge *to the test*, whether they are the humblest of shoemakers or [General] Secretary of the Hungarian Party, to take decisions and act after weighing up all the consequences of their decisions, which are material and spiritual and call everything they are into question – their ordinary lives, I say, but the whole of their lives, which are all they have and which are worth all the *cogitos* in the world; they are honest men who have come by their honesty in struggle and suffering, who have, by dint of effort, bloodshed, and will, *tested* their truth, who *say* their truth, show it, give it human names that everybody can understand, and point out to others who have not yet found it the concrete path that will lead them toward it, and which is in fact leading them toward it, wherever they may come from. There are thousands of us who can testify to this. Do you really think that you are not looking down on these men, that you are not betraying their suffering, their struggles, and their nobility, when you tell them: everything you are doing is fine and dandy, but there is a meaning to your actions that escapes you; you have lived through the Marxist history of Munich or Rajk, but I am going to tell you the spiritual history of Munich or Rajk! You are going to teach these men the truth of their own lives when they have acquired it through centuries of effort! And if they let you speak, what will you tell them? Are you going to write it some day, that spiritual history of Munich? If you have already written it, let us see it! If you haven't written it, keep quiet!

One doesn't, after all, have the right to tell people that they have erred without pointing them to the truth that will show them their error, without showing them how they can pass from their error to the truth, so as to redeem them from error. You appropriate words that have a meaning for men, you profit from the authority those words have, and from their profound human resonance, in an attempt to pass off a content that you are not only incapable of demonstrating, but even of defining for yourselves, a content which only the men you want to give lessons to are capable of defining for you: they are defining this content and they will show it to you, though it may not be the one you wish to see. They will say that philosophers and kings have always appealed to a history 'other' than the one actually experienced by men, to 'spiritual significance', to divine judgement, or to concepts shrouded in mystery, in order to justify a world or an attitude that these philosophers and kings have always been incapable of justifying to men in human terms. The history of θεία μοῖρα[38] is, you know, a long one. θεία μοῖρα has lent cover to Plato's obscenities, St. Augustine's slavery, Malebranche's and Leibniz's myths, Hegel's dialectic, and Hitler's foreign policy and massacres, and it has now become 'the Spirit of Truth' and 'the spiritual significance of history', it lends cover to Mounier's politics, it will lend cover to whatever you wish, it is a maid of all work, every impostor's fallback, and today, alas, it lends cover to even your own tergiversations.

That is what pains me. For, you see, θεία μοῖρα doesn't work any more, and if you do not relinquish it yourself, voluntarily, I would ask you to have the decency to consent to speak the language of men, to consent to share their language and their truth as you share their bread, not only because you *must* share their truth and their language if you want to bring them to share what makes up the bedrock of your life, but also because to do so is to *pay men back in kind*, to do them simple justice. Just as the workers give us bread, *so they give us the truth we live on, they give you the truth you live on*, the truth you use to make your philosophy, the human truth you use to make your reflexive philosophy, doubt and belief, the spirit of truth, the system, and existence.[39] 'Or what man is there of you, whom if his son ask bread, will he give him a stone?'[40] Can we give stones to those who give us bread? If we are not capable of giving back, as bread, the wheat men have given us, if we are not capable of giving back, *as truth they can live on*, as truth which they can see and feel is *the same truth*, ground up, sifted, and leavened, which men have furnished us so that we can live on it and give it back to them, then we are the ones who have betrayed them. Ultimately, everything comes down to this. There are men who make the truth, *fundamentally*, those who are at the centre of history because they are at the centre of life and bread: those who work and struggle. When we philosophers receive this truth, it has already been made, it comes to us by a long route, has passed from hand to hand; our task is to restore it to its original state, discover in it all the implications, all the possibilities it contains, and give it back to the men who have given it to us, who give it to us in its purity and richness, in their purity and richness. If they do not recognize it, if they cannot live on it in their turn, then we have *falsified* it, we have transformed bread into stone, the truth into the spirit of truth, historical judgement into a judgement about history.

These men are the proletarians, and it is they who are our judges, human judges who do not usurp God's place, as philosophers so often do, but who pass human judgement on the truth that we put at their disposal after having received it from them; who judge it by 'testing it out', as one judges a plough by 'testing it out'. And if these men, today for the first time, *know* that what holds for the plough holds for history too, they know it because *they make history the way a blacksmith makes a plough*,[41] because they have conquered, acquired, constituted the science of history by taking their own needs as their point of departure, through *praxis*, experience, and theory, proceeding exactly as a doctor does. And, today, when someone starts telling them that history has a 'spiritual meaning', that it is constituted by the Transcendent, they react to such talk with the same mocking calm that the blacksmith would display if someone told him that what descended in his hammer was the spirit of God. Don't laugh! It wasn't so long ago that God healed the sick using the doctor's hands and that the sick were 'possessed' by the devil. These proletarians could have answered you: the blacksmith who decides that a piece of iron is good enough to make into a plough, and who believes that he is quite simply performing a human task on the basis of an established body of knowledge – does that blacksmith pronounce a 'judgement transcendent to becoming' because of his mastery of the iron and the plough and men's accumulated knowledge? What would you have said? You would not utter such nonsense, because it is well known, and you too know, that if eternity is in the iron and the plough and the blacksmith, it is in them the way excipients are in certain substances we add them to in making pills; it is so much a part of them that it is quite as if it were not in them at all, as if, what with eternity on one side of the equation and eternity on the other, all I have to do is divide everything by eternity, and I will be left with the same problems.

You do not utter this nonsense when it comes to the blacksmith and the smithy because it is well known that nothing more is involved here than human knowledge, acquired through labour, experience, and reflection. But you do utter it in speaking of history, and the proletarians laugh! Their laughter is joyous and frank, don't be offended! They laugh because they have learned that they are blacksmiths in history, and because they have discovered the laws for beating the bourgeoisie as they have discovered the laws for beating iron! They laugh because they have forged a science of history out of their needs, experience, and reflections, and they handle history as the smith handles iron and the doctor the body; for them, it is a science as solid as the others, one they verify every day, even the least educated of them in the least little strike; this is clear as day, and every day God gives us they progress in their science, they create, as doctors create medical science, this prodigious science that is truly the science of all men, and required, required – but not to be had for nothing, ah, not to be had for nothing for all that! And when someone tells them it is necessary to consider the transcendent, and the 'spiritual significance' of history, they answer, he's a bit behind the times, he is, he's a man from the time before our science came along, or else they say he's 'off his rocker', as they would say of a blacksmith who told them it was necessary to hammer iron with the spirit of truth!

Yes, we are behind the times, and it is here, perhaps, that what I said a moment ago about these men becomes a little clearer: that *our truth* comes into being *in them*. So much so that if we do not stay in close contact with them, we not only risk distorting already established truth, but may *remain ignorant of* a truth that is coming into existence. Nowhere in your book do we see that history is now a science. This is a fact, an established fact, but it is a fact that has been established far from our studies *clausis fenestris*, and far from the *cogito*; no bourgeois stratagem will alter that one whit, not even the ploys of the jury for the *agrégation*,[a] which two years ago asked us whether 'a science of human phenomena was possible'![42] Quite a find! Here's an already established science: is it possible? Even a philosopher can laugh at that one. Well, we can laugh together if you like, but let us laugh at ourselves too, at how far behind and how isolated we are; and let us seriously and honestly ask ourselves whether all that we have written on this point counts for anything when weighed against the delighted surprise and calm strength of the proletarian in the face of this science that has now been created and that is being created, every day; in the face of this new-born human phenomenon which is turning our perspectives and our concepts and, perhaps, our books upside down, but which will amply repay us for devoting

[a] See translator's note, Preface, p. 16.

ourselves to it, for unreservedly devoting ourselves to it, out of our sacrosanct curiosity and for the simple love of mankind.

I am fully aware that this 'devotion' can carry one a long way. I don't hesitate to say that it should carry one a long way, and indeed, all the way to the end. What would most surprise someone who didn't know you at all is something I have experienced along with a number of your former students: namely, that in *actively* rallying to the working class, we have not only not repudiated what had been our reasons for living, but have liberated them by fully realizing them. I think we deserve our future, even from Wilde's point of view, in that *we have not disregarded our past*: we have watched our past grow inside us and bear fruit in a manner beyond the hopes of our youth. The Christian I once was has in no way abjured his Christian 'values', but now I live them (this is an . . . 'historical', not a divine judgement!), whereas earlier I aspired to live them. The sole difference lies in this 'aspiration', which you continue to make into a philosophy (doubt, belief, etc.), but which I can no longer make into a universal philosophy if I want to look my proletarian brothers in the eye and call their 'malaise' by its real name – the 'malaise' that comes from poverty and unemployment – or their 'doubt', which their combat, their encounter with the truth, and their direct contact with reality deliver them from, as they do every 'scholar', every 'man of art' or science, as they already delivered Descartes from his doubt (you give us a strange, distorted portrait of Descartes in your book). No, I do not have the impression that I have 'repudiated' anything at all; and, more than a year ago, I attempted to transcribe this experience, common to many young people of my generation, in a text I enclose with this letter.[43] I present you with my experience, along with the following thought: don't be afraid to *lose* what you most cherish. For my part, I am convinced that the forms of thought and consciousness I have criticized in this letter – sometimes harshly – mask a quest for values that will not be lost if you try to find a way out of your solitude; they will be given to you in the very presence they now lack, a lack that grieves you, that is obvious.

Let me add, for the edification of the 'philosopher' in you, that my experience of life in the Party – though quite short – has shown me the extraordinary richness of this world, and the extraordinary freedom that reigns in it. And I mean freedom in the sense that is the most suspect for the 'bourgeois', freedom of thought, intellectual freedom in the most 'scandalous' form, that of research which has to take into account the Party's guidelines and political orientations (in philosophy, art, literature, cinema), that of a 'partisan position' in science, art, etc. This may surprise you, but I must say, for example, that I read Zhdanov's essay on philosophy with a mixture of indifference and reserve two years ago. And then, three months ago, I wrote a long article on the crisis of philosophy[44] which summed up my experience, and drew up a balance sheet of the problems I had had to deal with over the previous eighteen months, coming to what I thought were important conclusions on a number of specific points. I had forgotten Zhdanov. I happened to reread him two months ago: I found, in Zhdanov, the essence of my conclusions and a great deal more, formulated in much more solid, powerful terms. What extraordinary *sensitivity* [*présence*] to our problems, even the most 'technical', the most 'philosophical'. I have remarked this fecundity of politically guided research on a dozen different occasions. Let me add that we can feel, that we can see, besides the extraordinary richness and fertility of the ideas put before us, the reason for them. It is that, thanks to the Party and the very conditions of its activity, its continued existence, its survival (the Party cannot resort to trickery in dealing with men or problems or reality, for if it does it perishes – and we can see this at the level of detail, it is an *ineluctable* rule: every 'dogmatic' party cell *inevitably* collapses), we are in contact with authentic human reality, with real life, its real problems, its prodigious 'imagination' which, at every moment, poses new problems, invents new situations that have a *meaning* and bear within them, in more or less developed form, the elements of their solution. This permanent contact with reality opens up an immense, constantly renewed arena of reflection, and, above all, an arena in which we can be sure that the problems we encounter are *real*, not false, problems.

I am not sure that you have ever given sufficient consideration to what the Party is. You say, after Villey,[45] that Marxism is the immanent philosophy of the proletariat. That is rather too hasty; it is not, of course, wrong, but it does not take account of the *theoretical* aspect of Marxism and the fighting organization the Party is; it does not take account of the fact that Marxism has ceased to be simply the 'immanent' philosophy of the proletariat in order to become its *theory*, the theory of its struggles, the theory of its strategy and tactics; it does not take account of the existence of the Party. It is one thing to construct the general theory of historical materialism, to say that 'Marxism is the philosophy of the proletariat' – it is quite another to provide the proletariat with the concrete means of waging its struggle, which is neither philosophical nor something of the past. The proletariat does not live on its 'immanent philosophy'; it can be Marxist unawares, and go to blazes all the same; one must give it, *at every moment*, without respite, without fail, in a way that takes its possibilities and situation into account, slogans to guide it in action; one must be attentive, at every moment, to the evolution of the situation, which has to be scientifically analyzed so that these slogans can be put forward; one must be in close touch with men and their problems to understand the situation; one has untiringly to explain, to demonstrate, to explain constantly, rationally, to appeal to the direct *experience* of the masses and their theoretical horizon, if they are to accept the slogans. One does not, you know, accept one's own 'immanent philosophy' all that easily! The entire history of the workers' movement, of reformism, splits, and F[orce] O[uvrière] & co. goes to show that![46]

It would seem you do not give due weight to the fact that *the whole force of the Party and the Communists lies in their intelligence and their capacity to prove, to show the truthfulness of their theory and politics.* The strength of other ideologies and parties is the force of the trusts, of the administration, army, and police, of 'myths' (moral and sometimes even religious), prejudices, and old habits. Nothing is harder to overcome than habit, Stalin says, and he knows it for having experienced such resistance during the construction of socialism. The Party has all these forces, these immense forces, ranged against it; this is the case even in the working class, which is not homogeneous, and for a long time looked toward the bourgeoisie and assimilated its aspirations. The Party has against it the immense force represented by the inertia of the workers, artisans, and the indifferent, the immense force of centuries-old habits of submission (think of the peasants!), the immense force represented by the moral and police pressures of the bourgeoisie. Have you ever experienced a strike and taken the measure of just what these forces represent, at the very heart of the working class? And I do not so much as mention another form of pressure exercised by the bourgeoisie, which daily tries to buy off militants (think of Jouhaux[47] and a thousand others), to offer them a secure place, *effective immediately*, in its world, to provide them immediate security in place of endless struggles for a still distant world!

Those who have *concretely* confronted these problems and forces without discouragement have a different conception of the 'immanent philosophy of the proletariat' than you do! That philosophy is so immanent that it has to be pulled out with iron forceps, amidst blood and suffering; we are badly mistaken when we affirm that it is already on hand, when the whole problem consists in drawing it out, bringing it into the world, making it become life, reflection, theory, and struggle – a struggle that needs to be pursued till victory, an intelligent, determined struggle! In the face of all these adverse forces, the power of the bourgeoisie and the habits, prejudices, and temptations of the proletariat, the Party is without force. The Party is condemned to do without the kind of force its adversary has; the Party is *materially* condemned to relying on the sole force of men stripped of everything, who have to be brought together through an understanding of the truth. *The Party is condemned to truth;* it is condemned to discover the truth, to base itself on it, to conceive its plans for action in its light, to show, to demonstrate the truth to men so that they will know what to do with their own two hands! It is condemned to *the test of truth*, condemned, at every moment, to put the truth it has discovered to the test; if it fails to, events will prove it wrong and the truth will turn against it.

No-one who has not lived in the Party can imagine to what extent discovering, demonstrating, and testing out the truth is its iron law. Elsewhere in today's world, you would look in vain *for men, other than the Communists, who are condemned to truth or death, for others for whom the truth is, as it is for the Communists, the elementary condition for the slightest act or the slightest objective judgement, the basic condition for their human existence.* And this is true not only here, where we can see the fate of the social-democratic parties, which were also awash, immersed, in the 'immanent philosophy of the proletariat' (and God knows they have turned out treatises and speeches!); not only here, where an honest bourgeois cannot seriously maintain that the Party is recruited through terror or 'interest' or police coercion! This also holds for the Peoples' Democracies and the USSR, for the whole history of the USSR, in which 'criticism and self-criticism' have become the law of social development, in which, that is, the truth, discovered, acknowledged, and demonstrated, is the very *condition* for rallying an entire people, whom the last war showed to be united as never before.

I would like you to understand that the truth, possessed and produced, is the iron law and the condition of the Party, and that we intellectuals, perhaps, do not always live in the same condition. The 'condition' that is ours does not require us, *materially, as a question of life and death, to possess the truth, to put it to the test of struggle, to share it with other men.* We say we 'seek truth', but if we don't find it today, it can wait and so can we; we do not have a pressing need for it because *we manage to get by*, going home with our salary and the *cogito* and our problems to boot. *We are not condemned to the truth.* Moreover, we say: this is what I think, I do not want to force you to think the way I do, I have too much respect for your way of thinking; and what is the result? You write me, I write you, we 'engage in dialogue', we have time, we need time for research as Mounier said, if I haven't persuaded you, if you haven't persuaded me, nobody dies, each of us goes home, see you next time, and we construct the theory of dialogue or of the pluralism essential to spiritual families, of the diversity of systems in which Truth is incarnated, the theory of Transcendence to top it all off and justify our behaviour: *we are not condemned to demonstrate the truth!*

Again, we say: there's a strike on, the strike of 25 November;[48] if we take part in the strike, we do so with the lingering consciousness [*arrière-conscience*] that we have shown 'solidarity', a lingering sense of our high moral purpose, a lingering sense that we have chosen the Good, and an aftertaste [*arrière-goût*] of secret merit [*arrière-mérite*] in our mouths; if we do not join the strike, we find every imaginable reason not to, and the best reasons at that (even, on occasion, valid reasons, but reasons the proletarian has no right to, as the proletarian has no right to what is – even in this case – our type of truth, a strange type of truth that is not universalizable!); and the best reason is, in the final analysis, that we do not take part in the strike because we are in a position not to. One more striker? One less? We go home and life goes on, and if the comrades have won the minimum living wage at fifteen thousand, we don't turn down the difference.... And the best reason is, again, that if we strike, we strike because the risk is a small one. We have a choice, and minor disadvantages, material and moral, in the one case as in the other, but, whatever we do, our lives, which are possible even if they are not easy, go on, and no-one fires us for being union militants, or smashes our windows because we 'scabbed'. And, after going home, we construct a theory of choice, a theory of doubt and apprehension, a theory of the will and unwillingness [*de la volonté et de la nolonté*],[49] of free will and the capacity to judge, which is the mark of God in us, a theory of commitment and freedom, a theory of belief 'which is sustained in us only through action', and constitutes a higher form of Doubt and Freedom, and we spell Belief with a capital B in order to show that there is no real difference between Faith and Belief. *We are not condemned to take action in truth!* And all this hangs together. *Because we are not condemned to attain the truth at all costs, to demonstrate [it] to men, to share it with them, we are not condemned to take action with them in truth.*

Am I wrong? I think that I can here invoke the gist of your initial reservation, 'that it is difficult to speak of the Party without being part of it', and carry it to an extreme. I will go further than you: I will say that it is not only the Party one understands once one has come to know it, but also those who confront the truth in the places in which truth reigns as the elementary condition of life and thought. I have understood a good many things about myself, and not only about the Party, by coming face to face with this world in which men are condemned to truth; and I have learned so much about myself, and in such forms, that I truly no longer believe that 'self-consciousness is, for man, the mode of self-knowledge'. And if I can, from time to time, render you this service, it is because others have done the same for me, because this too is our condition, and because this condition is such that we acquire knowledge of ourselves by way of our acts and by way of others, who are inseparable from the process by which we acquire the truth; inseparable from our lives, and our triumphs. This is the sense of our criticism and self-criticism: we do not separate the truth that has been conquered from the men who have conquered it, who defend it and practise it; we cannot put the whole of its human significance to the test without testing the men who are its body and soul; and we do not pass divine judgement upon them, just as we do not expect them to pass the Last Judgement on themselves. We ask them, and they us, to give an account of the truth we live on, of the way it has been employed and tested, which is to say, as well, of the way we have been proven and tested and have employed ourselves to serve the truth we live on.

I have a thousand other things to say to you, but I must bring this too lengthy letter to a close ... if only so that you will get it some day. Let me tell you, on behalf of all my friends, many of whom are your friends as well, that we expect a great deal of you and trust your judgement and courage. Let me add, speaking for myself, that you are assured of my deep affection and friendship, both for the past, and, especially, for the present and future, and for this world in which we must, all of us, show ourselves worthy of our admirable brothers, who are suffering and struggling for their freedom, for our freedom.

Yours,

Louis Althusser

I enclose with this letter an admirable text published in *La Nouvelle Critique* – the old article on religion that I've told you about is on the way – along with a picture of the Dijon railwaymen that appeared in *L'Humanité* a month ago.[50] I hope that people, observing the calm strength and dignity of these men, will not one day say of us that 'the philosopher missed his rendez-vous with the railwaymen'. I've made a copy of this too lengthy letter – which is why it is so late – so that I can refer to it and you can refer to it (note the page numbers) in your answer.

Yours

Notes

1. Jean Lacroix was active in the Resistance in Lyons.
2. Joseph Hours was Althusser's history professor in *khâgne* in Lyons [for *khâgne* or *cagne*, see Preface, translator's note, p. 14].
3. Lacroix's letter to Althusser has not been found. Apart from quotations from Lacroix's book, the quotations in Althusser's letter have obviously been taken from Lacroix's.
4. Lacroix had just sent Althusser his book *Marxisme, Existentialisme, Personnalisme*, (Presses Universitaires de France, Paris, 1950); the dedication is dated 13 December 1949. Althusser here evokes the last sentence of the book: 'To believe is to anticipate, in a present experience, a future that is in some sort already present; or, rather, because a belief that concerns the future alone ends up being nothing more than a deceptive mirage, to believe is to reconcile the temporal and the eternal in a present intensification of being, for the present is merely the presence of eternity in time.' The passages from Lacroix's book underlined by Althusser have been italicized in the present edition.
5. 'When we die, our relationship with eternity doubtless undergoes a change in mode, writes Thomas Dussance in *Témoignages*. But is it not a mere figment of the imagination to say that we enter eternity then? Time has never found itself outside eternity, any more than the creation can be outside God. Moreover, we must confess that we do not at all understand why people insist on taking men's deaths as the end of their history; men's history will end only when they do – that is, never.'
6. Marcel Cachin (1869–1958) was the director of *L'Humanité* from 1918 to 1958. In 1920, at the Congress of Tours, he was one of the principal advocates of the idea that the

SFIO [Section Française de l'Internationale Ouvrière] should join the Third International; this led to the foundation of the French Communist Party. Cachin was a member of the Party's Political Bureau until his death.

7. Laszlo Rajk, former Deputy General Secretary of the Hungarian Communist Party, Minister of the Interior, and later Minister of Foreign Affairs, was accused of being a 'spy for the imperialist powers and a Trotskyist agent', and sentenced to death in one of the big Stalinist trials staged in what were then known as the 'Peoples' Democracies'. He was executed on 15 September 1949, and rehabilitated in 1956.

8. The review *Esprit*, to which Lacroix was a regular contributor, vigorously condemned the Rajk trial in its November 1949 issue, which included an editorial by Emmanuel Mounier, 'De l'esprit de la vérité', and an article by François Fejtö, 'L'affaire Rajk est une affaire Dreyfus internationale'. In the January 1950 issue, Fejtö published a second article, entitled 'De l'affaire Rajk à l'affaire Kostov'.

9. Gustave Thibon was a Christian thinker, the author *inter alia* of *Diagnostics* (1940), *Destin de l'homme* (1941), *L'Échelle de Jacob* (1942). His analyses of the 'crisis of the modern world' were a source of ideological inspiration for the Vichy regime.

10. Jean Guitton had been Althusser's philosophy professor in *hypokhâgne* and his first months of *khâgne*; appointed to the faculty of the University of Montpellier in November 1938, he was later replaced by Jean Lacroix. If Lacroix was active in the Resistance, Guitton was summoned to appear before a committee charged with purging collaborators after the war and was demoted to a position in the secondary schools in August 1946. See Yann Moulier Boutang, *Louis Althusser: Une biographie*, Vol. 1: *La formation du mythe, 1918–1956*, Grasset, Paris, 1992, p. 230.

11. See Lacroix, *op. cit.*, especially ch. 2, 'Système et existence'.

12. In addition to the articles in the November issue cited above, *Esprit* published in its December 1949 issue, under the rubric 'Il ne faut pas tromper le peuple', an article by Jean Cassou about the 'Yugoslav affair' and the Rajk trial, 'La révolution et la vérité'. The article was followed by a reply from Vercors. Cassou's article ends with this sentence: 'I ask my Communist friends, to the extent that they are willing to listen to me, if democracy can only be brought about by anti-democratic means.'

13. Like most of the defendants in the big Stalinist trials, Rajk had indeed 'confessed'.

14. Jacques Doriot (1898–1945) had served as the Mayor of Saint-Denis and as a Communist Deputy in the French National Assembly; expelled from the Communist Party in 1934, he founded the semi-fascist French People's Party in 1936 and took part, during the war, in the founding of the Legion of French Volunteers against Bolshevism. He was shot and killed in Germany in 1945. Marcel Gitton (1903–41) had been an important leader of the French Communist Party, becoming a member of its Political Bureau in 1932. He left the Party with the Hitler–Stalin Pact, and, during the war, went over to the collaborationist camp. He was shot down by the Resistance in September 1941.

15. Koestler's *The Yogi and the Commissar* is frequently cited in Fejtö's article.

16. Mounier, *loc. cit.*, p. 659, writes of Fejtö: 'A shocked conscience is speaking here, a man who has striven to keep faith to the point of suffocation.'

17. See n. 2.

18. See 'Quelques remarques sur les aveux de Rajk', *Information et Documentation* of the Agence France Presse, 24 September 1949, and the *Blue Book* published by the Hungarian government. Fejtö's article includes long extracts from these two texts.

19. François Fejtö directed the press office of the Hungarian Embassy in France for some time.

20. Cardinal Joseph Mindszenty (1892–1975), Primate of Hungary, was sentenced to life imprisonment with hard labour in February 1949, then placed under house arrest in 1955. Freed during the 1956 uprising, he took refuge in the American legation in Budapest during the Soviet invasion, remaining there until 1971. A sharp polemic flared up over the way in which 'confessions' were obtained from Mindszenty during the trial; the Hungarian authorities were widely accused of having drugged him.

21. Since the Rajk trial took place in September 1949, Althusser is in error here. He may be thinking of the meeting of the National Council of Fighters for Peace and Freedom that was held in Ivry on 22–23 October 1949. Following rather lively discussions, the Council passed a final resolution which, it should be noted, did not condemn

Yugoslavia as such, but rather its election to the UN Security Council. A detailed account of the debates was published in the newspaper *Action*, dated 'week of 27 October to 2 November 1949', under the title 'Large confrontation sur l'affaire yougoslave'. *Action* cites, notably, Jean-Marie Domenach, whose picture may be seen on the first page; appearing with him in the photo are the other members of the 'resolutions committee'. '"*I am not yet persuaded by any of this*," says J.-M. Domenach, who was nevertheless *disturbed to see Yugoslavia elected to the Security Council with Western support*. "*Perhaps we should condemn Tito at the appropriate moment*," says Domenach, who, however, thinks that to do so now would be to lend support to the arguments of the enemy, who would like to regard those fighting for peace and liberty as an *echo chamber* for Communist propaganda.' Jean-Marie Domenach, a friend of Althusser's, was at this time editor-in-chief of the review *Esprit*; he became its director in 1956. In 1967 he invited Althusser to give a talk on the progress of his philosophical research before *Esprit*'s 'Philosophy' group.

22. See n. 8.
23. 'L'homme communiste', the first chapter of Lacroix's book, is a substantially revised version of a talk Lacroix gave in Paris during 'Social Week' in 1947, which was devoted to the position of Catholics 'vis-à-vis the major tendencies of the day'.
24. This is the first sentence of the first chapter; it may be found on p. 5 of Lacroix's book.
25. Father Henri-Charles Desroches was the author of a book that had a considerable influence on the Christian Left and the worker-priest movement, *Signification du marxisme* (Éditions Ouvrières, Économie et humanisme, Paris, 1949). He subsequently worked as a sociologist. He died in 1994.
26. In a note on p. 21, Lacroix does indeed write: 'Subjectively, the two attitudes may be analogous. Objectively, the difference is a radical one. This is due not to men's deceptiveness, but to the clash between their goals ... If simply holding a dialogue with the Communists is so difficult, it is by no means because they change society too profoundly, but rather because, in carrying the rejection of all forms of transcendence to an extreme, they ultimately bring about a perversion of language that makes *mutual comprehension* literally impossible.'
27. 'That history has a meaning enables us to make not only *historical judgements*, but also *judgements about history*, that is, judgements transcending process. It is clear that a value judgement cannot be based on a judgement about reality, and that one can judge a man's character to be "heroic or base" only with reference to a transcendent norm. It is not the historical judgement, but the judgement about history which strives to be the judgement of God – with, of course, all the risks of human error this entails.'
28. The note on p. 23 consists essentially in a long quotation from an essay by Jean Hyppolite, 'La conception hégélienne de l'État et sa critique par Karl Marx', *Cahiers internationaux de sociologie*, 2, 1947, repr. in Hyppolite, *Études sur Marx et Hegel*, Marcel Rivière, Paris, 1955 ['Marx's Critique of the Hegelian Conception of the State', in Hyppolite, *Studies on Marx and Hegel*, trans. John O'Neill, Basic Books, New York and London, 1969, pp. 106–25]. One reads there, for example: 'By some curious reversal of perspective, which becomes intelligible if one grants that at a given moment in his development Hegel, like Marx, imagined an effective end to the alienation of man but dropped the thought upon reflections over certain historical events – it is Hegel who in this case seems to be involved in an *endless dialectical development* in which the Idea would be reflected, whereas Marx looked forward to an *end of history*' (p. 116).
29. Cf. Karl Marx, 'Preface to *A Contribution to the Critique of Political Economy*', in Karl Marx and Friedrich Engels, *Selected Works in One Volume*, Lawrence and Wishart, London, 1968, p. 183.
30. Alexandre Kojève, *Introduction à la lecture de Hegel*, Éditions Gallimard, Paris, 1947 [partial translation in Kojève, *Introduction to the Reading of Hegel*, ed. Allan Bloom, trans. James H. Nichols, Jr., Cornell University Press, Ithaca, New York, 1969].
31. Althusser is citing from memory. Cf. Postface to the Second Edition, *Capital*, Vol. I, trans. Ben Fowkes, Penguin/NLR edn, Harmondsworth, 1976, pp. 102–3.
32. Althusser is again referring to Hyppolite, 'La conception hégélienne de l'État et sa critique par Karl Marx' (see n. 28 above).
33. Andrei Zhdanov (1894–1948), a member of the Politburo of the CPSU from 1935, was

one of the chief Soviet ideologues after World War II. Two copies of the text mentioned here were found in Althusser's library, both heavily annotated: the first was published in the December 1947 issue of the review *Europe* under the title 'Sur l'histoire de la philosophie'; the second appeared under the title 'Sur la philosophie', in Zhdanov, *Sur la littérature, la philosophie et la musique*, Les Éditions de La Nouvelle Critique, Paris, 1950. ['On Philosophy', in Zhdanov, *On Literature, Music and Philosophy*, Lawrence and Wishart, London, 1950; the passage quoted by Althusser can be found on pp. 107–8].

34. *Ibid.*, p. 107.

35. Lacroix cites Lukács, who writes that it is 'the objective content and the actual direction of history which determine whether the character of those who act in history is heroic or base' (*Marxisme ou Existentialisme* [1948], repr. Nagel, Paris, 1961).

36. Althusser is doubtless referring to one of the lectures organized by Abbot Brien, then chaplain at the École normale supérieure. Emmanuel Mounier was invited to give one of these lectures, as were, for example, Teilhard de Chardin and Gabriel Marcel. Althusser seems to have attended some of them. See Jean-Philippe Mochon's Master's Thesis, 'Les Élèves de l'École normale supérieure et la politique, 1944–1962', Université Charles de Gaulle-Lille III, 1993.

37. *Conscrit*, student slang for a first-year student at the École normale supérieure.

38. That is, destiny, to which even the gods were subject, according to the ancient Greeks.

39. See the essay by Emmanuel Mounier, *art. cit.*, as well as numerous passages in Lacroix's book – for example, p. 58: 'It is our habit of systematizing which leads us to believe that we can *possess the truth*; but the non-systematic philosophers, a St. Augustine or a Pascal, denounce this idolatry and show that we are not to possess the truth, but are to be possessed by it.... He who becomes true, who makes himself true, engages in communion between one being and another, and gradually makes his relations both with being itself and with other beings more adequate. But this intimate transformation of the subject reverses the attitude of the systematizers. That is the significance ... of Gabriel Marcel's objection to systems; it naturally leads him, throughout his work, to distrust the *idea of truth*, and to prefer to it the *spirit of truth*.'

40. Matthew 7:9.

41. A disconcerting affirmation for anyone who has read *Réponse à John Lewis*, Maspero, Paris, 1973 ['Reply to John Lewis', in *Marxism Today*, October and November 1972, repr. in Althusser, *Essays on Ideology*, Verso, London, 1984, pp. 61–114]. See, for example, p. 73: 'When a carpenter "makes" a table, that means he *constructs* it. But to *make* history? What can that mean? And the man who makes history, do you know that individual, that "species of individual", as Hegel used to say?'

42. The question set for the 1948 *agrégation* [see translator's note, Preface, p. 16] ran, 'Is a science of human phenomena possible?'. In September 1949, Althusser published, under the pseudonym 'Pierre Decoud', a sarcastic essay entitled 'La philosophie bourgeoise fait de son désarroi des sujets d'agrégation'. The essay deals with the evolution of the *agrégation* question from 1946, when the examination subject was 'The idea of truth' ('a vintage pre-war subject, a concept as empty and atemporal as one could wish'), to 1949, when the subject was 'An evaluation of rationalism today and the outlook for its future'. Althusser's essay includes, notably, this passage: 'Today the bourgeoisie has been hoist with its own petard. It created 'its' human sciences after the great fear of 1848 (Comte), the Commune (Durkheim), and communism (Anglo-Saxon psychologists and sociologists); these were mystified sciences, and yet the bourgeoisie had no choice but to pretend to believe in their laws. The whole problem, that is, the whole crisis of the bourgeoisie, can be summed up as follows: how was the science (even if mystified) that it wished to fashion to be reconciled with the ideology of disaster, blindness, and diversion represented by the ideology of subjectivity and the divided consciousness? Where is the answer to this question to be sought? "In the consciousness of the sociologist, which is likewise divided ..." (report [on the examination results] by M. Davy, a sociologist and the president of the jury) ... The conclusion is ineluctable: the bourgeoisie would rather abandon science, and even its claim to science, than the ideology which translates its fear. May science, even mine, perish, as long as I survive!'

43. According to Yann Moulier Boutang, who has consulted Jean Lacroix's archives in the

library of the Catholic University in Lyon, this essay has not been preserved with Althusser's letter. The essay in question may well be 'A Matter of Fact', published in the present volume.

44. This text has not been found.

45. Lacroix, *op. cit.*, p. 14, n., cites Daniel Villey's *Petite histoire des grandes doctrines économiques*, pp. 204–5: '[the proletarians] have never read Marx; but they understand him better than we do, perhaps. Not because they anticipated Marx, but because Marx anticipated them. Is Marxism not, in some sense, the immanent philosophy of the proletariat, of revolutionary proletarian action?'

46. FO (Force ouvrière), a trade union that split off from the Confédération générale du travail or CGT, was founded in 1948. Its full name was Confédération générale du travail – Force ouvrière.

47. Léon Jouhaux, General Secretary of the CGT, played a leading role in the foundation of Force ouvrière. At the time, it was widely believed that American money had been behind the creation of the trade union.

48. Allusion to the general strike of 25 November 1949, initiated by the CGT and Force ouvrière.

49. See Lacroix, *op. cit.*, p. 82: 'Thus it is in my powers of refusal and of non-adhesion, my power of negation, my *negativity*, as Hegel would have said, my ability to avoid all forms of feverish action, which Renouvier called *nolonté*, that my freedom first manifests itself: to be free is to be able to say no.' [*Nolonté* is a neologism meaning something like 'un-willingness'; cf. *volonté*, will.] ch. 3 of Lacroix's book is entitled 'The Significance of Cartesian Doubt'; ch. 4 is called 'Belief'.

50. These documents have not been preserved with Althusser's letter; see n. 43. The photograph referred to is probably the one that appears on the front page of the 24 December 1949 edition of *L'Humanité*, over the following caption: 'A group of railwaymen waiting for the official train in order to acquaint the Socialist minister with the railworkers' views.'

On Conjugal Obscenity
(1951)

Let us begin by noting the respective situations of the Church and religion in a number of western European countries – France, Italy, Spain. And let us also note the rule which says that the more solidly the Church is entrenched in the state, and the more deeply it finds itself engaged in the state-controlled administration of souls, the less it needs religion. Only when it is separate from the state apparatus, as in France, does it have to secure by means of religious life the voluntary consent it would otherwise obtain from the prestige attendant upon direct association with state power. In short, one of the most remarkable effects of the separation of Church and state in France is that (making necessity a virtue) it has cleared a path for religious life, that extra dash of spirit which makes up for the loss of state influence. If we compare the French with the Italian or Spanish Church, we will observe that the involvement of the last two in state authority acts as an influence strong enough to discourage them from promoting a new religious life amongst the faithful. It may, of course, be objected that the 'religious life' of the French Church finds its explanation not only in the separation of Church and state, but in other political developments from the Popular Front to the Resistance; and that the French Church has not been able to remain aloof from certain forms of political life that have had a considerable influence on it, affecting its religious life along with the rest. But this argument carries little weight when we consider, for example, the Italian Church, which has barely been affected by politics, and is content to exercise power while giving hardly a thought to religion. As for religious life in the Spanish Church, it takes the direct form of political opposition (for which it serves as a disguise and refuge), not only to the state, but even to the Church itself.

This exordium, too long and too vague, has only one objective: to make it possible to grasp *one of the senses* in which the renewal of 'religious life' has manifested itself in France, where we have experienced it both before and after the last war. Doubtless most of the events we are about to discuss would be unintelligible if considered in isolation from the grand project of the Church, which, so as not to be outstripped by the trade unions, political parties, and youth movements of the Left, took the decision to found *Action catholique* (around 1930? The exact date has yet to be determined[1]). This was a revolutionary decision, because, for the first time in its history, the Church was abandoning the kind of religious life that was centred exclusively on the *parish* in order to replace it with a new form of organization that made allowance for other kinds of groups – those rooted, for example, in 'milieux', students, peasants, workers, managers, bosses, etc., i.e., group forms that more or less took the existence of social classes, professional categories, or age groups into account. All the 'specialized' movements have their origins here: JEC, JOC, JAC, JP, etc.[2] That this was a general decision, not one restricted to France, makes the fact that these Catholic movements developed with incomparable rapidity in France (and Belgium) all the more significant. And the separation of Church and state figures, incontestably, among the features of French life that contributed to this rapid development – as does the fact that the Church had to appeal to religion, or, if one likes, to spontaneous forms, forms of voluntary commitment on the part of its flock. Church members had to leave the passive practices of parish life behind, and actively enrol in these specialized movements, making a personal commitment and experiencing this commitment as a new form of their religious belief. I do not think that anyone acquainted with the young chaplains who threw themselves into these movements heart and soul, or anyone who has experienced the 'religious life' of these movements, can deny that they really did involve forms of religious life, and, at the same time, forms of religious and para-religious relationships without precedent in the history of the Church – and, of course, in the history of our country as well. It has here been necessary, doubtless, to trace matters back to this point in order to bring out the contingent necessity that appeared, in France, as a need for an 'extra dash of religious spirit [*un supplément d'âme religieux*]' to compensate the relative decline in the Church's state role – and to bring out, as well, the profundity and originality of this supplementary 'life'.

I will consider only one of its particular forms, involving married life. Amongst the main themes of the new 'religious life', there emerged an entire neo-theology of marriage that was taught in the youth movements before being assigned an organization of its own, made up of young families and Christian couples. This theology had its theologians, the chaplains of the youth groups, who also served as leaders and confessors. What distinguished the way this neo-theology of marriage was propagated, taught, and sanctioned was the *public* character of the operation.[3] To be sure, the theology of the sacrament of marriage was not invented

between 1936 and 1940. But it was given unparalleled weight, prominence, and publicity in those years. It would not be an exaggeration to
say that, earlier, the papal encyclicals on love hardly concerned anyone
but the clergy, who had to be advised of the rules governing absolution,
and, consequently, of the duties of married Christian men and women.
These encyclicals were not, however, objects of the same sort of regular,
public instruction and commentary as they were later on. The couple's
relations continued to be a *private* affair; the priest had a role to play only
when it came to confession – or the special education he might give one
or another child at its parents' request. Would it be overstating matters
to say that one of the reasons for the phenomenal development, in all the
youth organizations, of courses or general commentaries on the encyclicals devoted to Christian love, the marriage sacrament,[4] etc., was the
special circumstance, peculiar to France, of the separation of Church and
state – as if the Church had sought, by assigning a profoundly religious
meaning to Christian marriage and proposing a Christian way of experiencing marital life, to obtain by the free consent of its members what it
could no longer obtain from an administrative authority that had been
denied it? Here again I would not hesitate to say that the Church sought
in this Christian way of experiencing conjugal relations that extra dash
of spirit capable of making up for its loss of power and influence.

In these conditions there developed, beginning with the specialized
youth movements and culminating in the organizations for young
couples, forms of instruction, commentary, and, later, pre-marital or
marital relationships (between young engaged couples in the youth
movements; between husbands and wives, and also amongst young
married couples in the Christian marriage movements), which were
absolutely new, unprecedented, and quite strikingly marked by what
might be termed an *aggressive exhibitionism*. It is not easy to account for
this phenomenon, but we need to try to zero in on it. Plainly, in this
attitude (adopted not only by the chaplains, but also by young people of
both sexes before, while, and after getting to know one another), a
defiantly emancipatory reaction to old taboos played a major part. It was
as if, on these matters, tabooed for centuries by, precisely, religious
morality, the Church militant of the young chaplains and their charges
was proving its broad-mindedness and audacity to itself by openly
addressing sexual questions: relieved that it could now speak of them as
others did, better than others did, it defiantly threw its own *public*
emancipation in their teeth. Yes, the Church had its theology of marriage;
yes, the popes had given it encyclicals about married love; yes, it was
necessary to speak out frankly and freely about this, calling things by
their real names and putting 'bourgeois' or even 'religious' prudishness
to shame (its time was past, but its time had always been past). Indeed,
to bourgeois marriage, ashamed of itself – to civil marriage (read:

marriage without religious consciousness), which was more or less hypocritical, and in any event [tainted] with hypocrisy by its own (purely legal!) status – to this marriage of interest or reason, which kept women in ignorance and gave men all the advantages of liberty and licence – it was necessary to oppose, unmistakably, religious marriage, which was self-aware, ensured the equality of man and wife, at liberty to administer the sacrament of marriage to one another, and confident of its objectives, which went beyond mere reproduction to the mutual sanctification of the spouses. Thus a *lawful lifting of repression* (lawful in the religious sense: authorized, sanctioned, and encouraged by religion) dovetailed with an *indirect condemnation* of non-religious forms of conjugal life; this can be taken as the basis for an explanation of the aggressively exhibitionistic form such propaganda assumed amongst young people.

Soon enough, however, the effects took it upon themselves to reinforce the causes. Something never before seen appeared: 'Christian couples' – I mean publicly Christian couples, who professed that that was what they were, and even came together in organizations for mutual assistance and spiritual exchange (on the basis of the Christian theology of the couple). These were couples who professed their convictions and advertised their principles, hiding nothing about them from anybody. They were, at all events, tempted by this *ordeal* suspended between triumphant witness and discreet martyrdom (which was, however, public too), meant to prove that they had the courage of their principles. But they put more than just their principles on exhibit: they also advertised their results – whether in their own concrete behaviour, or, more commonly, by parading their flocks of children around in public, thus demonstrating in sight of one and all that they made love, by the grace of God, and that, although the ultimate objective of marriage was the mutual sanctification of man and wife, they also could not help sleeping together – under, however, special conditions of human unrestraint, i.e., conscious abandon to the will of Providence. As to taking thought for the morrow, there were the family benefits, and the parable about God providing for the fowls of the air.

It is no exaggeration to say that this whole set of circumstances gave rise to what must be called a new and very particular kind of *conjugal behaviour*, which, unlike most of the preceding forms (of conjugal behaviour), had as its central, paradoxical feature the fact that it was *intimate public behaviour*. Not that couples made love out in the open, or confided the details of their lovemaking to all and sundry; but their way of conducting themselves in public served notice of the *natural* existence of their problems and of their intimate solutions. It was a form of public behaviour (right down to the conscious choice to have large numbers of children) which, far from concealing the existence of their private life and the principles guiding it, conspicuously gave it pride of place. When one adds to this the relations with (public) organizations of young couples, and the relations with the 'chaplains' (very different from those that had earlier been maintained with the parish priests), which were also conspicuously 'frank' and 'free', it will be admitted that this new form of conjugal behaviour could hardly go unnoticed.

The couple, the children, the chaplain, the groups of young husbands and wives, the lectures on theology, the religious ceremonies specially intended for these groups, the retreats, the exchange of 'spiritual' experiences – all this lent the new form of conjugal behaviour an incredible *indecency* and an incredible *lack of awareness* of this indecency. Here again there can be no doubt that this indecency was not at all consciously experienced as such by these young people. For, in their eyes, what was involved was not indecency or an exhibitionistic display of their private lives (even in the form of these 'phenomena'). What was involved was 'spiritual life'. The immediate identity (to put it in Hegelian language) between intimate sexuality and 'spiritual life'; the fact that emancipation from traditional sexual taboos came about under the aegis of spiritual sanctification; the possibility, which people now had for the first time, of speaking publicly about sex in spiritual terms (which also implied the possibility of speaking of the spiritual in sexual terms); or, in other words, the conjunction of the most purely sexual matters with the most purely spiritual sublimation; all this constituted the unconscious alibi, the legitimation of, and authorization for, a mode of behaviour which, taken out of this subjective context, was constantly in danger of lapsing into the exhibitionism of shamelessness – whether it was an exhibitionism of acts and modes of behaviour, or, quite simply, an exhibitionism of *principles*.

Moreover, just as Marx (and Bebel) say that the condition of women in their relationships with men permits us to judge the degree of freedom or unfreedom in a given society, so I would say that this unprecedented religious life manifested itself most clearly in the new status and behaviour of women. I mean that *it is woman* who found herself at the most sensitive point, the focal point of this exhibitionism. The reasons are simple. This neo-theology of marriage brought about a result far more equitable than the articles of the Civil Code: it made woman, religiously speaking, man's equal. We would have to study the history of this doctrine to determine when it appeared and developed. But it is certain that this sacrament, which man and wife administer to one another as equals in an exchange, had important repercussions on minds shaped by one hundred and fifty years of the Civil Code – by woman's legal inferiority. Heretofore, if the doctrine of the Church had not been concealed from women, its profound significance, at least, had been – and, in any case, even if it had been taught them, men, their husbands, would have been just deaf enough not to hear it. This time things were different: the chaplains taught everyone, young women, but young men as well, the theoretical truths about their union, and, along with the rest, the young men accepted the religious dogma concerning the equality of the exchange and of the partners in the exchange. The religiously motivated change in woman's status entered into men's consciousness, their relations with their wives, and their attitude towards other couples. One might say, in this connection, that *the conjunction* of this consciousness of equality – not only equality of status, but also equality in the grand spiritual enterprise represented by a life led in common, i.e., in the forging of the couple's future – *the conjunction* of the theology of procreation (as an uncontrollable side-effect of spiritual union), bringing in its wake the multiplication of children – the conjunction of the theory of children's education, considered in all its spiritual-religious profundity, and, generally speaking, the sacralization of the majority of everyday acts, which now overflowed with an excess of spiritual meaning – to say nothing of the more or less consciously assumed role of public witness (itself imbued with religious meaning) – this conjunction had as its overall consequence the paradox that, precisely because she was man's equal from a religious standpoint, the 'Christian' woman, overburdened by her children and the chores that consummated her own sanctification and that of the couple, became a *housewife*, giving up whatever projects she may have formed with a view to fleeing her limited existence, in particular her *professional* projects, together with all topics of interest and the social relationships they might have given her access to; she was literally transformed into a mother and homemaker.

But, *nota bene*, she was transformed into a Christian mother and homemaker, the Christian wife of her Christian husband. This was undoubtedly the circumstance that unconsciously reinforced the feature I earlier called the exhibitionism of shamelessness. I mean that mothers and homemakers are, as everyone can see, mothers and homemakers. But these particular mothers and homemakers had not become what they were either by accident or simply as the result of a sort of vague desire, or, again, of very precise intentions such as the wish to have one child or four children, etc. – the way most women, even traditional Catholics, simply *are* mothers and homemakers. These mothers and home-makers were such in consequence of a deliberate design that was religious in its essence, that could be set out, defended, and, if necessary, explained (or demonstrated) to anyone. They were mothers and home-makers essentially because they were Christian wives, who, as such, worked towards the spiritual perfection of the couple by having babies and taking them out for strolls, and wiping their bottoms, and bringing them up, as well as by doing the laundry, the cooking, and the washing-up.

I do not say that all of them spent their time *making that difference felt;*

some, thank God, found in this attitude something like a way to preserve their own natural modesty. But I do say that there was a big risk, a very big risk that became a reality for many of them, especially for those who *could have* done something besides having endless strings of children, who could have had a profession, a real profession, and developed as intelligent beings (and who therefore felt a deep need to make it clear *why* they had chosen the stupid option of the rabbit hutch and the kitchen sink, a deep need to come up with noble reasons for their obviously foolish mistake, that is, for their sacrifice, which *wasn't one*) – there was, I say, a very big risk that many of them would become *witnesses in their own defence*. In other words, that they would publicly profess their principles so as not to be accused of being fools, and would plunge all the more resolutely into the quagmire, with a resolve that was all the more manifest the more they felt the need to go through this semblance of an ordeal to convince themselves that, far from consigning themselves to perdition, they were securing their salvation. This was obviously a rather sad situation in itself, but it was precisely in this situation that all the latent forms engendered by this general context were gathered together and summed up. The cohabitation of the religious with the banal, or even with the least appealing aspects of daily existence – the cohabitation of the religious and the sexual, of religion and obstetrics, etc. – resulted in a constant back-and-forth from the sacred to the profane, the spiritual to the natural (outsiders could see and feel this, because the intention to demonstrate or defy, or else to bear public witness to something, ran through all these modes of conduct). Ulti-mately, because people could not always maintain, at the spiritual or religious level, the attitude required to put up with the rest or, if you like, to invest it with meaning, they came to acquire a sort of supplemen-tary shamelessness: they simply gave their attitude out as natural, though nothing in the world could have been less natural – as if 'nature' allowed one *to dispense with* the forms of respect and tact the most essential to social relations – in order to forge an immediate synthesis between what was noblest and what was least so. Thus one met couples (but especially women) who had no other ways and means of dealing with their own embarrassment than to put themselves forward as if they were, so to speak, *natural* institutions; they saw themselves as people who no longer had any problems to solve, at least as far as their relations with others went, and they paraded their children, and their 'problems', and their difficulties through the world, wholly preoccupied with themselves, barely mindful of outsiders, deaf, most of the time (and, it must be said, deafened, deadened, by the cries of their interminable families, whom they substituted for life and the world). They were, in event, confined to a world that was just as public, but they could no longer boast what had originally been their pride: the fact that they had made their world over into a spiritual one worthy of God's design. Thus they brought a new form of obscenity into the world with the help of the religion the French Church had mobilized to compensate its loss of power.

The designs of Providence are inscrutable. The shamelessness of these couples' 'natural behaviour', and the 'natural' character, as they saw it, of their public conduct, 'naturally' came to stand in for their religious life and religious intentions. Thus they lived out their married lives in exactly the same manner as certain couples who were forced to live in close proximity in dilapidated or semi-collective modern apartments, whom the constraints imposed by these deplorable living conditions transformed into family units given over to sex, feeding, and child-rearing, in full view of everybody. However, unlike ordinary people, who simply experienced their condition as a fact of life, they made a great show of experiencing it as the supreme spiritual epiphany, a manifestation of God's grace. They made a show of experiencing as something *natural* the attribution of a supernatural meaning to 'nature', to the point that parading nature about in its nakedness – that is, nature's public shamelessness – became the very presence of the supernatural, a way of announcing, if not advertising it. If we carefully consider this short-circuiting of 'nature' and 'spirit', and the public exhibition of their identity as simultaneously 'natural' and 'spiritual', we will not hesitate to identify it as the very structure of obscenity, if it is true that obscenity consists in the exhibition of a cultural phenomenon as something 'natural', the exhibition of the private as the public, the exhibition of forbidden behaviour as permissible or even eminently authorized, and, finally, the exhibition of the 'supernatural' as 'nature' itself. Obscenity, that is, consists in the 'natural' exhibition of the scandalousness of this perpetual confusion of orders.

I do not think anyone can seriously contest the idea that the Church has played an important role in creating these new attitudes and modes of behaviour. For it is the Church which has *permitted* this short-circuit, which has restructured earlier modes of behaviour by providing a new outlet for impulses that, only recently, were beaten back and repressed. The Church has taken hold of conjugal relations in the categories they were formerly caught up in: secrecy, intimacy, privacy, interdiction, silence, concealment, nature (assuming that these categories were pure) – that is, in the *form of repression*, generally speaking. And it has transformed these older categories into new ones seemingly in contradiction with them: the categories of the public, the authorized, the spiritual and the supernatural, of witness and manifestation. In other words, it has replaced the categories of repression [*refoulement*] with new categories which all have the properties associated with the lifting of repression [*défoulement*], particularly its aggressive triumphalism, its insistence on its rights, its proclamation of its claims to legitimacy, and a conspicuously good conscience rooted in consciousness of God's complicity.

But it cannot be said that the Church, in making this substitution, has extricated itself from the original situation: it has only 'inverted' this situation within the Church itself. The sole solution it has provided consists, in essence, in displaying the marks of its former servitude as so many proofs of its emancipation. But this public display, and all the meanings attached to it, could not have come about if the *interdict*, or, rather, the form of the interdict placed on certain subjects had not been lifted; it could not have come about, that is, without the official *authorization* of the Church. This lifting of the form of the interdict has been *possible* because the power that lifted the interdict is the one that established it: the authority that makes the laws can also unmake them. To be sure, in lifting this interdict, the Church pretended it had not established it, preferring to pillory the world, its materialism, etc., its false piety, hypocritical prudishness, etc. But no-one was fooled by that distinction, because the young couples passed from what was, for them, a false religious consciousness to a true religious consciousness; that is, they remained within the bounds of religion, simply declaring, as they passed from one form of consciousness to the other, that the first, the one they were abandoning, was not religious. However, what they failed to see – but, alas, showed everyone else – was that this authorized, and justified, lifting of repression, which was inwardly balanced by the absolution provided by *spirituality*, i.e., by the *sublimation* that sustained the edifice of these passions, had nothing emancipatory or 'natural' about it that was not contained in the very categories of authorization and sublimation. What these couples experienced as true emancipation was never anything other than a new form of servitude, but one experienced in new categories that made their private lives, sexual relations, and the conjugal division of labour a form of public witness and religious existence.

This is, without a doubt, one of the most serious forms of mystification of our day. To the earlier forms, which at least showed themselves for what they were, without even taking the trouble to conceal the hypocrisy at their root (the Civil Code in all its legal brutality), the modern forms have added the *illusion* of emancipation. But this emancipation is merely the authorization to *exhibit* what one had earlier been *obliged to hide*; its only effect has been to substitute the release associated with exhibition for the repression of desire, that is, to substitute one form of servitude for another, and, what is worse, a form of servitude that is experienced as true freedom. By thus replacing private repression with public sublimation, the Church has in fact *made it more difficult to criticize* the condition of the couple; by transforming what had hitherto been experienced in a context of moral asceticism into obvious, self-confident, and manifest 'nature', it has cut short criticism of the conjugal situation, and, in particular, of woman's position in the couple, eliminating the point of attack that the malaise caused by the contradiction of private repression had offered. By transforming malaise and bad conscience into 'nature', the Church has not produced the faintest stirrings of freedom; it has, for the most part, produced *inanity*, when it has not produced outright *obscenity*. It has terribly complicated the existence of the young people who have committed themselves to its myths, and it has posed the problem of their personal emancipation in terms which are all the more tragic in that these young people have had to break not only with traditional legal categories and obsolete modes of behaviour, but also with new modes of behaviour produced by this 'religious revolution' and the consciousness accompanying it. These young people have also had to cope with the surprise and ordeal of their solitude; they have not been able to understand why something 'natural' and 'unproblematic' in their eyes so often creates problems for others. When they have had the requisite courage, they have had to make an effort to learn to live again – in conditions that were worse than before; when they were not suited for freedom, they have had to go on living in their mythology, i.e., to continue to *forget about living*.

When, someday, someone draws up the balance sheet of the 'daring positions' of the French Church, I hope he will take this case as an object lesson: it demonstrates with perfect clarity that, to free one's hands, one needs to do more than turn one's gloves inside out.

Notes

1. Everything depends on what one means, precisely, by the 'founding' of *Action catholique*. The JOC was founded in 1925. According to the *Nouvelle histoire de l'Église*, Éditions du Seuil, Paris, 1975, Vol. 5, p. 879, the 1905 encyclical *Il firmo proposito* constituted '*Action catholique*'s first official charter'. According to Pierre Pierrard (*Histoire de l'Église catholique*, Desclée de Brouwer, Paris, repr. 1978), the main orientations of *Action catholique* were defined in 1922 in the encyclical *Urbi arcano*. Pius XI defined *Action catholique* as the 'participation of lay members of the Church in the hierarchical apostolate'.

2. The *Jeunesse ouvrière chrétienne française* was founded in 1926, the *Jeunesse agricole catholique* in 1929, the *Jeunesse étudiante chrétienne* in 1932.

3. On these questions, see, for example, *Histoire religieuse de la France contemporaine*, eds Gérard Cholvy and Yves-Marie Hilaire, Éditions Privat, Toulouse, 1988, pp. 138–40, 384–7. The authors evoke 'the deepening of the spiritual life of couples within the home-and-hearth movements and around the magazine *L'Anneau d'Or*' (founded in 1945 by Abbot Caffarel), the culmination of the 'efforts of an abbot, J. Viollet, of the Association for Christian Marriage, with its monthly, *Foyers*, and of Father Doncœur, both precursors of the great trend towards conjugal spirituality, already considered to be of major significance by the Congrès des Œuvres, held in Rennes in 1949'. The authors also mention 'the preparation of engaged couples for marriage, beginning in 1952, in the Centres for Preparation for Marriage, which emerged from the Équipes Notre-Dame' (first organized in 1938). Let us note, finally, the then recent publication of Jean Lacroix's book *Force et faiblesses de la famille*, Éditions du Seuil, Paris, 1948, an annotated copy of which was discovered in Althusser's library.

4. The encyclical *Casti connubii* (1930) on marriage and the family.

APPENDIX
On Marxism
(1953)

[A] On Marxism

Marxism constitutes one of the main currents of contemporary thought. By now, there is no counting the works that set out to expound, combat, or even 'supersede' it. It is already no easy task to find the path that cuts through this mass of polemical works and leads to the texts. Moreover, there are a great many of these texts. The (incomplete) French edition of the works of Marx and Engels published by Costes comprises some sixty volumes; that published by Éditions Sociales more than twenty;[1] the (incomplete) edition of Lenin's works includes some twenty volumes; the edition of Stalin's, some fifteen; and so on ... But the fact that there are so many texts is not the only problem. The Marxist canon spans an historical period that stretches from 1840 to the present, and raises problems that have fuelled polemics: the nature of Marx's early works; the problem of the Marxist tradition. Finally, the very nature of Marxism – a science and a philosophy closely bound up with (political or scientific) practice – represents an additional difficulty, perhaps the greatest of all. If one neglects the constant reference to practice, which Marx, Engels, and their followers insistently call to our attention, one is liable to misunderstand the significance of Marxism entirely, and to interpret it as an 'ordinary' philosophy.

Here we would like to provide a few guideposts that may make approaching and studying Marxism easier.

A few bibliographical pointers may be useful.

At the end of a work by H. C. Desroches, *Signification du marxisme* (Éditions Ouvrières, Économie et humanisme, Paris, 1950), the reader will find an introductory bibliography by C. F. Hubert.[2] This annotated bibliography is divided into two sections. In the first, the author presents us with an initiatory bibliography of selected works or chapters – the compendia of Marxism – by Marx, Engels, Lenin, and Stalin, organized under four headings: economy, theory of the state, general theory of history, and tactics and strategy. The second section (complementary bibliography) contains a chronological listing of the works of Marx and Engels, together with a very partial list of Lenin's works. This bibliography is quite serviceable. But it has a number of faults: it tends to sacrifice dialectical materialism to historical materialism; it is not up-to-date; and it does not include works about Marxism (with the exception of a text by Plekhanov and Auguste Cornu's dissertation [on the young Marx]).

The most comprehensive and interesting historical study of Marx is a book in German by Franz Mehring, *Karl Marx* (1918); it deserves to be translated. Henri Lefebvre, *Pour connaître la pensée de Marx* (Bordas, Paris, 1948), may also be consulted with profit; it is better than the short book by the same author, *Le matérialisme dialectique*, published before the war by NEP (Alcan, 1940). *Morceaux choisis de Karl Marx*, ed. Lefebvre and Guterman (Gallimard, 1934), has a serious drawback: texts from different periods, including extracts from Marx's early works, are grouped under the same heading, without any accompanying historical information.

Good accounts of Marxist economic theory may be found in Segal, *Principes d'économie politique* (ESI, Paris, 1936); Baby, *Principes fondamentaux d'économie politique* (ESI, 1949); and, especially, Benard, *La conception marxiste du capital* (Éditions SEDES, Paris), and Denis, *La valeur, la monnaie* (ESI).

I. The problem of Marx's early works

Contemporary philosophers have played up Marx's early works. These are doubtless more accessible than *Capital*. Moreover, they are 'philosophical' works, marked by the pervasive influence of Hegel and Feuerbach.

The importance we assign these early texts (in some respects, Hegel's work already throws up the same problem) will command our general interpretation of Marxism. If we hold that they contain Marx's basic inspiration, then they become Marxism's criterion of validity and the principle that will inform our interpretation of Marxism. Thus, to take two different examples, M. Hyppolite has argued that Marx remains faithful to his original philosophical intuitions right down to *Capital* (see 'Marxism and Philosophy'; 'Marx's Critique of the Hegelian Philosophy of the State;' 'On the Structure and Philosophical Presuppositions of Marx's *Capital*', in Jean Hyppolite, *Studies on Marx and Hegel*, trans. John O'Neill, Basic Books, New York and London, 1969). Conversely, M.

Gurvitch has defended the intuitions of the young Marx against his mature works, arguing that the inspiration of the latter is different and inferior (see 'La sociologie du jeune Marx', *Cahiers internationaux de sociologie*, no. 4, 1948). The problem of the Marxist tradition and the evolution of Marxist thought is posed by way of these theses.

If, however, we hold that these early works reflect the interests of the young Marx, who, like all his fellow students, entered the arena of thought in a world dominated by Hegel's philosophy, but, with the help of internal criticism, historical experience, and scientific knowledge, put this point of departure behind him in order to work out an original theory, then we will regard these early works as transitional, and seek in them less the truth of Marxism than the intellectual trajectory of the young Marx. This is, *grosso modo*, the thesis defended by Mehring, and also by Auguste Cornu in *Karl Marx, l'homme et l'œuvre: De l'hégélianisme au matérialisme historique, 1815–1845* (Alcan, Paris, 1934).[3] From this standpoint, the philosophical influences of Marx's youth are, in *Capital*, simply starting points he has left behind to forge an original conception of things (Lenin adopts this thesis in *Karl Marx* [1914]). So regarded, the Marxist tradition does not confront us with the same question as before.

We do not wish to deal with this important question here; it is matter for a detailed historical study. Let us simply take note of the judgement Marx and Engels passed both on their own early works and on the influences to which they were subject.

In the Preface to the *Contribution to a Critique of Political Economy* (a text dating from 1859, published by Giard), Marx examines his own development and early works, making the following points. To begin with, he underscores the importance of Engels' 'brilliant sketch on the criticism of the economic categories'. (The reference is to Engels' article 'Outline of a Critique of Political Economy', an empirical [*positive*] analysis of England's economic and political situation published in February 1844 in the *Deutsch-Französische Jahrbücher*. This crucially important article has not been included in the volume of Marx and Engels' philosophical works published by Costes.) Marx then refers to *The German Ideology* in these terms: 'When in the spring of 1845 [Engels] also settled in Brussels, we resolved to work out in common the opposition of our view to the ideological view of German philosophy, in fact, to settle accounts with our erstwhile philosophical conscience' [Marx and Engels, *Selected Works in One Volume*, Lawrence and Wishart, London, 1968, p. 193]. Marx thus considered all his texts prior to *The German Ideology* to be tainted by a 'philosophical conscience', and he regarded *The German Ideology* as a critique of this influence, which he had by then overcome. He adds, 'The decisive points of our view were first scientifically, though only polemically, indicated in my book published in 1847 and directed against Proudhon: *The Poverty of Philosophy*' [*ibid.*, p. 184].

These texts of Marx's would seem to make it possible to mark off the stages of Marx's thought as he himself defines them. 1) All the texts prior to *The German Ideology*, including *The Holy Family* and the '1844 Manuscripts' (which were left in the form of notes, and have not been translated in full by Costes), were more or less subject to the influence of German 'philosophy'. 2) *The German Ideology* is a critique of this 'philosophical conscience'. 3) *The Poverty of Philosophy* (1847) is the first scientific text Marx recognizes as being entirely characteristic of his mode of thought [*où Marx se reconnaisse entièrement*].

Marx and Engels often re-examined their relationship to, and disagreement with, Hegel. See, in this connection, *The German Ideology* (*passim*), *The Poverty of Philosophy*, ch. II, 1. 'The Method', the second Preface to *Capital* [the Postface to the second German edition], Engels' *Ludwig Feuerbach* (the beginning), and Engels' *Anti-Dühring* (Part I, ch. XIII, 'Negation of the Negation', a theme taken up and powerfully developed by Lenin in *What 'The Friends of the People' Are, Collected Works*, Vol. 1, Lawrence and Wishart, London, 1960, pp. 163–74).

One word more about the implications of this problem of Marx's early works. It is certainly not irrelevant to our understanding of Marxism today. This is evident when one considers notions like the *End of history*, bound up in turn with the notion of *alienation*. If Marx and his followers do no more in their works than illustrate and corroborate the still philosophical theses of *On the Jewish Question* or the '1844 Manuscripts'; if they merely attempt to 'flesh out' the Hegelian philosophical notion of the end of alienation and the 'end of history', then their undertaking is worth what this notion is. And, in that case, Marxism sacrifices its scientific pretensions, to become, in some sort, the incarnation of an ideal, which, although certainly moving, is utopian, and, like any ideal, gets entangled in both theoretical contradictions and the 'impurity' of concrete means the moment it seeks to bend reality to its demands. Conversely, if Marxism has nothing to do with any 'philosophical' notion of this sort, if it is a science, it escapes the theoretical contradictions and practical tyranny of the ideal; the contradictions it runs up against are no longer those resulting from its philosophical pretensions, but simply the contradictions of reality itself, which it sets out to study scientifically and solve practically.

II. Historical materialism

Historical materialism is precisely that science of history of which the early works are the 'philosophical' anticipation.

Here again, we would like to provide a few guideposts. Marxism has two aspects, which are profoundly united, yet distinct: dialectical materialism and historical materialism.

Marx and Engels use the term historical materialism to refer to the science of history, or the 'science of the development of societies' established by Marx. This term may seem questionable: we do not use the term 'physical materialism' to designate physics. In fact, Marx was using the term as a weapon. His aim was to counterpose his enterprise to the idealist conceptions of history of his day. He wished to found the science of history, not on men's 'self-consciousness' or the 'ideal objectives of history' (the 'realization of freedom', the reconciliation of 'human nature' with itself, etc. – see, on this subject, *The German Ideology, passim*), but on the material dialectic of the forces of production and relations of production, the 'motor' that determines historical development 'in the final analysis' (see the Preface to *A Contribution to the Critique of Political Economy*).

In a little known, highly instructive essay, Lenin discusses the scientific method of Marx's work at length, using Marx's own terms (*What 'The Friends of the People' Are*, pp. 129ff.). Historical materialism, says Lenin, is not an arbitrary conception. The science of history was constituted as the other sciences were; although it possesses its own methods and principles, it must meet the same standards of rigour. 'This idea of materialism in sociology was in itself a piece of genius. Naturally, "for the time being" it was only a hypothesis, but it was the first hypothesis to create the possibility of a strictly scientific approach to historical and social problems.' This hypothesis (the explanation of history through the dialectic of forces and relations of production) makes it possible to introduce the criteria of science into history: objectivity, repetition, generalization.

> Now – since the appearance of *Capital* – the materialist conception of history is no longer a hypothesis, but a scientifically proven proposition. And until we get some other attempt to give a scientific explanation of the functioning and development of some social formation – social formation, mind you, and not the way of life of some country or people, or even class, etc. – another attempt just as capable of introducing order into the 'pertinent facts' as materialism is, that is, just as capable of presenting a living picture of a given formation, while giving it a strictly scientific explanation – until then the materialist conception of history will be synonymous with social science (*ibid.*, p. 142; translation modified).

As such, Marxism cannot claim to do more than a science does:

> And just as transformism does not at all claim to explain the 'whole' history of the formation of species, but only to place the methods of this explanation on a scientific basis, so materialism in history has never claimed to explain everything, but merely to indicate the 'only scientific', to use Marx's expression (*Capital*), method of explaining history (*ibid.*, p. 146).

These theses enable us to articulate more precisely the objectives of Marxism and its claims to scientific status.

One further point needs to be clarified in this connection. Modern writers, taking up, consciously or not, a tradition whose representatives include Sorel and Bogdanov, have described historical materialism as 'the immanent philosophy of the proletariat' (Daniel Villey), as a theory that is valid for the proletariat and gives expression to its condition and aspirations. This thesis leads to the following conclusion: Marxism is a subjective ('class') theory, having no claim to scientific universality and objectivity; hence it is a myth in the Sorelian sense, rather than a science. Others have sought to ground the scientific nature of Marxism, 'the ideology of the proletariat', in the essence of the proletariat, the 'universal class' whose condition – whose very impoverishment – marks it out for universality and objectivity. Lenin had occasion to discuss this problem in a famous text, *What is to be Done?* (especially chs I and II; see Lenin, *Selected Works*, Vol. 5, Lawrence and Wishart, London, 1961, pp. 352ff.). Against the advocates of the 'spontaneity' of the proletariat, Lenin defends the absolute necessity of 'scientific theory'. He quotes approvingly the following passages from Kautsky:

> [For the spontaneists], socialist consciousness appears to be a necessary and direct result of the proletarian class struggle. But this is absolutely untrue. . . . Modern socialist consciousness can arise only on the basis of profound scientific knowledge. . . . The vehicle of science is not the proletariat [this was written in 1902], but the *bourgeois intelligentsia*: it was in the minds of individual members of this stratum that modern socialism originated, and it was they who communicated it to the more intellectually developed proletarians, who, in their turn, introduce it into the proletarian class struggle where conditions allow that to be done. Thus, socialist consciousness is something introduced into the proletarian class struggle from without . . . and not something that arose within it spontaneously (*ibid.*, pp. 383–4).

Lenin shows that, 'spontaneously', the proletariat cannot but be influenced by bourgeois ideology, and that Marxism, far from being the subjective theory of the proletariat, is a science that must be taught to the proletariat. Lenin and his followers have often drawn attention to the fact that the proletariat had existed for a very long time, and endured a thousand different ordeals, before assimilating Marxism and accepting it as the science that could account for its condition within the overall framework of capitalist society, securing its future as well as all humanity's. Only later did the proletariat produce, in its class organizations, intellectuals of its own, who developed Marxist theory in their turn.

This text of Lenin's is important for the study of Marxism's relation to the proletariat, class consciousness, the problem of 'economic consciousness' and political consciousness, 'spontaneity', 'partisanship', etc. If we compare it with the second Preface to *Capital* and Engels' *Socialism: Utopian and Scientific,* on the one hand, and the monographs Stalin has written on *Marxism and Linguistics* and *Economic Problems of Socialism in the USSR,* on the other, we can discern, in these theoretical works, a profoundly scientific conception of history, which rigorously defines its own domain while distinguishing it from others, determines the laws of its object, and submits its results to the test of concrete human practice:

> The criterion of practice, i.e., the course of development of *all* capitalist countries in the last few decades, proves only the objective truth of Marx's *whole* social and economic theory in general, and not merely of one or another of its parts, formulations, etc.; it is clear that to talk here of the 'dogmatism' of the Marxists is to make an unpardonable concession to bourgeois economics. The sole conclusion to be drawn from the opinion held by Marxists that Marx's theory is an objective truth is that by following the *path* of Marxian theory, we shall draw closer and closer to objective truth (without ever exhausting it); but by following *any other path* we shall arrive at nothing but confusion and lies (Lenin, *Materialism and Empirio-criticism,* Progress Publishers, Moscow, 1970, pp. 129–30).

This is doubtless the most profound characteristic of historical materialism: it is a science that not only inspires political action, but also seeks its verification in practice, developing and growing through political practice itself.

But this dialectic between scientific theory and practice brings us to the second aspect of Marxism: dialectical materialism.

[B] Note on Dialectical Materialism

Marxism comes forward not only as the science of History (historical materialism),[4] but also as dialectical materialism. Engels, Lenin, and Stalin have elaborated upon the latter aspect of Marxism in particular. It too is the object of lively controversies.

What are the most important of the Marxist texts dealing with this subject? The second Preface to *Capital*; Engels' *Anti-Dühring* (Part I), *Ludwig Feuerbach* (ch. IV), and *Dialectics of Nature* (*passim*); Lenin's *Materialism and Empirio-criticism* (chs I and II), *What 'The Friends of the People' Are* (pp. 163–74) and *Philosophical Notebooks* (*Collected Works,* Vol. 38); Stalin's *Dialectical and Historical Materialism* and *Marxism and Linguistics*; Zhdanov's 'On Philosophy' (in *On Literature, Music and Philosophy*); Mao Zedong's 'On Contradiction' (in *Selected Readings from the Works of Mao Tse-tung*).

I. The dialectic

A few preliminary remarks may facilitate an approach to the Marxist conception of the *dialectic*.

For Marx, Engels, and their followers, the dialectic is the most advanced form of *scientific method*. Marxist theoreticians affirm that they are heir to 'the Hegelian dialectic'. A first problem: Marxism adopts the dialectic from Hegel, and yet Marx himself declares: 'My dialectical method is not only different from the Hegelian, but is its direct opposite' (second Preface to *Capital* [the Postface to the second German edition], International Publishers, New York, 1974, Vol. 1, p. 19). After Marx, first Engels (in *Ludwig Feuerbach* and *Anti-Dühring*) and then Lenin affirm that the Hegelian dialectic is acceptable only if 'put back on its feet'. What is meant by this 'direct opposite', this 'inversion' of the dialectic? We can find a precise answer in a number of different texts.

What Marx, Engels, and their followers reject in the Hegelian dialectic is its *dogmatic* meaning, role, and utilization – in a word, the *schematism* for which Hegel himself criticized Schelling in a well-known passage of *The Phenomenology of Spirit*. This dogmatism does violence to reality in order to make it fit the dialectical schema at all costs. What if reality does not conform to the *a priori* structure of the dialectic? It is deformed to bring it into line. In certain cases, doubtless, reality may well conform to the Hegelian dialectical schema: this is why Marx distinguishes analyses that are of genuine scientific interest from 'the Hegelian hotchpotch' (for example, the conception of history as process, the critique of abstract ideals, the 'Beautiful Soul', and so on). Most of the time, however, the Hegelian dialectic is simply 'plastered onto' reality. This utilization of the dialectic is intimately bound up with Hegel's absolute idealism. 'According to Hegel the development of the idea, in conformity with the dialectical laws of the triad, determines the development of the real world. And it is only in that case, of course, that one can speak of the importance of the triads, of the incontrovertibility of the dialectical process' (Lenin, *What 'The Friends of the People' Are*, p. 167). It is precisely this utilization that Marx rejects: 'Responding to Dühring, who had attacked Marx's dialectics, Engels says that Marx never dreamed of "proving" anything by means of Hegelian triads . . .' (*ibid.*, p. 163).

Yet although they thus reject the dogmatic utilization of the dialectic – along with its philosophical foundations – Marx and Engels retain its 'rational kernel', the general content of the dialectic (interaction, development, qualitative 'leaps', contradiction), which, in their view, constitutes a remarkable approximation of the most advanced *positive scientific* method.[5] This puts us in a position to specify the meaning of the famous 'inversion'. It is neither reliance on a particular philosophical system, nor a sort of intrinsic virtue, an absolute 'logical' necessity, that makes the dialectic indispensable to Marx and Engels. *The dialectic is validated only by its concrete [positif] utilization, by its scientific fecundity.* This scientific use is the sole criterion of the dialectic. It alone makes it possible to speak of the dialectic as *method*. Marx, says Lenin, did not 'plaster' the dialectic onto reality:

> Marx only studied and investigated the real process ... the sole criterion of theory recognized by him was its conformity to reality.... What Marx and Engels called the dialectical method – as against the metaphysical – is nothing else than the scientific method in sociology, which consists in regarding society as a living organism in a state of constant development (*What 'The Friends of the People' Are*, pp. 163–5).

And Lenin cites the famous sentence from the second Preface to *Capital* in which Marx defines the dialectic: 'The whole matter thus amounts to a "positive understanding of the existing state of things and their inevitable development"' (*ibid.*, p. 167; translation modified).

However, if this is the significance of the 'inversion' of the Hegelian dialectic, one must go still further. Marx and Engels accepted the 'rational kernel', the 'laws' of the Hegelian dialectic, only as a remarkable anticipation of scientific method.[6] But if its utilization by science is the criterion of the dialectic, that utilization also determines its 'laws'; it alone can confirm, define, and thus modify, by making them more precise, the laws of the dialectic themselves. This requirement is not un-Marxist. Since Marx, we have been witness to an interesting effort to specify and define the 'rules' or 'laws' of the dialectic, an effort that has progressively eliminated the formalistic elements that continued to mark the initial definitions. Thus the 'negation of the negation' no longer figures amongst the rules retained by Stalin (see *Dialectical and Historical Materialism*). Thus Mao Zedong's most recent text ('On Contradiction') accentuates two new ideas: the 'principal contradiction' and the 'principal aspect' of the contradiction; they are intended to specify the concrete structure of the concept of contradiction, which had earlier been too abstract. This ongoing effort of definition, which is consonant with a positive scientific approach [*positivité*], is plainly not unrelated to the scientific nature of the dialectical method.

Another point merits attention as well. If the dialectic is a scientific method, it comprises, like any scientific method, two aspects. It cannot be a method of discovery or investigation *unless it articulates the structure of reality* known to science. *Method of discovery and structure of reality are here closely interlinked, as they always have been in the history of the sciences.* It is in this sense that Engels could speak of the 'dialectics of nature', and could write that 'in the last resort, nature works dialectically' (*Anti-Dühring*, Progress Publishers, Moscow, 1947, p. 33); or that Lenin could say that 'Dialecticis in the proper sense is the study of contradictions *in the very essence of things'* (*Philosophical Notebooks, Collected Works*, Vol. 38, Lawrence and Wishart, London, 1961, pp. 253–4; translation modified); or that Stalin could write, following Engels and Lenin, 'the dialectical method ... regards the phenomena of nature as being in constant movement ...' (*Dialectical and Historial Materialism*, Foreign Languages Publishing House, Moscow, 1941, pp. 4–5). This double aspect of the dialectic – *scientific method and structure of the real* – is at the heart of the definition of the laws of the dialectic given by Stalin in *Dialectical and Historical Materialism*.

But, by way of this conception, we have come back round to *materialism*.

II. Materialism

Without a doubt, materialism is the aspect of Marxism that has elicited the sharpest criticisms (see, in particular, J.-P. Sartre's essay in *Les Temps Modernes*, nos 9–10 [June–July 1946; 'Materialism and Revolution', in *Literary and Philosophical Essays*, London, 1968, pp. 185–239].

Let us, first of all, try to avoid certain misconceptions.

Simply to mention the arguments of the 'vulgar materialism' denounced by Marx, which come down to denying the reality of thought, consciousness, and ideals, is to reject them. Marxist materialism refuses to assimilate thought to matter, and attributes a very important historical role to consciousness (see Engels, *Ludwig Feuerbach*, ch. III, *in fine*, the letter to Conrad Schmidt [of 5 August 1890], etc.).

But let us take a moment to consider another argument. Materialism, it is said, is a 'metaphysics of nature' that reconstitutes the world by starting out from a material element regarded as an absolute substance (atom, body, matter). In short, it is an 'Absolute Knowledge' in which matter plays the role of the Hegelian idea. Marx and Engels criticize this conception, which they call 'metaphysical materialism'. Lenin, for example, writes: 'The recognition of immutable elements, "of the immutable essence of things", is not materialism, but *metaphysical*, i.e., anti-dialectical, materialism' (*Materialism and Empirio-Criticism*, p. 249). One of the essential features of dialectical materialism is precisely that it refutes all dogmatism grounded in 'Absolute Knowledge'. Materialism radically rejects the idea that there can be any '"immutability", "essence", [or] "absolute substance", in the sense in which these concepts were depicted by the empty professorial philosophy' (*ibid.*, p. 250). It is not for a metaphysics of nature to *deduce* the structure of reality; it is the role of the sciences to *discover* it. Thus only physics can determine and develop the *physical* notion of matter, with which the philosophical notion of matter must not be confused.

Accordingly, Marxist materialism does not have the same object science does. Its aim is not [*il ne répond pas à*] the discovery of the structure of reality. It responds, says Lenin, to the *fundamental 'epistemological question'*: primacy of matter or mind? Primacy of existence or consciousness? The answer to this question – posed and debated in all the theories of classical philosophy that bear on the problem of knowledge – lies, for Marxism, in scientific practice itself. Defining the 'materialist standpoint' in opposition to Hegel in *Ludwig Feuerbach* [Marx and Engels, *Selected Works*, p. 618], Engels shows 'it means nothing more than' the scientific analysis of the real world, of facts 'conceived in their own and not in a fantastic interconnection'. Lenin, echoing Engels, tirelessly repeated that 'the sciences are spontaneously materialist' (*Materialism and Empirio-Criticism, passim*).

Here, as we have seen, the notion of practice comes into play. Indeed, we cannot consider scientific truths apart from scientific practice (itself the most abstract form of human practice in general), which is their basis. Only by articulating the implications of this practice can we propose a valid response to the 'epistemological question'. For this practice constitutes, *in actual fact*, the origin and criterion of all truth. In *Materialism and Empirio-Criticism*, Lenin energetically addresses this theme, the subject of Marx's famous second thesis on Feuerbach: 'The question whether objective truth can be attributed to human thinking is not a question of theory but is a practical question. In practice man must prove the truth, that is, the reality and power, the "this-sidedness" of his thinking. The dispute over the reality or non-reality of thinking which is isolated from practice is a purely scholastic question' (Marx and Engels, *Selected Works*, p. 28).

Thus this position, which is distinct from pragmatism, radically excludes all questions about the 'possibility of knowledge', i.e., all transcendental philosophies. Affirming that the fact of practice envelops* all questions as to the legitimacy [*droit*] of knowledge, it rejects any *philosophical* reflection that purports to arrive at the truth, the truth of this fact included, by seeking a *de jure* foundation [*un fondement de droit*] for knowledge beyond this *fact*. At this level, rigorous reflection, in conformity with the truth it seeks to attain, can by itself do no more than articulate the reality of the practice that engenders truth.

The theses of materialism consequently do no more than articulate and consciously draw out the implications of the 'spontaneous practice' of the sciences, itself a particular instance of human *practice*. This practice involves confronting two terms joined in a profound unity: *the ideas (or*

---

* A passage from Althusser's DES thesis on Hegel sheds some light on his use of this word: 'The Hegelian concept is the movement through which the result recovers its origins by internalizing them, by revealing itself to be the origin of the origin. This process of envelopment implies that the initial term and the reflected term are *aufgehoben* in the result' (see above, p. 88).

the consciousness) of scientists (of men) – *and external reality*. This confrontation entails recognition of the *primacy of external reality* over ideas or consciousness, which, in this practice, models itself on reality; and the recognition of the objectivity of the laws established, in this practice, by science. 'The recognition of the priority of nature, not mind, is the distinguishing feature of materialism *par excellence*,' says Lenin, who insists heavily on the 'epistemological' as opposed to the dogmatic aspect of that thesis: 'One only has to formulate the question clearly to realize what sheer nonsense the Machists talk when they demand that the materialists give a definition of mattter which would not amount to a repetition of the proposition that matter, nature, being the physical – is primary, and spirit, consciousness, sensation, the psychical – is secondary' (*Materialism and Empirio-Criticism*, pp. 133–4). Ruling out all dogmatic definitions of matter, Lenin repeatedly affirms that 'the sole "property" of matter with whose definition philosophical materialism is bound up is the property of *being an objective reality. . . .*' (*ibid.*, p. 248); 'matter is a philosophical category denoting . . . objective reality' (*ibid.*, p. 116). The basic significance of this 'epistemological', rather than dogmatic, conception of the primacy of existence over consciousness stands out even more clearly when Lenin underscores the 'limits' of this thesis: 'Of course, even the antithesis of matter and mind has absolute significance only within the bounds of the fundamental epistemological question of what is to be regarded as primary and what as secondary. Beyond these bounds the relative character of this antithesis is indubitable' (*ibid.*, p. 134).

Here, however, one might hesitate. Does Lenin's emphasis on the 'bounds of the epistemological question' not justify a transcendental reflection *à la* Kant? More: is the analysis of what we have called the 'implications of practice' not reminiscent of an 'analysis of essence' of the Husserlian kind (an explanation of scientific 'praxis' as constitution; objectivity as an 'intentional' structure)? Undeniably, Husserl too contested the subjectivist, pragmatist, and empirio-critical interpretations of the great crisis of physics at the turn of the nineteenth century. Were not the struggle against dogmatism, the concern to provide a foundation for, and so save, the objectivity of the natural sciences, and the 'description' of scientific practice and its 'claims' among his major concerns? Manifestly, Husserl's disciples could have found an echo of their doctrine in certain of Lenin's formulations taken out of context.[7]

It is nonetheless clear that Lenin's analysis is not an 'analysis of essence' which refers us to its ideal conditions of possibility, or even, from foundation to foundation, to an original intention. Practice, which, for Marxism, is the source and criterion of all truth, and 'envelops' the epistemological question, does not provide a *de jure* foundation for the materialist thesis in the idealist sense of the term. The *fact* of practice points back, not to an originary legitimation [*droit originaire*], but to *its own real genesis*. It is here that materialism is radically counterposed to all transcendental philosophies. No-one, perhaps, has put this better than Engels, in connection with the problem of the definition of life: 'From a scientific standpoint all definitions are of little value. In order to gain an exhaustive knowledge of what life is, we should have to go through all the forms in which it appears, from the lowest to the highest...' [*Anti-Dühring*, p. 104]. The same holds for practice. It is not the immediacy of an act or structure, but *its own real genesis*. Inseparable from human practice (broadly conceived: social production, daily social practice, class struggle) in its contemporaneous forms, scientific practice, which is the most abstract refinement of practice, can be defined only in terms of its real evolution, that is, its history. That is why Lenin also declares that the answer to the *'fundamental epistemological question'* is simultaneously provided by human practice and by the history of knowledge (*Materialism and Empirio-Criticism*, pp. 89, 122–4, 143, 147, 217, 239, etc.).

This history defines 'the limits ... revealed by practice' with respect to the 'objective truth we are capable of attaining' (*ibid.*, p. 177). Mao Zedong, for example, shows (in 'On Practice') that the knowledge a given period is in a position to produce is always subject to the determinate forms of existing practice (*bound up, above all, with the existing social mode of production, i.e, with the dominant mode of the transformation of nature*). But within these historical limits, the truths acquired through practice are absolute (there is no truth outside them). It is this dialectic of the historical conditions of knowledge which Lenin worked out in his frequently misunderstood theory of relative and absolute truth.

'The "essence" of things', writes Lenin, 'or "substance"'

is *also* relative; it expresses only the degree of profundity of man's knowledge of objects: and while yesterday the profundity of this knowledge did not go beyond the atom, and today does not go beyond the electron and ether, dialectical materialism insists on the temporary, relative, approximate character of all these *milestones* in the knowledge of nature gained by the progressing science of man. The electron is as *inexhaustible* as the atom, nature is infinite but it infinitely *exists* (Lenin's emphasis) (*ibid.*, p. 250).

Whence the conception of knowledge, intertwined with practice, as the progressive 'adaptation' of men, in history, to an inexhaustible nature, itself caught up in a process of endless development (see *ibid.*, pp. 174, 175–7, 260–61).

The features of dialectical materialism are perhaps coming into sharper focus. The materialism that responds to the 'epistemological question' does not escape the metaphysical dogmatism it proscribes only to succumb to a new scientific dogmatism. The history of knowledge does not constitute, any more than the other sciences do, a new 'Absolute Knowledge'. It does not contain the 'absolute essence' of current practice: it is the science of that practice, and, as such, is itself enveloped in a current practice and its development.

What form, then, does the relationship between *the sciences and the materialist theory of knowledge* take?

Let us, to begin with, make one point more precise. The materialist theory of knowledge is not the 'science of sciences', nor 'a science over and above the others' (Zhdanov). It is not a set of principles from which we can, by deduction, arrive at scientific findings capable of taking the place of the truths the sciences discover. This point radically distinguishes the materialist theory from the theories of knowledge of traditional philosophy. The theory of knowledge licensed Kant to deduce the laws of Newtonian physics (see *The Metaphysical Elements of Natural Science*), Hegel to deduce the scientific categories of mathematics, physics, biology, history, etc., Husserl to determine, *a priori*, the eidetic regions and the structure of the object of the sciences. The materialist theory of knowledge refuses to substitute itself for the sciences.

Nevertheless, if Marxists do not permit themselves to treat materialism as the 'science of sciences', they do say that 'materialism is verified by the sciences' (Engels, Lenin, Stalin). What does this statement mean? It must be understood in two senses: materialism is verified *by* the sciences and *in* the sciences.

The sciences do not verify the materialist theory of knowledge as a set of propositions which they demonstrate, a body of laws they establish in their respective domains. The sciences verify the materialist theory *practically*, inasmuch as they only ever make progress, in the final analysis, by submitting to the authority of reality.

In a different sense, the sciences verify the materialist theory of knowledge *within their own domain*: 1) by showing that lower forms of life (for example, physical corpuscles) have no use for the determinations of higher forms (for example, freedom); 2) by showing, conversely, that the higher forms of life (biological existence, consciousness) come about through the development of their sustaining structures (physical and chemical conditions, biological and social conditions).

Thus the primacy of reality is verified at two different levels *by* the sciences and *in* the sciences. It is this double envelopment (*of the progress of the sciences in the principles of materialism, and of these principles themselves in the reality discovered by the sciences*) which makes it possible to understand the philosophical and scientific nature of materialism – initially captured in this phrase of Stalin's: materialism is a 'scientific philosophical theory' (*Dialectical and Historical Materialism*).

Thus understood, materialism stands in a fundamental relation to the sciences: reminding them of their true nature, it ensures their survival and progress. We will better grasp the import of this if we bear in mind that materialism implies:

1. *A rejection of all 'idealist crotchets'* (Engels). This requirement not only entails the rejection of any concept that is not in strict conformity with, and limited to, its scientific content (the problem of the rigour of scientific concepts). It also implies a radical criticism of all idealist philosophies and of philosophy as such in its classical form: the critique of philosophy as pure 'theory' or pure 'interpretation' which 'gives an account of' reality in order not to have to *account to reality for itself*, and which is exempt from the obligation to submit to the criterion of practice and verification – the critique of the philosopher as the man who rules over the words that, for him, take the place of the world, the fictitious demiurge of a pseudo-world. It is in this sense that Marx wrote: 'One has to "leave philosophy aside" ... one has to leap out of it and devote oneself like an ordinary man to the study of actuality. ... Philosophy and the study of the actual world have the same relation to one another as onanism and sexual love' (*The German Ideology*, in Marx and Engels, *Collected Works*, Vol. 5, Lawrence and Wishart, London, 1976, p. 236. On the subject of philosophy, see *ibid.*, pp. 28, 36, 37, 45, 54, 101, 145, 171, 196, 236, 250–52, 282, 293, 330, 449, 461).

2. *Criticism of all scientific dogmatism*, which drags along behind it, like its shadow, the idealist exploitation of science and its 'crises'. The primacy of reality implies that a scientific theory does not exhaust reality, but remains always approximative (Lenin). Materialism reminds science and human practice of their own limits (not transcendental, but historical), and bars all 'philosophical' exploitation of concepts, problems, or scientific or social crises. At the turn of the twentieth century, the philosophers loudly announced the 'divine surprise' that the 'atom had disappeared'. Materialism excludes this self-seeking flight into philosophy (or religion); it understands the crises of the sciences and history, not as a 'divine victory' of Spirit, but as a moment in the concrete development of the sciences and history.

3. *The rejection of all abstract formalism*. Materialism reminds every science of its real source: the world men transform. No science can, whether in its history or its object, grasp its own origins within itself or constitute itself as a closed world, exhaustively defined by internal rules. Materialism refers every science and every activity to the reality they depend on, even if this dependence is masked by a great many abstract mediations: mathematics as well as logic, aesthetics as well as ethics and politics.

To safeguard the endless development of the sciences, and, with it, all 'living human practice' (Lenin, *Materialism and Empirio-Criticism*), to preserve the sciences from all forms of dogmatism and idealism by reminding them of their fundamental reality – such is the aim of materialism:

> You will say that this distinction between relative and absolute truth is indefinite. And I shall reply: it is sufficiently 'indefinite' to prevent science from becoming a dogma in the bad sense of the term, from becoming something dead, frozen, ossified; but at the same time it is sufficiently 'definite' to enable us to dissociate ourselves in the most emphatic and irrevocable manner from fideism and agnosticism, from philosophical idealism and the sophistry of the followers of Hume and Kant (*ibid.*, p. 123; see also p. 129).

We hope that these all too brief remarks, however insufficient,[8] will give some idea of the characteristics of Marxism, of its rigour and fecundity. 'A method for science', 'a guide to action', and 'a scientific and revolutionary theory', Marxism articulates the most exacting demands of scientific activity and, simultaneously, the living bond that unites them to human history and practice. These are amongst the reasons for the prestige of a doctrine that today deserves better than to 'be learned about by hearsay': it merits attentive and meticulous study.

Notes

First published in the *Revue de l'enseignement philosophique*, Vol. 3, no. 4, April–June 1953, pp. 15–19, and no. 5, October–November 1953, pp. 11–17. Where appropriate, English-language references have been substituted for Althusser's references to French-language works.

1. The texts published by Éditions Sociales are preferable to the other versions, because of their critical apparatus and the quality of the translations.
2. In the first part of this work, M. Desroches examines the relationship between Marxism and religion – interpreting it from a 'religious' standpoint.
3. M. Cornu believes that *The Holy Family* is the first 'Marxist' text. This is a debatable position. See our remarks below.
4. See 'On Marxism' [i.e., the first part of the present essay, originally published in two instalments].
5. '... it is precisely dialectics that constitutes the most important form of thinking for present-day natural science, for it alone offers the analogue for, and thereby the method of explaining, the evolutionary processes occurring in nature, inter-connections in general, and transitions from one field of investigation to another.' Engels, *Dialectics of Nature*, Progress Publishers, Moscow, 1954, p. 43.
6. Here, obviously, a problem arises. How does it happen that, despite his system, Hegel is able to state dialectical laws that, generally speaking, lend themselves to positive scientific use? In *The Young Hegel*, Lukács has tried to give a partial response to this question by pointing to the role Hegel's study of political economy and history played in the genesis of Hegelian dialectics. Marx insists on the influence Hegel's knowledge of science had on his method. Engels shows that the Hegelian 'inversion' is not an isolated instance in the history of human knowledge (see *Dialectics of Nature*, pp. 48–9).
7. In certain respects, Tran-Duc-Thao's *Phénoménologie et Matérialisme dialectique* seems to us to be based on, and to perpetuate, this ambiguity.
8. In this last section, we have focused on the materialist theory of knowledge. A fuller

account would have to show how dialectical materialism conceives the system of scientific knowledges that must be put in place of the old 'philosophy of Nature' (Engels), as well as the crucial role this theoretical synthesis plays in the development of human practice and knowledge. On this point, the reader should consult Engels' *Ludwig Feuerbach* and *Dialectics of Nature*.

Index

Absolute Consciousness 210
Absolute Content 98, 143
Absolute Knowledge 68, 96–8, 104–5, 114, 132, 143, 147
  dialectical materialism 250, 254
Absolute Spirit 207
Absolute Subject 207
Absolute Totality 91
abstraction of the void 49, 52, 55, 56–7, 130
Aesthetics 5
Alain (pseudonym for Chartier, É.-A.) 26, 174
'aleatory materialism' 10
alienation 131–3, 137, 140, 206–9, 244
Althussser, Hélène 10, 15, 16
Anaxagoras 69
Andler, C. 173
anti-humanism 7
Aquinas, St. T. 187, 188
Aragon, L. 8
Archimedes 65
Aristotle 42, 79, 85, 100, 188
Aron, R. 180
Aubier 5
Augustus, St. 187, 212, 218

Bachelard, G. 15
Ballard, J. 16
Bebel, F.A. 235
Begriff see concept
Bergson, H. 173
Bismarck, O. von 176
Blum, L. 30
Bogdanov, A. 246
Bossuet, J.B. 24, 27, 204, 211, 212, 213
Bottigelli, É. 17
bourgeoisie 174–82

Breton, S. 8
Bruno, G. 79
Brunschvicg, L. 173, 174

Cachin, M. 198
Camus, A. 22, 23, 24, 25, 28–30
capitalism 31, 137–9, 178
Catholicism 6, 8, 14, 19
Caveing, M. 7
'Certainty of Truth and Reason' 131
Chesneaux, J. 7
Christianity 49–51, 52
Church/religion 97, 185–96
  practical reduction perspectives 193–5
    reconquest of religious life 194–5
    social liberation 193–4
  reflections 49
  religious problem 46–7
  theoretical reduction 186–93
    ideological situation 187–90
    political situation 190–93
    social situation 187
  see also Philosophies of Religion
circularity 88–9, 118–19, 128, 146, 147, 150
civil society 118–23, 125, 175, 180
Claudel, P. 112
cognition of concept *see* 'On Content in the Thought of Hegel'
Communism 8, 14, 137–8, 204–5
Communist Party 7, 9, 18, 221–5
concept (*Begriff*) 84–90, 107
  see also philosophies
'Conjugal Obscenity' (1951) 1, 19, 231–40
  Church 231
  Civil Code 239
  emancipation 239
  exhibitionism 233–40
  France 231–3

'Conjugal Obscenity' (1951) (*cont.*)
  Italy 231
  Spain 231
  status and behaviour of women 235–6
consciousness 112, 210
  see also self-consciousness
content
  countenancing 140–56
  as given 64–72
  of history 133
  as reflection
    logic 73–47
    man 80–4
    nature 77–80
  as self 84–98
  see also Absolute
contradiction 77, 86, 131
Cornu, A. 242, 243
Costamagna 180
Critique of Practical Reason 58
Croce, B. 174

Danton, G.J. 202
death 93–6
decay/decomposition 37–9
Decoud, P. (pseudonym) 229
Deism 45
Derrida, J. 9
Desanti, J.-T. 8
Descartes, R. 188
  cognition of the concept 64, 65, 71, 81, 84,
    85
  'Latest Word in Academic Revisionism'
    173, 178
  'Letter to Jean Lacroix' 198, 221
  misapprehension of the concept 100, 103,
    132, 149, 154
Desroches, H.-C. 205
Diatkine, R. 10
Dilthey, W. 179
divine judgements 213–14
Domenach, J.-M. 204
Doriot, J. 202

Ehrenburg, I.G. 21
Encyclopædia 69, 72, 112, 117, 173, 180
end of history 206–9, 211, 244
Engels, F. 175, 207
  'International of Decent Feelings' 17, 23
  'On Content in the Thought of Hegel' 37,
    133, 140, 155
  'On Marxism' 241, 242

dialectical materialism 247, 248, 249,
    250, 251, 253, 254, 255
  early works 243, 244
  historical materialism 245
Enlightenment 44–7, 52, 55, 59–60, 80, 103,
    132, 144–5
Epicurus 9, 70
error 117–23
  necessity 124–30
Esprit 201–4, 217
eternity 214–17
exhibitionism 233–40

Faith and Knowledge 54, 57, 72
Fejtö, F. 201–2, 203
Fessard, G. 5, 174, 180, 181
Feuerbach, L.A. 208, 242, 251
Fichte, J.G. 56, 58–9, 65, 77, 82, 112, 147
for-itself 120–22, 135–6, 152, 174
form–matter relation 75
formalism 112, 114, 255
freedom 90
friendship 198–200

Gall, F.J. 80
Gentile 180
Georgette (sister of Althusser) 18
Gestalt psychology 62, 75
Gitton, M. 202
Glockner, H. 179, 183
Goethe, J.W. von 44, 57
good conscience 200–201
Gramsci, A. 9
Grappin, P. 17
Greeks 47–8
Guitton, J. 200
Gurvitch, M. 242–3
Guterman, N. 5

Haering, T. 179
Hamelin, O. 148
Hartmann, N. 38, 112–13, 115, 133, 174
Heidegger, M. 9, 171
Hellenism 79
Herr, L. 173
historical judgement 211–26
History 175
  cognition of the concept 93, 94–5, 97–8
  'Letter to Jean Lacroix' 207, 210, 220
  'Man, That Night' 170
  misapprehension of the concept 134–5,
    144, 149, 153

History (*cont.*)
  see also end of history; *Philosophy of History*
Hitler, A. 198, 215, 218
Hoffmeister, J. 179
Hölderlin, J.C.F. 42, 45, 47, 49
Hours, J. 191, 197, 202, 203
'Human Front' 22
Hume, D. 76–7, 256
Husserl, E.G.A. 67, 112, 115, 252, 254
Hyppolite, J. 5, 16, 18, 173, 174, 179, 181, 206–11 *passim*
Idea 182
  cognition of the concept 68, 70
  misapprehension of the concept 108–9, 111, 121, 125–7, 130, 139, 148
idealism 82
'idealist crotchets' 255
ideology 28, 151
imagination 57
in-itself 120–22, 135–7, 174
'International of Decent Feelings' (1946) 6, 14, 21–35
  capitalism 31
  ideology 28
  proletariat 23–7, 31
  servitude 25–6
  socialism 30–31
  war 29–30
intuition 84–6
Izard, G. 6

Jacobi, F. 85, 114
Jankélévitch, S. 5
Jaurès, J. 173
Jesus Christ 47–50
Jews 48, 50, 53, 56, 244
Jouhaux, L. 223
Jourdain, M. 214–15, 216

Kant, I.
  cognition of the concept 63, 65, 69, 71, 76–7, 81, 85, 86, 91
  'Latest Word in Academic Revisionism' 176–8, 183
  misapprehension of the concept 102, 104, 124, 132, 145, 147–8, 150, 153–6
  'On Marxism' 252, 254, 256
  origins of the concept 47, 51, 52–60
Kautsky, K.J. 246
Kierkegaard, S.A. 100, 151, 216
Knowledge

superficial 63
  see also Absolute Knowledge; *Faith and Knowledge*
Koestler, A. 22, 23, 28, 30, 202, 203, 204
Kojève, A. 5, 16, 171–2, 174, 181, 207
Kroner, R. 87, 179

labour 135–6, 138–9, 156, 175
Lacroix, J. 1, 18–19, 174
  see also 'Letter to Jean Lacroix'
Lasson, G. 179
'Latest Word in Academic Revisionism' (1950) 16, 173–84
  bourgeoisie 174–82
  capitalism 178
  civil society 175, 180
  labour 175
  liberalism 176–8, 181
  positivism 176
  Prussian monarchy 175
  scientific socialism 175, 181–2
law 140
Leclos, R. (pseudonym) 6
Lefebvre, H. 5, 17
Leibniz, G.W. 42, 68, 204, 213, 218
Lenin, V.I. 17, 202, 241, 242, 243, 244
  dialectical materialism 248, 249, 250, 251, 252, 253, 254, 255
  historical materialism 245, 246–7
'Letter to Jean Lacroix' (1949–50) 8, 18–19, 197–230
  Absolute Consciousness 210
  Absolute Subject 207
  alienation 206–9
  Communism 204–5
  Communist Party 221–5
  criticizing Marxism 212
  divine judgements 213–14
  end of history 206–9, 211
  Esprit 201–4, 217
  eternity 214–17
  friendship 198–200
  good conscience 200–201
  historical judgement 211–26
  History 207, 210, 220
  Nature 207
  self-consciousness 207–8
  Spirit 204
  truth 197–204, 217–21, 223–5
liberalism 176–8, 181
life of Hegel 41–4

Logic 174
   cognition of the concept 68–70, 73–7,
      92–3
   misapprehension of the concept 106,
      109–10, 128, 143, 146, 149
   see also Science of Logic
Logos (word) 106–7, 109–10, 141
love 48–9, 81–2
Lukács, G.S. von 142, 213
Lysenko affair 8

Macherey, P. 10
Madonia, F. 1, 15–16
Malebranche, N. 188, 200, 204, 218
Malraux, A. 14, 21, 22, 23, 30
man 80–84, 107, 128
'Man, That Night' (1947) 16, 170–72
Mandouze, A. 7
Mao Zedong 247, 249, 253
Marcel, G. 22, 27–8, 204
Martin, J. 5, 6, 15–16
Marx, K./Marxism 37, 43, 106, 235
   communism 182
   countenancing the content 141, 147, 148,
      150–51, 152, 153, 155, 156
   Critique of Hegel's Philosophy of Right 180
   humanism 19
   'International of Decent Feelings' 1, 2, 5,
      9, 16, 17, 23, 27
   'Latest Word in Academic Revisionism'
      173, 175, 181, 183
   'Letter to Jean Lacroix' 198, 204–7, 208,
      209, 211–14, 217, 222
   'Man, That Night' 171, 172
   'Matter of Fact, A' 189, 193
   Molitor translation 6
   sins of the content 116
   error 117, 118–23
   necessity of the error 124, 126–7, 129–30
   necessity's revenge 131–2, 133, 134–8,
      139–40
   see also 'On Marxism'
mathematical method 61–2
Matheron, F. 1–11, 14–19
'Matter of Fact, A' (1949) 1, 18, 185–96
   Good News 185, 191–3
Mauriac, F. 28, 30
mediation 100–105
   of the dialectic 110–16
   of language 105–10
Mehring, F. 17, 242–3
Meinecke, F. 180

Mendelssohn, M. 175
Merleau-Ponty, M. 1, 16
Mind 70
Mindszenty, Cardinal J. 203
misapprehension of concept 99–156
   countenancing content 141–56
   sins of the content 116–40
   sins of the form 100–16
Molitor, J. 6
Monarchy 121–2, 124–7, 148–9, 175
Montesquieu, C. de S. 19
Montuclard, M. 7–8
Mounier, E. 201, 202, 203, 204–5, 217, 218,
   224
Mussolini, B. 180, 215

Napoleon III 176
naturalism 93
Nature 171–2, 207
   cognition of the concept 69–70, 72, 77–80,
      81, 91–3
   misapprehension of the concept 107, 110,
      122, 128, 130, 139–40, 146, 149, 155
   see also Philosophy of Nature
Nazism 200
necessity's revenge 130–40
negativity 115, 140
Newton, I. 112
Niel, H. 5, 174
Nietzsche, F.W. 21, 42, 48, 142, 170
Nohl, H. 179
Novalis (pen name for Hardenberg, F. von)
   44

Oedipus 50
'On Content in the Thought of Hegel'
   (1947) 15, 36–169
   cognition of concept 57, 61–98
      content as given 64–72
      content as reflection 72–84
      content as self 84–98
   decay 37–9
   Hegelianism, advanced 37
   misapprehension of concept 99–156
   origins of concept 41–60
      Hegel and Kant 52–60
      Hegel's life 41–4
      Hegel's times 44–51
   truth 38–9
'On the German Constitution' 45

'On Marxism' (1953) 241–57
  dialectical materialism 247–56
    dialectic 248–50
    materialism 250–56
  early works, problem of 242–4
  historical materialism 244–7
origins of concept *see* 'On Content in the
  Thought of Hegel'
panlogism 93
Parmenides 101, 118
Pascal, B. 81
Phenomenology of Spirit 5
  cognition of the concept 62, 66, 68, 78,
  89
  countenancing the content 141–3, 149–50,
  154
  dialectical materialism 248
  'Latest Word in Academic Revisionism'
  174, 180
  'Letter to Jean Lacroix' 207
  'Man, That Night' 171
  origins of the concept 42, 44, 45, 49, 51,
  52, 56
  sins of the content 122–3, 129, 131, 132
  sins of the form 101, 103–6, 111–12
philosophies of the concept 85–6
philosophy 61, 63
Philosophy of Art 129
Philosophy of History 101, 103, 112, 146
Philosophy of Law 140
Philosophy of Nature 78, 93, 112, 129, 140
Philosophy of Religion 129, 140, 174
Philosophy of Right 5, 116–18, 140, 141–3,
  146, 174
Philosophy of Spirit 69, 93, 105
Plato 48, 188, 218
  cognition of the concept 61, 64, 66, 68, 71,
  84, 86, 87, 94
  misapprehension of the concept 99,
  101–3, 108–9, 111, 125, 132, 149, 154
Plekhanov, G.V. 242
plenitude, excess of 43
political life 82
positivism 176
proletariat 23–7, 31
Proudhon, P.J. 244
Prussia
  bureaucracy 116–21, 124–6
  monarchy 175
  state 128, 146–7, 156
psychology 62, 75

Rajk, L. 8, 18–19, 200, 201–2, 204, 217
Rancière, J. 2
realism 82
Reason 106, 120, 131
reflection 82–4
  see also self-reflection
Reign of Freedom 171
Reinhold, K. 65
religion *see* Church
Renaissance 80
research 153, 155
Reynal, A.O. 2
Ricci, F. 7, 14
right *see* Philosophy of Right
Rimbaud, A. 61
Riquet, Father M. 181
Roberval, G. 215
Robespierre, M.M.I. de 145
Romanticism 44
Rousseau, J.-J. 44, 145, 177

Sade, Marquis de 144
Sage 104–5, 132–3, 144, 150
sandglass dialectic 75–6
Sartre, J.-P. 5, 250
Say, J.P. 176
Schelling, F.W.J. von 45, 63, 65, 79, 82, 112,
  248
Schérer, R. 17–18
Science 108–9, 112, 144, 147, 155
Science of Logic 60, 64, 70
scientific
  cognition 63
  dogmatism 255
  socialism 175, 181–2
Self 107, 114
self-consciousness 111, 207–8
self-reflection 87, 101
servitude 25–6
sins of the content 116–40
  error 117–23
  error, necessity of 124–30
  necessity's revenge 131–40
sins of the form 100–116
  Hegel's mediation 100–105
  mediation of the dialectic
  110–16
  mediation of language 105–10
Smith, A. 176
socialism 30–31
  scientific 175, 181–2
Socrates 47, 110–11

Sorel, G. 246
Spinoza, B. de 65, 71, 72, 82, 101, 102, 111, 138, 175
Spirit
  cognition of the concept 68, 91–7
  countenancing the content 141, 143, 146–7, 149, 153
  dialectical materialism 255
  'Letter to Jean Lacroix' 204
  'Man, That Night' 170–71
  sins of the content 117, 120, 122, 131–2, 138, 139, 140
  sins of the form 104–5, 107, 110
  see also Absolute; Philosophy of Spirit
Spirit of Christianity and its Fate 49
Stalin, J. 241, 242, 247, 249, 250, 254
  'International of Decent Feelings' 8, 9, 17
  'Letter to Jean Lacroix' 198, 200, 202, 211, 223
state 180
  see also Prussia
Stoics 107, 131
Storr, G. 47
subject 207
Substance-Subject 171–2
Supreme Being 45, 55

Thibon, G. 200
Tito 204
Torricelli, E. 215
totality 91

train metaphor 9–10
transcendentalism 153–4, 156
triplicity 86–7, 112, 115, 128, 140
Trotsky, L. 182
truth 38–9
  'Letter to Jean Lacroix' 217–21, 223–5
  misapprehension of the concept 104
  countenancing the content 142–3, 144, 147, 148, 149, 150
    sins of the content 125, 131, 132, 140
    origins of the concept 41, 52, 53
    of the unity 57
Tübingen period 45–6

Umschlagen 75–6, 79, 81, 91
unity 57, 58–9

Van Gogh, V. 99
Véra, A. 5, 173
Villey, D. 222, 246
void see abstraction

Wahl, J. 4, 174, 179
war 29–30
Wilde, O. 198, 221
Wilhelm II 180
Word 110

'Youth of the Church' 18

Zhdanov, A. 8, 17, 173, 210, 221–2, 247, 254